MEDITATIONS OF A TRAVELER

Lewis Codington

PREFACE

My great-grandparents were missionaries in China in the 1880s, until Richard V. Lancaster was asked to take on the Presidency of Belhaven College. Before my Grandmother moved to China and married my Grandpa, her family grew up in Clinton, South Carolina, where her father, William G. Neville, was the president of Presbyterian College. Between bandits, a firing squad, and evacuations, my grandparents had some stories to tell. I wish they had written more of them down for us. Our middle child, Marianna, kept pestering me to record some of these stories. So, I need to dedicate this book to her, trusting that she will now leave me alone. Our oldest son, Wim, compiled and arranged it all, so I want to thank him as well. These stories are dedicated to all nine of our children, so they will know where they came from, and most of all, understand the importance of walking with God and living with his Word. Additionally, I want this book to be for our many friends from China and North Korea, so they will hopefully come to understand the Bible a little better. Finally, I want to thank our North Korean friend, Eugene, who, while in hiding, read through the Bible five times in three weeks. His example challenged and inspired me to read through the Bible (only once) in two weeks. The meditations from those readings are included at the beginning of each month's devotionals.

The paintings at the beginning of each month's writings are by Martha Stewart, whose parents were also missionaries in Korea alongside the Codingtons. She desires to see her art glorify our Creator God and to bring his light into our world.

The cover drawing is by Wuzzy Wu, who worked with the Codingtons in CLC and has lived and served in Asia for many years.

Of course I also need to honor my wife, Elsbeth Schaffers Codington, who, with her Dutch "flink", has held our family together all of these years, providing us with the wife and mother we could not do without.

JANUARY

During this two week quarantine lockdown time in Seoul, I was challenged by one of our NK friends to read all the way through my Bible. While he was in hiding for three weeks some years ago, he read five times through a Bible someone had given him! So, I figured I should be able to read through it once in two weeks.

Starting at 8:00 this morning, I read until 8:00 p.m...(with breaks for meals and exercising). In my 2626 page study Bible, I will need to read close to 200 pages a day (or less than 100 pages in a regular Bible). Today I read through Genesis and Exodus. Tomorrow I hope to read Leviticus, Numbers, and Deuteronomy.

So what spoke to me in my reading today?

*The Bible is a wonderful treasure that God has given to us.

*We discover who God is: all powerful, dazzlingly creative, holy and righteous, all knowing, and sovereign over everything.

*We discover who we are: God's crowning creation, we reflect God's character in many ways, we are extremely precious to God, and we have an internal bent toward running away from God.

*God communicates with us what we need to know. But there is much he chooses not to tell us about the world, and how and why he works the way he does. Frequently, this is frustrating to people.

*God is relentless in his pursuit of a relationship with us...which he desires but does not force on us.

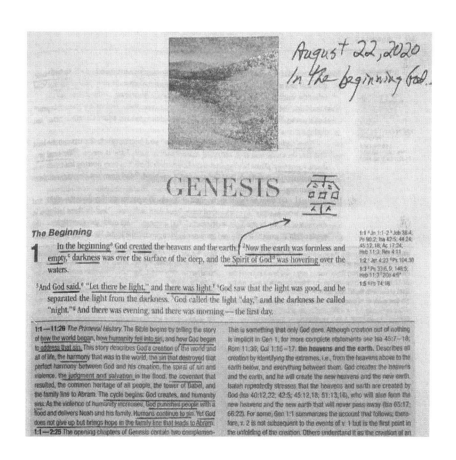

JANUARY 1

In Korea, nearly all the old people keep their hair dyed jet black. I don't know if they think they are somehow less "Asian" without black hair, but they don't seem to dare be caught with any white hair. However, on rare occasions, I'll see an older lady sitting alone on the subway...with white hair. Invariably, I'll sidle up to her and whisper in her ear about what beautiful hair she has. Usually, they respond with a sheepish grin and fluff up their hair a bit. (Lest you worry, I do it only when my wife is with me!) Occasionally, it will backfire. Once I was walking past three older ladies sitting by the side of the road. One had white hair. I walked over and gave her the usual compliment. However, this time she berated this impudent foreigner who would dare come on to her. It took me aback a bit...but I expect it was to save face in front of her mates next her. At any rate, I try to notice and compliment older folks because the truth is...most people don't notice them, much less give them the time of day. Some of our kids are even more blunt than that, as they proclaim, "I never want to grow old!"

That's why I like this little verse tucked away in Ecclesiastes 11... It tells us that there is actually something to be glad about in growing older. I've sometimes wondered myself what that could be. But God is slowly, in his time, beginning to open my eyes. What's so great about growing old? I suppose we could come up with a long list of things: no more rushing out the door for work, no more feeding the 5,000 at meal time, no more trying to juggle 8-10 passports at one time, no more traveling across the globe with 20+ duffel bags... But I'll leave all that. So what is so special about it all?

It's God's Word...it's the assurance of his presence...it's the greater certainty of my final destination. Whereas in my younger days I knew these things and had them appropriately filed away in my brain...today they are what I live for. They are what keep me going, what get me up in the morning, what consume my thoughts throughout the day and sleepless nights... God is near me, he is with me...and this, my friends, I would not trade for all the healthy days I lived in my toned and chiseled 20s...

JANUARY 2

> January 2
>
> 1 Corinthians 16:23 Message   Jesus has his arms wide open for you.
>
> Am I holding back from going to Jesus? What is distracting me or delaying me? Run to him right now. Bring to him all that is part of my life at this moment.

I remember as if it were yesterday, seeing my ancient father, with his snow white hair (He was in his early 50s...) arriving to attend my high school graduation over 45 years ago. At that tender age, life seemed to spread far out into an endless distance, as if it would go on forever. My parents had always been there, no doubt would always be there. But suddenly, one day, I find my parents are long gone (...and how I wish I could sit down with them and enjoy just one more cup of coffee with them!), and now I am in my 60s, coming into the twilight zone of life! And these words in Ecclesiastes 12 ring very true...remember God while there is still time; we are all headed on a one way train to eternity, and we don't know when our arrival date will be; when all the dust has settled and we have passed through life, walking with God is really what is important, is really what life is all about...

JANUARY 3

> Day/Date — Be sure to remember five things to be grateful for every day. January 3
>
> Psalm 5:3 Message — Every morning I lay out the pieces of my life on your altar.
>
> What a beautiful picture of the best way to start the day with my imperfect life — to put all its parts in God's hands so that he can make something good out of them.

As a teenager, my older brother introduced me to the passion contained in the words of the Song of Solomon. I saw that passion in him and his wife as they courted and then moved into marriage. Later, I discovered the reality of this same passion toward my own wife. Now, imagine God welcoming us into his own presence, as if we were being escorted into the throne room of the greatest king on earth. (That's about as far as we can imagine, but, of course, it will be dazzlingly, immeasurably greater...for in the Bible, when people encountered God, their usual response was to fall over, comatose...) But here in Solomon's words (and he certainly knew something about dazzling riches and rooms), we catch an image of God's incomprehensible, nonsensical love for us! It's so great as to leave us staggered, speechless, yes, even comatose...yet, there it is...God loves us that much...

JANUARY 4

Due to having lived in several countries over the years, we have been on lots of airplane rides. Most transpire just fine, but occasionally you experience a real doozy! Two flights, I remember in particular. During one, we were flying straight through a violent thunderstorm. The plane was bouncing around like a corked bottle in the ocean. Lightning flashed around us, and several times you could see it hit the plane and explode. I knew it was over. We were not going to make it back alive. We were going down, for sure. (Somehow, we got through it...)

Another time, I was on a small Uzbek prop plane. The flight started badly when they bused us out to the plane...then made us wait on the bus because they had forgotten to tank up the plane with fuel! (If they could overlook that, I wondered, what else had they overlooked?!?) Well, we finally took off...sort of. It was a bad start that left me terrified. First off, there were no assigned seats. Just find one... Then, when I sat down, I discovered that my seat could rock back and forth...(and it wasn't because I was in First Class!) As we started to lift off, the real terror began. There was the distinct smell of burning electrical wire or rubber...I couldn't be sure, but it couldn't be good... Then, as we rose up into the air, the plane started to shudder, like it just couldn't quite get the umph needed to really lift off. I knew we would fall out of the sky. So I calmly pulled out my book, opened it to my bookmark, gripped it...and never turned a page during the entire flight! Just stared at and read and reread the same paragraph over and over again. Somehow we made it home then, too...

On both of those flights, as well as all our others, having a measure of peace and calm came down to trusting the pilot. Could I trust him to see us through? Could I leave the uncertainties and unknowns and terrors in his hands?

Which brings us to Psalm 37...

In this psalm, the situation in difficult, uncomfortable, dangerous... And yet, strangely, seemingly unwisely, we are told to relax, not be afraid, be calm. Not because of the circumstances...but because we can trust the One who holds our lives in his hands. We can, and we need, to trust the One who has the world, and our futures, in his safe hands. He is trustworthy. He will see us through the storms and turbulence...

JANUARY 5

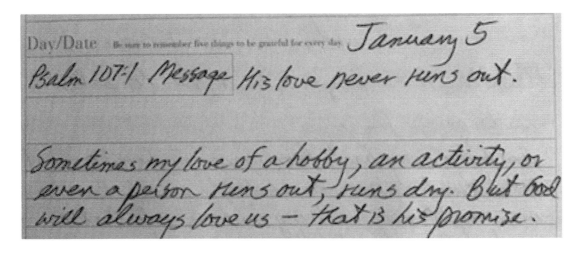

Day/Date   Be sure to remember five things to be grateful for every day.   January 5

Psalm 107:1 Message   His love never runs out.

Sometimes my love of a hobby, an activity, or even a person runs out, runs dry. But God will always love us — that is his promise.

When I pull out Bibles I've read before, I can flip through them and notice by the underlinings (something I love to do as I read), which psalms and passages have meant a lot to me. Psalm 39 is not one of these such passages. There's not much I find in it that I want to underline. However, it does speak to us, and especially to us in this noisy era of social media. The deafening level of hostility we hear being flung back and forth across our world today is disheartening. The politics, the issues that divide us, even comments tossed between family and friends...

Apparently, this is not something new. David, who lived about 3,000 years ago, was talking about this exact topic. He says that he carefully watches over his life, so that he won't misstep with his mouth. How many of us are so conscious of possibly saying the wrong thing, that we guard how we live? Why does he do this? In addition to knowing the damage that words can cause, David is aware that his life will quickly pass. His words will quickly be forgotten (except that in his case, they haven't been forgotten, to his great surprise, I'm sure, as well as to our great blessing!), but the damage done can remain. He also is very aware of the fact, as was Job, when God finally answered him, that before God's greatness, he has nothing to say. He is speechless. So, why would he, why would any of us, rant and rave, knowing that the all holy God, who knows my every inner thought, is watching, hearing, and seeing everything in me...and everything that comes out of me? As Solomon says in Ecclesiastes 5, "So let your words be few."

JANUARY 6

Day/Date · Be sure to remember five things to be grateful for every day. · January 6

2 Corinthians 1:4 NCV · He comforts us every time we have trouble.

Trouble can be frightening, costly, and painful. But in the middle of it, when it visits me, do I remember to notice how God is comforting and blessing me at the same time? God always comes to us in our trouble.

A few years ago, my wife and I were privileged to be able to visit Israel. We wanted to walk around Jerusalem as much as possible to see the places mentioned in the Bible. I remember leaving the Old City, walking down the hill to the Kidron Valley, and then walking up the hill on the other side to where the Garden of Gethsemane still exists today, with some of the same olive trees. In John 18, Jesus did the same thing. He and his disciples crossed the valley and hiked up to the garden, where he spent his last night of freedom on earth. When Jesus left heaven, he shed all aspects of divinity to become a man, and came to earth to save us. This simple passage speaks loudly of his humanity. Any king or high official would ride down the hill, across the valley, and then back up the facing hill. Jesus was Almighty God...and he walked down the hill, across the valley, and up the other side, something no king would likely ever do. He was demonstrating his complete humanity, the full taking off of his divine rights, to walk as the most common man would, across a dusty valley. Yes, Jesus became fully man, because that was what he had to do in order to be the perfect sacrifice for you. As he walked that dirty little valley, he was thinking of you...and me. And he knew that his task was to not lose one single soul that he came to save. (That's why I know that he was thinking about you!)

Further on in chapter 18, we see again that Jesus is thinking of us, rather than himself. When soldiers come to arrest him, his friend, Peter, responds by drawing a sword. Even after three years with Jesus, the disciples were thinking of Jesus in terms of an earthly king and an earthly kingdom. But Jesus assured them that his kingdom was not here on earth. He was not here to preserve himself for earthly power, but rather for his heavenly kingdom...which is also why he spoke openly before often hostile crowds. We tasted a small glimpse of that as well, when we spoke out in public in China when we lived there, knowing that not everyone who heard was friendly.

So we're reminded, as we read these events, of what Jesus gave up in order to lay down his life for us.

JANUARY 7

January 7

Psalm 18:20 Message · God made my life complete when I placed all the pieces before him.

Life is rarely perfect, it seems. But when I put my messy life in God's hands, he can make something good out of it. He can form me into the person he wants me to be.

When we lived in China, I enjoyed taking one or two of our students with me to translate, and we would walk into the streets looking for someone to talk to, to interview. One day, we encountered an elderly man, who turned out to be a retired Geology Professor. Uncharacteristically for Asia, he invited us into his home...which looked something like a rock museum. He proudly showed us his collection, then told us something rather startling. We were living in a beautiful corner of China, at the foothills of the mighty Himalayas. This professor told us, "Do you see those mountains rising up behind us? I found all these stones at the top of those mountains. And I can tell by examining them, that all of them were once under water!" The two students I had with me were stunned into silence by that statement. For you see, we had just been teaching them about Noah and the flood, which covered the tops of the mountains! Now, our Bible story was being confirmed by a secular scientist. This statement that we heard spoken that day reminds me of the beautiful verse that we read in Isaiah 11:9... A day will one day come, when everyone will know God. The knowledge of him will be so complete, that it will be like the flood of Noah's day that covered all the tops of the mountains. What a beautiful picture! What a wonderful hope and future to look forward to!

JANUARY 8

2 Corinthians 12:9 NCV   When you are weak, my power is made perfect.

Embrace my weakness. Be thankful for it. God loves us when we are weak. Then he can work out his good plans in us and through us because we recognize that we're not perfect and that we need his help.

Before we leave on a trip, my wife is always going over and over the logistics and the preparations in her mind...which means that she has restless nights. I'm sure it must have been the same for Mary Magdalene in John 20, following Jesus' crucifixion. She would have tossed and turned all night, wondering what had happened. So she got up...while it was still dark...and ran all the way to the tomb where Jesus' body had been put to rest. Had he really come to life again, as he had said he would? Could it possibly be? She did come and see, as did the other disciples. But they still didn't get it. After all that Jesus had done, after his body was no longer there...still they didn't understand. But then a beautiful thing happened: the same thing that will happen to each one of us when we arrive one day in heaven. Jesus showed up and spoke her name: "Mary!" That is how he will welcome each of us...calling out our name! Won't that be an amazing day! After all our stumbling, failures, and doubts...he will put it all to rest by opening his arms to us and calling our name!

Later, when Jesus is with the disciples, these unbelieving and full of fear followers...he tells them: "Don't be afraid! I'm sending you out!" Isn't that's beyond remarkable! It is us, in our weaknesses and failings, that he has chosen and placed his mark of approval on...to be his messengers, his ambassadors, into a lost world...to share the most important, most wonderful, most amazing news in all of history. He has selected you and me for that most amazing and noble task!

Jesus then goes one step further... When we have specific struggles and doubts, he comes to us and meets us exactly, precisely, where we are. Jesus returned, for all of us down through history to see, when Thomas had specific doubts, especially so that he would be reassured and comforted. Thank God...he knows us, and he meets us and welcomes us right where we are.

JANUARY 9

January 9

Psalm 18:24 Message God rewrote the text of my life when I opened the book of my heart to his eyes.

When I open my heart and desires to God for him to work in me, he changes the whole focus and direction of my life into something infinitely better.

When I was a little boy in Korea, our family lived in an old missionary house that I remember with great fondness as my home. Thinking back, it probably was not quite as wonderful as my memory leads me to believe. We didn't have central heating, on cold winter mornings we could see our breath, there were a good number of rats that lived with us (I hear them still, gnawing at night while I lay in fear...), on occasion our feet got splinters from the rough wooden floor, mosquitoes held sway in the summer, and electricity and water were both prone to go off for long periods of time throughout the year. A dark winding stairway led to a long upstairs hallway, at the end of which, we younger boys lived. I don't know how long that hall was...15 feet, 20 feet?...but after feeling my way up the stairs in the dark, and then feeling my way in pitch darkness along the hallway, it seemed to stretch on forever. And I knew that little rodent eyes were watching my every step. Finally, at the end, I could reach up, swing my arm back and forth, and hopefully come in contact with the thin string hanging down from a single bare lightbulb. A tug on the string...and light would suddenly make the hall visible (not bright, mind you, but at least visible). I would let out an audible sigh of relief and head into my room. Made it through the darkness once again!

As I read the few short verses of Psalm 43, I am reminded of that scary journey along that hallway in thick darkness. The writer is feeling very sunken down in depression. He is pleading with God to bring light into his circumstances..to restore him to a place of praising God. That is just how I felt along that dark, scary passageway as a boy. I couldn't wait till light shone into my lonely world and shooed the darkness away.

This also reminds me of the present dark tunnel we seem to be going through in 2020. Many people have felt lonely, depressed, with diminishing hope... We need God's light to shine on our desperate situation! He does promise to respond when we call. Let's keep putting our hope in God. At the right time, he will come and answer us. And one day, we will see and understand more clearly what the purpose in this trying time has been.

JANUARY 10

2 Corinthians 4:18 NCV We set our eyes not on what we see but on what we cannot see.

The world is filled with things that occupy our attention. It takes a deliberate choice and decision to focus on spiritual things that are lasting — and doing this completely changes the direction of our lives.

As I reflect back over my childhood, and even into adulthood, I cannot recall a single instance when I felt fearful or afraid of some outside threat or situation, while at the same time being in my father's presence. (I might have been fearful when he was angry at something I had done, but that's a different story!) I felt completely safe and secure in his presence. In my mind, he could handle anything that might come against us, so I was completely safe. Years later, after I became a father, I realized that there certainly were times when I was afraid or anxious about a situation. Did my children feel safe in my presence during those same anxious moments? I hope so. But the way we feel as little children in our father's presence can be a beautiful picture of how we should feel in God's presence.

In Psalm 44, we encounter a desperate picture of outside threats and despair. Yet, the writer knows, even in these terrible moments, that God is trustworthy, that he can be counted on. God is his sure salvation...not weapons, armies, or strategies. Is that the confidence we have in God when we are experiencing times of threat, despair, and uncertainty?

And the writer says that even if it were possible for him to forget God, God would not forget him. And that also is the way it is with parents, isn't it? I have found, as a grandparent, that I still am just as concerned for my children as when they were young (probably more so, actually!).

The writer also says that he learned about God from his parents and grandparents. That is how he knew who God was. That's a challenge to us as parents, isn't it! Are we passing on to our children the truths about God? For that indeed is our duty, our challenge, our privilege. That is surely the most important task we have as parents.

JANUARY 11

> Day/Date Be sure to remember five things to be grateful for every day. January 11
>
> Psalm 103:6 Message God makes everything come out right.
>
> Life throws a lot of challenges at us. Very often things turn out differently than we expect or desire. But God uses all circumstances and events to weave his good plans into our lives.

My children will tell you that I'm a fanatic about Facebook...and they run for cover whenever I pull out my phone to take a picture, wondering what I'm going to post next. And I flatter myself, imagining that I have so many Facebook "friends". What if, one day, my greatest sports hero or the actor I loved the most...suddenly friended me in Facebook. Then, not only that, but they started writing me, calling me, wanting to come visit me, and so on. Suddenly, I would really think I am something great!

Psalm 45 paints a short picture of the grandeur of the king...the perfect king, who is always good, always beautifully robed, always attended by admiring assistants and servants, always cheered everywhere he goes. Now imagine that this king is coming into town in a great procession...and he comes right up to your home, asks for you, and says that he's come a long way specifically because he wants you to be his best and closest friend. Goodness, what would you think? What would your family think? What would your friends think?? Suddenly, everyone would want to be your friend!

Now...imagine that the one Supreme Being in all the universe, the one who spoke the galaxies into existence, who by a look can heal any disease, who with a word can stop dead any storm, who can instantly call millions of angels to his aid, who is worshipped and praised in heaven continuously...imagine that this greatest of all rulers came to seek you out. And he kept seeking you out. And he wanted to have a close relationship with you...so close that in some sense it could be described as a marriage. Imagine that this greatest, most benevolent, and most powerful of all rulers ever...wanted to have a relationship with you! Wouldn't that be amazing! How would you respond? Would you keep it quietly to yourself? Or would your excitement prompt you to let the whole world know??

JANUARY 12

Day/Date — Be sure to remember five things to be grateful for every day. January 12

Matthew 18:14 NIV   Your father in heaven is not willing that any of these little ones should perish.

God wants the whole world to have a relationship with him because he loves everyone. But he leaves the decision to pursue a relationship up to us. He even allows and gives us the privilege of sharing his great plans with others!

When I was nine, our family returned to the US for a furlough year, after a five year missionary term in Korea. That summer, without my gang of buddies back home in Korea, I was banging around the house restlessly without much to do, and irritating my parents and grandparents. My father hit upon the great idea of sending me to a kids' club to keep me occupied and out of trouble...and out of their hair. I was terrified. I begged and pleaded not to be sent off to be with a bunch of kids I didn't know, didn't want to know, and didn't want to be with. Apparently, I had become a greater nuisance around the house than I had realized, because my normally easy going Dad wouldn't budge. So off I went, upset that my father had made a big mistake...and at my expense, no less. Well, surprisingly, to me anyway, I enjoyed myself and still have good memories of that time spent with those kids. With many years of hindsight, I understand that my Dad really did love me (He was not punishing me because he hated me!), and quite surprisingly, he apparently knew better than I did what was good and needful for me at that time.

The account in Isaiah 23-25 unfolds for us a similar, if far more serious, series of events. God is shaking the earth's foundations, upsetting the seas, leaving people terrified. But, surprisingly, it's not just a display of chaos and calamity.

God has, from long before we were even born, laid down carefully thought out plans...for our good, for the good of the world... So we find ourselves in the same predicament I did at age nine. Will we trust God to work out his good plans... when all that we see around us tells us a different story...one of disaster and loss? I didn't believe my Dad...I knew he had it wrong...he was forcing me into a bad situation unnecessarily. But, much later, I finally realized that he was right all along. Through all the unpleasantness and angst, he had something good planned for me...because he loved me, he knew what I needed, and he cared enough to even go against my will...for my own good.

This is the picture we see in this Isaiah passage. And truly, this is the reality of what we're living in the world today. We are living in extremely unpleasant conditions, people are suffering...and seemingly God is out on a tea break. Or is he? Do I really imagine that the Almighty God of the universe, who has loved us immeasurably from all time, who only has plans for good...is leaving us in the lurch, is abandoning us, doesn't care about us? No...I can never believe that. We see otherwise in the God of the Bible. He is the God who always brings good out of seemingly impossible circumstances...he is the one who will prevail, who will conquer evil, who will welcome those who trust him into his presence...and into an eternity of never ending good, joy, love, hope, and happiness.

This is the God of the Bible...the God we hope in. Whenever I hear of someone who rejects God, even a Christian leader who turns away from God, I am reminded of a scenario like this one in Isaiah. Can we, will we, trust in the God who loves us...but who we don't yet understand? Apparently, for some people that is too much to ask...so they turn away. I might have turned away from my father a time or two if I had had my way...but thankfully, he held onto me too tightly and wouldn't let me go. Our Heavenly Father does the same for us as we trust in him...

JANUARY 13

Psalm 119:1 Message You're blessed when you stay on course.

Following the way of life God has revealed to us doesn't make life easier and may not make life happier. But our lives will grow spiritually and in maturity as we follow his path. There is greater joy and contentment when walking with God.

Earlier this year, we were driving to visit my brother and his family. As we approached South Carolina, there were tornado warnings in the weather forecast. Suddenly, the violent storm caught up with us. I've never experienced anything like it. The interstate highway was covered with branches and debris that were swirling around. Visibility was zero...we slowed to 20-30 miles an hour. My shoulders tensed, as I hunched over, gripped the steering wheel, and strained to see out the front of the car. Branches were sailing across the windshield horizontally. They were also hitting us on the side, sounding as if someone was peppering us with buckshot. It was truly terrifying. But I didn't want to stop. I knew that tornadoes are narrow swaths of wind and storm that I figured we could drive through if we kept going. We also looked around frantically for some place, any place, such as an overpass, that we could hide under, to ride out the storm. We found none, so kept going.

Eventually, we got through it, and breathed a great sigh of relief. It was the most terrifying ride I had ever been on. One thing I clearly remember, though...the whole time, we were straining to look for some kind of shelter...some place of protection out of the storm.

This is the picture we see in Psalm 46. God is our refuge. He is the one we need to be looking for when we are frantic for protection. He is also ever present...he's already here with us. Am I looking for him, to him, when I feel panicked? God tells us to be still...even when the mountains are tumbling into the sea! Now that takes real focus! Why should we be that focused? Why should we be at peace when a tornado is wrapping its vise around us? Because it's the God of Jacob...the God we see performing wonders, demonstrating power, stopping armies in their tracks, banishing storms...it's this God of the Bible who is with us! Let's trust him, let's focus on him; he is with us in the storm, in any storm, we are enduring.

JANUARY 14

One of my favorite places to visit when I'm home is McKay Used Bookstore. I'm always on the lookout for New Testaments for 5-10 cents that I can give out to people I meet (as well as for any goodies in their free throwaway bin!)... Another thing we enjoy doing is going through their piles of DVDs (Yes, we still have a DVD player...), some for as cheap as 25 cents...can't make too many mistakes at that price. Especially during this COVID lockdown time, we have been watching some of these random movies in the evenings, after our teaching is done for the day.

One thing I've noticed is that movies are not the same today as they were back in our childhood days. We'll be watching a movie, and the narrative will be moving along...and suddenly it will just end, seemingly in mid-story... That's not the way they went in our day. Back in the old days, you saw clearly and quickly who the good guys were and who the bad guys were...and by the end of the tale, the good guys had decisively cleaned up and done away with the bad guys, and the heroes usually ride off into the sunset.

OK, so they weren't very true to life, but at least they left you with a warm fuzzy feeling in your heart as you turned in for the night!

Or were they? Could they, in fact, have been true to life?? When we look at the world around us, sometimes it's hard to locate the good guys...or the upbeat storyline. But it's interesting what the Bible says. In Isaiah 26-28, and all through the Bible, really, there is definitely trauma and terror (the "bad guys"), but in the end, God's good plan (the "good guys") does, all indications to the contrary, prevail! Just like in those old, apparently unrealistic, movies we used to love. Perhaps God is a bit sentimental, too... Actually, no...he's just righteous, good, and all powerful. So the bad guys don't stand a chance. We look around us and see messes everywhere. We throw up our hands, thinking there is no hope in certain situations.

But Isaiah tells us a different story. Chapter 27:6 says: "In days to come, Israel (that is, God's people) will blossom and bloom and fill the whole world with fruit." (CSB) And 28:21 says: "The Lord will rise up...to do his work, his strange work, and perform his task, his alien task." (NIV)

What an interesting God we have! He seems to enjoy surprising us, doing the unexpected, to ratchet up the odds, then, boom, he sweeps aside all the bad guys. Because we know the end with certainty, we can let our minds be at peace, we can rest in his care and certainty...and wait for him to carry out his good plans. Now that's the kind of ending I like! Amen!

JANUARY 15

Day/Date Be sure to remember five things to be grateful for every day. January 15

Psalm 139:3 Message I'm never out of your sight.

Whether in the dark of a sleepless night or struggling to keep calm in the middle of a difficult trial, we can often feel very alone as we walk through life. But our feelings are one thing – reality is another. God tells us that he always knows where we are and what we are going through. He is watching over us.

When I was in ninth grade, in 1971, we spent a year of furlough, from Korea, in Atlanta. In January, President Nixon visited Atlanta and was briefly at the Georgia State Capitol, with the Governor at the time, Jimmy Carter. We drove downtown to join the people gathered there in front of the Capitol, as both men came out briefly to wave to the crowds. I remember straining against a fence that had been put up to control the crowds, simply to catch a glimpse of these two famous men. So much effort, by so many, to just see these two passing historical figures for only a moment.

Imagine now the contrast, when the Ruler of all the earth, the King of all history, will one day appear before the whole world, in such a spectacular way that everyone will see him, everyone will recognize him, all the nations will cheer for him. That is the picture we see described in Psalm 47...when, at last, the whole world will know who our greatest of all kings is, the Almighty Sovereign of all the earth, who has, and will continue, to reign all through history and eternity. What a day that will be! Let's keep hoping for and anticipating that great day, when all people will know, when all things will be made right...

JANUARY 16

Day/Date   Be sure to remember five things to be grateful for every day   January 16

2 Timothy 2:10 NCV   Patiently accept all these troubles so that those whom God has chosen can have the salvation that is in Christ Jesus.

Paul was a great example for us. He willingly and eagerly endured all kinds of trouble so that he could share God's message with many people who had never heard it.

I love history and a good story. I especially enjoy seeing how people react and rise to the occasion in dramatic and unexpected ways when adversity and enemies come against them. There are so many great stories of how a tattered, weakened group of people or soldiers will suddenly pull together and shift the whole tide of a developing war or battle. We see this happening in many great battles, such as, Thermopylae...Joan of Arc and the siege of Orleans...the Battle of Tours...Yorktown...Waterloo...Stalingrad...and Normandy...

The picture we are given in Isaiah 29 & 30 is similar. The self-confident, disobedient people of Israel are unexpectedly surrounded and devoured by God's overwhelming presence and power. It reminds me of the people in Noah's day... suddenly overwhelmed, with nowhere to turn, no way of escape. In contrast to human actions and battles, however, God always has our good in mind. After God devastates, Isaiah 30:18 says he rises to show compassion to us. I can picture a great king, rising up from his throne when a weak beggar comes into his presence...rises to show him unexpected mercy and compassion. One day, the God of all the universe, the God of all the armies in heaven, will rise up from his throne in heaven and reach out to us...because he wants to show us compassion. Isn't that a beautiful picture! Of course, he has already done this, by sending his Son to pay the penalty for our disobedience. But he will do it again, finally, on that last day, when, once and for all, he puts all things right. Let's look to him and wait on him!

JANUARY 17

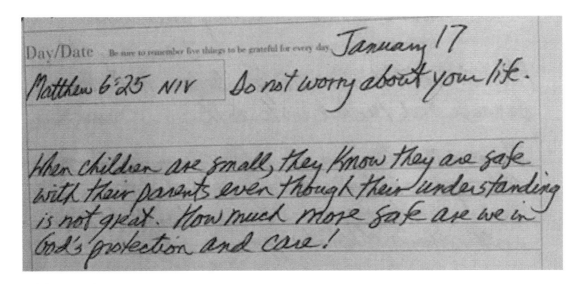

Day/Date — Be sure to remember five things to be grateful for every day — January 17

Matthew 6:25 NIV — Do not worry about your life.

When children are small, they know they are safe with their parents even though their understanding is not great. How much more safe are we in God's protection and care!

When we were teenagers, we used to hear alarming predictions that the world would be so overpopulated by the year 2000, that there would hardly be more than standing room left for anyone. Now, 50 years later, the population has more than doubled. But it's interesting…when you fly over most of Europe, North or South America, Asia, Africa…anywhere, really…what do you see? Vast areas of empty, seemingly uninhabited land. I remember once flying to Kazakhstan from Europe…and looking down over empty landscape for hours and hours, on what looked like an empty planet. The big picture certainly looks different than the downtown area of any major city.

When we look at the Bible, we can get the same feeling…a lot of details and individual interactions taking place. But what about if you take a quick flyover, as if in an airplane? What do you see?

You see the Almighty God of eternity operating in stunning power and control…

Speaking light into existence.

Creating man from nothing.

Carrying Enoch away up to heaven.

Opening the heavens...and flooding the whole earth in Noah's day.

Elevating the slave Joseph to the height of power in the kingdom of Egypt.

Leading Moses and two million Israelites out of Egypt and across the Red Sea with spectacular miracles.

Stopping the sun in its course...and even making it retreat.

Tumbling Jericho's thick stone walls.

Saving Daniel from the mouths of famished lions.

Raising Jesus...and others...from death.

Saving Peter and Paul from imprisonment and other perils.

But do you know what I find almost more amazing than any of those great exploits? It's what we read in a short verse at the end of Psalm 48: "This God (Yes, the very same one who so easily spoke all these great events into happening...) is our God forever and ever. He will be our guide to the very end." Now, if this great God we read about is the one who is with us, who will never abandon us...why do I get so easily worried? It's no wonder that nearly every time a messenger comes from God to speak to someone on earth, his first words are, "Don't be afraid!" These angelic messengers know, far better than we do, who it is that is with us!

JANUARY 18

> **Day/Date** Be sure to remember five things to be grateful for every day. January 18
>
> Isaiah 26:3 NIV You will keep in perfect peace him whose mind is steadfast, because he trusts in you.
>
> When I look around at all the parts of my life, it is easy to quickly become anxious or worried. The remedy or cure for that situation is for me to focus and reflect on who God is and what he has promised us.

Many of our friends in Asia find it hard to read the Bible. It's such a big book, heavy in more ways than one. And if you are not used to reading it, it seems like a hard thing to do. Why, really, did God have to make it so big, I have sometimes asked myself? Perhaps for the same reason we tell our kids the same thing over and over again, 27,000 times! Because they still don't get it...and because we love them too much to give up on them. Why, I wonder, do we keep turning away? Why are we so hard of hearing? Maybe because we are so set in our ways (as Paul related, when he said he kept doing what he knew he shouldn't do...), that we simply become blind to the truth of what God tells us.

We have a North Korean friend, living now in South Korea, who has managed, via China, to call her parents, who are still back in the North. What I find interesting is that she can't tell them about some of the realities of life here in the South. They have been told all their lives that North Korea is the greatest...so, obviously, there is no way that anything in the South could be better. They are blinded and just wouldn't believe it.

But we are exactly the same. God has told us endlessly, "Follow my ways. Then you will find peace, security, joy..." Do we believe it? Sadly, many times not. When we read the opening verse of Isaiah 31, we can almost imagine God's sigh of frustration and impatience with Israel. "What? Don't tell me you're going to

Egypt for help again? Haven't I told you already (a few zillion times!) that they are the wrong place to go for help?" Thankfully, we're not left there. Chapters 32 & 33 follow, with the little word, "will". One day, the King will rule over the whole earth, one day people will listen, one day we will live in peace and security. Let's keep looking toward that day...and reminding each other not to give up or turn back, as we are so prone to do. And let's especially pray for those, like in North Korea, whose eyes are so closed that they keep returning to "Egypt" for help.

JANUARY 19

When I was in high school, the most burning question that we all wanted an urgent answer to was: "What is God's will for my life?" I don't know for sure if I ever really discovered the answer to that question...until today...in Acts 9! I know I am a slow learner, and I don't know if that's even the pivotal question facing today's young people...and, aside from that, it's a bit late for me now, anyway...but at least I do finally have the answer to that question...right there in verse 5.

God stopped Saul dead in his tracks, converted him dramatically, and then told Saul his will for Saul's life (and I think for ours as well). Saul (later we know him as Paul) was used by God to arguably make the greatest impact in God's kingdom since Christ's life and death and resurrection. So God had to very clearly and thoroughly show Saul what his will for him was. Do you know what God told him? Yes, it's right there in verse 5: "Get up and go...you'll be told what to do later." On top of that, God struck him blind, and he had to be led to a place to stay. In the meantime, God told another guy, Ananias, to meet up with Saul, and that God was going to give Saul further instructions: "You are really going to suffer." So there it is, God's will for Saul: "Get up, go, and you're gonna suffer." No five year plan...no support raising...no...well, really nothing else. And it occurs to me that this is exactly how God leads most of us. He has told us to go into all the world, sow seed, reach the lost. So now we just have to get up and go! Very often, as with many of God's servants down through the ages, he tells us what to do along the way, as we get up and go. That certainly gives us a strong impetus to trust God, doesn't it...since we don't always know where he's taking us or the task he has for us to do! Lord, help us to trust you...as you lead us...and as we get up and go.

JANUARY 20

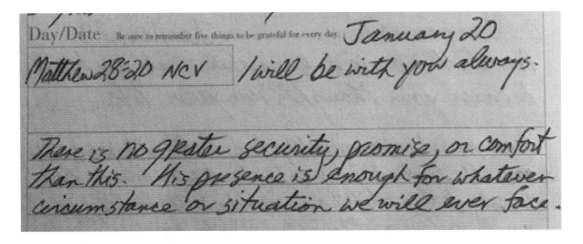

Day/Date   Be sure to remember five things to be grateful for every day.   January 20

Matthew 28:20 NCV   I will be with you always.

There is no greater security, promise, or comfort than this. His presence is enough for whatever circumstance or situation we will ever face.

Coming from what they have experienced in their former lives, it's perhaps not surprising, when we ask our North Korean students what they want to do in life, that most of them say, "I want to make money." It always makes me sad when I hear this. It's very hard to convince a person who has suffered greatly in poverty that this is true, but as we see in Psalm 49, riches aren't the answer to life. How many wealthy celebrities have we heard of, seemingly with everything life could offer, who end their own lives...surely in part because they have come to the realization that, having arrived at the pinnacle of what this world has to offer, they've discovered that, in fact, it's not enough. I read just the other day of one self made billionaire who said that it was satisfying (literally) for a few days, but after that his riches were meaningless. Money is useful and helpful, for sure, but it's not satisfying, and will be terribly disappointing if that is what we are living for. As much as we may try, for as long as we may work at it, chasing what this world has to offer will bring us up short...just as God tells us in his perfect and loving Word.

JANUARY 21

Mark 10:45 NCV   He came to serve others and to give his life.

Father, help me to use my life as Jesus did — pouring it out so others can know you. God has given us this same task that Jesus had — to give up our lives for others.

When we were young, we loved to run around outside and play...and put out of our minds, that day of reckoning in school that would always come at the end of the term. It must be human nature to be that way, because we see it all through the Bible as well...God warning the people of a day of accountability, and the people not wanting to hear it. God warns the people of this in Isaiah 34. A day of reckoning is coming. Sometimes that day of reckoning comes in the form of a natural disaster. In chapter 36, however, we see the King of Assyria threatening Israel with calamity. But, whereas we may give up on something that seems like a lost cause to us, or something that doesn't look like it will produce a return that will justify the expense...God never gives up on us. Never mind that we will never produce a useful return to God. God is a God of holiness, who requires a day of reckoning. But he is also a God of hope, who provides for us a way of escape from judgment...as we see in chapter 35. Thank God...he loves us and does not give up on us, even when we don't deserve his rescue!

JANUARY 22

January 22

Romans 8:39 NCV | Nothing in the whole world will ever be able to separate us from the love of God.

The trials and challenges that come to some people are daunting, insurmountable, overwhelming. But they will never put us into a place where God's love cannot reach us.

When my father passed away, I remember going through some of his old papers and coming across a letter he had kept from Corrie ten Boom. Wow, I thought, Dad heard from Corrie ten Boom?? That's pretty amazing. Some years ago, I came across a verse in the Message Bible as I was reading through it, and I was a little puzzled about the choice of words the author had used. So I thought, I'm going to write and ask author Eugene Peterson about this verse. I wrote him, not really knowing if he would even receive the letter. Well, to my surprise, he wrote me back a couple of weeks later. So, again, I thought, wow, that nearly makes me a celebrity, doesn't it...getting a letter from him?!? (When I was quite a bit younger, I once wrote to my favorite baseball player, Hank Aaron...who my grandmother also was a fan of...asking if he would write my grandmother a birthday greeting. I was so excited to think that our hero would write a personal greeting to my grandmother...alas, he never did.) But we do get excited, don't we, if we happen to be noticed by someone who's famous.

Now imagine how Cornelius must have felt, in Acts 10, when an angel from heaven showed up and told him, "Almighty God who sits enthroned in heaven and reigns over all eternity...he has heard your prayers. And not only that, he has received them as a offering of sacrifice from you...and he has sent me, his heavenly messenger, to come tell you that." No wonder Cornelius was afraid when he received a messenger like that. What's even more amazing is that when we offer up prayers to God, the Sovereign God who reigns over the universe, this God, hears and receives our prayers as offerings of incense coming up to him. Isn't that amazing! We should make frequent use of this privilege...and offer up our prayers to him all day long...and throughout our sleepless hours at night.

JANUARY 23

> **Day/Date** Be sure to remember five things to be grateful for every day. January 23
>
> **Proverbs 4:23 NCV** Be careful what you think, because your thoughts run your life.
>
> Our minds can quickly be filled with good things or with evil. In his infinite care for us, God wisely tells us to fill our minds with healthy, positive, and uplifting thoughts. That's because our thoughts determine the flavor of our lives.

Our boarding school was located outside of one of the larger cities in Korea. Amusements were few and far between, but probably the main one was to hop on a bus for the dusty, bouncy ride into town to catch a John Wayne movie at the local Korean theater...or to go onto the US Army base, where they tolerated these kids coming to the snack bar for real American hamburgers and ice cream from home. That was a big treat, worth the effort of getting there. One day, my older sister took me to the Stonestown Army base, and we headed to the snack bar, as usual. As we were enjoying our heavenly burger in the company of a few other soldiers, suddenly, one soldier stood up and made this announcement: "Everyone who is eating here right now...the bill is on me!" I don't think our bill was more than a dollar or two (I seem to remember that the pints of ice cream we got cost 25 cents.), but still...it made us feel like millionaires or like someone who had just won the lottery! More than 50 years later, I still recall that exhilarating moment.

Psalm 50 starts with a similar announcement...but one which is mega-times greater than the announcement we heard that day, long ago. The Almighty God of the universe stands up to summon everyone on the earth, including you and me. Now that is quite a summons...and worth a whole lot more than one or two dollars! In fact, God summons us, is calling us, everyday, through his Word that he has given to us. Are we listening? Are we in awe that the Great God of all the universe is calling us? So often, in the Bible, when people encountered God, they were struck down as if dead. That is how awesome and devastating it was to come in contact with this great Divine Being. And this is the same God who calls us...let's be sure we are listening!

The final verse of this same chapter 50 has become very precious to us, and especially to my wife. Every time we read it, we recall our intense and frightful struggle with her breast cancer 17 years ago. After she heard her doctor tell us that she had life-threatening cancer, and wondering how she would cope with it, she read this verse. "He who sacrifices thank offerings honors me." She decided right then to make a list of things she was thankful for. Number one on the list was the pain she had felt in a little lump in her breast. Quite often, cancer starts out without pain. She might have missed it if there had been no pain. But she felt pain, went to the doctor, and very quickly started treatment on this particularly aggressive, fast moving cancer. Nearly 20 years later, we are still thankful for the pain God gave her, and which got her attention. And that last verse continues to have precious meaning to us. What are you thankful for today? Is there some offering of thanks you can offer up to God, even in the midst of serious struggles and pain? These offerings are precious to our Heavenly Father...start making a list!

JANUARY 24

Having little kids is a battle, isn't it? (OK, OK, so it is wonderful, as well...but sometimes it does seem like a battle!) Certain ones of our kids (who will, of course, go unnamed...) were a little bit more of a battle than others. I can still remember saying once or twice: "All right...you can do it the easy way or the hard way...but either way, you will obey!" I would then explain that they could obey agreeably (to eat their food, clean up their room, or whatever)...or, if they chose not to, I would make them obey anyway...that was called, "doing it the hard way"...and then it probably wouldn't be quite so pleasant. I am reminded of this battle with our kids when I read Isaiah 37:29. God told the king of Assyria: "I'm going to stick a hook in your nose and drag you back!" Apparently, King Sennacherib chose to do things the hard way. He could have obeyed easily...or not...but either way, God was going to have his way! Sometimes it can seem comical (except that it's really not!) how far we think we can go in not being obedient to God. Do we really imagine for one microsecond that we can outfox or outfight the God who commands the sun to stop or a storm to quiet down? Heavens, no! Why don't we just go easy on ourselves...and do things the simple way... God's going to have his righteous and good way, anyway...so we might as well go along sooner rather than later.

And once we have finally come around, can we, will we, be able to say, as Hezekiah did in chapter 38:17: "I realize that it was actually for my benefit that you allowed me to suffer. You have cleared away all my sins and put them behind you." God sometimes allows us to go through trials...to suffer, even...for our own benefit and good. Let's reflect on that and remember that when we have been struggling.

JANUARY 25

Day/Date   Be sure to remember five things to be grateful for every day.   January 25

Deuteronomy 31:8 NKJV   The Lord, he is the one who goes before you.

When we put our lives into God's hands, who are we following? We are following the one who spoke the universe into existence and who controls the actions of all those who have power.

As soon as I woke up this morning, I started thinking about Psalm 51, knowing that it was where I am in my Bible reading. One of the better known psalms, it was written after King David recognized his terrible actions toward Bathsheba and her husband, Uriah. Three things strike me powerfully about it.

It's terribly sobering (and frightening, really) to realize that this "man after God's own heart" (What better description could God make of someone, really?) could stumble so badly and blindly. And we are all susceptible to this same blindness to our own actions and are capable of falling badly in this way. No one is immune, and God help us if we imagine that we are.

Secondly, David sinned terribly against Bathsheba, using his power of position to force her...and even to destroy her family by having her husband killed deliberately in combat. But what is so startling, really, about David's words in this psalm, is that his great grief and repentance seem to be directed only toward God. Of course, he knew he had sinned badly against Bathsheba's family. That was not at all a light matter. But David knew his God...this holy, righteous, Almighty God who is incapable of living with sin and disobedience. David recognized that he had broken trust with God, that he had gone against everything that God is and stands for...that, in fact, truly, his sin was against God.

In one sense, it's remarkable that God would include all the details of David's horrible sin in his holy Word. But it is for our instruction and sober warning. When we disobey God, we aren't just making a mistake or a bad decision. We are going against everything God is and stands for. I wish I knew that in my heart. Usually, when I get angry, impatient, or do anything else, really, my first thought is about the possible "human" damage it may have caused. I forget or ignore completely what David understood in this psalm...that the real devastating consequence of his action was against God.

Thirdly, as bad as David's sin was (both against God and against Bathsheba...and never mind the terrible example it was before the whole nation)...and it was terrible...the most remarkable point of all is that David knew that God's grace and mercy were greater. Few of us will actually commit both murder and adultery...so David's sins cover just about anything bad we could possibly do. But the big message of this psalm is that God's grace is greater...greater than anything we could do. If I could come up with the worst possible sin I could think of...God's grace stretches farther. We are never outside of his mercy if we turn back to God for forgiveness as David did. What an amazing grace God we have!

JANUARY 26

When we were kids in Korea, many of the missionaries would seek a respite from the oppressive summer humidity in the cities by heading to the beaches or the mountains. In August 1967, we were at the beach, and my Dad and another doctor had to leave us and head back to their hospital duties in Kwangju. Just as they were on their way, my little brother was pulled out to deep waters by a strong ocean current and drowned. An urgent message was sent to a police office, and they managed to intercept my Dad along the road and sent him back to us. That must have been an awful journey back for him and his colleague, because both of them knew that a serious emergency had occurred to one of their families...but they didn't know the details of what had happened or to whom.

I remember that day as if it were yesterday. One thing that stands out, among others, is that a young missionary nurse came to our cabin with us and would not leave my mother until Dad arrived back home. She just stayed with us to comfort my Mom. She refused to leave us.

That is the picture that comes to me when I read these opening verses in Isaiah 40. A terrible tragedy has befallen Israel, as it had to our family many years ago, but God told them not to worry. He was with them...he would not leave them. And he would make things right. He would hold onto them and not let them go.

That's how it is with all of us, isn't it? Life throws a lot of hard stuff at us...it's a broken world, after all, and we're all sinful people. But God promises to be with us, to fix things, to make things right...when we trust him. Lord, help us to do that, to fix our hope on you, through the storms of life.

JANUARY 27

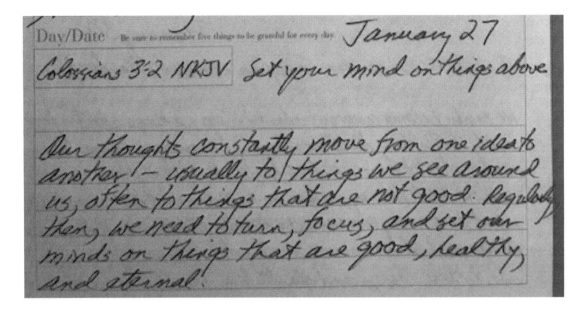

Day/Date — Be sure to remember five things to be grateful for every day. January 27

Colossians 3:2 NKJV — Set your mind on things above.

Our thoughts constantly move from one idea to another — usually to things we see around us, often to things that are not good. Regularly then, we need to turn, focus, and set our minds on things that are good, healthy, and eternal!

Would you like to take a break from some serious passages and read a more light, convoluted, almost comical chapter in the Bible? Try Acts 12. I don't know if anyone (except perhaps Mr. Bean) could come up with a more unlikely tale...

King Herod wants to score some points with the Jews, so he arrests and executes James, who becomes the first disciple to be martyred. This pleased the Jews, so next Herod arrested Peter, who, you would imagine would have been mildly anxious by now. He was pretty much dead meat, all chained up in a dungeon, presumably the next in line to be executed. But God won't have it...so he sends an angel to rescue Peter. But Peter is so totally unconcerned about his predicament that he's sound asleep...and the angel has to bang him upside the head to wake him up. Even then, Peter thinks it must be all a dream. But, sure enough, it's really happening! Now Peter knew that the believers were worried about him and praying fervently for him all through the night. So he headed straight to where they were gathered and knocked on the door. In her excitement over seeing Peter at the door, poor Rhoda opened, then slammed, the door in Peter's face and ran back inside to tell everyone the great news. But poor Rhoda, they all thought she was a nutcase. Peter at the door?? Don't be silly! Of

MEDITATIONS OF A TRAVELER

course he's not there! He's in prison...why do you think we're praying to God to let him out...exactly because he is still there. No way he's gotten out! (Which makes me wonder...in all their fervency, did they really believe God was going to answer their prayers?? It seems not.) Well, when they finally did go open the door, there was Peter...and they were astonished...(i.e. they didn't believe in their own prayers!) Then to finish off the strange saga, the great king gets eaten to death...not by a lion, as would befit a king, but...by worms.

What to make of this funny tale? I've always wondered why God rescued Peter and not James. Clearly, it was not due to anyone's great faith. The believers didn't believe Peter had been rescued...if fact, Peter himself didn't even believe it. So, it's obvious that God is not limited by our great, sporadic, wobbly faith. He will carry out his good plans in spite of us. It's also pretty clear that, in this life, we aren't going to understand God's ways...so we might as well just trust him and not be worrying so much about trying to figure him out...(which seems to be a particular human trait). And, finally, I don't care how great you are...you're treading on very dangerous ground if you start to imagine that you're as great as God.

JANUARY 28

January 28

Psalm 105:4 NCV | Depend on the Lord and his strength.

God gives us great strength, wisdom, and guidance in his Word. Trust in what he makes available to us rather than in our own changeable and unpredictable thoughts and feelings.

Hebrews 11 talks about seeing things through the "eyes of faith"...seeing something that we can't yet really see. My Dad was good at that. Perhaps that's what kept him going. He saw things from an eternal perspective...in ways that weren't yet evident to most of us. Maybe that's why he seemed to me like he was an "eternal optimist". He saw things that the rest of us didn't see...he saw things from an unseen, eternal viewpoint. I remember once asking him, after he had returned from a visit to Bangladesh, where he started up a couple of medical clinics, how things were going there. He responded, "Things are going well. I believe there's a lot of hope for optimism. Things are looking up." I remember, without responding, thinking to myself, "The situation looks like a basket case to me!" He clearly saw things I didn't see...things that, without the eternal perspective, just weren't evident.

Perhaps this is what David is seeing in Psalm 52. As was not unusual, David was being chased all over kingdom come by Saul, David had been betrayed, and some of God's priests had been murdered. It all sounds like a terrible disaster to me. After lamenting the outcome of these wicked people, David ends the psalm by saying, "Who me? Oh, I'm doing great! Couldn't be better! I'm flourishing, in fact. Everything's great." David reminds me of my father...here he was, on the run for his life, betrayed, a fugitive, in desperate straits. What in the world is going on here? Simply, David seeing through the eyes of faith. He has his eternal spectacles on. He knows who's in charge. He knows who's calling the shots. He knows who is holding him in his hands. It only looks like a disaster. (Yeah, right, David...) But that is really what it comes down to, doesn't it? Frequently (too frequently for my taste!), we don't know what God is doing. We don't see much of any good going on. Things look like they are crumbling, desperate...and they would be, if God wasn't in the (eternal) picture. We often can't see him. But he's the one who made it all, planned it all, is working even bad things into his good plans. One day we will see more clearly, as Paul reminded us. Until then...Lord, help us to trust you. All too often, Lord, I forget to put on my eternal spectacles, which you regularly remind me to do.

JANUARY 29

Day/Date Be sure to remember five things to be grateful for every day. January 29

James 3:17 NCV

But the wisdom that comes from God is first of all pure, then peaceful, gentle, and easy to please. This wisdom is always ready to help those who are troubled and to do good for others. God's truth and wisdom usually go against what we first want or think will make us happy. But following his message will give us a richness, depth, joy, and peace that other passing desires are unable to deliver.

In August 1974, my sister dropped me off at the Castle in the Clouds (better known today as Covenant College) with a suitcase and a trunk, all my earthly belongings, and drove off back down Lookout Mountain. I had never even been to Chattanooga before and knew virtually nothing about it or the college. I was a teenager off the boat, so to speak, from a childhood in Korea, which was a world and a half away. It would have been so easy for me to have gotten in with the wrong crowd, to have lost my way, to have spun out of control. But something unusual happened, which to this day I don't understand or am able to make sense of. One of the early patriarchs of the college, RFS, took me under his wing. It's a mystery to me, because there was certainly nothing in me he could have seen that would warrant his attention. Somehow, I managed to get through the program, and still not quite knowing what to do, I applied to an MBA program in Delaware (which I also knew nothing about except that a certain gal was living there). Remarkably, to me, the U of D gave me a free ride and a teaching assistantship (a well paying job to this boy from Korea). I sometimes wonder whether they just felt sorry for me and so offered me this position. But I suspect, though again I'm not sure, that RFS might have had something to do with it, with an over the top reference and recommendation. At any rate, somehow I managed to squeak through there as well. I expect I will be forever indebted to RFS, probably for more than I am even aware of. And this is what I am reminded of when I read those first words of Isaiah 42. They are utterly unbelievable, really. God says to us, "Ah, look at this! He is my most precious person in the world. I just absolutely delight in this person and have specifically chosen him over everyone else. In fact, I have specifically placed my Holy Spirit, my perfect all powerful Comforter and Sustainer, Supporter and Warrior, to look after you, to go with you, to go before you through life." What God has done for us is totally and completely unwarranted and unable to be explained...which is why it reminds me of RFS... But God's love and good plans for us are beyond our understanding and comprehension.

Now, one place we often stumble at, is thinking that, because God loves us, life will be easy and fun. We expect God to either be Santa Claus or a Coke machine that gives us exactly what we want. But just as loving parents do, God knows what we need, and gives us that, rather than what we want. Chapter 43 says that God will be with us when we pass through water and fire. I don't know about you, but that doesn't sound like something I would happily sign up for. But there it is. God says life is going to be trying, a crucible, even. But he's going to be right there with us, holding our hand. And on top of that, he has decided that he won't even remember our sins and shortcomings...again, reminding me of that saint who looked after me in college. What an amazing, undeserved Heavenly Father we have...

JANUARY 30

> **Day/Date** Be sure to remember five things to be grateful for every day. *January 30*
>
> **Psalm 55:22 NCV** | Give your worries to the Lord.
>
> We easily become anxious about things we know about — tests, family difficulties, hard relationships, money problems. And we worry about things we don't know about — what job we will find, who we will marry, where we will live. But God already knows about each worry we have and every situation we will face. He has good plans for us — so why not let him be concerned about these things and thank him already for his plans for us?

When I read a sad passage such as in Psalm 53, it reminds me of Jesus' words of lament at the end of Matthew 23, where he appears to weep over Jerusalem's rejection of his message of compassion. Or it reminds me of Paul's words in 2 Timothy: "Everyone in Asia has deserted me." What sad words! Often, I puzzle about why people reject God. As with our own children, we seem to have an independent streak in us that wants to be its own master, that doesn't want to be told what to do, that doesn't want to be accountable to someone else. (Come to think of it, that's exactly how I am!) Lord, open our stubborn hearts to you, take away our blindness, heal our spiritual illness...help us to respond to you, as Lydia did on that riverbank outside of Philippi...

JANUARY 31

Day/Date	Be sure to remember five things to be grateful for every day.	January 31
Colossians 1:18 NCV	In all things Jesus has first place.	

If we make a conscious and deliberate choice to please God primarily each day, it will change the way we live and the entire direction of our lives.

In the old days, we used to cross the ocean in ships…a voyage that might take a week or more. In 1966, our family returned to Korea, following a year in the US, from San Francisco, aboard the California Bear (which was a ship, not a real bear!). That was quite an experience…watching dolphins arch out of the waters, playing marathon, days on end, Monopoly games, sometimes (certain ones of us) hanging off the slim railings out over the ocean… One of my most vivid memories, during a very tumultuous ocean storm, was climbing to the top of the ship with my Dad, to a position where we could look down over the whole ship. I remember watching the great masts swaying first to the left, then way over to the right, as if the ship would suddenly flip over on its side. It was an awesome experience, one that could certainly bring fear into anyone's heart. But I remember clearly feeling not an ounce of fear. I was only ten, but the great, angry waves gave me no fears. Why was this? It was not because I was brave. I'm sure if I was in that position again today, I would be afraid! It was simply because I was standing next to, holding on to, my father. He was with me. What could I be afraid of? I knew that if I was with him, I was safe. In his presence meant safety. So, waves, thundering, swaying…all that didn't matter. Nothing could touch me. I was with my father.

And this is very much the picture we are given in Isaiah 44-45. We are with God. He controls everything. So we are safe. Yes, there will be tumults. There will be shaking. There will be collapse. But in God's presence, we are safe. Let's remember that one great truth. It is not any human or temporal circumstance that makes us safe. It is being in the presence of God. That is where we truly have nothing to fear.

FEBRUARY

Quarantine day 2...

Thoughts from Leviticus, Numbers, Deuteronomy:

*God is more active and involved in our lives and in the world than we realize.

*God loves us more than we realize.

*God is more holy and to be revered than we realize.

*God is actively at work to show himself to us and to teach us.

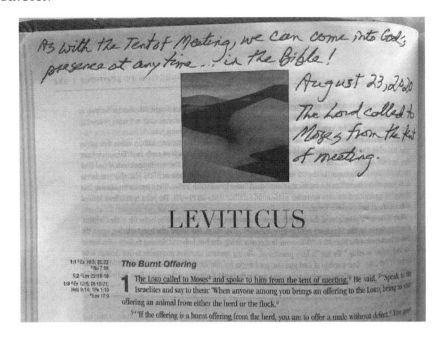

As with the Tent of Meeting, we can come into God's presence at any time... in the Bible!

August 23, 2020
The Lord called to Moses from the tent of meeting.

LEVITICUS

The Burnt Offering

1:1 ᵃEx 19:3; 25:22
ᵇNu 7:89
1:2 ᶜLev 22:18-19
1:3 ᵈEx 12:5; Dt 15:21;
Heb 9:14; 1Pe 1:19
ᵉLev 17:9

1 The LORD called to Moses and spoke to him from the tent of meeting. He said, "Speak to the Israelites and say to them: 'When anyone among you brings an offering to the LORD, bring as your offering an animal from either the herd or the flock.

³ "'If the offering is a burnt offering from the herd, you are to offer a male without defect.

FEBRUARY 1

> **Day/Date** Be sure to remember five things to be grateful for every day. February 1
>
> Colossians 1:25 NCV God gave us a special work — to tell fully the Message.
>
> The most precious, important concern that God has — to have a relationship with everyone — he has entrusted to us = the privilege of sharing this great news with others.

In our earlier days of marriage, I knew that my wife was such a saint that she would never get cancer. I was going to get cancer, given how prevalent it is in our generation, and I was such a much bigger sinner than she was, that I was sure to get it. Well, low and behold, she got the cancer...life threatening cancer. I still knew she was more of a saint than me, so obviously I had to adjust my theory... I realized then that, in fact, God allows his choicest saints to suffer the most. And, really, that's what we see all through the Bible, isn't it? In Acts 14, Paul healed a person. But it caused such an uproar, that a crowd was stirred up and ended out stoning a Paul, and nearly killing him. In fact, God told Paul that everywhere he went, he was going to suffer and be persecuted. And, of course, it was the same with Jesus. God does allow his choicest saints to suffer...just as Jesus also did...because we are representing him. He loves the world so much that he's willing to suffer, even willing for those he loves to suffer, to reach out to those who don't yet know him.

FEBRUARY 2

Day/Date Be sure to remember five things to be grateful for every day. February 2

Colossians 2:3 NCV In him all the treasures of wisdom and knowledge are safely kept.

The key to living a full life as we were made to live is to know Jesus, to discover the truth contained in his Word, and to apply it to our lives.

During the 1980s, I owned and managed a small Christian bookstore in Tennessee. Shortly after taking it over, sales took a dip (before later rebounding), and I began to feel a bit panicked. I remember turning to Psalm 115 at the time ("The Lord has been mindful of us, and he will bless us." RSV), and being greatly blessed and encouraged by it through those uncertain days. (Elsbeth cross-stitched it for me, and that framed verse has remained precious to me ever since.) I can't say that God came to my rescue by suddenly doubling my sales...but perhaps that was not what I really most needed. What I do still remember from those days, nearly 40 years later, is turning to God and being encouraged by that psalm. Every time I read that psalm, even today, I am reminded of seeking God's comfort during those scary days and being encouraged by his promises of support and being with us. I expect that was the help I needed then...to be reminded to turn to God...rather than a doubling in sales.

I'm reminded of those days when I read Psalm 54. David was running for his life (probably slightly more terrifying than experiencing a little drop in sales), and his hiding place had just been reported to Saul, who was hunting David down with his elite soldiers to kill him. What is truly remarkable (and quite an example to us), is that at this desperate moment, David turned his attention to God, reminded himself that God was with him, and was so confident and sure that God was going to answer and deliver him, that he gave an offering to God...and said, "God has (already) delivered me." Now if that isn't amazing faith, I don't know what is! Perhaps it's a good reminder to us right now in 2020. We are feeling unease, uncertainty, some have lost family members, many have lost jobs. Are we so confident that God is with us and will rescue us that we can begin already to thank and praise him? Who knows, one day we may look back and see that 2020 was a defining moment in our spiritual walk, in that of our nation, perhaps even across the world! Let's trust and believe in God and his good plans...even before we can see things being worked out. Let's trust God as David did during his hour of trial.

FEBRUARY 3

> **Day/Date** Be sure to remember five things to be grateful for every day   February 3
>
> **Colossians 3:16 NCV** Let the teaching of Christ live in you richly.
>
> We can learn a lot of knowledge in the Bible. But to make it a part of my life, to allow it to change and direct my life, that is what will really make my life full.

When we were in college and starting to get interested in each other, my wife and I used to visit a nursing home on Sundays. I can't exactly say it was the highlight of my week, but it was something good we could do together. One ancient lady we met there was Mrs. Gould. A retired missionary from India, she still treasured the tin cup that she long ago used to take with her when she went on trips out into the countryside. From any worldly measure, Mrs. Gould was old and washed up, just waiting to die. But I remember her glowing and radiant face, as she told us about India and reflected on her relationship with God. Truly, in her last earthly days, she had joy in her Lord. I expect she knew and understood Isaiah 46, where God tells us, "Don't worry…I'll be just the same when you're old, as I am now. I'll take care of you then, just as I do now." That's Mrs. Gould's God…still the same God we have today.

FEBRUARY 4

> **Day/Date** Be sure to remember five things to be grateful for every day. **February 4**
>
> **James 4:3 NCV** When you ask, you do not receive because the reason you ask is wrong.
>
> When my children ask me for good things, I love to give them these things. But often they ask for things they desire which are not healthy, wise, or best for them. These things I don't give to them. God answers us in the same way, by giving us what is best instead of what we want.

There are not too many people who would accuse my missionary doctor father of over planning. Although he grew up in a refined and cultured Southern family in the early 1900s, he must have inherited or picked up somewhere along the way that peculiar Asian trait of doing things, of changing course, last minute. I remember hearing the story about him having to give a medical lecture…but on the way he got sidetracked by stopping to help someone in need…and he forgot about his appointment altogether. I doubt if anyone waiting for him that day forgot that lesson! (And surely no one waiting for Jesus to show up when Lazarus was dying ever forgot that he was too late…and what then happened after that.) I don't know the details of that story about Dad, but it certainly doesn't surprise me. Once I was walking with him through town…and he stopped, seemingly forgetting all else, to talk to and help a man with a large goiter. Another time, we were on a train together at night. Near us, a lady was struck by glass in the eye…(Someone outside must have launched a stone at the passing train.) Again, Dad forgot all else to tend to this lady, even escorting her off the train to a hospital, if my memory serves me correctly. I don't remember where we were going or if we arrived there in time!

My (frustrating to many) Dad reminds me of Jesus and Paul...always on the look-out for the needy, seemingly oblivious to his plans and responsibilities, aggravating more than a few along the way.

This little statement in Acts 15 reminds me of my Dad. The apostles had been sent on a particular and rather urgent trip. But, seemingly, they forgot all about it and stopped all along the way to talk to and encourage many other folks. They didn't allow their plans to interfere with the fields which were white and ready to be harvested. Neither did my Dad.

FEBRUARY 5

Day/Date Be sure to remember five things to be grateful for every day. **February 5**

1 Thessalonians 4:7 NCV   God called us to be holy.

God's plan is for us to be dedicated to living the good and wise life he prepared for us — not just to live selfishly, restlessly, and for ourselves.

When John Kennedy was President, his children were still very young. Perhaps many of us remember seeing the pictures of his kids playing in the Oval Office, in one of the most important places of power in the entire world. Did his children actually realize where they were? To them, it was just the room where their Dad went to work, to meet with other folks. But, primarily, it's where their Dad was. I doubt if they even began, really, to understand who their father was, to understand the complex and varied issues that he grappled with every day. They just wandered in and out because that's where Dad was.

If any of us were to enter the presence of a king, president, or prime minister, we would come with a certain amount of hesitation and trepidation. It's striking to notice how David addresses the Almighty, All Powerful, Sovereign of the universe in verse one of Psalm 55. None of us would address a sovereign or leader this way. David comes demanding, with a hint of impatience in his voice. "Listen to me, God!" None of the aides surrounding President Kennedy would have dared approach him like that...yet, very probably his kids would come scampering in, with that exact tone in their voices. Their relationship to the President was everything. Then, toward the end of the chapter, David tells us: "Unload your problems and worries on God!" I picture a dump truck, unloading a mound of dirt onto the ground. Again, we are invited to do that because of our relationship with the King. None of us can begin to comprehend fully who God is, the complexities of running the universe, the fact that he knows how many hairs are on the heads of 8 billion people. Yet, it's our relationship, as we are his children, that permits us to be welcomed into his presence, at any time, with any concern, and, no matter how occupied he is with affairs of the universe, to receive his full attention and compassion and power in response. What an amazing, Almighty God, our own Father, we have.

FEBRUARY 6

Day/Date	*Be sure to remember five things to be grateful for every day.*	February 6

Isaiah 55:7 NCV · Come to God, because he will freely forgive.

God is happy to clean away my evil and badness if I really want him to do so and am serious about him changing my life.

It's a painful second or two, to be driving along a road at night, and to suddenly see a squirrel try to dash across the road. It will dart in one direction, hesitate, turn, and thud! Too often there's the sickening sound of it's body hitting the car. I think of that tragic squirrel as I read Isaiah 47 & 48. God is watching us try to run through life on our tiny little legs, thinking we can find our way on our own, and then...boom...we're hit by disaster. Sometimes it comes sooner, sometimes it comes later...but we're in for a bad ending if we're trying to scamper through life on our own.

Life is hard and challenging either way. But the difference, when we follow God, is that he is with us, he goes before us, his presence guides us, when we experience desert or storm, as we keep our eyes on him. Lord, keep us from the foolishness of imagining that we can be the little squirrel, racing confidently as the beams of a freight train come bearing down on us. How much better and more secure to be led and guided by his Spirit, as we walk the road of life.

FEBRUARY 7

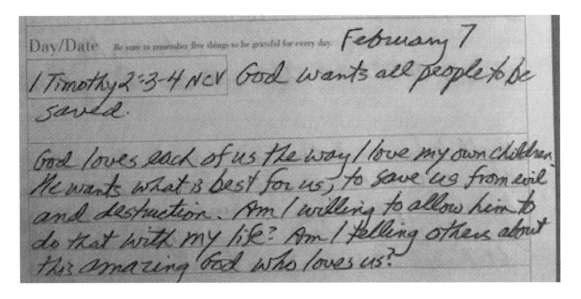

When I visited Dali, China, for the first time, in 2009, I was struck by and excited about the foreign students I encountered there. Looking at a map, I realized that there were six or eight countries very close to this spot in southern China, and students from these countries were coming up into China to study. Many were from countries not very reached with the Gospel, and all of them wanted to learn English. I was gripped by this possibility, this opportunity. Within a number of months, we moved to Dali and began what were to be seven of the most exciting, exhilarating, and rewarding years of our 30 years serving as missionaries.

But what is interesting, and a bit ironic, is that nearly all of our outreach with the Gospel was to Chinese students...not to the ones that had drawn me to that location in the first place. Was I mistaken? Did I get it all wrong? Did I allow myself to be sidetracked or distracted?

I am reminded of our own experience in China when I read Acts 16. Paul was passionate about reaching the lost, the unreached, those who hadn't heard the Good News before. He made plans to visit those people, started on his way, and then discovered, midstream, that, in fact, God had other plans for and designs on his time and his life. Things turned out looking very different from

Paul's original plans. He made plans...but he didn't block out God's overruling of his carefully laid plans. He held his own plans loosely, and stayed attentive and open to the doors that God opened to him along the way. Paul didn't miss too many opportunities, because he was alert to what was happening around him...he knew that his carefully crafted plans and goals were subject to God's plans and wishes, as they came to Paul on his way.

So often, I realize in a passing moment that I have missed an opportunity that God has brought across my path. I remember still, with some regret, encountering two Ukrainian gals passing through Dali. After engaging them in conversation, they went on their way...and I realized I had missed the moment to share the Gospel with them. They were not part of my plans and goals...but clearly God brought them across my path...and I missed that moment that was staring me in face. Lord, help us to be alert and attune to you, caring so much for those around us that we seize opportunities, regardless of whether or not they fit into our goals.

FEBRUARY 8

Day/Date Be sure to remember five things to be grateful for every day. February 8

1 Timothy 6:18 NCV Be generous and ready to share.

My natural desire is like a squirrel — to save up as much for myself as I can. But God made us and gave to us so we would give and share. Ironically, doing that makes us richer and more content in ways we never thought possible.

One thing I like to do when I travel is to take coins with me to give out to kids that I encounter along the way. I know I loved getting coins when I was little, and I expect many kids still do as well. I also like it that US coins state: "In God We Trust." (It helps, too, that most people the world over have heard of Abraham Lincoln, so they would probably prefer to get a penny than a more valuable US coin with some lesser known figure on it! So, I load my pockets up with pennies as I go out into the streets. Occasionally, Customs officials will look at my rolls of coins in my bags and eye me suspiciously. He's got to be hiding something here with all these worthless pennies, they seem to be thinking...) Who knows if someone may see that statement on the coins and have their attention turned to spiritual things...

David uses those same words in Psalm 56, saying that when he's afraid, he trusts in God. For being a great king in his time, for still today being remembered as Israel's greatest king, for having defeated so many other kings in his day, it's remarkable how often he talks about being afraid. Even being a great leader, in a powerful position, does not, apparently, prevent one from being afraid. And it must have happened often to David. For he says that God keeps track of every single one of David's tears. There must have been a lot of them if God was keeping a meticulous record of each one. And, again, it's remarkable that, as he does in other places such as Psalm 54, David talks about already having been delivered by God...even though he was still very much in the thick of his problems and troubles. What does this tell us about David...(and about how we should also be)? For one thing, David, God's specially chosen leader, was not immune to fear, danger, hardship, and terror. Perhaps one of our most common questions as humans...as believers...is: "Why is this happening to me?" And David at times asked the same question. But it's clear that he had many instances when he could indeed have asked that question. He says, "When I am afraid..." In other words, he must have felt that way pretty often. But he also knew exactly where to turn when that happened. He had no doubt, even though it wasn't easy and he still struggled, that God was the one he needed to turn to. And it wasn't like God was somehow out to lunch or had missed the boat this time. God knew about ever detail of David's suffering...every single tear that he shed! But David, again, even though his sufferings and trials were very real, knew with total confidence that God had his back, as we say. God had him covered. So much so, that David, still in the middle of his stresses, could say, "God, here are my thanks for what you have already done. You've already sent your angels...I have already been delivered and saved"...(though the circumstances may very well have suggested otherwise). Can we do this with David? Can we already offer thanks to God for his delivery...even though we don't see signs of his delivering angels yet?

We may wonder why David had to so frequently go through all these trials? Couldn't God have just easily swept aside all his enemies? Yes, he could have. But, no doubt, God was thinking of you and me, even as he recorded David's tears. God knew that we also would have to learn these same lessons of trusting in God. So, in his love for us, God allowed his servant (and his own Son, later, for that matter) to suffer. Are you and I suffering today? Do we wonder why God is allowing us to suffer? Is it because he is allowing us the privilege and opportunity to be an example to someone else God loves and wants to reach with his love? Perhaps...probably...definitely! So, let's, with David (and later with Paul, who reminded us to be patient in tribulation), trust God as we suffer. Look to him in our trials. Thank him for his deliverance, which he promises, now...even though we can't yet see it.

FEBRUARY 9

Day/Date — Be sure to remember five things to be grateful for every day.

February 9

2 Timothy 1:8 NCV — Suffer with me for the Good News.

To save someone from an empty, destructive life with no hope and no future — to tell them how they can have a rich, meaningful, contented, saved life — that's worth going through some trouble and inconvenience for.

Fashions and fads sure are funny things, aren't they? I remember in high school, we had a drill sergeant of a coach who loved wearing pencil thin ties. This was in the day when ties were about six inches across...the wider the better. He seemed to delight in wearing his thin ties and belts, and we all thought he was pretty cool for being different and proud of it. He would tell us, "Keep your things long enough, and they'll come right back in style!" Years later we often look back on styles and wonder, "How could we possibly have thought that looked good??"

I must confess that there is one fad that makes my skin crawl...the current rage with tattoos! Sometimes I'll see a pretty outlandish tattoo and wonder, "What is that guy going to think of his tattoo when he's my age??" If I had gotten a tattoo when I was a teenager, it would have no doubt been a giant Atlanta Braves emblem right across my chest. As much as I liked them then, I sure am glad today that my chest doesn't have a huge "A" painted across it.

But there is one tattoo that I will be forever grateful for... God tells us that he has our names tattooed on himself. Yeah, right, you're thinking! But it says so, right there in Isaiah 49...God has us carved right into the palms of his hands! Will he ever forget us? Not likely. I would be reminded of the Atlanta Braves every single day if I had their giant "A" across my chest. Probably we don't look at any part of our body more times in a day than we do our hands. Is that why God carved our names into his hands? More than likely so...how could he ever, ever forget us, when he is constantly staring at us? Isn't that amazing? God wants to be sure that he is always thinking about us, that he never forgets us...so he put our names right where he will always see us. Let's not forget that. Let's take comfort in that. He loves us. He will never forget us.

FEBRUARY 10

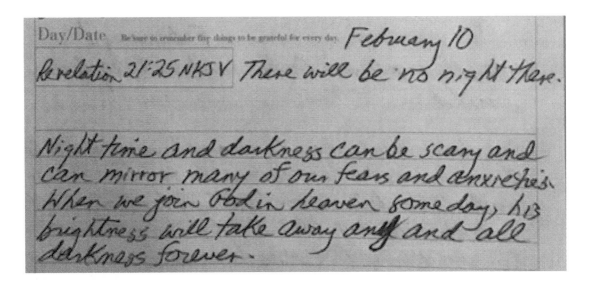

Day/Date Be sure to remember five things to be grateful for every day. February 10

Revelation 21:25 NKJV There will be no night there.

Night time and darkness can be scary and can mirror many of our fears and anxieties. When we join God in heaven some day, his brightness will take away any and all darkness forever.

Somewhere along the line, we seem to have lost our way in regards to church. We have the odd idea that we should avoid anyone different from or disagreeing with us...anyone who is deficient or who has a problem of any kind...especially those who are hypocrites. What I find interesting about Acts 17 is that Paul had exactly the opposite attitude. Everywhere he went...Thessalonica, Berea, Athens...he immediately sought out the gathering places of religious people. And some of them clearly didn't agree with him, some of them were not believers in the Gospel, some even tried to kill him. But everywhere Paul went, he sought out people who he could encourage, bless, serve, minister to. His thought was always about how he could be a blessing to others. It was never about: do they agree with me, are they perfect, are they going to please me?

So, what about me? What do I think about church? Am I avoiding any group that has hypocrites? Anyone who doesn't match me perfectly? Anyone I don't like? If I'm honest, any group with me in it will automatically be deficient, hypocritical, undesirable. Thankfully, Paul would have still welcomed me. He would have seen my hypocrisy...and reached out to me anyway. Would I do that? Do I do that? That, really, is what God has done for all of us...welcomed us in our imperfection and unpleasantness. Let's do the same to others, shall we?

FEBRUARY 11

Day/Date Be sure to remember five things to be grateful for every day. February 11

Psalm 116:1 Message I love God because he listened to me.

God knows what we are thinking about, knows what we need, has available what is best for us... and wants to give it to us. It's hard not to love a heavenly Father like that!

Psalm 57 is remarkable and crazy! David bursts into praise and shares words of great confidence...while he is hiding in a cave and on the run from his great nemesis, Saul. It reminds me of stories I heard from my parents in Korea and grandparents in China...tales of bandits, firing squads, invasions, evacuations, losing all their possessions including wedding gifts, fleeing into unknown destinations, panic, burglars...seemingly endless disasters. What is interesting and surprising, though, is that invariably these stories are related with a sense of nostalgia, with a smile, with confidence, almost a sense of longing, as if they were great highlights in their lives. I remember hearing old people in England share with warm sentiment about their days lived during the panic and desperation of World War 2...and saying that those days of bombing and destruction were the best days of their lives. How could that have been so? What they remembered was that people came together, cared for each other, were one as a people, all in it together. In some ways, those were special times.

In a similar way, the stories of my parents and grandparents were precious because they remembered, not so much the panic and alarm, but, the presence of God with them...the way God brought them through, his care for them. And those were life defining moments that they never forgot, that remained precious to them throughout their lives. Perhaps David was experiencing the same thing. In the midst of intense danger and alarm...he knew God was with him. He knew that God had a purpose. He knew that God would receive glory and honor through this crucible. And so, already, though still in the middle of it, David could offer praise to God. He knew that his experience of trial and panic would provide an opportunity to tell the world of God's goodness and greatness...and so it did. Thousands of years later, we are still being blessed by the torments that David endured.

That's a good lesson for us as well. When we feel without hope, abandoned, stretched to the end of our resources...we haven't been abandoned. God hasn't forgotten us. It most likely means that God has plans to use our trials in his good purposes to bless us and many others. Can we trust him, as David also did, even as we are still in the furnace, on the run, seemingly deserted, and enduring disaster? God, help us to keep our eyes on you. When the circumstances tell us otherwise, help us to remember that you are still with us, you will redeem this difficulty, the final chapter has not yet been written.

FEBRUARY 12

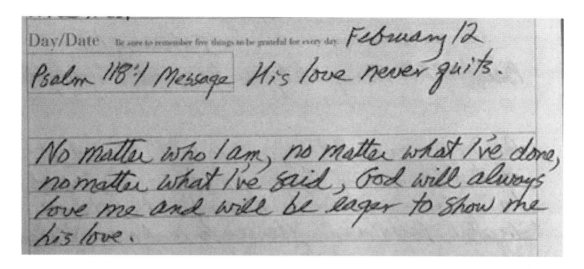

Day/Date   Be sure to remember five things to be grateful for every day   February 12

Psalm 118:1 Message   His love never quits.

No matter who I am, no matter what I've done, no matter what I've said, God will always love me and will be eager to show me his love.

I still see my old, snow white haired grandmother, Nai Nai, we called her, using the Chinese name for grandmother, recounting tales from China, with a twinkle in her eyes and joy in her voice...

Those were dangerous, unsettled, alarming days in China's history, some 75 years ago. Conflicting forces were clashing, advancing, retreating, wreaking havoc wherever they went...a frightening time. One story Nai Nai told us was when my Grandpa had to leave for a few days to transact mission business, as he frequently did. While he was away, word came that military forces had swept in and overwhelmed the city where my Grandpa was. And then silence fell over the area. No one quite knew what was happening, news had ceased to filter out, and Nai Nai realized that Grandpa was somewhere in the thick of it. Days inched by...no word. What was happening? Where was he? Was he OK? It must have been a most frightening time for her.

Then something happened which reminds me of some of the verses I read in Isaiah 52-55. These chapters talk about a time of alarm, uncertainty, danger-...but all the while, God's good plans were being worked out, were unable to be thwarted or stopped.

One day, a disheveled, dusty, dirty figure came walking up the driveway. As he approached, Nai Nai saw the most beautiful sight she had ever laid eyes on. It was my Grandpa! He had come home. Somehow, he had made it through the danger zone. He was safe again at last. This filthy figure...was the most beautiful sight she had ever seen. Suddenly, all the uncertainty was gone. The danger had passed. The alarm had evaporated.

We see that same picture in these chapters in Isaiah. God's Servant, his Messenger, our Savior, was unattractive, beat up, seemingly without hope and lost. But he came through. He conquered sin. He saved us. And things were made right. God's good plans could not be deterred. His Word, his Decree, accomplished what he sent it out to do. God's good plan prevailed. Perhaps one day we will look back at our dark days of challenge, testing, and despair...and we will recognize that, in fact, God was working his good purposes out. He had not abandoned us after all. Evil had not overwhelmed us, or him. God's love prevailed. Let's keep hoping in him...one day the dust will clear...and we will see what God has been accomplishing all along.

FEBRUARY 13

> Day/Date Be sure to remember five things to be grateful for every day. February 13
>
> James 4:4 - NCV   Loving the world is the same as hating God.
>
> When the Bible talks about loving the world, it is referring to loving those things which are worldly rather than spiritual like God is. It means loving things which are against God, the opposite of God, things that are selfish and evil.

I don't doubt that the apostle Paul would have said that all his steps and all his days were carefully directed by God. But sometimes we read his stories, and they sound like a litany of crazy coincidences, random events and encounters without any rhyme or reason. The story in Acts 18 is something like that, and in fact it brings to mind a rather crazy experience that happened to me once... something that I have no doubt that God had a hand in...

In 1993, we were living in France, and I was feeling very discouraged, wondering even if I should just pack it up and return home to the US. At the same time, I planned a trip that took me from France to Romania, to neighboring Moldova, and then on to Moscow, before returning back home to France. Following the visit to Romania, I took an overnight train to Kishnev, Moldova, where I stayed with a family that knew precious little English. It was a bit challenging, but my hosts seemed to be grateful for the visit, and at the end, the man went outside to his yard and returned with a bag of walnuts and a jar of honey, parting gifts to me. I had only a small carry on bag with me, so, really, the last thing I wanted was more stuff to carry with me on to Moscow. But it was clear that he was giving me what he had, as a generous gift to his guest. So I received it gratefully.

In Moscow, I stayed with a retired couple who had been school teachers, in their top floor apartment in a high rise complex. There was a tiny elevator up to their apartment, so small that we couldn't fit in together. So, as I ride up with his wife, the retired PE teacher bounded up the eight or nine sets of stairs and greeted us at the top. It was a rather grim, weather worn building from the outside. But when we arrived inside their apartment, a different sight greeted my eyes altogether. Their shelves were lined with beautiful volumes of books, and it was indeed clear that this was a refined and cultured family. They began to recount to me the trials they had struggled through in recent years. With the collapse of the Soviet Union, life had become very difficult for people like them, dependent on their pension layout. The value of their retirement income had shrunk to a microscopic $30 a month, this in one of the most expensive cities in the world, and they had been reduced to peddling their precious books on the streets.

On top of that, their 13 year old granddaughter was living with them. She had a serious condition where she had been born with three kidneys. They did not have the money to pay for her needed surgery or treatment. I never sensed that they were asking me for money...they were just sharing their hearts and their lives with me. The doctor had related to them that without surgery or treatment, there was really only one thing left that he could advise them to do... give their granddaughter walnuts and honey. What?? "Just a moment!", I said. I jumped up from the little kitchen table and ran to my bedroom. Out came the walnuts and honey from my bag, and I brought the gifts in to them. Their jaws dropped, as did mine as well. We were both stunned. How could this be? How could I, just off the plane from Moldova (Where else?), have on my person, literally, exactly, what the doctor ordered? Neither of us could believe it.

I still remember those moments, nearly 30 years ago, as if it were yesterday. I don't know what happened to the family after that. I lost contact with them. But I will never (and I'm sure they won't either) forget that, in my moment of deep discouragement, God gently touched me on the shoulder and said, "I haven't forgotten you. I'm still right here...still watching over you. I still have good plans for you. Things are going to be OK."

Paul may at times have wondered why he, along the way, encountered this person or that, why his plans took him out of the way to this or that seemingly random place. But I don't doubt that he sensed God's nudge as these things happened. In the midst of all the chaos, beatings, and shipwreck...God was still with him...just as he is with us today.

FEBRUARY 14

Day/Date Be sure to remember five things to be grateful for every day. February 14

2 Timothy 3:12 NCV Everyone who wants to live as God desires, in Christ Jesus, will be hurt.

The world we live in, the people we live with, we ourselves, have all been damaged and stained by sin, by disobedience to God. That means that when we want to please God, we will come into conflict with everything around us — and we will get hurt.

Many years ago, I was sitting in the left turning lane at a large intersection. One car was in front of me, waiting for a chance to turn as we got a green light. The left turn signal had gone off, but we still had a green light in the event there was a break in the oncoming traffic. There were two lanes of traffic coming towards us. On the inside lane, closest to us, a large truck was coming towards us. There was a break in the traffic following it, and I could see the car in front of me starting to inch out as the driver waited his chance to turn left across the intersection. But, sitting back far enough behind the guy in front of me, I could see something that apparently he couldn't. In the outside far lane, behind the truck coming toward us, was a car also coming towards us, which the driver in front of me couldn't see. As soon as the truck zipped past, the guy in front of me pulled out across the intersection...and was hammered, broadsided, and then pushed all the way to the side of the road, by the car he hadn't seen, hidden out of view from the truck. It all happened so fast, in a split second, that I wanted to warn the guy in front of me but didn't know how. If I had honked my horn at him to get his attention, he, no doubt, would have thought I was impatient for him to hurry up and move into the opening as the truck sailed past. At any rate, it happened so fast, that I could see in a flash that the guy was going to get smashed...but there was nothing I could do about it.

Sometimes, we have perhaps seen videos of folks playing in the beach, while a giant tsunami is racing in above the waves...and the people on the beach are completely oblivious of what is about to hit them.

When something like this happens, it gives us a sickening feeling as we watch disaster about to strike from our vantage point.

But what about if something really good, but also unexpected, is about to strike? That's what's described in Psalm 58. There is violence, evil, and injustice everywhere...in fact, it's how I sometimes feel as I look around our world. But after describing the sickness we see in the world around us, David, in this psalm, ends by saying, "But wait! I see something coming that the rest of you can't see from your perspective. A tsunami of justice and righteousness is on its way. It's coming, and it will put everything right again. Hang on until that day!" Lord, help us to keep our eyes on you. When the oncoming traffic all looks bad, help us to remember that we can't see the whole picture from where we stand. You are also in the picture...coming to set all things right. Let us hope in that.

FEBRUARY 15

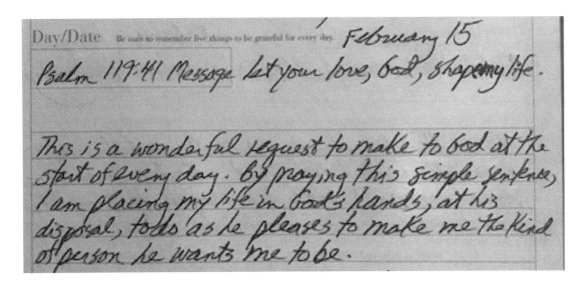

Day/Date Be sure to remember five things to be grateful for every day. February 15

Psalm 119:41 Message Let your love, God, shape my life.

This is a wonderful request to make to God at the start of every day. By praying this simple sentence, I am placing my life in God's hands, at his disposal, to do as he pleases to make me the kind of person he wants me to be.

My mother grew up in China, where her parents and grandparents were missionaries. They were in the same mission group, and in the same province, that the Nelson Bells were in. Their daughter, Ruth Bell, eventually met and married a young guy from North Carolina who she met at Wheaton College, a guy named Billy Graham. Ruth Bell Graham's sister was a missionary in Korea, and I was in school with her kids. So that almost makes me famous, right?!? I mean, I knew the folks who were related to Billy Graham...so that must count for something!

Occasionally, I've observed Billy Graham's children...I think just about all of them have grown up to have ministries of their own. In my self-pitying moments, I'm tempted to think, "Man, it's not fair. They all made it...they all arrived...just because of their name!" (Now, of course I'm too spiritual to actually say that...but, just on occasion, that thought crosses my mind.)

But do you know what is really remarkable? If I want to think about unfair...do you know what is really unfair?? It says it right there in the opening words of Isaiah 56. Chapters 56-58 go on and on about how the Almighty, holy God hates injustice. He hates sin and evil. But in 56:1, God is talking to you and me...us in all our sinfulness...and he says, "You fix the problem of injustice." Now, if I think Billy Graham's kids had an unfair advantage...what about us? The Almighty, perfect, all knowing God of the universe and all eternity...that same God who knows every single one of my selfish thoughts...yes, he invites me to participate in his perfect plan to bring healing and righteousness into a broken world. Talk about an unfair advantage! Who am I (aside from being a big time sinner), that God would reach down and choose me, loser that I am, to participate, not from the sidelines, but in actively carrying it out, in his perfect plan of redemption? Now that is what I call privilege. Forget about Billy Graham. The God of all the angels in the heavens, the God of all eternity, has invited me to be a part of his perfect plan for the world. That is an unfair advantage. So, the question is, what am I doing about this golden opportunity and privilege and responsibility that God has placed in my hands?

FEBRUARY 16

"Paul took the road through the interior." Acts 19

A few years back, I had a meeting in Sofia, Bulgaria. Especially if I have a trip to a far off destination, I will often look at a map to see if there is anything else interesting nearby that I can stop off at to make the trip a little more worthwhile. When I pulled out my map to Bulgaria, I noticed that Thessaloniki and Philippi, Greece were only a couple of inches away. Wow, wouldn't that be cool to see where St. Paul visited once upon a time, I thought. So my plans started coming together. I lured my niece into my plan as well. She was living in Albania at the time (just a couple more inches over, on the map), so I figured we could meet up in Greece and enjoy the fun together. It really did turn out to be a significant milestone in my life. One thing I noticed, as the bus took us on the hour or so ride between Thessaloniki and Philippi, was how many other little towns there were all along the way. I thought to myself, I wonder how many of these little towns Paul passed through and visited, that we've never even heard about. One of the towns we passed through, one I had never heard of, I noticed, did in fact have a monument stating that the apostle Paul had stopped there at one time. Sometimes it seems that Paul deliberately chose the longer way around, perhaps out of curiosity, but certainly so he could meet and share the

Good News with more people...as he did at the beginning of Acts 19. I wonder how many strange sounding tongues or languages he must have heard on his journeys.

Language is actually a fascinating thing. I hated it in school, but I have to admit that it is pretty interesting. Just the other day, I was part of a zoom meeting with a number of folks from around the world, including a couple of Japanese men. One of the men said that after he had gotten his funds together and paid off some bills, there would be "giddy giddy" left (zilch, nada, zero). Isn't that a great word for "nothing"!

When we lived in China, I struggled (not enough, apparently) to learn the language. There were a couple of words I came to love...they just seemed so perfect. When we ask somebody how they're doing, it's perfectly fine to respond, "So so..." Well, the Chinese have the perfect word for that: "Mamahuhu". Literally, it means, "horse horse tiger tiger". In other words, a little of this, a little of that...so so. But doesn't manahuhu just have a nicer ring to it than so so does?? Another fun Chinese word I like is the word for ice cream. Now anyone who knows me, knows that ice cream makes me happy. And it's hard to say the Chinese word for ice cream without a smile on your face: "bing-jeling". Isn't that great! I was famous at the school I taught at in China for sneaking out after lunch for some bing-jeling.

Maybe Paul had certain words he liked the sound of, too. But just think, one day we'll be in heaven, and we can spend the rest of eternity listening to and learning all these cool words! After all, Revelation tells us that in heaven there will be a great multitude of people there from every tribe, nation, and language... what a chaotic cacophony that will be! Can't wait!

FEBRUARY 17

Before we moved to China, I used to tell my wife that she would understand the Bible better after living in Asia. Because the Bible was written and happened in an Eastern, an Asian, context, many of the events and cultural nuances related in its stories can be better understood from an Asian perspective. One example of that is the walls of Jericho. My wife used to wonder, what's the big deal about some flimsy wooden or brick walls toppling over. When we arrived in the city where we lived in China, there was a new, modern part of the city...and there was an older part, dating back to the time of when Kublai Khan had his base there, nearly 1,000 years ago, as he was uniting all of China. The old city of Dali is still there, with a wall around it, perhaps much like the walls of Jericho. But this wall is nothing like a modern brick or wooden wall we might find in the US today, and what my wife was picturing. This wall was formidable, virtually impregnable, especially considering there were not mechanized vehicles 1,000 or more years ago. The walls around Old Dali are massive stone edifices, which must have taken years to erect. A car can easily drive around the top of them. These are not walls that a trumpet blast could topple, even with hurricane winds aiding the sound of the trumpet. These walls will likely still be there 1,000 years from now. But the powerful old empire of Kublai Khan, along with all his soldiers, is long gone. They didn't last.

So often, as fragile human beings, we look for something that will give us a sense of security, don't we...the latest alarm system, the most sophisticated computer security program, a Swiss bank account (OK, OK, so I'm not talking about myself, but you get the point...)... But, really, all these things are passing. They don't really provide us with lasting security.

That's something that David understood in Psalm 59. I don't know what it was about David, but he sure seemed to have an unending flow of thugs coming after him...it would be a great plot for some action movie. Even though, I dare say, most of us don't have that level of opposition...still, we sometimes feel like we do. So we can take comfort in the same thing David did. When David felt and saw enemies all around him, what did he do? Build bigger walls? Hide his gold in Sheba or Babylon? Build a stronger army? No, his security was simpler, and perhaps more difficult, than that. He knew that his security was in the Lord, his God. That's easier than building a massive wall. But it's also harder. We fragile humans don't find it easy to lay our burdens, to rest our anxieties, at the feet of someone we can't see or touch. That's a real challenge for us. But in his most desperate of moments, when disaster and doom swirled all around him, David knew that his hope was beyond human institutions, beyond human cleverness or strength. Only God could save him. The last thing I want is more trouble. But sometimes God allows trouble in our lives so that we will come to the end of our rope, the end of our resources, as David did. Then, truly, we realize, we have nowhere else to turn. God is all that's left. And David found that his God was enough. Lord, may we, in our challenges and trials, also discover the same...

FEBRUARY 18

> Day/Date Be sure to remember five things to be grateful for every day. February 18
>
> Hebrews 4:12 NCV God's Word is alive and working.
>
> We should offer and dedicate our lives to serving and honoring God. One of the most important ways to do this is by sharing his Good News. His Message will accomplish his good plans in people's lives. That's our hope and confidence — what his Truth will do in others' lives.

Parenting puts on us challenging tensions that at times feel like they will pull us apart. Many times, I wanted to just reach out and draw one of my children to me and brush all the problems away. But, at the same time, their little selfish wills had to be tempered, molded, and guided. They had to learn that they were not the king of the castle in life...that life requires us to get along with others, and that frequently means giving up what we want. And so, the tension and battle had to continue.

I expect it's the same in the way God deals with us. We catch glimpses of this in Isaiah 59-61. God's overarching loves for us is sweeping and deep...and yet, our sinful disobedience separates us from him. Our holy God can't just brush it aside and ignore it. It must be dealt with. As we well know, we are not capable of fixing this problem. And rather than giving up on us and throwing up his hands in frustration, God provided the fix that was needed. We see his massive, overwhelming love for us through the verses of these chapters. Although God had to deal with our sin...his bottomless love couldn't leave us alone. I remember that same dilemma. I was frustrated at our kids' little selfish hearts...but my love for them overwhelmed and outlasted any frustration I may have felt from time to time. There was no way I could leave them alone or abandon them. And so it is with our Heavenly Father...

FEBRUARY 19

> **Day/Date** Be sure to remember five things to be grateful for every day. February 19
>
> Genesis 50:20 NIV But God intended it for good.
>
> In the darkest days of Elsbeth's battle with cancer, it appeared to us that our family might be destroyed, that life may never again be the same for us. But at the same time, God gave her many opportunities to share his love and support with many others also battling cancer. This deep valley in our lives was used for good purposes by our loving heavenly Father.

Paul's life, as it is recounted for us in Acts...for example, in chapter 20...must have been a whirlwind of activity, false starts, chaos, stress, alarm...and blessing. And he tells us to follow his example...now, that's a scary thought. Some time ago, I was flipping through Reagan's Diaries, an amazing record of his activities while he was President. Ronald Reagan had a way of looking so charming and carefree, with his hand constantly reaching for the jellybean jar, that it can seem easy to write him off as a lightweight. But his diaries tell a different story. From sunup to sundown, all day long, he was moving from appointment to appointment, with one head of state after another. It boggled my mind. And he made notes and comments and observations all along the way. How in the world did he do it all? I can see how the jellybeans must have been essential for him to maintain his sanity.

Paul's life was similar...on the go, long days, meeting people here and there...it makes my head spin. How did he do it...and before the days of jellybeans, no less.

Well, Paul tells us that his passion, his mandate, his heart, his life...was sharing the wonderful truth, the Great News, about God's love, to those who hadn't heard it before. I don't know how he did it. But he tells us to follow what he did.

I certainly couldn't begin to do it on my own. Lord, as you did with Paul...fill us with your Spirit, change our hearts, make us the people you want us to be...so that we can follow in Paul's footsteps, and, of course, in his Savior's footsteps.

FEBRUARY 20

Day/Date   Be sure to remember five things to be grateful for every day.   February 20

Matthew 6:33 NCV   The thing you should want most is God's Kingdom and doing what God wants.

More than anything, our desire should be that God is ruling in our lives and reigning over the world around us. Am I asking him and allowing him to rule in my life today?

The world is an interesting and amazing place, isn't it, with all its strange people, places, languages, and cultures. Sometimes I wonder where they all came from...and perhaps the only plausible explanation is that God scattered and confused people all across the globe, as is recounted for us in the story of the Tower of Babel. In Central Asia, in the area around the Caspian Sea, there appear to be a bunch of random languages that leave people scratching their heads, wondering how they all could have gotten there. One local tale, which perhaps may not be far from the truth (!), is that when God was dishing out languages across the globe, he stumbled at the Caspian, and all his leftover letters of the alphabet dropped out of his basket and scattered across that region. Who knows??

I am reminded of the puzzle of languages as I read Psalm 60. Now, this is not really a psalm about languages. Rather, it's more of a lament over losses, battles, enemies, and tragedy. But a number of seemingly random places are mentioned that remind me of all the odd locations and languages around the world. What is remarkable, to me, is that God says to us, "Oh, Gilead? Yes, that's mine. What, Moab? That's mine, too. And Edom? Sure, that's mine as well." It all belongs to God. He cares about and loves the whole world. As small, finite human beings, we quickly think in terms of what's right and wrong, who is for us and who is against us, who the good guys are (us, of course), and who the bad guys are.

And God, being a righteous God, certainly does punish evil. But sometimes, in our zeal to help God out, we start hating the ones who are not like us. We did that as kids...we still do that as adults...and even nations continue to do that. But let's not forget that God loves the whole world. It all belongs to him. And he wants to bring all the people home back to himself. Will we join him in that task?

FEBRUARY 21

February 21

Psalm 121:3 NCV Your Guardian God won't fall asleep.

God is always with me, watching me, protecting me, going before me, and giving me what I need. He never tires, never gets distracted, never gives up. He promises to always, always be with me.

One thing I really enjoyed about Europe, when we lived there, was how close together and small most of the countries were. I'm sure the locals thought these Yanks were rather touched in the head, but I used to love hopping over to this country or that, for a quick visit. While Elsbeth was in the hospital in France, following the birth of our number six, I remember piling the other five into our van...and driving down to Barcelona, Spain, for a quick daytime visit from southern France, where we lived (with a stopover in Andorra, along the way, of course). Another time, again from the south of France, we took all our kids, including our, by then, ten day old number six, up to Switzerland, to Interlaken, and back, in a day. (A few other harebrained excursions, I'll leave unmentioned.)

By the time we moved to England, a few years later, I had settled down a bit and limited my excursions mostly to the local countryside. Britain was so filled with history that relates to our American culture, though, that I wanted to take as much of it in as I could as well. So, again, on Saturdays, I would sometimes pile everyone into our 12 seater utility van and head off down the English lanes to here or there. The local cars would scatter when they saw our big rattletrap vehicle coming down the road, especially since this French machine had the steering wheel on the wrong side!

One day, we passed through Oxford, and I remember seeing the monument where Latimer and Ridley were burned at the stake for their commitment to the Gospel. I remember, too, hearing about Eric Liddell, Olympic runner and missionary to China, who died while imprisoned by the Japanese. Even my grandfather, another missionary to China, was stood up before a firing squad during those tumultuous days...

Why would these people do those things? Why were they willing to give up all, and to die an excruciating death? Well, it tells us why, right there in the opening phrase of Isaiah 62: "For Zion's sake I will not keep silent." For God, for his plans, for his people...these people, down through history, would not keep silent. And we go on to see more of who this great God is in chapters 62-65. He is a God who relentlessly pursues, who never gives up on us, whose compassion stretches and lasts longer than any sin or rebellion we can conceive of. That is the God these ancients believed in. He is the one they refused to keep silent about...

FEBRUARY 22

> **Day/Date** Be sure to remember five things to be grateful for every day. February 22
>
> Psalm 136:1 NCV   His love never quits.
>
> In the 26 verses of Psalm 136, God tells us 26 times that his love will never run out. Even if he had told us only once, it would be true. But he repeated his statement of love for us again and again and again. Why? Because he wants us to be sure, to really know and understand, how much and how permanent his love for us is.

Occasionally, we'll see someone who just seems a little bit of a misfit in society. (And I certainly feel like that at times, as well.) One story I heard was of a guy who was traveling, and he was so scatterbrained, that when he arrived back home, he had no shoes on...and he couldn't even recall what happened to them along the way! Now, my wife nearly forgot and lost her phone in a bathroom stall the other day...but how could you leave without your shoes?? There was a really brainy guy in one of my high school classes...probably a genius, in fact...and one day in PE, as we were running laps, I noticed that he had one shoe on...and the other foot was shoeless. And somehow he seemed oblivious to his situation. He just kept churning out the laps.

When I read about Paul in Acts 21, traveling here, traveling there, running here, running there...I am reminded of the same thing. He just seems to be running around, a little bit crazy, like a chicken with his head cut off. What was the deal, Paul? Why didn't you just settle down and chill a bit? Paul felt such a blinding compulsion, didn't he? Such a burning passion to finish the race, to complete his course... He knew, deep down, the stakes that were involved...people's eternal destinies. How he may have looked as he ran around the globe was not important to him. The compelling task was all that consumed him. I wish I had a quarter of his passion! Lord, help us to see what Paul saw. Help us to see and know that people's destinies hang in the balance. Light a fire under us that will never go out. In your Son's name, for your glory and for your kingdom, amen.

FEBRUARY 23

Day/Date   Be sure to remember five things to be grateful for every day.   February 23

Jeremiah 31:33 NCV / will put my teachings in their minds and write them on their hearts.

Repeatedly and regularly, God tells us to remember his words, to obey them, and to make them part of our lives. We are often quick to forget, so he keeps reminding us. But one day, when we are with God in heaven, he will put his Word permanently in our minds and on our hearts. Then we will never forget it.

It was still cold and dark when I woke up this morning. Quietly, I reached for my phone, trying not to make a sound or movement that would stir my wife. If she is sleeping soundly in the early morning, it may mean that she had a restless night and is now finally sleeping deeply, so I didn't want to wake her with my carelessness.

As I glanced at my emails, one caught my eye...with the heading, "Sad News." One of our dear friends in China, whose family is currently at home in America, was out for a run, when he collapsed and was called home to heaven. But he leaves with us still on earth his dear wife and three children.

I thought of them as I read Psalm 61 just now. David is crushed...at the very ends of the earth, as he says. That's where our friend is today...at the end of the earth, left alone with her three young children. Lord, she has nowhere else to turn but to you. You understand her tears, and you weep with her. Lord, wrap her family in your comforting arms. You know the end from the beginning, nothing is a surprise to you. But this is devastating to our friend. And you understand that. So comfort her, dear Lord, wrap your arms around her...and lead her to the Rock that is higher than where she is... In your Son's name, we ask.

FEBRUARY 24

Day/Date Be sure to remember five things to be grateful for every day. February 24

Matthew 7:12 NCV — Do to others what you want them to do to you.

The greatest way we can show our love for God is by loving others. Parents love their children by providing them with what they need. What is it that all people need most? To know that there is a God who made them and loves them. The best gift I can give to others is to share with them this Good News.

February 25

I love history, and I enjoy reading about times of testing and trial. That sounds macabre, I'm sure, but really, I just am blessed at seeing how people rise up to the challenge, somehow find a way to endure, carry on with life when so much comes against them. But it's one thing to read about the Civil War or World War Two...it's an utterly different thing altogether to actually live through it, to find a way to survive in the midst of it. My wife is reading a Holocaust survivor book right now, and while we were out walking yesterday, she told me about a family in Poland during the start of the Second World War. The father was arrested, beaten, and then died. The mother sent her young ones to safety on a boat that was evacuating children to the Netherlands and England. She was eventually put in a concentration camp, where she didn't survive the war, never seeing her children again. In the meantime, the war eventually caught up with her children in Holland, and they were captured and shunted around during the course of the fighting. Somehow, they managed to survive. I've never experienced anything remotely close to that.

Yet, at the end of Isaiah and the beginning of Jeremiah, we hear similar stories of disaster and tragedy. But woven through the calamity, God speaks comforting words. Listen to what God says to us in the middle of turmoil and destruction.

"Heaven is my throne, and the earth is my footstool."

"I will extend peace."

"As a mother comforts her child, so will I comfort you."

"As the new heavens and the new earth that I make will endure...all mankind will come and bow down before me."

"Before I formed you in the womb, I knew you, before you were born I set you apart. Do not be afraid, for I am with you."

"I am with you and will rescue you," declares the Lord.

These words speak of God's control, his plan, his understanding, his comforting love, his assurance about the future. So much around us happens that we don't understand, that we can't fathom, that doesn't make sense. But, somehow, it all makes sense to God. We can trust him, even when our senses tell us otherwise. Lord, give us your peace in the storm, your comfort when all around us things are shaking. Help us to trust in you...

FEBRUARY 25

Day/Date — Be sure to remember five things to be grateful for every day. — February 25

Matthew 10:39 NCV — Those who try to hold on to their lives will give up true life.

It is a sad thing to watch someone grow old who has only invested in himself and his possessions. As he comes to the end of his life, it seems to shrink in significance while his possessions become more meaningless. He has given up what is most important for that which does not last.

I like to follow Gmb Akash on Facebook. He is a top photographer in Bangladesh, with an amazing ability to catch people from all walks of life, as they go about their daily lives. But what I find so gripping about him is the stories he relates. See, he doesn't just go out and look for interesting photos to record. He goes way deeper than that. He will go to the prostitutes, the day laborers, those who've suffered great tragedy, those barely holding on to life, with no resources to fall back on...and he shares their remarkable, tragic stories. With his compassionate heart, he has a way of drawing them to open up their hearts to him. But not only does to capture amazing photographic glimpses of their lives, not only does he get them to open up about their grindingly hard lives...he goes even deeper than that. Akash is an amazing example to us all. He supports, with his own money (along with donations from his fans), students who need supplies, beggars who need a tool or a bike to help them eke out a living, a shopkeeper who needs a hand up to start his own business...Akash is astonishing in his heart for those who are mostly passed by in life by the rest of society. I keep following his page so that I won't forget. In the busyness of our daily lives, we are prone to forget so many others around the world who are so much worse off than we are. We can forget that there is a needy and desperate world out there. I don't want to forget that.

Paul, in fact, faced the same situation in Acts 22. He was sharing his story before a crowd of devout Jewish leaders. He recounted how he had been such a zealous follower of God...how he wanted to kill all the misguided Christians. Then, he told his audience, God got hold of him, changed him, and sent him on a mission to tell the nonJewish Gentiles about God's love. As soon as Paul mentioned the Gentiles, the crowd had heard enough. They roared their disapproval and drowned Paul out. He had to be rescued from the crowd by the Roman commander who had Paul in his custody.

What I find interesting about all this, though, is the Jewish leaders' response to the mention of God reaching out to the Gentiles. This was blasphemy of the highest order. Everyone knew that the Jews were God's chosen and select people. His message of salvation and redemption was for them. How could this scoundrel Paul say anything otherwise?

But, obviously, the Jews had forgotten God's Word about reaching out to the Gentiles. He clearly states in the Old Testament, Jewish, Scriptures that his Message was also for the Gentiles. But in their preoccupation with themselves, they had forgotten this. And that's why I need Akash's stories to keep reminding me. This life is not about me. There is a much bigger world out there that God cares about. Let's not forget that. Let's let our hearts be consumed and burdened by the things that are also on God's heart.

FEBRUARY 26

Day/Date Be sure to remember five things to be grateful for every day: February 26

Psalm 51:17 NCV God, you will not reject a heart that is broken and sorry for sin.

When our eyes and our understanding are opened to who we are before God — disobedient sinners — then he can accept us and make us into people who are pleasing to him.

Jesus must have been exasperating at times. The disciples would see a big problem or developing crisis (How are we going to feed this massive crowd following us around, now that it's approaching evening??), and they did the right thing. They came to their Master with the problem. But instead of instantly solving it or making it evaporate, he would invariably tell them, "You figure it out!" Or he seemed to love sending them on a wild goose chase by telling them, "Look for someone carrying a jar..." No clear instruction on what would happen or what to do next.

Once in Moscow, I had a similar experience. I was with a Russian coworker, going through the subway. All the signs were in Russian (I mean, it is Russia, after all!), and Moscow is known to be a challenging city for tourists without a knowledge of the language. We had been through the subway a time or two before, so she figured I should know my way around by now. So she said, "OK, I'm not telling you anything else...you figure out where we need to go!" I thought, what?? How am I supposed to figure out where to go when I can't read a thing?? Thankfully, she didn't follow through on her statement...or I might still be there to this day, trying to figure my way out of there.

I'm reminded of Jesus in the boat. A hurricane was raging around them on the Sea of Galilee, these seasoned fishermen who were his disciples were panicking...and Jesus was sawing logs in the back of the boat. What a crazy time to be sleeping! How could he be sleeping at such a moment? Well, their utter lack of peace of mind was completely determined by their immediate (and rather intense) circumstances. Jesus' was not. He was at peace, at rest…because his heart did not find rest in his circumstances. So he could be calm and at rest even with a tsunami approaching.

David declares the same thing in Psalm 62. Now, we do know that David was scared to death at times. Not only does he tell us so, but sometimes he literally shakes his fist in exasperation at God because God is not showing up to save him in a crisis. But at least David does tell us the right thing to do in this psalm. He says, "The only place where I am at rest, calm, quiet, secure, and at peace…is in my relationship to God…when I'm trusting in God." He knows that when the earth is shaking, when his kingdom is collapsing, when people are coming against him…his security is not contingent on those things around him. Uncertainty is very scary to us human beings…but our security, our peace…is rooted in something, someone, who can't change, who can't be shaken, who can't be taken away. Will we trust him? Will we say, as David did, that we can now lay down in peace and go to sleep, because our trust is in God? Lord, help us, indeed, to keep our focus and our heart on you…even when our surroundings tell a different story.

FEBRUARY 27

The museums of the world are fascinating places, with incredible treasures in them...jewels, unbelievable art, sculptures, writings, pieces of history... I remember seeing two really cool things once when I was wandering through the British Museum with my family. One was a paper napkin...a piece of rubbish, really...except...that on it was scribbled the original words to one of the songs that the Beatles composed! Amazing! So great that it was kept for us to see, years later. Another piece of paper was perhaps even more amazing. It was an original composition written out by Mozart himself. Wow! Hard to believe that I was looking at the actual musical score of the wizard himself.

But there is something else I've had the privilege of seeing that, in actuality, is far more priceless than all the treasures in the Louvre or the British Museum put together. It is the divine, supernatural, actual Words of the King of Kings and Lord of Lords himself.

In Jeremiah 2, the prophet records for us that God's words came to him. Thankfully, Jeremiah wrote them down, and we still have them today...and they are just as relevant for us today as the day they first came to Jeremiah. Chapters 2 & 3 tell a sad story (a story that is also true for us) of the people who God loves turning away from him and living in rebel against him. But he is still waiting for them to return to him.

That same story...that same truth...speaks to us today. And the God of all the universe has written those words to us, to you and me. That should really, really excite us...more than a few words scribbled by John Lennon, more, in fact, than anything else on earth. Almighty God invites us, wants an audience with us, wants a relationship with us. And we can read his Words to us every single day. Priceless. Beyond measure. What are we waiting for!

FEBRUARY 28

Day/Date   Be sure to remember five things to be grateful for every day.   *February 28*

Matthew 7:24 NCV   Everyone who hears my words and obeys them is like a wise man.

The God who designed us and made us and has wonderful plans for us has not left us in the dark about who he is. The Message he gave us explains who we are and why we are here and how we can have a full life. We will find rest and wisdom and joy by hearing his Word and making it the center of our lives.

Ceremonies are special events in life, and graduations are among the best. For at least one day, you feel on top of the world, like you've conquered Mt. Everest...until you come back down to earth the next day and realize that life continues on, pretty much right where you left it, a day or two before. I don't know if they remember it, but when our kids were pretty small, we had little graduation ceremonies for them at home, after they completed one of their school years. We wanted to acknowledge and celebrate their accomplishments. They were fun memories.

Then there were high school and college graduations, where I really didn't need the ceremony, thank you...I knew that I had arrived at the pinnacle of life and of accomplishment without anyone having to remind me.

Well, then, finally, there was graduate school. Maybe it had at last dawned on me by then that I wasn't the only, or even the most important, graduate in the whole wide world. At any rate, for whatever reason...I didn't even bother to attend that ceremony.

But there is one ceremony that is still coming up. Paul alludes to it in Acts 23. It's the one that comes at the end of our lives. Paul didn't know exactly which day that would be, but he knew he was getting close…and there were plenty of people around who also wanted to be sure he arrived at that day in plenty of time. They seemed eager to help him along in any way they could.

What amazes me about this final ceremony for Paul, though, is that he says, as he anticipates it, "I'm all ready for graduation. I've fulfilled all the graduation requirements, everything's been checked…all that's left is the ceremony." Honestly, I can't imagine ever being able to say, "Got it! I've completed everything that God expected me to do. All I have left is the trip up to heaven." I tremble in fear just thinking about what God expects of us. I realize, with all sincerity, that I am wholly dependent on his mercy and grace. Nothing I could ever do could bring me close to what God expects of us. And yet, Paul was so consumed with serving and following God that he could say in all sincerity, "I have run the race. I have finished the course. All I have left to do is to collect the crown." Wow, I find that amazing that he could even say that. I really better get on the stick and make my life count for God, for eternal things…as Paul did. God, help me!

FEBRUARY 29

> Matthew 13:22 NCV — February 29
>
> That seed is like the person who hears the teaching but lets worries about this life and the temptation of wealth stop that teaching from growing.
>
> We live in a complex world that puts many, strains, burdens, and distractions in our lives. Jesus warned us in this story that we can lose sight of what is really important if we allow all these intrusions and demands to become the main focus of our lives.

Some time ago, I turned around during our church service to greet the visitor behind me. She was from New York and was visiting her roots and some of her remaining relatives back here in Korea. As I shared by background of having grown up in Korea and of my father having been a missionary doctor who worked primarily with tuberculosis patients, an amazing story came out. The mother of this young lady I had just met had at one time been suffering very seriously from tuberculosis. In those days, it was a very serious malady in Korea, with many suffering and dying from it. Her mother was told to head for the Kwangju Christian Hospital, where my father was the Director. She made her way there, was cared for at the hospital, and eventually recovered. And now, so many years later, her daughter and the doctor's son had a chance encounter that was a wonderful moment for both of us.

It seemed perfectly normal to me, because I didn't know any different and just assumed it was this way for all fathers, but many people used to come seek out my Dad. Sometimes they would hang out, just hovering around, for hours, for days even, waiting to see him, to be with him, to receive his healing touch, his healing words, his healing treatment. In those dangerous and precarious days, word had filtered out that if you had a serious TB ailment, if you were beyond hope, even if you were just down and out or at the end of your rope...there was a doctor who could, who would, help you. So people came and kept coming. It seemed normal to me. It's just the way things were.

But thinking back on my Dad reminds me of the words of David in Psalm 63. David says he was thirsty for God. David saw and experienced many things...nail biting panic, hanging by a thread escapes, spectacular military victories, stunning wealth and opulence...about anything you could imagine in life. But through it all, he knew that his security, his hope, his true life...was in God. Kind of like those gravely ill folks who knew that if they could just be with my Dad, they would be OK...if they could just find some time in his presence, their needs would be met, would be dealt with.

For David, it was to be in God's presence. And it's the same with us. God is the one we need to seek. He is the one in whom our soul finds rest. He is the one we need to come to.

MARCH

Quarantine day 3...

Thoughts from Joshua, Judges, Ruth, and 1&2 Samuel:

*God goes with us; he doesn't send us out alone.

*God does not give up on us.

*We don't have to worry; God has already worked things out according to his good plans.

*God expects us to actively participate in his plans.

*God delights in using and involving the least, the most insignificant, and the most unlikely people.

August 24, 2020
I will never leave
you nor forsake you.

JOSHUA

Joshua Installed as Leader

1 After the death of Moses the servant of the LORD,[a] the LORD said to Joshua[b] son of Nun, Moses' aide: [2]"Moses my servant is dead. Now then, you and all these people, get ready to cross the Jordan River[c] into the land I am about to give to them — to the Israelites. [3]I will give you every place where you set your foot,[d] as I promised Moses. [4]Your territory will extend from the desert to Lebanon, and from the great river, the Euphrates[e] — all the Hittite country — to the Mediterranean Sea in the west.[f] [5]No one will be able to stand against you[g] all the days of your life. As

MARCH 1

Day/Date *Be sure to remember five things to be grateful for every day.* March 1

Matthew 11:28 NCV | Come to me and I will give you rest.

These are such simple words, like a cup of refreshing water or a mother welcoming her child into her arms. But they are also very profound, meaningful, and life-changing words, if we will do what they tell us to do and come to Jesus for rest and peace for our lives.

When we lived in England, we had kids of all ages, with one year when all nine were together at home. After that, they started, one by one, leaving for college. As you can imagine, it was a bit of a challenge keeping up with all their passports. I used to keep a chart to make sure I renewed them on time as each one expired in turn. On top of that, we needed British visas for each one, and occasionally, one child would have two passports, as they would receive a new passport, but their current British visa was still in their expired passport. So sometimes we traveled with my hip pack bulging with 12-14 passports.

Once, when we were checking in at the Manchester airport, probably in 2000 as we were taking our oldest to college, I pulled out my stash of passports and laid about 13 of them on the check in counter. Without even looking at the passports, the lady behind the counter simply looked at me and said, "We've been expecting you!" Apparently, our long list of names had completely lit up her computer screen, so she was just waiting for us to show up and plunk down all our documents.

Now, when I was young, along with passports, we always travelled with another document. This was the dreaded Vaccination Certificate. It was much more than a simple certificate. It was a whole foldout booklet with a painful record of all the "shots" that we had been inflicted with…in those days, that included cholera, small pox, tuberculosis, typhoid, tetanus, polio, and probably a few others I don't remember. Once a year, we had our shot day, when the missionaries would gather in a room, and we would all get the needed injections that had come due. It was the most scary day of the year, bar none…a day which seemed to circle around again all too quickly each year. Why in the world couldn't Mom and Dad have just taken these shots for us? How come we had to go through all these painful stabs? Well, apparently, it was what we needed. It was hard for me to imagine, but seemingly, it could be much worse for me if I didn't get them, than if I did. So each year, we nervously trudged off to the appointment, somehow, hoping beyond hope, that maybe we would be overlooked or missed…which never did happen, by the way. The nurse was very careful to shoot each one of us as many times as necessary. It took a lot of faith to trust our parents when they told us we needed these things, that, in fact, they were good for us. But, aside from the faith, we really had no choice. It was going to happen, faith or no.

Now, in Psalm 64, David talks about something that in some ways is similar to that dreaded memory I have. He is complaining to God that painful threats, swords, and arrows are coming against him. In truth, he didn't really need to tell God about this. God knows everything, and so he knew that this unpleasant thing was happening to David. But, for whatever reason, God let it happen anyway. David didn't understand why, he just knew that God said things would work out in the end, that there was a good purpose to all this discomfort and pain. It would all be OK in the end. In the meantime, David had to hold on to God, trust him, and get through this painful trial. A little like those dreaded shots we used to get. I didn't fully understand why we had to get them. Mom and Dad definitely knew I wasn't happy about them…but, somehow, they knew that this was necessary, that it would pass, and that one day things would be OK. So I had to trust them, knowing that they loved me, put my bravest face on, roll up my sleeve, and step up for the medicine. God frequently doesn't tell us either why we are going through some trial or testing. But he does understand our pain, and he tells us to trust him, and that it will all work out. Can we trust him? Will we? Really, it's the best choice and solution we have, even if it's not quite what we might choose.

MARCH 2

High school and college were full of carefree days...parties, Halloween carnivals, picnics, a moment of glory on a sports field or court, a movie out with someone special...and many other good memories. But, invariably, the school term would wind down, and the day of accountability would approach.... If we hadn't stayed on top of things...well, then that would be a dreaded moment. I remember a few folks in college who seemed to have more carefree days than most of us. But then, curiously, at the start of the next term, they were nowhere to be seen. Apparently, the day of accountability had caught up to them, and they weren't ready, and had been unable to answer the bell. Perhaps, that's part of our human nature, because it seems to happen a lot.

Jeremiah 6-7, in a way, are talking about the same scenario. Early in chapter six, it says that the daylight is fading. Time is running out...the day of accountability is nearly upon us. If we're not ready, it can be a scary moment indeed...like if we're caught out in the woods somewhere, and nighttime suddenly catches us unawares. In this case, God is warning the people: "A day of reckoning is coming...and so far you haven't been paying attention. Don't you know that you're running out of time? I've told you what you need to do to get ready. But you haven't been listening. Get yourselves ready! The daylight is vanishing! Time is running out!"

What about us? Are we about our Heavenly Father's business? Are we living as we should...so that when we are called forth, we will be ready? I do hope so...for God tells us that that day is surely coming...

MARCH 3

March 3

James 4:7-8 NCV   Give yourselves completely to God. Come near to God, and God will come near to you.

Sometimes we feel as if God is far away. But when we give ourselves to him, he promises to be right with us. How we feel is not really what matters — it is what he has promised that is important, and he has promised that he will be with us.

Paul had a challenging task in Acts 26. (The same task that God gave the prophets…and gives us.) It is the difficult job of explaining to and convincing someone of something they can't see, don't understand, and don't believe in. That is the hard task God has given to each of us, in fact.

My wife and I were reminded of this very thing just moments ago. We live in a major world city, Seoul, that most of the time is very calm and orderly. But this morning something happened that reminded us that there is an unseen reality that we are often told about but which we can't see and, really, have to take in faith. It's the reality of North Korea, sitting just a handful of miles to our north, a political and military threat that is easy for us to forget about in the day to day goings on, here in the big city. We are told that North Korea is there, that it's a threat, but we can't ever see, hear, or feel it in any way…until just now, this morning.

We were calmly going about our usual Monday morning routine, when suddenly it sounded like World War 3 was breaking out all around us. There was a very loud roar, that rose louder and louder, until it was nearly deafening. In a split second, it sailed right over us. Then it was gone. What was it? My wife knew instinctively: "Those are fighter jets." Repeatedly, they swept over us, and we kept running to the window to look up into the sky. I saw one jet sail overhead on its side, but mostly all we saw was a tail of smoke they left behind. Finally, I got smart and went outside with my phone, prepared to catch them next time around. I raised my phone and waited. Suddenly, the high pitched roar came again...and this time I got them on my camera. A beautiful, an awesome sight indeed. Those F-16 fighter jets (a reliable source informed us) reminded us of something we can't see...North Korea is close by. They are a sign to us that another world exists that we can't actually see in our day to day lives.

And that was the message Paul was trying to get across to his audience. There is another world out there...the spiritual world. Much of the time we can't see it, perhaps aren't even aware of it. But it is real, it is out there...and it's as real as the North Koreans just to our north...

MARCH 4

Day/Date — Be sure to remember five things to be grateful for every day. March 4

Psalm 116:5 NCV — The Lord is kind and does what is right.

Sometimes as a child, I remember thinking that my parents did not care about me because they didn't give me what I wanted. I began to understand their perspective much better when I had my own children. I give them what is right and what they need, but of course this is often not what they want. Our heavenly Father treats us in the same way. Trust him, for he is good and loves us dearly.

Psalm 65 starts off in a rather strange way. Perhaps it's an appropriate beginning in Hebrew, in which it was originally written, but it's not how we would express something in modern day English: "Praise waits for you, O God." What in the world does that mean? I don't really know. Looking at a number of different translations of that verse, I get the impression that they are not quite sure either.

There are certainly many things in life that require waiting. Becoming a mother stretches and strains and tests a lady in ways few other things do. Your body does things, reacts, and behaves in ways you would not have imagined before. (Obviously, I'm not speaking from personal experience, but from a lot of close at hand observation!) Then, it slowly starts to feel as if your body is going to burst. And, on occasion, at the last moment, something dramatic, alarming, or urgent might happen that suddenly causes the medical staff to shift into intense high gear until the danger is dealt with or under control. We had that happen a time or two as well. Then, suddenly, an amazing thing happens. A little life appears…and all the pain, struggle, and anxiety is forgotten and vanishes like a puff of smoke. Instantly, the waiting is over, the uncertainty has ended, the angst has evaporated.

There was another kind of wait associated with the small Christian college we attended. It was established on the grounds of a luxurious mountaintop hotel...which had the misfortune of being built and opened right at the tail end of the "Roaring 20s", just as the Great Depression was about to descend. The hotel never quite fully got off the ground, and it was in for a decades long wait before it really found itself, reborn as an institution of higher learning.

The same thing can sometimes happen in our relationship with God as well. The wonderful thing about waiting for God is that, with him, it will always end well...when we trust, believe in, and obey him. We may feel like we are in the midst of a long pause, a long wait for something, like our relationship with God is stuck in the wilderness. So what do we do? Well, one thing that never hurts us is to pray. Remember Paul telling us to pray constantly? Perhaps one aspect of the first verse of Psalm 65 is that praise is waiting, in a sense, to be offered to God. Who offers it to God? We do...when we pray. So let's pray, and praise... let's not let our praise for God wait too long. Let's go ahead and offer it to him now...all day, all night, in good times, in bad times, in season, out of season, any time, all the time. Don't let your praise to God wait! And then let's wait on him and see what he does...

MARCH 5

> Day/Date Be sure to remember five things to be grateful for every day. March 5
>
> Isaiah 55:1 NCV The Lord says, "All you who are thirsty, come and drink. Those of you who do not have money, come, buy and eat!"
>
> When we become weary of this life, depressed about the evil we see in the world, even discouraged at times with ourselves – this is when Jesus invites us to come to him for refreshment, for renewal, for true meaning in life. Give yourself to him today.

More than a dozen times, in Jeremiah 8&9, it says: "God declares", or "says the Lord." You definitely get the impression that God wants to tell us something...yes, he does, in fact! These are sad chapters, really, relating how God's people have turned away from him. But this is not just a statement or declaration. You very much sense that God is talking to us, wanting to dialogue with us. In the midst of these lamentable statements, God asks us questions: Don't you understand? Can't you see? He also throws out expressions in seeming exasperation, as if he's waiting for us to answer. The Bible is full of statements by God. But just as parents want a two way dialogue with their kids, that is also what God wants with us. Sometimes, it seems that God puts us in situations (stress, sleeplessness, disappointment, illness) that give us a great opportunity to talk to him, to open up ourselves to him.

I remember one such experience I had as a boy in Korea.

When I was young, there were two things that the missionaries loved to do during the sultry dog days of summer: run to the beach...or head for the hills. In the south of the country, there were some beautiful mountains that provided wonderful getaways for the foreigners...provided you didn't mind roughing it a bit (i.e. no AC, no running water, no heat, no electricity at all, for that matter).

The first time I went up those hills was when I was ten, invited by a buddy, along with several of his other buddies, to celebrate his tenth birthday. It was quite an adventure, starting with a coal powered chugging train ride from our town to his...alone and on my own as a ten year old. (It scares me now to even think about it.) We had some wonderful adventures up there on those mountains, and soon it was over, and we began the daylong trek back down. Part way down, I had to answer the call of nature, so I told the guy I was walking with to go on ahead, that I would catch up shortly. Now, the thing I hadn't fully realized, was that, as we got closer to the bottom of the mountain, rice paddies dotted the landscape, and there were little trails running this way and that, all around those fields. Confidently, though, I headed straight on down the mountain on the wide, broad trail. After some time, and seeing none of the other guys anywhere in sight, panic started rising in my chest, and I began to realize that I was not, after all, on the right trail. I had no idea where I was in these endless hills around me. Now, thinking back over 50 years later, I can see that this would have been a great time to start talking to God. And now that I think about it, very likely, that is why he put me in that situation, so that I would reach out to him as he patiently waited for me to do so. Did I start talking to God at that point? I have to admit, I don't remember doing so. What I did do, though, and which did calm me down some, was to begin to whistle loudly the theme tune to "The Bridge on the River Kwai", a cool movie that we had recently watched. So, on I went, whistling loudly to myself, as I got closer to the road at the bottom of the mountain. I arrived in the wrong place at the bottom, but thankfully, it was not too far from the church which acted as our "base camp", in fact, I could see it in the distance, and so I confidently wandered into the church courtyard and joined the rest of the crew, a while after they had arrived. Whew, what a relief that moment was!

I sometimes wonder why things like that experience of momentarily getting lost happen to us in life... Why do we misplace something? Why do we turn onto a wrong road and waste 15 minutes finding our way back, seemingly for no reason at all? These kinds of things occur all too frequently for our liking. But what if we used them for a good purpose? Sometimes, when I lie awake in the wee hours of the dark night, I like to imagine that God has nudged me awake because he wants to talk to me. I've told myself that so many times, actually, that now I really do believe it. So, what if we used every irritating or frustrating moment as a reminder to talk to our Heavenly Father? I dare say that he won't mind the interruption. Even if I keep approaching him multiple times on a really frustrating day...I doubt if he will mind at all... Shall we try it and see what happens?

MARCH 6

My wife will tell you that wherever we are...Tennessee, China, Korea...my book antenna goes on full alert until I hunt down a little corner where I can find books to please my hunger for the printed page. Thankfully, just down the lane and around the corner from where we presently live in Seoul, I have again located a gem to meet my cravings. This is a simple place, called "The Book", that almost has no room to stand in. Books are jammed into every corner, piled on the floor, spill out onto the sidewalk, and sliding shelves have even been installed that allow you to move a section of books along...and reveal a whole additional section of books behind the one you've just pushed aside. An older gentleman, whom I have become friends with (and spent a good sum of money on), started this shop about 50 years ago, when I was a teenager. It appears to still be in the same location, and perhaps some of his books have been sitting on the shelf for most of those 50 years. It is a used foreign language bookstore, which to my ears, suggests that it's products are cheaper than elsewhere, and most of the titles are in English. So, many days, when we walk by on our way to the subway, heading out to teach, I'll pause briefly to give him a greeting and poke through one or two books.

But there's one thing that makes me sad about this place. He has a good selection of study Bibles and other resources, and I've purchased a number of them to help me with my Bible studies, small group meetings, and personal devotions. But, I'm always a little sad when I pick up a Bible, flip through it, see someone's name written in it, and notice that the pages are still very crisp and hardly touched. God's precious Message was given to someone...and they laid it aside, cast it off, not realizing the precious treasure that they are missing.

Jeremiah 10-12 seems to convey some of the same sadness. God has told his people again and again and again that they need to listen to him, to follow him, to obey him. But, as is our common nature and habit, we too often cast aside God's Word, forget his words to us, go in our own different direction. It's no wonder the Bible is such a big book...God has had to remind us over and over again to pay attention to his important message to us: when we trust and follow him, we find and fulfill our purpose and peace in life. When we don't follow him, invariably we get ourselves into trouble, turmoil, or restlessness. God is saddened when we don't listen to his truth and counsel. And it makes me sad, too, when I see evidence of the same thing.

MARCH 7

Day/Date. Be sure to remember five things to be grateful for every day. March 7

Daniel 2:28 NCV But there is a God in heaven.

The story of Daniel in the Bible is one of incredible opposition and persecution. Through it all, including being thrown into a cage of hungry lions, Daniel demonstrated remarkable and unimaginable calmness and courage. Why? Because he knew that God in heaven knows all things and is in control of all things.

When I read Paul's words in Romans 1, I wish in some ways that we were all like him...well, not entirely. I'd be happy to skip the chains, flogging, and shipwrecks. But his life reminds me of some athletes and musicians I've seen. I'll watch them and think, "I wish I could do what they do." But do I really? Probably not. I remember hearing about a famous cello player, who would spend all day alone, in a hotel room, practicing over and over and over again to get one little part of his piece exactly perfect. I could not do that. I wouldn't want to do that...in other words, if I was honest, I wouldn't really want to be like him. It's the same with athletes. I love tennis, and used to enjoy playing it a good bit in my younger days. I'll sometimes watch one of the pros and think, "I wish I could play like that." But would I really? I've heard of some of these guys, spending hours and hours practicing, drilling, and working on one particular stroke. If I'm honest with myself, there is no way I would want to do that, aside from not having the tenacity to do it.

And then there is Paul. Paul's life was so consumed with following God, all he did was so caught up in honoring God, that, that was all you saw in his life. I look at my life (as well as others around me), and think, man, I'm just constantly distracted, always thinking of unhealthy things, doing things that are probably not really what God would want me to be doing. It's no wonder that Paul could say (in a way that I could never say), "Follow my example. Do what I do." Of course, he knew that he wasn't perfect. He knew he needed God's grace and forgiveness in his life, just as much as we do. But, for whatever failings he may have had, he certainly was consumed with following God. His heart was in the right place. That is how we need to follow Paul. Lord, may it also be the same with us as well.

MARCH 8

> **Day/Date** Be sure to remember five things to be grateful for every day. **March 8**
>
> **Isaiah 53:5 NCV** He was crushed for the evil we did. The punishment, which made us well, was given to him. In past history, a lamb might be offered as a sacrifice to clean a person of his sins. But God loves us so much, he himself provided the perfect sacrifice to take away the stain of our sins once and for all. Jesus was sent from heaven to die in our place, to pay the penalty of our sins by sacrificing his own life for us.
>
> March 9

One of my most beautiful memories of our years in China was a time when we took a short excursion up to Shangrila. Yes, there really is a town called Shangrila, tucked away in the mountains close to Tibet, a beautiful little tourist spot for backpackers and other adventurers...and the occasional missionary. When we lived in China, anytime I was out on the streets, I would stuff my pockets with God's Word and look for people I could connect with. This time was no different. As we walked the interesting cobblestone alleyways of that backhills town, we came upon a small eating place where a young Tibetan lady (evidenced by her headdress) worked and looked out the doorway at passersby. She was looking for, hoping for, customers, so we stopped for a chat...and offered her God's Good News. It thrilled me to realize that it was our privilege to share God's love with her, for most likely the first time in her life.

Moments later, walking down a nearby street, I spotted a young, well dressed couple...no doubt tourists from a bigger city. I generally looked for people like that to approach because they tended to be more open, more likely to speak some English, and more friendly to strangers. It turned out that they were engineering students from one of the largest cities in China, well educated and conversant in English. After a brief chat, I gave them a Bible and moved on down the road. Almost immediately, he came running after me and wanted to get a photo together. He proudly held up his Bible, and it reminded me of the story of the one leper who came running back to Jesus to thank him for healing him. They both told me that they had never even heard of the Bible, much less having ever read it. It stunned me that educated folks in a large, modern city in China would have never heard of the Bible before.

When I read Psalm 67, it reminds me of these brief encounters. It speaks of the excitement that will take place when the peoples of the world hear the Message of God's salvation. What an amazing privilege God gives us to participate in a small way in his wonderful plans.

MARCH 9

life for us.

Day/Date   Be sure to remember five things to be grateful for every day.   March 9

Matthew 28:19 NCV   So go and make followers of all people in the world.

An ambassador is a very important person. He is sent by the king or president to deliver a vital message or to represent the King or president in some significant way because he can be trusted to do so. When Jesus left his friends to return to heaven, he gave them (and us!) the job of being his ambassadors in the world. He wants us to share his Message because it is so important and he trusts us to do it.

One summer day, many years ago, a teenage gal took a dive...and her life was never the same. And I thank God that it happened, in spite of how excruciating that trial was for her. Joni Eareckson dove into the water and broke her neck...and God has chosen to bless countless people through her suffering. God sometimes asks his servants to travel painful and difficult paths...for a good purpose. On occasion, God asked his prophets to do some pretty strange things as well, such as in Jeremiah 14, when God told the prophet to go buy a belt and put it on...as a symbol of the people's misbehavior toward God. Thankfully for us, though she wrestled and struggled a lot, Joni recognized God's sovereign plans in her life, and she has used her painful life in amazing ways to be a witness to who God is, to many, many people.

These examples cause me to wonder about things that happen to us. One of our friends just recounted a frustrating incident with their car...which God used as an opportunity for them to praise God...and for her children to recognize that this aggravation was actually being used by God for their good. So, I wonder about us. When frustrations come along, when calamity hits, when disaster strikes...obviously, we are terribly uncomfortable, perhaps even panicked. But, at the same time, are we able to pause, like our friend, like Joni, like the prophet...to reflect on God's plan in all this? Perhaps, if we think on God and wait patiently for how the matter will turn out...we may actually discover that God is still there, still working his good purposes out, that there really are good reasons why bad things sometimes happen.

MARCH 10

> Day/Date — Be sure to remember five things to be grateful for every day.
>
> March 10
>
> Philippians 3:8 NCV
>
> I think that all things are worth nothing compared with the greatness of knowing Christ Jesus my Lord.
>
> This is an astonishing statement for Paul to make. Paul was one of the best educated, most zealous, most successful, and most respected religious leaders of his day. Yet when he met Jesus, he suddenly could see the truth clearly. He understood that all his own efforts and accomplishments were worthless compared to the real life that Jesus had to offer him. May we also have this same understanding!

We sometimes talk about the "tip of the iceberg," and certainly there are many things in life which are like that. One friend, many years ago, recounted a story to me which kind of exemplifies this expression. When he was a manager once, he was talking with one of his workers, and he asked him what he hoped to aspire to one day. The worker replied, "I want to be the manager someday." "Oh, why?", my friend asked him. "Because the manager gets to just sit at his desk with his feet up all day!" Talk about the tip of the iceberg, clearly this guy had not quite understood all that was entailed in being the manager.

When we lived in China, we lived right at the foot of the Himalayan mountains. They soared straight up behind us, so close you felt like you could reach out and touch them. They were just right there.

Occasionally, we would follow a path up the mountain. After walking up, up, up for several hours...we actually had hardly made a dent in the side of the mountain. It was far higher than it appeared from a distance.

Paul points out the danger of judging and highlighting the faults of others, in Romans 2. It's so easy for us to see every little thing that other people do, that's out of line. But as Paul points out, we really are barely seeing the tip of the iceberg in our own behavior. It's frightening, really, to think of how many ways my thoughts, desires, behavior, and life are contrary to what God desires. Usually, I'm oblivious to my own behavior. So, I hope God would open our eyes to our own shortcomings...rather than us focusing always on everyone else's imperfections. Lord, help us to see things as you do. Forgive us for skipping over our own sin...and seeing what everyone else is doing wrong. May we all, more and more, be pleasing to God and seeking his pleasure, rather than focusing on things that dishonor him.

MARCH 11

In my younger days, we must have been a bit of an odd family to behold. At one time, there was a crazy lady living with us in the front room (later my parents' bedroom). I remember, in fear, hearing her scream and yell as several folks tried to hold her back and reign her in. Another time, the tiniest wisp of a boy, with severe tuberculosis, stayed with us for a while. He was so weakened by the disease, that he had to hold onto the wall as he shuffled along from his bedroom toward the bathroom. Then, for some years, we had another guy, who originally had been taken in off the streets by American soldiers, come live with us, and for all practical purposes, become part of our family. To this day, even though he passed away some years ago, we think of him as part of the family. One time, my father brought into our home a former gangster, who was saved from tuberculosis by my father and had become a believer in Jesus. We had a paper thin partition put into the upstairs boys' room (where my brother and I lived), and that is where this former gangster lived. I remember lying awake at night, listening to his hymn singing. Later, he went to seminary, got married, and started a church not far from our hometown. A few years ago, my wife and I visited him and his church. Now in his 80s, and I being in my 60s, we both wept when we saw each other. His words were: "I owe everything to your father."

When I read Psalm 68, I think back on all these people. These words of David speak of a grand procession, of "captives being led", and I think of people who once were captives to sin and evil, being brought to God. I think of my Dad, how well he did that, bringing those who were slaves to sin and brokenness, home to God.

And that is the business who should also be about...

MARCH 12

Day/Date Be sure to remember five things to be grateful for every day. March 12
Psalm 139:1-2 Message God, investigate my life. I'm an open book to you.

When we pray this with sincerity, God opens up a whole new world to us. We see ourselves differently (and not always a pretty sight), view the world around us differently, and gain a new understanding of who God is. It can be an unsettling ride, but God goes with us, and he promises that it is for our good.

I remember hearing the story of an older Korean gentleman, arriving at our mission community, and asking to see Dr. Codington. Apparently, as he was nearing the end of his life, he wanted to be sure that his personal, spiritual house was in order, so he wanted to see the good doctor. What was interesting about this story was that there were some full time evangelists also living in our community. But he didn't ask to see them…he asked to see my father.

(Now, that's not in any way to take anything away from those evangelists. In fact, when I travel around Korea today, everywhere I go, I see crosses on churches, rising up in every village, town, and community. In my day, they simply were not there. More often than not, you would see a Buddhist temple here or there. And this makes me think of those evangelists who lived among us, away so many weeks, toiling endlessly in the far off fields that were ripe for harvest…and today you see the fruit of their labor, all across the land. Those were amazing men. So this little story about my father is not meant to speak lightly of those self sacrificing evangelists.)

I expect that the older gentleman who wanted to see my father knew that he would receive compassion, understanding, and grace from my father. That's just who my father was. So he didn't want to see anyone else. In Jeremiah 15, God, in his exasperation with his people's disobedience, says, "Even if you folks had Moses or Samuel speak on your behalf, I would not listen to you. You guys are just so bad, so disobedient, that your best professionals aren't enough to fix your wrongs!"

Thankfully, we know that Christ was enough. What he did for us on the cross was enough to cover our disobedience and rebellion against God. Jesus is the safe place for us to be, the one we can come to, to receive the grace that we need. (And I expect that the older Korean gentleman thought the same thing about my Dad.)

MARCH 13

Many years ago, I used to visit our bookstore team in Pakistan every year. Although I grew up in Asia, still, Karachi was a world away from where I was raised. What an amazing, teeming, alive city it was! Something interesting was happening everywhere you looked. From time to time, I would enjoy just standing outside our bookshop, watching life go by…rickshaw drivers pumping their bikes past us, sellers peddling their wares, impeccably dressed conservative Muslims on their way to afternoon prayers…what an amazing world. Bewildering, to me, as well. Thankfully, on those trips, I usually found a welcoming haven to stay at, away from the hustle and bustle of the bursting city. One of my favorite places was the home of an elderly, very proper English couple. He had built up an engineering business over many years, and now they were approaching retirement. They lived in a good sized home above his business office. And they had turned several of their bedrooms (probably because their children had long grown and departed) into Airbnb lodgings, long before the term had been invented. So it was a wonderful way to find refreshment at the end of the busy days, in their quiet home. (And I loved their British breakfasts, as well!)

One day, I met another young man at their home, who was spending a night on his way to the countryside. He had grown up in Pakistan, and came from a long family line of folks who had served there. The next morning, he was on his way again, and I quickly forgot about him.

Not long after that, I heard some tragic, heartbreaking news. This young father, who I had just been with, had been out with his family and some friends, for a picnic and relaxing afternoon by the river. Several of the kids were swimming, and at one point, his daughter started to yell for help. She was in over her head, and the water was pulling her away. The young man jumped up without a second of delay, and dove in the water after the girl. Apparently, the current was strong there, and he struggled to save his daughter, as well as to return to shore. In the end, she was saved...but he went beneath the waters and never came back up, until later, when his body was recovered. Life can turn tragic so suddenly and unexpectedly at times.

David's life was no different, and he unfolds such a scenario in Psalm 69. "Save me, God, the waters are rising up to my neck. I'm sinking down in the mire!" I can't help but think of that young father in Pakistan when I read those words. It also reminds me of what Jesus did for us. But not only did he jump in after us when we were drowning in our sins...he jumped in, knowing beforehand that it would cost him his life in the process. And not only would he lose his life, he would lose it in the most horrible of ways...being scorned and tortured and abused by the very people he loved and was dying for. (Most of us weren't, after all, anything close to what that father's little girl was to him, from a human perspective.) Then, as a final, and the greatest, part of his suffering, his own perfect Heavenly Father turned his back on Jesus and abandoned him. Would I give up my life for any one of my children? I'm sure I would. But would I knowingly, willingly, intentionally, lay down my life for thugs who hated everything about me. I have to be honest and say, that would surely give me serious pause!

But that is exactly what Jesus did for us. He dove into hell, seeing us drowning in our sins...because of his great love for us.

How deep the Father's love for us, how vast beyond all measure...

MARCH 14

Day/Date Be sure to remember five things to be grateful for every day. March 14

Psalm 139:5 Message / I look behind me and you're there, then up ahead and you're there, too — your reassuring presence, coming and going.

When I was a boy, it was a fearful thing to walk alone along a dark road at night. Panic would on occasion rise up in my chest. But God says that when we love him, he is all around us, watching over us. Whatever my circumstances, I do not need to be afraid.

Occasionally, a series of "coincidences" will come your way that leave you scratching your head and wondering, "How in the world did that happen?" Just such a series of unusual events came our way last December. Our youngest son was visiting us in Korea during his Christmas break from college, and we had off for our winter break from teaching. We live in Seoul, in the northern part of South Korea, but I wanted to show David my childhood hometown, down in the south. So, we took a two hour comfortable train ride (which, in the old days took six long hours) down to Gwangju. There, I showed him the same trees I used to climb, the cemetery where my younger brother is buried, the little chapel building where I had elementary school, the clay court where I began my storied tennis career (OK, OK, that's a mild exaggeration, but I can dream, right??), the hospital where my father toiled for many years...all part of my DNA, and a glimpse into his father's life, for our son.

After a few hours of this, we were tired and needed a sit down and a coffee break. Just at that moment, we spotted a cafe down the street from us, and so figured that would do the trick. As we walked into the cafe, I glanced to my left and saw a bunch of colorful paintings displayed on the wall. Out of the 30 or so pictures displayed, my quick glance landed on one that instantly caught my eye. It was the house I had grown up in, our family home, which had long since been torn down. But someone knew of it and had painted it! I moved in closer and read the caption in Korean, below the picture. It said, "This was the Codingtons' house, and I lived next to it." "What?", I thought. "The artist lived next to us??" There was only one person who lived next to us when I was little. Her name was MiHwa, and her father worked for us as our gardener. Over to the right of all these paintings was a sign in Korean that said, "These paintings are for sale. If you would like to purchase any of them, please call this number." And the name next to it was...MiHwa! We called her right up, she came over, and I had a tearful reunion with the little girl I grew up with more than 50 years ago! What was perhaps even more amazing than meeting her again, was the fact that she now lives in Seoul, where we live. She happened to be down in our old hometown during the same couple of days we were also visiting. And of all the coffee shops in Gwangju (and believe me, there are more than a few in this city of well over a million inhabitants...), she had just displayed her artwork in the exact cafe that we happened to walk into. All of that is amazing enough... But, in the briefest moment, as I was walking past the jumble of paintings, my eyes fell onto the one of our old house...and I recognized it instantly. MiHwa and I were both stunned to make this reacquaintance...no doubt both never imagining that our lives would again interconnect after so many years.

Sometime later, MiHwa showed me a letter that she had received from my father in his retirement, about 25 years ago. It was remarkable for me to see my father's own handwriting, written in the old style Korean, which was to write vertically, and from right to left on the page.

Somehow, as I read the opening words of Jeremiah 18, my thoughts drift back to this old letter, written especially to MiHwa, and that she has held onto and treasured for so many years. For in Jeremiah, the prophet records that the words of God came to him as well. God wrote him a letter, especially to him, with a very important message. Thankfully, Jeremiah preserved it, and we still have it 2,500 years later! Now, if MiHwa preserved my father's letter for 25 years, and to my eyes, it still has a lot of value...well, imagine how much more valuable God's letter to us is, written 2,500 years ago, and just as relevant today as it was then! Have you read Jeremiah lately? I do believe that God has a message in it that he's waiting for us to receive...

MARCH 15

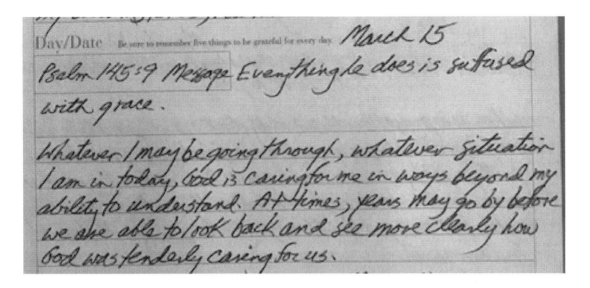

Day/Date   Be sure to remember five things to be grateful for every day.   March 15

Psalm 145:9 Message   Everything he does is suffused with grace.

Whatever I may be going through, whatever situation I am in today, God is caring for me in ways beyond my ability to understand. At times, years may go by before we are able to look back and see more clearly how God was tenderly caring for us.

We don't seem to be getting any younger, and trudging across this sprawling metropolis to teach English (or even teaching online) can wear us out. It certainly doesn't get easier as the years pass. One thing we enjoy doing on the evenings we're not teaching is to sit on our bed, put on some old movie, and eat our supper together as we watch. So, when we're back in the US, we do the occasional poking around at our favorite used bookstore, to find cheap DVDs to bring back to Korea with us. One series we've been watching a bit of (and which I don't particularly recommend, by the way…) is called, "Justified", about a Deputy in the backwoods of Kentucky. I'm not quite sure where they got the name for the series from, but there certainly doesn't seem to be too much that's justified about it…

Especially, when I compare the story line to the way Paul talks about "justified" in Romans 5&6… Paul tells us that God dumps his excessive love out on us…even when we don't deserve it…and then provides our justification because of what Christ did on our behalf. It is truly beyond our human comprehension, beyond what is sensible.

But there is a catch to this…

All too often, and we've seen this in our Chinese and North Korean friends, as well as with folks back in the US, we get the idea that, since God has forgiven all our sin, and given us a fresh start, now life should be all hunky dory, as my older brother used to say. No more problems, no more pain, all smooth sailing. But nearly in the same breath that Paul talks about God's over abundant love and about our justification, he adds, "Oh, by the way, suffering is good for you. It helps build perseverance!" Great, thanks a lot, Paul…(sounds like what some high school principal would say). But that is, in fact, important for us to remember. Although God forgives and saves us, we still live in this very fallen, very messed up world…and, I'm increasingly aware, I live in this world enveloped with my messed up self. That's important for us not to forget. We're forgiven…but it's still hard work, and includes plenty of suffering, to live in the broken world. So, as Peter tells us in his first letter, don't be surprised by your suffering!

MARCH 16

Day/Date Be sure to remember five things to be grateful for every day. March 16

1 Timothy 1:15 NIV Jesus Christ came into the world to save sinners.

Paul had about the most impressive credentials and resumé of anyone around time. If anyone was a good man, he surely was. But one day God opened his eyes and showed Paul that all his good works still left him a sinful man in need of God's saving mercy and grace. And that was exactly the kind of person Jesus came to save.

My parents arrived in Korea in 1949, shortly after their wedding (and not too many months after they met in missionary candidate school). Then, within months, the Korean War enveloped the land. By the time the dust and bombs had settled, in the mid-1950s, Korea was utterly destroyed and was one of the poorest countries in the world. Mom had evacuated to Korea during the war years, Dad had mostly stayed behind in Pusan, helping refugees with whatever expired medicines he could get off the hands of the US military. Occasionally, he was able to hop across the Korea Strait to visit my Mom. Somehow, by the mid-1950s, they found themselves with five little kids…not sure how they managed, but we all showed up, one after the other (five kids in six years!).

By the early 60s, things were still very primitive in Korea, and I remember Dad being pretty taken up with his hospital duties, as the Director of the Christian hospital there. Our family lived among the missionary community, just across the dirt lane from the hospital. It was close enough, that Dad was able to dash over for lunch with us, and then hustle off back to the hospital. Thinking back on those days reminds me of stories we read of Jesus. Anytime he showed up, crowds scrambled after him, looking for help, for compassion, for sympathy… The same was true with Dad. In those busy days at the hospital, I remember watching him walk swiftly back to work after a meal with us, with a Korean man running after his long strides, trying to keep up and to get Dad's attention. Other times, folks would just come and hang around our front porch, waiting for a chance to unload their hearts and worries. One man who hung around, we called, "The Crazy Man". I was scared to death of him. He called himself, Harry Truman...not quite sure how he latched onto that name. Another man, a sweet small man we called, "The Little Elder", always put a smile on our faces, when we saw him peddling up the dirt path on his bike. Invariably, he would bring us a large gift of chestnuts or persimmons.

In those difficult days, all these folks came looking for a listening ear, a healing touch, a little financial help. They knew they could get that in the presence of Dad.

David must have known that as well. Every time he needed something, he came running to his Heavenly Father, where he knew instinctively that he would receive consolation and help, and a safe place to rest. That's the picture we get in Psalm 70, when David once again calls out, "Hurry up and come, God! I'm desperate and have nowhere else to turn!" Isn't it truly remarkable that we have exactly the same Almighty God that David had, the very same one who delivered David from the lions and from Goliath, just waiting for us to run to him! That's what I call, amazing grace!

MARCH 17

Sometimes God says, "No!", doesn't he. That's what happened to King Zedekiah when he appealed urgently to God as the armies of King Nebuchadnezzar of Babylon were closing in around Jerusalem, in Jeremiah 21. "Help your people, God! Enemies are about to overwhelm us!" But the king got a no, in response. "Sorry, I won't. As badly as you want and need rescuing, in fact, you need something even more than that. You need to turn back to me." As difficult as it may seem, sometimes, just on occasion, the Almighty God of the universe may know something we don't...and may know our needs better than we do.

When I was a boy in Korea, one year we got an old push lawn mower, with a rotating blade. I don't know where Dad found it, but it was an amazing piece of equipment, the latest in high tech lawn care. You see, up to that time, we hired an old man, probably for not more than pennies, to squat down in the blazing sun, and cut our expansive lawn with his own muscles and sweat, one fistful of grass at a time, with a simple one blade sickle. I still remember our old "Grass-cutter", (the actual name we called him), pausing for a cigarette break in the shade, puffing on one he had formed from discarded cigarette butts and rolled himself. I never thought about all his toil and effort...but I did notice his sickle. Now, that was about the coolest tool, the coolest blade, I had ever laid eyes on. And I knew that I needed one for myself. As any good missionary kid would do,

I took my request directly to God. (I don't know why I didn't ask Dad...probably I was smart enough to know what his answer would be before I asked him...) At any rate, I took my request straight to the source. I can still remember, all these years later, how excited I felt, lying in my bed, after I had prayed, knowing with certainty that God would give me what I needed (the sickle, of course). For some reason, my excitement quickly wore off...and that beloved, longed for, sickle never arrived. I dare say, now that I have a gray head of hair with its accumulated wisdom, that God knew that a sickle was not quite what I needed. Close, yes, but not quite. So he withheld it from me. That was actually an important lesson to me. I realized that you don't always get what you want, what you think you need, what you ask for. God actually knows better than I do what I need. So sometimes he holds back on the urgent...and delivers what I really need. In the meantime, will I trust him for his answer? I hope that King Zedekiah did, before it was too late.

MARCH 18

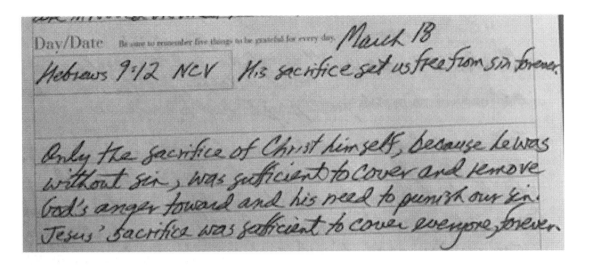

Day/Date   Be sure to remember five things to be grateful for every day.   *March 18*

Hebrews 9:12 NCV   *His sacrifice set us free from sin forever.*

Only the sacrifice of Christ himself, because he was without sin, was sufficient to cover and remove God's anger toward and his need to punish our sin. Jesus' sacrifice was sufficient to cover everyone, forever.

When my wife and I visited Israel a few years ago, we entered a world we had never experienced before. In many ways, it reminded me of New York...a real melting pot of nationalities, religions, languages, and peoples. It was startling to stop and ask an Israeli soldier for directions...and have him answer in a perfect Chicago accent. Jews from all over the world have descended on Jerusalem to make it their home.

While we were there, two things made a big impression on me...the Sabbath, and the conservative Jews. Our visit happened to include a Sabbath, and as we were walking the streets on a Friday at dusk...we had no idea what was about to take place. Just at the moment the sun dipped down below the horizon, what sounded like a loud shofar suddenly filled the air for a few brief moments. Then, all went quiet. And when I say things went quiet, I mean the city was suddenly deserted...no people, no trams, no cars...just deathly silence. I thought, "Wow! They take the Sabbath seriously in a way that we Christians can't begin to comprehend. Talk about a Sabbath rest...the whole city ceased functioning.

The other thing I noticed, that really struck me, was the Orthodox Jews. You would see them rushing down the streets, with their prayer tassels, long hair on the sides of their heads, with their black hats and outfits on, and with their heads buried in the Holy Scriptures. My, oh my, they took their religion seriously. They were devout followers. Me, on the other hand...on occasion, when

I travel, I'll pull out a Bible furtively, and take a quick glance around, as if I'm ashamed or embarrassed to actually be holding a Bible in public. Not these wholly committed followers of the Old Testament. If the Bible said do it, they simply responded, "How high and how often?" Their devotion certainly was convicting. Even walking down a busy street, their eyes were on their Scriptures. They fulfilled the whole law like no one else I've ever seen.

Paul also was very zealous about obeying the whole law...and more. But God knows we're still big time sinners. And, thankfully, he paid the price himself, for our sins...for a bill that was really ours to pay. So, now, we are free from having to fulfill the law...yet, sadly, those devout Jews in Israel apparently don't realize it.

But that's not the end of the story. Paul tells us in Romans 7 that when we choose to follow Christ, we are actually freed from slavery to keeping the law...to become slaves to God (which is a good thing, by the way, because it's what we were made for and the place where we find true peace and purpose). Paul reminds us that our new slavery to God (which is freedom from the slavery to sin) involves serving God, and bearing fruit for him. So, we've been given a task and a purpose. How are we doing in our new slavery/freedom? Are we even seriously aware of our new status as believers? Lord, open our eyes...give us the zeal, the passion, the dedication, that those Jews in Jerusalem have...so that we will follow you.

MARCH 19

Day/Date Be sure to remember five things to be grateful for every day. March 19

Mark 1:38 NCV We should go to other towns around here so I can preach there, too. That is the reason I came.

During Jesus' life on this earth, he was poor materially, living in a Roman occupied land, and daily facing religious opposition. Additionally, life was very difficult. Food was limited, clean water mostly didn't exist, plagues and diseases scourged the people, and travel was by foot on dusty, dangerous roads. But in spite of these many hardships, Jesus always remained focused on completing the task before him. How do our priorities compare with his?

Near the end of his life, my father voiced a question that puzzled him, that had, in fact, puzzled him for a long time, that he really didn't seem to know the answer to. But, now, finally, he could express it, because he had finally discovered the answer to his own satisfaction. The question he asked was: "Why has God been so good to us? Why has he blessed us so richly?" Now, really, a lot of folks would have looked at him, looked at his life, and thought to themselves, "What? You blessed? Are you kidding me? Your life has been tragic!" Why would they have thought that? Well, here are a few reasons:

*Dad grew up in a cultured, prominent, privileged Southern family. His father was well known in the city, had built up a surgical practice, and had it all planned that my father, as his first son, would take over the practice. Instead, Dad latched on to a far fetched idea of throwing it all away to pursue some pipe dream in China (or Korea, as it turned out). My Granddad was so disappointed that he didn't even come to see his son off, when, newly married, he sailed for Korea. No doubt, that was painful for them both.

*Shortly after arriving in Korea, war broke out, my parents had to flee, which meant they lost all their possessions, and they spent those early married war years mostly separated from each other.

*After the war, Dad reopened and built up a Christian hospital, of which he became the Director. But after a couple of decades, it was decided, in his absence, that he wasn't the right one for the job, and so, he was told to step down. Now, the folks who came to that decision were upstanding folks who no doubt had the best intentions and reasons in mind, and they saw that the hospital had grown beyond Dad's limited administrative abilities. So, I'm sure, they were correct in their assessment. Still, it would have been hard for him to have to travel that experience after all he had poured into the hospital to raise it from the ground up.

*Just about at the same time as the hospital leadership change was taking place, my parents lost their youngest in a drowning accident. That is a crushing experience to any parent.

*Years later, my parents lost their oldest daughter when a drunk driver hit her head on, as he drove the wrong way down an interstate highway at night. How could they cope with, not one, but the tragic loss of two of their dear children?

*Not too long after that, after he had started a new medical work in Bangladesh, his mission organization required him to retire, against his wishes. (As it turned out, though he was officially retired, he kept on serving in Bangladesh until age 79.) But, even though he was able to continue his work, it must have been painful to have the organization he had served so long, so faithfully, in the most trying of circumstances, say to him, "You're done. Hang it up."

So...it would not have been surprising, perhaps, for someone to look at my father's life, and think, well, that was a series of unfortunate tragedies...

What I find remarkable about my father's life, is that he only thought about the blessings. Almost like a little kid who wins some prize, he seemed genuinely surprised and puzzled that God had apparently singled him out for so much blessing. It never seemed to cross his mind that he had, after all, encountered one or two pretty major hiccups along the way. Life really does, as is often said, depend on our own attitude, our own choice of how we respond to the twists, turns, and tragedies that it throws at us or drags us through.

We see something of the same attitude in Psalm 71. The writer speaks of troubles, accusers, enemies...clearly, he's had his share of bumps and bruises. But, at the same time, he reflects on the added fact that God has always been with him, God has always been his refuge, his secure place. So, really, the psalmist has made the deliberate choice to focus on how much God has blessed him all through his life. And that was what my Dad chose to do. And, before I forget it, do you know what conclusion Dad came to...about why God had blessed him? He realized, at the end of his life, that God had poured blessing on him...so that he could be a blessing to others. So that he could use the blessings God placed in his hands, to be a blessing to others. And that is certainly what I saw him do with his life...

MARCH 20

Day/Date Be sure to remember five things to be grateful for every day. March 20

Jeremiah 17:14 NCV Lord, heal me, and I will truly be healed.

This is a more profound prayer by Jeremiah than it may appear to be at first glance. We can be healed medically or in other ways. But to be truly healed by God means more than physical healing. It involves complete healing—physically, spiritually, emotionally, and mentally. God can heal us in every way when we come to him.

Sometimes I wonder what it was that Jesus had against the Pharisees. I mean, for such a peace loving, warm hearted, compassionate person, he sure could get his blood pressure inflamed as soon as he encountered one of them. What was the big deal about them? They were conscientious, meticulous, fastidious, passionate in keeping, in honoring, in revering God's law. Wasn't that what life was all about? What could have been more important? Apparently, they missed something along the way that really got Jesus' goat, as we say.

Perhaps it might have been the same with Hitler or some other leader down through history. At the time when Hitler was rising into prominence, Germany was a basket case of the worst kind. Unemployment was at 30%. Inflation ran something like 300%…every month! Repeatedly, the government would have to drop a string of zeros off the currency and start over with a new one. I have one or two of those old German Marks, as curiosity pieces, that seem to be covered in zeros. I've heard stories of people pushing wheelbarrows of bills because it took so many just to buy a loaf of bread. So Hitler came onto the scene at the worst possible time. Not long after he came into power, however, things had changed unimaginably. It seemed that he had worked a miracle. Germany was powerful and prominent again in Europe, the people had their pride in country returned to them, most everyone was working, inflation had been tamed...truly an economic, national miracle. It almost seemed true that, indeed, Germans did have pure blood running through their veins. So, Hitler was amazing, right? Well, as most people would recognize, that wasn't quite the whole story. Along with the successes, Hitler had forced international slavery on millions of people, he had introduced the idea that some humans were not worth the air they breathed, and he had plunged Germany, Europe, and the rest of the world, into the worst and most devastating war ever known.

And, perhaps, that was the problem Jesus had with the Pharisees. On the surface, they seemed to have done all the right things. They were leading the people religiously, they were examples in how they followed God's laws...exemplary, and able to be looked up to. But, along the way, their attention to detail had so distracted them, that they had forgotten their basic purpose and job. As we read in Jeremiah 23, the shepherds were destroying and scattering the sheep they were supposed to be caring for.

These examples are sobering reminders to us as well... We can be so focused on completing every task, covering all the bases, checking every box...that we end out missing the main job we are actually supposed to be doing.

So how did Hitler miss the mark? In all his triumphs and successes, he didn't care for the needy people, the people he should have been shepherding. And that was the problem with the Pharisees as well. In all their attention to detail, they forgot the two great commandments that fulfill the whole law. They were so taken up with checking every box, that they forgot that they were supposed to love God primarily...and to love others as much as they loved themselves. Now, in their defense, we all fall short in those two departments. Not a one of us fulfills those two commandments. We are all dead in the water. But with the Pharisees (and certainly with Hitler, as well), they really believed that they had fulfilled the whole law. They thought they had done everything...and more, thank you very much...that God expected of them. But they forgot that obeying God was not about themselves. It was to die for, we might say...to give up their lives to God, and then to lay down their lives for others. That's something that I fail in and need reminding of every single day.

MARCH 21

> Day/Date   Be sure to remember five things to be grateful for every day   March 21
>
> **Mark 2:17 NCV**   It is not the healthy people who need a doctor, but the sick. I did not come to invite good people but to invite sinners.
>
> Jesus was always focused on reaching out to and helping the needy, the sick, the lost, and the outcasts. We also have been given the task of serving the same kind of people — the ones who are costly to serve, marginalized, and who will not make us very popular according to society's standards.

A number of years ago. I went to a counselor a time or two, and in the course of our conversations, I told this young, successful professional that I was looking forward to going to heaven. Her response made me think that perhaps she thought I was suicidal. I mean, who would want to walk away from all that this life has to offer us, right?

Now that I am that much older than I was back then, I am more eager than ever to get to heaven. I can certainly understand Paul's sense of longing for heaven. Just in the past few weeks, we've received news of a sweet friend who is dying of cancer, a young father of several small children who came home after a run and fell over dead, a very young friend who was discovered dead in her hotel room, a Christian lady whose partner has slipped in and out of drug battles, a wonderful lady who is far from her kids and has troubling symptoms that could suggest cancer...it just seems like life is full of trouble and hardship, that each day brings more bad news. Even my wife is beginning to agree with me about heaven...so you know that life is troubling, if she is starting to feel that same way!

As I've been reading through Romans, chapter 8 has hit me in the face...and now I really, really want to get to heaven! What Paul says sounds truly unbelievable. Especially, when we remember all of his excruciating trials, it's astonishing what he says in these verses.

Paul tells the readers, "You know all the hardships I've been telling you about that I've suffered...yes, all those trials? Well, let me tell you a secret. Heaven is going to be so, so much far better than anything we've experienced down here in this life, that we'll realize that all our difficulties in this life are just trivial events that we might as well not even bother mentioning. God's going to make every single little irritation...as well as all the big whoppers...to help bring about nothing but good for us. Every single bad thing, we'll be able to look back on and see how they were all actually part of God's strategy to bring about great things. Not only that...it's a done deal. Nothing and no one can possibly derail the spectacular blessings that God has all stacked up for us to unpack during all of eternity."

Oh, come on, Paul...quit pulling our leg. Quit making light of all these hardships we're going through right now. That's not a very sensitive thing to be doing.

And Paul comes right back at us: "Honestly, I'm not pulling your leg. In fact, I haven't even begun to tell you the half of how amazing it's going to be in heaven. You wouldn't believe it if I really told you what it's going to be like. But, trust me, you're going to be so staggered that you won't even remember your struggles down here. You'll look back and think, 'Goodness, what was I so fussed about back then?'"

So, that's the way it's going to be. It's making heaven look sweeter and sweeter. And every day, as we trust in Jesus, we are one day closer to it. Hurry up and get here, Jesus!

MARCH 22

Day/Date   Be sure to remember five things to be grateful for every day.   March 22

Isaiah 53:11   NCV   My good servant will make many people right with God; he will carry away their sins.

Jesus, the almighty King of the universe, became a lowly servant because of his love for us. At the cost of unspeakable pain and suffering, he offered himself as the perfect sacrifice to carry the stain of our sins far from us. In doing so, he provided the means for us to have a restored relationship with God.

I can still picture the little boy, aged 6 or 7, with his bright scarlet hooded sweatshirt on, running around the soccer field with all the other boys. I wanted so much for him to perform well, that if I could have willed my strength and power into his small body, I certainly would have. My whole heart was focused on him at that moment, as I watched from the sidelines. Many years later, all of his family cheered by the side of the road, with banners and whistles, as this same little boy, now a grown young man, sailed past us with the rest of the runners in the Boston Marathon. Again, my heart was all in it with him, willing him to succeed, to win, even. For, you see, this little boy, this young runner...was my firstborn son. Especially coming from an Asian background, as I do, I wanted my eldest son to succeed.

And this is the picture we see in Psalm 72, where Solomon, the king, waxes eloquent about his own son. Clearly, Solomon had bigger dreams than I did. He anticipates his son reigning as long as the sun will, and that his righteousness will cover the whole earth like rain. In fact, all the rest of the rulers of the world will bow down to the king, his son. I must say that Solomon had slightly bigger hopes and dreams for his son than I did. I just hoped that my son would play well and not break his leg at the same time. Not exactly visionary, I confess.

But, perhaps Solomon recognizes the truth, the reality of the situation, even as he goes on about his own son's greatness. For he ends his beautiful psalm by acknowledging that, really, it is only God Almighty who does great things, whose name will be lifted high and recognized through the earth.

As we think of our own children and loved ones, it's truly a comfort to know that God is in control, he will have his righteous and loving way, that his plans will succeed. That is something we can hang our hopes on. (Of course, it would be real icing on the cake if one of our children became a king or prime minister, as well!)

MARCH 23

> Mark 1:41 NCV — Jesus felt sorry for the man, so he reached out his hand and touched him.
>
> As a boy, I remember walking through the town with my father during a poorer time in Korea's history. His great compassion reached out repeatedly to those he encountered who were in need. Usually I never even noticed these people. Jesus, also, saw and reached out in compassion to the needy. They were the ones he came to be with and serve.

When I was in seventh grade, I had really arrived. I was far from home, in boarding school, all on my own. On top of that, my roommate was the most amazing athlete I had ever seen. He certainly could have given Michael Jordan a run for his money on the basketball court...but, really, he excelled in every sport. Now, boarding school back then was a little like army boot camp must be...they ran a very tight ship. (Of course, I didn't think it was bad...all this newfound freedom, having my own money, being out from under my parents...well, I could certainly have counted my blessings if I had thought to.) In addition to cleaning our room daily, making our beds trampoline tight, taking care of our own wash and homework...the day ended at ten o'clock sharp. No exceptions. Not a peep. Dead silence.

Well, one night, my roommate and I just couldn't contain ourselves. I have no recollection, whatsoever, of what it was that tickled our funny bones so intensely. But we couldn't keep it in. We started giggling...and giggling...and giggling. Maybe it was a little more than giggling, I don't know. But our dorm parent, a young Mr. Bean sort of a guy, apparently heard us from his apartment, all the way down at the other end of the hall. He came down and issued a warning. We got quiet...for about 15 seconds. Then, the giggling started again. (I'm sure it must have been my roommate's fault...I can't imagine myself being so insubordinate...) Well, not too many minutes later, Mr. Bean...I mean, our dorm parent, padded down the hall again. "All right, boys, get up and get dressed!" (At this hour? What in the world does he have in mind? What is the man going to do to us? Suddenly, Mr. Bean seemed a lot more menacing than he had a few moments ago.)

"Come on outside." By outside, he meant outside, outside...not just out of our room. I don't remember what time of year it was...but, if my memory serves me correctly, I do seem to recollect snow falling...so it was a bit cool outdoors. He took us outside the men's dorm, and around in front of the main class building. There was a large lawn out in front of it, an open area, where not too many years later, this same roommate and I stood to receive our high school diplomas. But I don't want to get ahead of myself...back to that snowy seventh grade night. Mr. Dorm parent crossed his arms, planted his feet, stood like a drill sergeant under the outdoor lights, and barked at us, "OK, boys, now start running laps until I tell you to stop!" Well, the whole scene was just too much for my roommate and me...and we just kept giggling the whole way. We just were not getting the message. Our dorm parent didn't return the following year. Maybe we made him feel like such a failure that he couldn't take it anymore, I don't know. But for me, anyway, it was one of the most entertaining and pleasant memories I have of all my boarding school years.

But the point of this whole story is that my roommate and I just weren't listening. Now, at age 12, if we don't always listen, it's probably not the end of the world. But a much more serious tale of not listening unfolds for us in Jeremiah 25. It's really painful and tragic in its seriousness. Jeremiah tells the people of God, "You know, folks, I have been preaching God's message to you for 23 years...and you have refused to listen. God's been patient with you. He's come down the hall to warn you, so to speak, and you just have not paid attention. I'm sorry to have to tell you this, but now it's too late. God's gonna lower the boom on you...and you're gonna start running laps until you drop!" (Except in Israel's case, it was the armies of Babylon that God recruited to carry out his punishment.)

Occasionally, it's not too big of a deal if we don't listen. My roommate and I got a comical memory out of that one night so long ago. But when we persist in not listening...well, then, the time clock eventually runs out, and the day of reckoning arrives.

Generations and ages later, those words of Jeremiah still speak to us. Will we hear them? Will we listen? God tells us that a day of reckoning is coming. Let's make sure we're ready when it does.

MARCH 24

Mark 12:30 NCV   Love the Lord your God with all your heart, all your soul, all your mind, and all your strength.

If you want to love and serve God, we cannot do so halfheartedly or while we also have set our desire or affection on other things as well. Loving God involves and requires our whole self, every part of who we are.

When my kids were little, I loved playing games with them, teaching them fun new things to do together. But it was a bit of a tricky business... it was a fine balance between teaching them, letting them win on occasion, and keeping their heads from swelling too big if they won too much. So it was a bit of a tap dance to get the balance just right. It didn't want to crush their spirits, but I didn't want them to imagine that they would automatically win every time, either. My parents did the same with us, I seem to recollect. Occasionally, they seemed pretty lame at things... but just when we were pretty sure that, that was indeed the case, they would remind us with a flash that, actually, not all their screws were totally loose yet.

We used to enjoy a good Easter egg hunt with the little ones. I loved watching them run all over the yard, squealing with excitement at the prospect of finding their very own egg to put in their little baskets. Obviously, I could have hidden the eggs so well, that they never would have found a single one. But that would have been tough...both on them and on me, frustrating them and taking away my pleasure at watching their mounting excitement.

I can almost imagine God doing the same thing with us. If we're really honest with ourselves, I expect most of us would admit that we hold onto a fair bit of selfishness, impatience, and pride...the Bible comes right out and just calls it sin. God hates sin. His holiness can't cope with dirt. And, besides, he loves us too much to stand by and watch us get eaten alive by it. Romans 10 is pretty amazing...and reveals God's big parent heart to us. It says he unloads his blessings on all of us. It's kind of like he just flings Easter eggs out everywhere for us to pick up. And more than even that, God says, I'll let you find me even when you're not looking for me, even when you're not asking for me. I mean, what else could he do for us?? But as with our kids, even though I tossed most of the eggs out in plain sight, they still had to get up and run after them. And we have to do the same. God tells us we'll find him if we look, that he's not really very far away...but we still do have to look for him, seek him. Let's not delay...let's get into this serious game before it's too late.

MARCH 25

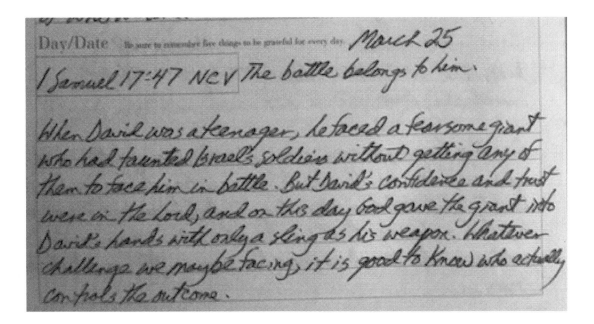

Day/Date   Be sure to remember five things to be grateful for every day   March 25

1 Samuel 17:47 NCV   The battle belongs to him.

When David was a teenager, he faced a fearsome giant who had taunted Israel's soldiers without getting any of them to face him in battle. But David's confidence and trust were in the Lord, and on this day God gave the giant into David's hands with only a sling as his weapon. Whatever challenge we may be facing, it is good to know who actually controls the outcome.

Back in 1990, when my wife and I decided that we wanted to help the people in the former Communist countries of Eastern Europe get the Bible more freely, our quiet life in Tennessee was thrown upside down. For the better part of the next couple of years, we got rid of belongings, arranged for our business to be left in the hands of someone else, sold our house, joined a mission organization…definitely stirred up the waters of our quiet little life with four small children. But in our excitement and preoccupation of getting all ready to go, perhaps we didn't pause to fully think about what we were doing. Finally, the day arrived for our send off to France, and we boarded the flight along with our now five kids, passports, bags, school books, and, hopefully, everything else that we would need in a strange new world.

As we lifted off from the tarmac, I suddenly had an overwhelming sense of dread... What in the world had I done with my life...with my whole family's life?? What were we doing? What were we thinking, throwing it all away?

I don't remember how long that feeling stayed with me, but, now, 30 years later, I can look back over the decades and see God's presence, hand, and guidance with us. There have been plenty of bumps, curves, surprises, and disappointments along the way, but as I look back on it all, I realize that God was right there with us the whole way. In moments of panic, feelings of abandonment, or unexpected disappointment, God has been there, walking with us the whole way.

The writer of Psalm 73 must have felt the same way. He felt like he was slipping, as if he was losing his foothold. But, as he pondered it further, he realized that God had been with him all along. God was even holding his hand the whole way, step by step. As scary as it seemed along the road, there was actually nothing he had to fear. God knew what was happening...God was right there with him. What a wonderful reminder to us, as well, when we chart our path through life, to know that God is right here with us. He is holding us by the hand, he won't leave us, he won't abandon us, and he will stay with us right up until the moment we arrive in God's presence in heaven.

MARCH 26

> Daniel 6:10 NCV Three times a day Daniel would kneel down to pray and thank God, just as he always had done.

What had been a routine habit for Daniel actually became a life threatening exercise. Being seen praying from the street beside his home, his activity was reported to the King, who had proclaimed that worship of anyone other than himself would be punishable by death. But Daniel worshipped and trusted in God, so he continued to pray even though it placed him in grave danger.

As we have come up on, and passed, 40 years of marriage, my wife and I have had successive opportunities to observe our own children travel the same journey of entering and experiencing marriage for themselves. As we look back over our own life together, with all the things life brings across our path, we want more and more to steer our kids and walk with them through this process. There is so much involved in marriage...it's more complex and deep than we imagined when we first embarked on the journey.

As we read Jeremiah 27-29, we observe that there are significant, and perhaps, complex aspects of having a relationship with God as well. One very startling phrase in chapter 27, is when God says, "King Nebuchadnezzar of Babylon is my servant." How could God possibly say that? How can God speak of an evil, pagan king as his servant, as a person who is carrying out God's plan? It's actually a very comforting thought. It would be downright scary if there were things or people that were outside of God's control, things that happened that he didn't have power over...that would be a pretty disturbing, troubling scenario. But nothing is outside of God's knowledge or control. All things really do work together for good. That gives us tremendous encouragement and hope.

Additionally, is the serious and sobering reality that God doesn't shrug his shoulders at disobedience. He will address it, it will be punished, sometimes in very painful ways. Whenever we are tempted to think of sin lightly, whenever we imagine that we can do something in secret, let's be reminded of this passage, where God assures us that disobedience will face a day of reckoning.

And, finally, as he so often does, God reminds us that his good plans will indeed come to pass. He has not forgotten us, he won't abandon un, he will bring us safely home one day, as we trust in and follow his leading. As usual, God's grace, mercy, and love covers and pours over us.

MARCH 27

> **Day/Date** Be sure to remember five things to be grateful for every day. *March 27*
>
> *Isaiah 35:10 NCV* — Their happiness will last forever. Their gladness and joy will fill them completely, and sorrow and sadness will go far away.
>
> Life brings us many good events and experiences. At the same time, life is full of hardship and suffering. But one day, when we are with God in heaven, all evil and sadness will be swept away, to become a thing of the past. All that will be left is happiness and joy. What a day that will be!

On occasion (probably not more than a few times a day!), I feel weighed down by the cares of the world, by the things that worry me and give me anxiety. When I give into that temptation of worrying and feeling pity on myself, perhaps I am doing what Elijah also did. After a spectacular victory from God, he began giving into worry, and thought, "Poor me. I'm the only one left who is still following God." And we do exactly the same thing, too, don't we, when we imagine that we're all alone, the only one left. We are making the colossal mistake and oversight of forgetting that God is part of the picture, a big, big, big part of the picture, as a matter of fact! We are not alone, it is not all on us, the working out of God's good plans is not only dependent on us. I think of this when I remember back to the day I dropped our little six year old off at French school. The panic in her face told me that she thought she was all alone in the world, that I was abandoning her, that there was no one else left…(just how I sometimes feel as I go through life). But I knew that I was still with her, watching over her, that I would never abandon her. That is how God is with us. We do, for sure, feel all alone at times. We feel the weight of everything hanging on us. But when we feel that way, we are forgetting the truth that God is with us, that he is, in fact, working his good plans out…and we are part of that plan.

MARCH 28

Day/Date   Be sure to remember five things to be grateful for every day.   March 28

Jeremiah 31:3 NIV I have loved you with an everlasting love.

Our love for people can grow, decline, or go through ups and downs. It can be a very fragile and uncertain reality. But God loved us deeply before we were even born to such a degree that we can't even imagine it. We will never be loved so much as or in the way that God loves us.

My wife's mother grew up during the years World War 2 was roaring all around her as a little girl in the Netherlands. Her father's business was bombed...they were reduced to eating tulip bulbs...then her father was marched off to work in a German factory, an experience he was never able to talk about when he eventually returned home, almost unrecognizable, and with his youngest son not even knowing who he was. Those were life defining moments in the hearts of everyone alive at the time. My mother in law admonished her children never to forget those years, those experiences, those memories. She wanted her children to be sure that they passed on her history to future generations.

Franklin Roosevelt also told the American people never to forget December 7, 1941, which we still today celebrate as "Pearl Harbor Day". Perhaps the year 2020 will be a similar year...a year we will long remember and find hard to forget.

The writer of Psalm 74 was also living through a time of disaster, most likely after the Babylonians had come and ransacked and destroyed Jerusalem. He asks if God has forgotten and abandoned them. He feels so crushed and demoralized that he doesn't end the psalm on a high note of reassurance, as most other psalms end. There doesn't seem to be much in the way of hope or comfort here. But, in fact, there is. Because when life has become unbearable, when the unthinkable has happened, the writer knows where to turn. He hasn't received an answer yet, but he knows that he can bring his problems and sorrows to God. Why? Because he knows that God is good, full of compassion, loving and faithful, that he will never abandon his people. So, even when there doesn't appear to be any sign of God in what is happening all around us, still, we can turn to him for help. That is what the psalmist did...and that is what we can do, even in a year like 2020.

MARCH 29

Surely, it's the understatement of the century...or the millennium...to say that God is inscrutable, that he is beyond our understanding. And, of course, he says as much, himself. God tells us, "There's no way you will understand me or what I'm doing, so you might as well not even try." Jeremiah 30&31 are good examples of that. God comes to the prophet and tells him, "You folks are dead in the water, kaput, terminated, incurable..." Then, almost immediately, he seems to say the opposite: "I'm going to restore things, I'm going to bring you back, I'm going to create something new out of you." No hope, no solution, time has run out...but, actually, there is hope, there is still time, I am going to make something happen after all. It's like one of those crazy basketball games... A last shot goes up at the buzzer...and bounces off the rim. The opposing team grabs the rebound, game over. But, then, just as the fans start filing out, a whistle is blown, the refs huddle...and six seconds are added back onto the clock. There was a foul...and with it, another chance. Your team gets the ball back, a jumper goes up, again it bounces, but with the final second winding down, hands unexpectedly reach up...and stuff the ball in. Game over, no last second whistle, you've won after all, and the place goes bonkers.

I never asked him, but I wonder if that's how my Grandpa must have felt. In China during the 1940s, there was turmoil, chaos, and hardship everywhere. It was not a good time to be a foreigner. They had been the cause of much of

China's suffering, in the eyes of many. The Communists and the Nationalists were in a death struggle for control of the land. One day, soldiers marched up to the mission community and apprehended my grandfather. He was marched off...and stood up in front of a wall to be shot. But at the last moment, just as time was running out, there was an interruption, a disturbance. The soldiers were quickly called aside...and at just that moment, a loyal Chinese friend, who had been following at a distance, grabbed my grandfather and squirreled him quickly away. Saved at the buzzer. Terminated...but given new life. Grandpa was a soft spoken man, who almost never raised his voice or got rattled. But, I expect, that the events of that day must have shaken even him...and surely given him renewed confidence in God's control.

The point about this passage in Jeremiah is that even when time has run out, even when it's all over, when there is nothing left to hope in...there is still God. He, in fact, is all that matters. Because he's calling the shots, he's pulling the strings, he has the final say. Don't count him out.

MARCH 30

> **Day/Date** Be sure to remember five things to be grateful for every day. **March 30**
>
> Romans 12:2 NLT — Don't copy the behavior and customs of this world, but let God transform you into a new person by changing the way you think.
>
> Part of trusting God to save me is offering my life to him to work in me and make me the person he wants me to be according to his good plans. If I am really doing this, I won't at the same time be acting and living in a way that is contrary and opposite to how God wants me to live.

When we were young, we used to kind of smile and snicker when airmail folder letters would arrive from NaiNai (our grandmother), longtime China missionary, now retired in the US. And arrive they did. As long as I can ever remember...and my Mom always confirmed it...a blue aerogram letter would arrive weekly, all the way from America, to our doorstep. Talk about dedication, loyalty, devotion... And that is what made us kids snicker. NaiNai would always, but always, sign her letters to her daughter, our Mom, "Devotedly, Mother". We even, between each other, got to calling NaiNai, "Devotedly". There could not have been a more loud example, sermon even, to me of what the word "devotion", means, than those letters, which arrived for years, 52 every year, to our home in Korea. NaiNai was committed to supporting her daughter, to staying in touch with her, to being there for her...that's what devoted means, I learned through this unspoken demonstration.

The question it makes me ask myself is, how devoted am I? How committed am I...to my beliefs, to the Bible, to my family, to God's family, to my children? How devoted am I to what I say I believe? Does my life reflect my words?

In Romans 12, Paul uses this same word that my grandmother was so fond of. He tells us to be devoted to each other. Are we this way? Do our lives reflect what we say we believe? Lord, help us, in our weakness and our stumblings, to be devoted to you...to be devoted to the same things that you also are. My that be what our lives look like.

MARCH 31

March 31

2 Chronicles 16:9 NCV The Lord searches all the earth for people who have given themselves completely to him.

God sees us, watches us, and knows us. And he is looking for those of us who want to honor him with our lives and with the decisions and choices that we make every day in our lives.

This weekend my wife and I are heading down to the southern coast of Korea. Several of our former North Korean students are now in university there, so we are going for a quick visit to see them. We're planning to stay at a hotel she found near the beach. My wife dearly loves the ocean. It seems to breathe life and peace into her. She remembers with great fondness, days at the beaches in Delaware as a child. She also has memories of rather harrowing experience on a family vacation in Florida. Shortly after the Cuban missile crisis, her father got the idea in his head of driving all the way down to the south coast of Florida in the family car...just as hurricane Cleo was rattling its saber. They were staying at a residential cottage area as the storm approached. Very wisely, and according to weather warnings, everyone there fled as quickly as possible...except for this hardbitten Dutchman who happened to be my wife's father. "I paid for it! I'm staying!", he declared with authority, while shaking his fist at the cyclone. Nothing and no one was about to spoil his family vacation. As the storm approached, they stuffed what they could under the doors, boarded up the windows, and hunkered down. As a little girl, my wife remembers being terrified all night. As morning finally dawned, a quiet settled over the land. They peeked outside...and saw a thick blanket of sand covering everything. The new station wagon had undergone a paint removal job...the entire covering of paint had been stripped off by the sand blistering past it. Later, my wife recalls finding before unseen treasures all along the beach. No telling what might get washed up by a hurricane.

Storms can be terribly fearsome things. Remember Peter, in his impetuousness, stepping out of the little fishing boat, to start walking across the water toward Jesus, and then becoming terrified by the waves?

What is very easy to forget, yet imperative for us to remember, during frightening storms of any kind, is who actually controls the storm and everything swirling around us. Whether the storm is weather related, an epidemic, an international crisis...whatever...it is God, in truth, who is holding the reigns. When our vision is impaired, when our hearts are wildly pounding, let's remember and keep our focus on the words we read in Psalm 75: "When all hell breaks loose, when the whole world is shaking and quaking, keep your eyes on me. I'm the one who's holding it together." That's God's promise to us, that is the fact, that is what we can rely on, even as the storms boom around us.

APRIL

Quarantine day 4...

Thoughts from 1&2 Kings, 1 Chronicles:

*Start your life's journey with God...and continue it with God. Starting well is not enough.

*As with any relationship, our relationship with God reflects how much or little we invest in it.

*Pass on our knowledge of God to those who come after us, especially to our children.

*Whatever goodness and greatness we may have...comes from God, not us, to use for his honor.

*God warns us for our protection and because he loves us.

*We better take God seriously!

*God works in many different ways in different people's lives. What happens to one person may not necessarily happen to another person.

*God sees everything I do...even the things I do "in secret".

*God is greater...greater than any situation, problem, crisis, opposition, need...simply because he is the greatest.

*God does what he says. That gives us hope...as well as being a sober warning to us.

*God warns us...and then punishes us...because we disobey him.

*It's been tried, but it's not possible...we cannot serve two Gods...God and something else...one or the other, yes...but not both.

*When we pray, we should acknowledge who God is: Almighty and All Powerful God, our Benefactor, our merciful and grace-giving Sovereign, the Holy One who is beyond our understanding and is unapproachable (except that Jesus made it possible!).

August 23, 2020
The heavens cannot
contain you.

1 KINGS

Adonijah Sets Himself Up as King

1 When King David was very old, he could not keep warm even when they put covers over him. ²So his attendants said to him, "Let us look for a young virgin to serve the king and take care of him. She can lie beside him so that our lord the king may keep warm."

³Then they searched throughout Israel for a beautiful young woman and found Abishag, a Shunammite,ᵃ and brought her to the king. ⁴The woman was very beautiful; she took care of the king and waited on him, but the king had no sexual relations with her.

⁵Now Adonijah,ᵇ whose mother was Haggith, put himself forward and said, "I will be king." So he got chariotsᶜ and horsesᵈ ready, with fifty men to run ahead of him. ⁶(His father had never rebukedᵉ him by asking, "Why do you behave as you do?" He was also very handsome and was born next after Absalom.)

⁷Adonijah conferred with Joabᶠ son of Zeruiah and with Abiatharᵍ the priest, and they gave him their support. ⁸But Zadokʰ the priest, Benaiahⁱ son of Jehoiada, Nathanʲ the prophet, Shimei and Rei and David's special guardᵏ did not join Adonijah.

⁹Adonijah then sacrificed sheep, cattle and fattened calves at the Stone of Zoheleth near En Rogel.ˡ He invited all his brothers, the king's sons, and all the royal officials of Judah, ¹⁰but he did not invite Nathan the prophet or Benaiah or the special guard or his brother Solomon.ᵐ

¹¹Then Nathan asked Bathsheba,ⁿ Solomon's mother, "Have you not heard that Adonijah,ᵒ the son of Haggith, has become king, and our lord David knows nothing about it? ¹²Now then, let me adviseᵖ you how you can save your own life and the life of your son Solomon. ¹³Go in to King David and say to

APRIL 1

Day/Date — Be sure to remember five things to be grateful for every day. — April 1

Proverbs 3:5 NIV — Trust in the Lord with all your heart. Do not depend on your own understanding.

God works in ways that are frequently beyond what we can understand. He works on a level and dimension that often brings good out of tragedy and suffering. If we only live according to what we understand, we are missing out on what God can and will do in our lives beyond what seems possible. Trust him!

Has life come crashing down?

Have the storms of life strained your moorings?

Had disaster struck, beyond your capacity to cope?

Have you just received devastating news?

Has your last ounce of hope been used up?

Do you have no reserves left?

I remember a frightening day when we were living in China. We were visiting some friends, and I suddenly began to have a sharp pain inside my belly. It was too much to ignore, I had to go home. My wife and our son were not quite ready to leave, but that was OK. I would just take the motorbike home on my own, then they could follow later. I weaved my way back through the streets, feeling almost delirious, and when I got home, I stretched out on the bed...and started writhing in pain. That's the only way I can describe it. I called my wife and said, "You've gotta come home. I don't know if I'm going to make it." I was being crushed and enfolded by an invisible anaconda...sneezing me so tightly that I was twisting and groaning in agony. Mercifully, a nearby friend told my wife, "Oh, yeah, I had that once. I took some apple cider vinegar...and, boom, the pain evaporated." So, as soon as she got back home, she gave me some of that magic potion...and sure enough, it happened to me, too. Boom, the pain evaporated...and I fell into a deep, exhausted sleep like a baby. Sometime later, we asked a couple of doctors about it, and as they diagnosed gall stones (twelve to be exact, which I called the twelve disciples, and which were surgically removed), they smiled knowingly and assured us that apple cider vinegar was just an old wives' tale that carried no substance whatsoever. Maybe...but it sure seemed to save my life just in the nick of time. On occasion, we are in such a desperate position that we are feeling strangled and utterly without hope.

Sometimes, we may even get the idea that, in fact, this is exactly the place God wants us to be...

In Jeremiah 32, the situation could not have been worse. The invincible armies of Babylon had a visor like grip around Jerusalem...that was bad enough. But for God's anointed servant, the next words out of God's mouth had to have been the worst he had ever heard. What did God say to him? Just this: "Jeremiah, now you know that these people are my chosen, special people, right? Well, you see those ferocious armies outside the city walls? Of course, you know I could flick them aside with a word or a nod, right? Well, I'm not going to do that. In fact, I'm going to give those brute savages free reign in my holy city. They're going to come in and ransack the place, destroy everything... And when they're done? When they've laid waste to everything, they are then going to drag off the king and everyone else into captivity as slaves in Babylon. It's going to be curtains for the whole nation."

Jeremiah must have become close to comatose upon hearing these words. How could this be? How could the Almighty God of the universe allow this to happen to his own people? How could the covenant keeping God of eternity do this to his own chosen people?

And God continues on: "You know why this has got to happen, right? It's because you folks have turned away, have been utterly unwilling to listen and obey, have persisted in being completely rotten to the core. I've got to make a clean sweep...then, we'll start all over, I'll bring you back, I'll restore you as my people, and we won't remember anymore all the bad things my people did. This calamity will never happen again. You will be brought back to a good place as my people once again."

When life comes crashing down all around us, let's remember Jeremiah 32.

When it's all over, when there's nothing left...God still reigns. He promises us that he's still bringing about his good plans. Let's hold on tight to him and trust him with our lives.

APRIL 2

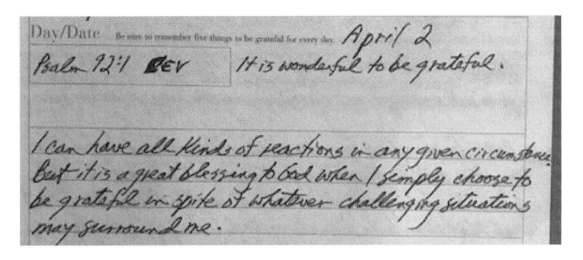

Day/Date Be sure to remember five things to be grateful for every day. *April 2*

Psalm 92:1 REV — It is wonderful to be grateful.

I can have all kinds of reactions in any given circumstance but it is a great blessing to God when I simply choose to be grateful in spite of whatever challenging situations may surround me.

Life is simple...but hard. God made us and loves us...that's pretty simple. But, man, it's messed up and complicated...because of who we are. As I read the words of Romans 14&15, I think to myself, "I wonder what would happen if we all just decided, and acted upon that decision, to take God's Word at face value, to do what God tells us to do..."

What does God say to us in these verses?

"Accept anyone who is weak."

"None of us lives to himself."

"Whether we live or die, we belong to the Lord."

"Why do you criticize your brother?"

"It's a noble thing not to do anything that causes your brother to stumble."

"Bear the weaknesses of those without strength."

"Even the Messiah did not please himself."

"May God grant you agreement with one another."

"Accept one another, just as the Messiah also accepted you."

It's all about putting others before myself. Or, as Jesus told us, "Love others in the same way I loved you." (Well, we all know what he did for us, don't we?) The real clincher, to me, is that last statement above..."Accept others as Christ accepted you." He ignored our sin and loved us anyway. He loved us though we were spiritually dead. Against all reason, good sense, and justice...he made the choice to love us anyway, to die for us, to save us.

Wouldn't it be amazing if the whole world suddenly acted on these words in the Bible! Would wars cease? Would borders open? Would hunger end? Would we all live in the way God meant for us to do so, all along?

What a wonderful world it would be!

APRIL 3

> **Day/Date** Be sure to remember five things to be grateful for every day. **April 3**
>
> Philippians 4:11 NRSV — I have learned to be content with whatever I have.
>
> Because so much of what Paul did was contrary to the established politics and religion of the day, he faced hardship and persecution on an ongoing basis. But he knew that in uncertain and difficult circumstances, what really mattered was his relationship with God. Because that was secure, he knew he could be content.

I see the whole world out of my two tiny eyes. Perhaps it's not surprising that very often our eyesight, our viewpoint, our perspective, is rather small and limited. The other day, we visited a part of Seoul we hadn't been to in a couple of years. As we walked the bustling streets, my wife commented that everyone was busy about their business...and had been so every day since we had been away, though we hadn't seen any of it. Shops had changed, streets had been redone, even our own perspective on things had changed. Last time we were there, we had just landed in Korea, and we were straining to figure out how to survive in this strange new place. Now, after two years of living here, everything seems simpler and more straightforward. A lot happens in different parts of the city that we are totally unaware of. And how about some of the other places where we've lived before...China, England, and so on? Life has carried right along in those places as well. And, of course, there are also the myriads of places where we have never lived...in those places, as well, people get up everyday, go about their business, and return home...day after day after day.

It's mind boggling to think that God knows about each person, in every place, and all that is happening to them, day after day after day. It's also interesting, amusing even, that I can get so agitated when something doesn't go exactly as

I expect or want it to. It's as if I expect and assume that everything revolves around me, that everything's happening for me and because of me. If I would pause for half a second, I would remember and realize that there's a pretty big world out there, with a lot of differing needs and priorities, many of which may take precedence over or contradict what I think is important.

I can imagine something of the same thing happening in Psalm 76. The writer says that God is judging the world. The whole world suddenly grew quiet, most likely out of fear or panic. No doubt they were thinking, "Wait a minute, God! This isn't working for me! This is not what I want to happen. What in the world do you think you are doing??" We respond this way, don't we, when things aren't going as we want or expect. But we so easily forget that there are many other dynamics going on as well. This psalm continues, after saying that God is judging the earth, by adding that he is also working to save "the lowly of the earth". Isn't that interesting? You mean, God isn't just being reckless and careless? He is also doing something good? Surprise, surprise...it isn't just about me, apparently. God may be judging some folks (surely not me!?!), while at the same time working to save the most needy, lowly, marginalized folks around the world.

So, I guess I'll just need to trust God for what I don't see and understand from my limited perspective...and realize that he may be helping some folks big time, while appearing to be stepping on my toes (or at least my desires), at the same time.

Lord, help us to trust you for what we can't see, what we can't understand...

APRIL 4

Day/Date Be sure to remember five things to be grateful for every day. April 4

Hebrews 10:14 NCV   With one sacrifice he made perfect forever those who are being made holy.

This is the tension and paradox that will always be with us on this earth. Our perfection has been purchased; but we still live with our sinful natures. Our salvation is accomplished; but it is still being worked out in our lives.

We really do live in two worlds, don't we? Probably our default is to live and move through and mostly just think about the physical world. But sometimes (well, always, really), what is happening in the physical is radically different from what is happening in the other world, what God calls the spiritual world. Or, as it talks about at the end of 2 Corinthians 4, the seen and the unseen world. I'm sure most of us go through life thinking and believing (or at least we certainly live like it...) that what we see around us is what is most important. But, interestingly, God says, "No, no, no, no...you don't seem to understand. It's the unseen world that is actually more important. In fact, that's really where most all the action is taking place!" "What?? You're kidding, right, God?" I'm sure that's how Jeremiah must have felt in chapters 33&34. Jerusalem was being squeezed, the life was being sucked out of it, the Babylonians were breathing down their necks, and...God said, "Oh, by the way, I'm starting on some new plans! Do you want to hear about them??" "Uhh, come on, God, just help us get the heck out of this mess right now! Then, we'll sit down and talk about those other plans of yours..."

Isn't that really how we usually feel? It amazes me, really, when I read about all the hardships and difficulties God allowed his servants to live through in the

Bible. Was God unaware of what they were going through? No. Did he not care? Again, no. It's just that what was going on in that other world, the unseen world, the one that God says is most important...that is usually where God's main focus is.

So, hang on. This physical world that we see and experience around us can be a pretty wobbly, unpredictable, uncertain place. It can definitely give us some panicked moments. But, thank God, not only does he control things...he is also working out some much better things in the world that we are so often prone to forget about. So, let's keep our focus on that world. After all, God tells us that this seen, physical world is passing away, it won't last, it's really not the thing that is most important.

APRIL 5

> **Day/Date** Be sure to remember five things to be grateful for every day. April 5
>
> Genesis 15:5-6 NCV Abram believed the Lord. And the Lord accepted Abram's faith, and that faith made him right with God.
>
> Abraham was far from a perfect person. But he did trust in God, and that made him acceptable to God in spite of his weaknesses and disobedience. God knows we are not perfect. But he counts Jesus' perfection in our behalf.

Whenever I pick up something by one of the Puritans or saints of old, I'm struck by how little they think of themselves and how big and troublesome their sin is to them. It's certainly not the language we use or the attitude we have these days. In today's world, we would rather be encouraging, supportive, and uplifting toward others, rather than focusing on their weaknesses or shortcomings. But it's hard not to agree with the old writers when we read a couple of phrases in 1 Corinthians 1.

It's clear that some people are more talented than others, some have been more successful than their counterparts. But these verses tell us that, really, God's the one who has made us rich and successful. It's not something we've accomplished through our own efforts or hard work. Everything we have, or have gained, or have accomplished, comes from God. No wonder the Puritans recognized that they were nothing. They understood the depth of their own sinfulness...that all that we have truly is a gift from God...that we really are undeserving of anything from God, that he alone is worthy of all praise, of all boasting.

Lord, open our eyes to who we are (big sinners), to who you are, and for all that you have done for us. Amen.

APRIL 6

Day/Date Be sure to remember five things to be grateful for every day. April 6

Jeremiah 31:34 NCV Their sins and the evil things they do — I will not remember anymore.

Although they trouble me no more, I still remember small hurts and slights that were done against me over the years. Regrettably, I also recall times when I was unloving and mean toward others. Isn't it wonderful that when we trust him, God completely erases all our past wrongs and imperfections? And it's amazing to think that a perfect and holy God would do that — what great love!

We talk often about having 2020 vision, about seeing things sharply and clearly. Perhaps as we come to the end of this year of 2020, the idea of "2020 vision" will take on a whole new meaning. As I think back to just a year ago, no one would have imagined or predicted what this year would look like. Probably even the most creative fantasy writer would have been hard pressed to come up with a plot like what we have lived through this year. Professional sports brought to a standstill, industries and economies collapsing, things that have taken place methodically and like clock work all our lives...suddenly suspended. I've talked with several old folks (even older than me...), and no one remembers anything like what we've seen in 2020. Let's hope it sets on the horizon and never shows its face again!

Someday, I wonder what we'll reflect on as we look back over our lives, and especially over this period. We have been a very blessed generation, so we are mostly unused to this kind of trauma and turbulence. But, certainly, and thankfully, we are not the first to have traveled these waters. So many times, scary and horrendous things have taken place down through history, events which have shattered, scattered, and crushed people. And tragic as they have been, at least we can learn from some of those events and gain some perspective on our own unsettling experiences.

The writer of Psalm 77 describes a similar situation in his day. In his desperation, he is yelling loudly for God...and, nothing. No response. Deafening silence. He starts to ask himself...has God forgotten about us? Has he rejected us? Does he no longer love us? Things must have gotten pretty bad for him to have come to this point in his thinking. But then he starts to recall, to reflect, to think back. He remembers how God was with him in the past, the great things that God did. But, at the same time, he doesn't deny his difficulties. He acknowledges that God has led him through deep and troubled waters. But as he thinks back over it, he suddenly realizes something marvelous. Though he had missed God, though God seemed to be hidden...actually, God was with him the whole time. The writer says that God's steps were hidden...he was there, but he couldn't be seen. So God had not really abandoned him, as he had first thought. In fact, he could see now, as he looked more closely, that not only was God with him the whole time, God was actually walking with him and holding his hand. Whew! What a relief! The same relief I remember feeling as a child when I felt panicked or afraid...then caught a glimpse of the lights of home on the road up ahead, and I knew I was safe. Lord, even when we can't see you, even when our vision is blurred and less than 2020, remind us that you're there, that you're with us, that you're holding us in the palm of your hand, that you won't let go of us. Our trust and our hope is in you.

APRIL 7

Sometimes a seemingly simple gesture or action can speak very loudly and powerfully about something much greater that is actually taking place. I think of the time when the Nazis gathered up Jewish books and burned them in huge piles of flames. It was a tragic loss of ancient and treasured holy documents and manuscripts. But, in reality, the greater significance of the event was what it represented...a loss of freedom, religious persecution, the belief that some people were not valuable enough to live in society...some very scary statements about what was descending on the nation at that moment.

In Jeremiah 36, a very similar event is taking place. God says to the prophet, "Record this message I'm giving you, and take it and read it to the king so that he will understand what I am doing. Hopefully, he will come to his senses and turn back to me." God's message is written down, taken into the king, and read in his presence. And, then, a shocking thing happens. The king takes out a knife, slices off parts of the scroll as they are read aloud, and tosses them into a fire. It's a dramatic demonstration of what the king thinks about God, about his total disregard of and condescension toward the things of God. At that point, he certainly had earned whatever punishment God had planned for him.

Now, thankfully, I've never done anything so reckless and callous as that, scorning God right to his face. Or have I? I've been privileged to read, to learn, to know God's Word most all of my life. So, when God tells me to love others as much as I love myself...and I don't do it...what is happening, really? It may not seem like a big deal. After all, nobody really sees or knows what I'm doing...no one, that is, except for the one who counts the most, God. What I'm really doing, when I refuse or neglect to do what God tells me to do...is to cut up his Word and toss it in the flames. Have I thought about that? Probably not. But my actions are reflecting my heart, and I'm saying, "No thank you, God. I know what's best, I can handle it. I don't need you or your Word telling me what to do." That sounds frighteningly close to what King Jehoiakim said to God...frightening words, frightening actions. Lord, keep us from our own foolish, blind, selfish hearts. Keep our hearts sensitive and soft toward you!

APRIL 8

Day/Date   Be sure to remember five things to be grateful for every day.   April 8

Luke 1: 50, 53 NCV   God will show his mercy forever and ever to those who worship and serve him. He has filled the hungry with good things.

In what ways has God shown me mercy? What good things have I received from him? His mercy and goodness are so vast and deep that it is a good exercise to think about these things and to thank him regularly for them.

I guess it's our human nature to want to be remembered. Everywhere you go in the world, you see things that are put up, constructed, carved…so that someone will be remembered. And let's face it, there are some pretty impressive people that should be remembered. People who've done great things. People who've accomplished previously unimagined heights of success or beauty. They deserve to be recognized and remembered. It's interesting, though, how quickly we forget people. When we read history, we find out about people and events that were clearly spectacular and world changing in their day…yet, we can hardly remember them or perhaps have never even heard of them.

But, lest anyone of us is tempted, just on occasion, to imagine that we are worthy of being remembered or recognized…Paul sets the record straight in 1 Corinthians 3. He says that whatever happens that is important…it's because God did it. Anything worthwhile or of note…is due to God. Now, on the surface, this can sound as if God is not very appreciative of our substantive contributions. But, I doubt if that is really the case. It's just that God realizes and knows that what we do is passing…and really a bit silly, like some little sand castle on the beach that is here today, gone tomorrow. What God does is great, it lasts, it's righteous, it's wise, it's beneficial. Any great thing we do…well, compared to what God does, it's very trivial and probably just as well to be forgotten. All the great things down through history and creation, all of them, come from

God and point back to God. Lord, help me to remember that when I'm (daily) tempted to imagine that I am really somebody pretty important...

APRIL 9

Day/Date   Be sure to remember five things to be grateful for every day.   April 9

Hebrews 10:34 NCV   You even had joy when all that you owned was taken from you, because you knew you had something better and more lasting.

Can I say this? This is truly difficult, if not nearly impossible, when family, health, or jobs are taken from us, such as in the extreme case of Job. But even in the midst of terrible suffering, it does give us a balanced perspective to remind ourselves that this life is passing and that ultimately our hope is in something much more permanent.

I can still picture my white haired grandmother, hunched over her tattered King James Bible, almost surely reading from the Psalms, which she loved so dearly. I also remember seeing Dad's burgundy hardback Bible, which he had underlined throughout, in different color pens. One year, in my youth, I went all the way through Dad's Bible, and underlined my own Bible, which he gave me for my tenth birthday, in all the same places and verses where his was underlined. I suppose I thought that I might somehow be more spiritual if I had the same looking Bible that he had. I still have that Bible...and now it's all the more precious, as I can see his underlinings in my own old Bible.

Although my parents and grandparents did talk about the Bible and passages they loved, I don't remember too much specifically about what they said. What I do recall well, though, is those images of them with their Bibles, and that has stayed with me and become imprinted in my mind. Today, the Psalms is my most beloved book. And, also today, I love underlining and scribbling notes into my Bible...habits formed early from those who went before.

That is what Psalm 78 is talking about. It contains a long recounting of Israel's up and down history...God talking to them, them turning away, God punishing them, them turning back, God forgiving and restoring them. Sometimes it can almost seem wearisome, reading all these same stories. But the psalmist begs us, implores us, to tell our children, to recount all these stories, so the next generation will hear and know and learn...and then also pass it on to the succeeding generations. It's of paramount importance for us and our children to know who the sovereign God is, and to know of his love for us. But they won't know unless we are deliberate in and determined to tell them. Am I doing that? Will the generations that follow know the most important truths in life? It's up to you and me to see that they do.

APRIL 10

Day/Date — Be sure to remember five things to be grateful for every day. April 10

Lamentations 3:22-23,25 NCV The Lord's love never ends; his mercies never stop. They are new every morning. The Lord is good to those who hope in him, to those who seek him.

My wife is about the most loyal person I know. Long after a friendship has run dry or run its course, she stays and keeps pursuing the friendship. In spite of all my shortcomings, I know that she will always be there for me. That's how God is toward us. He keeps giving and loving long after we have given up.

How quickly we forget...

When we were young, a large percentage of the world lived in hunger. Yes, there are still many living in hunger, and it's every bit as tragic. But there is more food today, more have access to it, and less are hungry and starving than in previous generations. As we have more and more of our needs and desires provided for, we forget that this has not always been the norm, and may not even be what's normal in the future. It's remarkable how many of God's servants down through the ages have suffered...that God allowed to suffer, as part of his larger plans for the salvation of the world. Probably we shouldn't be surprised about this. After all, Jesus told us: "Follow me...and you will suffer." As I read Jeremiah 37, I'm reminded of this same thing. God certainly allowed his servant to suffer greatly. As soon as Jeremiah told the king (the king of God's own people, no less) the message God had given to him to pass on, he was tossed into a dark, mud-filled hole in the ground. And I think back to my grandparents in China, a hundred years ago. Their only desire and intention was to share God's Good News with those who had never heard. What did they get for it? Abuse. Repeated evacuations (i.e. running for their lives). Scorn and attacks. Loss of belongings and homes. Separations. Uncertainties.

So, let's not forget. Remember history. Remember how God worked in the

Bible. And don't be surprised when hard times come.

APRIL 11

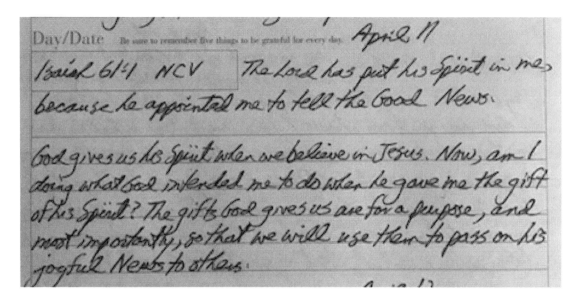

Day/Date   Be sure to remember five things to be grateful for every day.   April 11

Isaiah 61:1 NCV   The Lord has put his Spirit in me because he appointed me to tell the Good News.

God gives us his Spirit when we believe in Jesus. Now, am I doing what God intended me to do when he gave me the gift of his Spirit? The gifts God gives us are for a purpose, and most importantly, so that we will use them to pass on his joyful News to others.

We are funny creatures...insecure, at best... We wonder, ponder, puzzle... whether or not someone loves us. After over 40 years of serving me, laying down her life for me, demonstrating in ten million ways her love for me...I can still catch myself thinking...does my wife really love me??

And I think of the apostle Paul in 1 Corinthians 4, pouring out his heart to these people he had served and suffered for, who he has brought along in the faith so tenderly. He says he was weak for them, hungry, brutally treated, slandered, treated like dirt...all because he loved and cared for them.

Then, if we think of what Jesus did for us...leaving the perfect harmony and peace and joy of heaven...not only coming down to this evil world for us, but also being willing to be trashed, scorned, brutalized, tortured, and painfully murdered for us...we, who are so imperfect, rebellious, so quick to turn away...it is astounding to consider the endlessly wide and deep love that God has for us... And, yet, there we go again...we wonder, out loud, shaking our fist even, whether or not God loves us...

Indeed, we are strange creatures. And that only highlights and emphasizes all the more, as the hymn says:

"How deep the Father's love for us,

How vast beyond all measure,

That He should give His only Son

To make a wretch His treasure."

APRIL 12

> Day/Date Be sure to remember five things to be grateful for every day. April 12
>
> Luke 2:10 NCV Do not be afraid. I am bringing you good news, that will be a great joy to all the people.
>
> How often we are reluctant to open ourselves up to what God has for us — to what he wants to do in us. We are afraid that his best will not be good for us nor bring us joy. Why is this? Because we don't believe him; we don't see beyond our small world. But God's goodness and salvation extend much further and deeper than we can ever imagine.

As I think back to my high school years, around 50 years ago, it's amazing how much I knew and understood about life already, at such a young age. I'm not quite sure what happened in the intervening years, but today I find that I understand almost nothing, especially when I think back to how much I knew back then. How is it possible to lose so much understanding in just a few decades?? However, there is one thing I am starting to understand now that I apparently didn't understand back in those days. And that is this simple truth: I am blind to myself. I see everyone else clearly (or at least I have an opinion about everyone else), but seemingly, I'm blind to myself.

I remember one day in boarding school, sitting in a science class. In my usual self confident way, I was letting loose clever comments and remarks, not believing that the teacher could really be serious when she gently admonished me to pipe down and quit interrupting. Finally, after she returned our recent tests (which I scored quite well on, by the way), she docked me a few points because I had just not listened and kept my mouth shut. I didn't say a word in response, but I recall so well feeling the injustice of her action. I mean, how could she penalize me on my high scoring test…for actions unrelated to my academic performance? It just wasn't fair. Well, whether it was fair or not…it sure got my attention. I still remember that deflating day. I have never forgotten it.

Now, in Psalm 79, we encounter a very similar scenario...mind you, on quite a bigger scale. The writer is complaining to God at the injustice of Jerusalem having been flattened by the Babylonians, Israel's enemies. I mean, come on, God, how could you allow these heathens to tarnish your good people, your holy place, your own reputation? But what the writer is seemingly blind to, is that God was using these heathen Babylonians for the purpose of punishing and getting the attention of his self centered and disobedient people. At times, God allows or uses something or someone, which on their own may not seem appropriate, for his purposes in getting our attention or disciplining us in some way.

No doubt, that is what was going on with me in my science class once upon a time. And I have to wonder if that is also what is going on in our world many times. We get so frustrated and impatient with a bump in the economy, a disappointment in our career, a let down in a relationship, an unfair political outcome... But is God more concerned about getting our attention, of turning us back to him...rather than whether or not we are comfortable or getting what we believe is due us? Yes, there are messes in the world, things we don't like, situations we think we don't deserve... But rather than ranting and raving against God, perhaps we need to pause and consider...why might God be allowing this to happen? Why is he trying to get my attention? What does he want to see changed in my behavior and attitudes...more than whether I happen to get what I think I deserve?

Lord, open our blind eyes to your perspective, your priorities, your heart. Take away our self blindness, which seems to affect us all. Put us in tune with who you are.

APRIL 13

Luke 5:8 NCV   Go away from me, Lord. I am a sinful man.

Do I realize who I am before God? When I see my sin and disobedience against our holy God as he sees it, I will begin to realize, as Peter did, that I don't deserve even to be in his presence. How great then is his love, mercy, and forgiveness, that he should accept me with open arms instead of turning his back on me as I deserve.

As I was just reading Jeremiah 39, a Billy Graham message came on, from nearly 30 years ago. What struck me about his message is how much it sounded just like what is happening around us today...it was a time of chaos, change, uncertainty, alarm, panic, worry. I look back now to that time 30 years ago, and I think, what was the big deal? What was the great alarm? Nothing much was really happening... But at the time, things seemed alarming. When you don't know the future, everything out of the ordinary, the predictable, seems worrisome. We're in the same situation today...anxiety, uncertainty, fear...worry about the future. To the people listening to him that day, Billy Graham gave the reassuring message that what counts, isn't going to change. God is still on the throne. We don't need to worry. And Jeremiah is addressing a very similar situation in his day. In fact, his was a much more worrying situation. Jerusalem has just fallen. Everything, literally everything, had collapsed for God's people. It was as bad as things could possibly get. No one could have painted a more grim scenario. And yet, God gave this message to his people. "Don't worry. I am still in control. I am still going to carry out my plans. I will save you. I will rescue you. It may look like all is lost, but really, the important, lasting things, still haven't changed. I'm still with you, I'm still at work. I will still have the last word."

When our world feels like it's rocking today, when we feel like things are slipping away...let's not forget one thing. That same God who came to Jeremiah in the worst possible conditions...he is still with us when we trust in him. He's still in the driver's seat. He will still have the last word. Let's keep our trust focused on him.

APRIL 14

As I was nearing the end of my MBA program at the University of Delaware, I got a job offer at Covenant College. Now, when you're in school, you don't get a job offer every day of the week, so I decided to take the job. In doing so, I realized that I would have to finish my last couple of courses at the University of Tennessee. So, I went to my academic advisor to get clarity about what I still needed to take in order to complete my program. Well, when I went in to see him, I got a rather severe shock. He looked at my transcript and said, "You've been taking all the wrong courses! You'll never graduate!" I don't know if he was just thinking out loud as he looked at my courses and saw that I hadn't taken any of his classes, or what... But if you really want to shake a student up or cause all his neatly lined up ducks to scatter...tell him just before graduation that he's totally blown it! I was so rattled that I decided to take my situation right to the top. In fear and trembling, I went to see the head of the whole program. Almost like a frightened mouse, I approached the venerated professor to receive his verdict. Thankfully, he was available when I arrived, he invited me right into his presence with a smile, and...he glanced over my courses, and, seemingly, with a flick of his wrist, swept aside my worries and alarm by stating, "You'll be fine. Your courses are just right. You only need two more marketing classes, and then you'll graduate. Congratulations!"

I call tell you...even 40 years later... I remember how my heart lifted, there was a spring in my step, and I walked out of his office with a smile on my face! After I dutifully completed my final two marketing classes (with "A's", no less), my coveted MBA diploma arrived in the mail. The moral of that little incident, to me, was, when in trouble, don't mess around...go to the top!

Now that's the very same message we get in Psalm 80. The people had a big mess on their hands (slightly more serious than deciding which graduate classes to take), and so the writer went right to the top...also without bothering to get an appointment, just walking right in, carrying his problems with him. In this case, he had the audacity of really going straight to the top...to the God Almighty of all the universe. And was he received? Was he heard? Yes, indeed! Remarkably, the Potentate of all eternity received his plea with such importance that...he recorded the man's request for us forever to see and read and learn from. Apparently, Almighty God thought it was so, so, so important that we all learn that his door is open, that his appointment book is always clear, that he decided that this little incident needed to be in Holy Scriptures for us all to see. Honestly, it would probably do us all good (me, anyway) to read Psalm 80 every single day to remind us that God's door is always open.

It's interesting, isn't it... Everywhere we look in the world, people clamber to their leaders for hope. They are so certain that their leaders will fix their problems, restore order, heal their land, that they seek their attention in any way they can. Meantime, God's door stands open. He's patiently waiting with his arms spread wide. He is right there, thinking, when will my daughter, my son, come into my presence?

APRIL 15

Day/Date Be sure to remember five things to be grateful for every day. April 15

Luke 6:44 NCV Each tree is known by its own fruit.

What kind of fruit am I leaving behind? I may think I am good, living a good life, or at least appearing to be good before other people. But ultimately I will produce the kind of fruit that reflects what is really in my heart. It's worth thinking about and then examining ourselves to see what our lives are really like.

"Patch Adams" was a fun movie...I enjoy watching the seeming underdog, the one everyone counts out, the one least likely to succeed...triumph in the end. And I recall the comical episode when his roommate in the psychiatric hospital is frightened...of squirrels. We can be frightened of the silliest things sometimes. And I am first in line for becoming afraid of silly things. This morning I woke up from dreaming that I was taking an exam in school...and I didn't know the answers to the questions! Talk about feeling panicked... Now, why in the world would I dream something like that...especially since I've been out of school for 40 years...and also since I can count on one finger (yes, one finger) how many tests I took when I didn't know the answers to the test questions.

God seems to wonder, too, why we are afraid so often. In Jeremiah 42, after Israel has been clobbered by Babylon...in fact, after they have been done in worse than any of us will likely ever experience, God tells them, "Don't be afraid. I am with you. I will have compassion on you." That's it. That's all he says. God seems to be puzzled that we would be afraid when our entire world has collapsed around us...while at the same time, we still have him. I mean, what's to worry about, people? What's to be afraid of? From our small, finite perspective, it's no wonder that we are afraid about so many things. But God sees the whole picture. He sees and knows everything. And he tells us there's nothing to worry about. Will we trust him. Will we lay our fears at his feet? Or will we allow the squirrels to hold us in fear?

APRIL 16

> Job 12:10   NCV   The life of every creature and the breath of all people are in God's hand.
>
> With so much evil, uncertainty, frailty, and turmoil around us and in the world, there is nothing better or more comforting to know that we are securely in God's safe and loving hands.

If there is one thing we learn in our Western nations, it is that we have rights. I am important...it is my right...therefore I deserve to be heard. I am worthy of getting what belongs to me. So, it startles me, when I read in 1 Corinthians 8&9, how strongly Paul lays aside what is rightfully his, what he deserves, what he knows to be right...for the sake of others, for the sake of love, for the goal of advancing the Gospel. How little we look like Paul today! Everything seems to be about what I deserve, what is rightfully mine. So, I have to wonder...what am I doing? Am I trying to live and look like the world? Or do I want to follow Paul's example? I wonder, I do wonder...what would Paul think (or Jesus, for that matter) if he came into our midst and looked around...what would he see? Would he see in us what we see of him in these chapters?

APRIL 17

> Day/Date   Be sure to remember five things to be grateful for every day.   April 17
>
> Luke 6:46   NCV   Why do you call me, "Lord, Lord,"
> but do not do what I say?
>
> Just as people clamber around politicians and celebrities
> for favors or friendships, we also quickly scurry to God when we
> want him to help us out in some way. But God is not fooled by
> us. He sees into our hearts even better than we can. If we
> really desire God's favor, we should trust him and obey him.

It's amusing and puzzling to me when I hear people say that babies are born "good"...that they pick up their bad habits and behavior from society around them. It always makes me wonder who taught the very first humans to be bad, if there was no society for them to learn bad habits from. In China, they used to tell us that babies are born with a clean slate, and they gradually learn bad behavior from everyone else.

We certainly had our opportunities to observe little babies, as we had nine of them along the way. One thing that appeared very clear to us was this: we didn't teach them to be bad. Not to say that we were perfect, mind you. It's just that the little ones demonstrated quite successfully on their own that they could be selfish creatures, without any help from us. Give two little kids the same toys, and what may happen? They want what the other kid has, even though they are holding the same toy in their own hands. Give them enough to eat, and what do we observe? They want what their sibling has. It's fascinating to watch and does leave you scratching your head and thinking, "Now, who in our neighborhood has been in here to teach them that behavior??"

It almost seems like God tilts his head and wonders the same thing. Take Psalm 81, for example. God is puzzled: "I don't get it. I give them everything they could possibly need. I even drop food from heaven, squeeze drink from rocks...and what happens? They're unimpressed. They keep wanting to look for something else, invariably where trouble is lurking, some place that takes them far from me. I just don't get it!"

As God ponders our bad behavior, he also issues a warning: "Choose to go your own way, turn away from following me, and what will happen? You will get stuck in a quagmire of trouble. You will experience maggots that will eat you alive. If you know what's good for you (which obviously you don't...), you will hear and listen to and obey me...not because it will please me (which it will), but because you will save yourself from being skinned alive. Don't even think about going there."

So, what do we do? We do what Samson did, when his parents warned him about the dangers of the Philistines. We turn confidently on our heel, seeming to say, with a nod of our head, "Relax. Don't be so uptight. I know what I'm doing. I can handle it."

Samson is about the saddest story in the Bible. God blessed him with some amazing talents, including parents who cared about him. He knew what was the right thing to do...and he confidently, flippantly, chose to stride away into the winds of trouble. And reading the rest of the story is sad and painful. His life is one long and tragic litany of trouble and sorrow.

Will we learn from Samson? Will we listen to God's words in the psalm? I don't know...but God has warned us of the consequences of going our own way, with oodles and oodles of sad examples throughout his Word. We better pay attention.

APRIL 18

Day/Date Be sure to remember five things to be grateful for every day. April 18

Matthew 6:34 Message Give your entire attention to what God is doing right now, and don't get worked up about what may or may not happen tomorrow.

When we look at everything around us, it is easy and natural for us to become anxious and worked up over the things that affect our lives. But God instructs us to look beyond what we see around us — to take in what He is doing in the world — then the unimportant things won't trouble us, and our focus will be on what is important and lasting.

There is something that frightens me as I think back to my childhood in Korea. A few short years after the Second World War and the Korean War, the land lay devastated and desperate. It's inconceivable to imagine today, as Korea stands as one of the wealthiest nations on earth, but at that time, scarcely 50 years ago, it was among the very poorest countries on the planet. Everyone lived hand to mouth, most lived without electricity and running water, I don't remember anyone owning a private car or even a black and white television. Who had pets, when they couldn't even feed themselves (answer: no one)?

There were no foreigners around (other than American G.I.'s and missionaries). I mean, there were no jobs to be had, which today brings the whole world to Korea's doorsteps. Who would want to come to Korea in those drab days? Now, the missionaries were by no means wealthy at the time. Today, we would be shocked if we looked back to how they lived in those days. But...they did have steady, relatively guaranteed income from the West...and that was the clincher. To any Korean, wondering how they would find food to feed their family tomorrow, the foreigners looked wealthy, exceedingly wealthy, even. My Dad used to say that, as a missionary doctor, he was wealthier than any of the Korean doctors. But just 25 short years later, when he left Korea, all the local doctors were richer than him...that's how quickly things were changing.

But what frightens me, as I reflect back, is the attitude that was so easy to absorb without even realizing it. Local folks were constantly coming to our foreign doorsteps, always hanging around hungrily, forever sharing a desperate tale without an answer. And, they knew that we had possibilities, we had sources, we had backing...really, we held the possibility of life. What is so dangerous and scary is that, when everybody clambers to be heard, when everyone cranes for your attention...you begin to believe it. You begin to take on board the thought that you really are something special, you really are the answer to people's problems...in short, that you really are better and more valuable than anyone else. And that is a scary thought...that the world around you seems to be validating in your mind.

That was the problem we see...and should take note of...in Jeremiah 45. God specially chose the children of Israel to be his own people...and it promptly went to their head. Man, oh man, look how great we are. Even God himself gives us special attention. Goodness, are we great, or what! But in these short few verses, God warns them. "Even though I have chosen you and carefully taken care of you, I'll take that all away from you if you don't turn back to me. Don't think that you are immune or somehow impervious to being uprooted, taken down, and tossed aside, just because you are my special people. You need to follow me just like everyone else does. You don't have a special inside track that keeps you beyond the law, beyond justice. You need to do what's right, just like everyone else does."

Do we sometimes imagine that, because we're one of the chosen, the elect, that we're on the inside, immune to sin, to disobedience? That's a dangerous place to be in. It's scary to be in danger...but, at the same time, to be blind to its presence. It's like an animal being hunted, and yet totally unaware of it.

All I can say is, Lord, keep us humble. Keep us from pride. Help us to have a right understanding of ourselves...as Paul did, when he cried out, "Wretched man that I am, who can save me??" Thankfully, he knew the answer to his own question, and he let us in on the answer as well. It's not because of who we are...but because of who Jesus is and what he did for us. That is really all that matters.

APRIL 19

> **Day/Date** Be sure to remember five things to be grateful for every day. April 19
>
> Isaiah 51:13 NCV Have you forgotten the Lord who made you, who stretched out the skies and made the earth?
>
> The history of the Israelites is long, and sometimes we may wonder why so many tedious details are included in page after page of the Bible. But sadly, much of Israel's history is the story of how they, time and again, forgot and turned away from their great and almighty God. God does not want us to follow in their same footsteps!

Probably my favorite pastime is giving Scripture to people I encounter along the road. Since we've been living in Asia for the past ten years, and since people are polite to strangers here, it's really an easy and a rewarding activity. People nearly always thank me with a smile and a bow, as if I have really made their day. I like to give them a Bible in English because everybody seems to want to learn English, so they get excited about a gift in English...and hopefully will be more likely to read it. Occasionally, when people politely decline my offer, it's because they feel bad that they don't have something they can give to me in return, and they don't want to feel beholden to a stranger. But, it's indeed rare to have someone just flat out refuse my offer. So, like I said, it's a fairly easy and rewarding task...especially, when there are eternal benefits promised. I do always feel a little sad when someone occasionally holds up their hand and says, "No, no thank you...I don't need that."

It makes me sad because of what we are told in 1 Corinthians 10. Paul tells us he's writing...so that we won't be ignorant, so that the examples given to us will teach us, so that we will understand that life is all about living for God. Fairly simple, really. It's sad to think that some people don't want to hear that. And, in case we are worried about bills, pandemics, or elections, God tops it off by saying, "Really, you don't need to worry. It all belongs to me anyway. There will always be enough. I will always take care of you. I will always be with you. Don't worry." I wonder what would happen if we just decided to take God's words (his Word) at face value? What if we just believed what he said? Are we willing to try it? Paul implores is to do so!

APRIL 20

Day/Date — Be sure to remember five things to be grateful for every day.   April 20

Psalm 24:1 NCV — The earth belongs to the Lord, and everything in it.

If I was using something that belonged to a King or a president, how would I take care of it or treat it? No doubt I would never want to return it damaged or broken. How much more care should I take in using and treating the world that God has allowed for our usage ... but that belongs to him?

The summer of my tenth birthday, my family of eight individuals climbed into an old VW bus in Wilmington, North Carolina, on the Atlantic, and headed west on an epic journey (long before interstate highways and convenient rest stops) that eventually landed us in San Francisco, California, on the Pacific Ocean. We were on our way, in the blistering heat of July, without AC or seat belts, on the start of the voyage that would take us back to Korea after a year in the US. What an amazing adventure for us kids who had seen and knew little about our own country. Among many other memories, one eerie day in Kansas sticks in my mind. I don't remember where it was, I just remember driving through that town in Kansas, on the plains, in the middle of tornado country. I will never forget that day. As we drove through that town in complete silence, I recall only two gas pumps that were standing. The rest of the town had disappeared...flattened and carried away by a tornado that visited it before we did. We drove by nothing but brick foundations of houses, one after another...everything else, gone. I don't remember any of us saying a word. The sight before our eyes is all that consumed us.

Now, no doubt, just five or ten miles away, there were other Kansas towns scattered across the landscape, carrying on as they always had. Nothing had changed, it was all business as usual. The devastating tornado had missed them.

Life can certainly seem random, haphazard...unfair, even...in what it dishes out here and there, to this people and that people. Why are some countries so regularly ruined by hurricanes, others never able to rise above corrupt governments... It all leaves me shaking my head and not able to make sense of it all.

And then I come to the first verse of Psalm 82...and here is my answer. Like a little child, for a moment lost in Walmart, who suddenly spots his Mom and realizes everything will be all right after all, we read the beautiful words of verse one. "God presides in the great assembly."

Now, it's one thing if a good judge or ruler is over us. We can hope, with a fair chance of reason, that the right thing will happen, that the ruler will know what to do to bring about good for most people. But that's not the way it is at all with God. You see, the Lord Almighty is perfect. No only does he not want injustice. Not only does he not like it. It is incompatible for God to live with injustice. And he is all powerful, in control, in the driver's seat, and will outlast anyone or anything else.

"God presides." That's enough. For those unlucky Kansas farmers who were in the wrong path at the wrong moment...things will one day be made right. God will deal with and make right all the wrongs. As we look around our messed up and, in so many ways, wrong world, as bad as it may be...in the end, we don't have to worry. The bad guys, the bad storms, the bad stock market, the bad virus...nothing and no one will stop, interrupt, or circumvent God's righteousness and his love. He presides...he will have his way...that's enough. God will make all things right.

APRIL 21

As I was leaving, I turned back to wave to my hosts, and the thought came to me, "They are living in prison." It was 2005, and I had just passed through Customs in the airport in Pyongyang, North Korea. Following a visit to that country with a humanitarian group, I was returning home, and turned back for one last wave to the guys who had been our hosts during our visit. That moment stays with me, as well as the thought that they were still there, their whole world, a prison. Since that visit, I have prayed often for the people of North Korea, that the light of the Gospel will once again shine brightly in their land. In the early 1900s, revivals broke out there, and the future looked promising. But politics and armies swept over them, and the people have suffered greatly during most of the intervening years. I remember wondering if North Korea would open up 50 years ago...today, we still wonder. But I have hope. As hopeless as things may at times look from a human perspective, God will have his way. And I believe he has a future, and hope, for North Korea. The prospects of Moab, in the Bible, give me hope. They were a wayward, sad people, whose history took them down painful roads. But God gives the final word on Moab at the end of Jeremiah 48, and that gives me hope for North Korea today as well. Though God declared that Moab would be destroyed for their disobedience, he closes the chapter by saying, "Yet I will restore the fortunes of Moab in days to come." Out of time and hope, with their lives and nation destroyed...God says, "Yet I will restore..." That is what gives us hope...not the circumstances, not the situation, not the prospects, not the chances...but God's Word. He will do what he says. He will bring hope, he will restore...and that's why I have hope for North Korea as well.

APRIL 22

Luke 15:20 NCV While the son was still a long way off, his father saw him and ran to him.

God is not sitting back uninterested, waiting for us to come to him. He is doing all he can to reach out to us, looking for any sign of interest or trust on our part toward him. When he sees this in us, he welcomes us with open arms into his presence. What a warm, safe, and peace-filled place to be!

Several times in his letters, Paul says something remarkable, that is hard for me to imagine any of us saying: "Follow my example. Imitate me." That's how he begins 1 Corinthians 11. Who of us can say that? Perhaps we could say that if we were referring to our study habits, how we handle money, or how we improve our tennis game. But Paul certainly seems to be saying more than, "Write letters like I do, travel where I travel, or sew tents like I do." He seems to be saying, "Copy me in how I am living, in what I am doing with my life…" In all honesty, could I say that? Would I really even want people to live their lives the way I have lived mine?

So, what was Paul saying, what was he meaning, by these words?

Here are a few suggestions:

1. Give yourself to God, with all you have.

2. Learn, live by, and make God's Word an integral part of your life.

3. Focus your attention on God.

4. Be thankful…always.

5. Invest your life in other people.

6. Live your life for what counts for eternity.

7. Hold onto this life loosely. Things can change quickly, and it's not really this life that counts, anyway.

8. Don't ever forget that God wants to save everyone...and he's given you the privilege and responsibility of being involved in that task.

9. Be willing to give up what you deserve or have earned or that belongs to you.

10. Someday you will be gone. What will you have left behind? What will those following after you see in your life?

Perhaps this was what Paul was saying to us...

APRIL 23

Day/Date — Be sure to remember five things to be grateful for every day. 'April 23'

Romans 8:31 Message — So, what do you think? With God on our side like this, how can we lose?

As children, we played games requiring us to choose teammates. As we chose, we considered our chances of winning based on those who were now on our team. Being on God's side takes the guess work and uncertainty out of life completely. Although the process and the journey may look different than we envision, the success and victory are sure.

As the Watergate scandal swirled around us in 1973, and as Nixon's presidency hung in the balance, my primary focus, during those high school years in Korea, was...how my beloved Atlanta Braves were doing. OK, OK, so they were mired in the bottom rungs of the baseball standings, but there's always hope, right?!? We returned from a Junior/Senior getaway during my final year, and the front page news on the US military newspaper that we went to for our news was that Vice President Agnew had just resigned. I didn't even notice that headline until one of classmates gently chided me for turning straight to the sports page first, seemingly (and correctly) oblivious to the historic events overtaking us at the time.

Given how little I knew, or cared, about politics back then, it was a real revelation when, not long after, I got to college in the US and immediately began to hear from every corner how important the upcoming election was, how so much hinged on the outcome, how, apparently, all that was important to me was politics...and not the Atlanta Braves, as I had mistakenly believed.

In Jesus' day, too, the Israelites were straining for a political solution to their difficulties. Would Jesus be the one who would bring them relief from their burdens under the Romans? They waited in anxious expectation. And right up to the present day, we are still doing the same thing. We wonder, "Will the new administration bring us relief, bring us justice, bring us salvation (!), from all that ails us?"

Psalm 83 starts out with the very same urgent appeal to God for a solution to their current problems. "Come on, God, do something. Get us out of this mess! Fix our dilemma." Then, it ends with God's response to them, and to us: "All you need to know...all that really matters...is that I am ruling over the whole earth. That's it. Leave the details to me. Things are going in just the way I want them to go. I will make things come out right. It's not some politician, government, party, policy, or anything else that will fix the problems you see around you. Trust me; I will handle it...I am handling it."

So, from where does our help come from today? Are we like the Israelites, hoping against hope for some way out of our problems? I really like what Robert Browning said, and I think he got it right, when he said: "God's in his heaven. All's right with the world." Really, that's simply all that matters. Yes, there are messes everywhere...injustice, evil, and too many other problems to count. But the most important thing is where God is...he's presiding in heaven...so let's look to him, let's wait on him.

APRIL 24

Day/Date   Be sure to remember five things to be grateful for every day.   April 24

Daniel 3:18   NCV   But even if God does not save us, we want you, o king, to know this: We will not serve your gods.

The Old Testament contains many instances of people who trusted God when they observed him blessing and caring for them. Often we behave the same way. We find it easier to trust God when we sense he is blessing our lives. But what about when we don't easily see or feel God's care for us? Daniel made it clear that whether God rescued him or not, he would still trust in God. Is that something I could also say?

I enjoy history, and especially stories from the American Civil War. Of course, there was horrible suffering, and the issues at stake were terribly profound and weighty. But, what I like, at least from the distance of time and settled issues, were the dramatic, dashing, unexpected, and surprising stories that came out of it. I suppose anyone, stepping back and examining the opposing balance sheets (The North owned the industry, the shipping, much of the military, 70% of the population...), would have known the final outcome. But war is made of emotion, not necessarily reason, and passionate politicians and soldiers will see it through, no matter what the cost, the tragedy, the almost certain final result.

It seems that many in the North knew it was a done deal even before it started. I mean, how could those silly ragtag Southern states, with nothing but cotton plantations, expect to accomplish anything against the might and right of the national government and military? Senators from Washington even brought picnics along in their carriages to watch and then celebrate the first major battle of the war...the First Battle of Bull Run. (Perhaps, the place and name of the battle should have given them pause...) At any rate, as the day drew to a close, and the Rebels had given the Yankees a good spanking, the stunned and scared Senators hustled back to Washington, perhaps beginning to realize that this might not be the festive fight that they had carelessly anticipated.

As the war unfolded, President Lincoln was faced with a simple, but serious, problem. He couldn't seem to find a general who would take hold of the army and press the fight to the rebels. His commanders just were too cautious and frightened of these sneaky, unpredictable Southerners. They couldn't find the resolve to go after those scallywags. At one point, in exasperation, Lincoln blurted out to his top general, "If you're not going to be using them, do you think I could borrow your armies so I can go after the Confederates??"

Well, finally, finally, eventually, Lincoln found what he needed. Grant and Sherman showed up. They were not the guys we might have expected to win the war. They didn't look dashing, they weren't impressive, and Grant was known as much for his drinking and his business failures as he was for anything else. But one thing they were, was no nonsense. Even looking at their photos today can bring fear into your heart. These two were here to fight…and they were going to hang on till the job was done.

And that's what makes the end of the war pretty surprising. Grant tenaciously hunted down the dashing General Lee, until Lee and his armies were out of bullets, horses, food…out of gas, really. And, finally, painfully, Lee knew he was done, beaten. He knew it was going to be a humiliating meeting he had to have with Grant to discuss "terms"…Grant wasn't known as "Unconditional Surrender" Grant without reason. Robert E. Lee arrived for the meeting in his best battle dress gear and sword. Grant, rather surprisingly, showed up in a dusty, frumpled, uniform, hardly befitting the Commander of the entire, victorious army. But, most surprising of all, were the terms Grant laid out. It's almost as if he was saying, "Just kidding…it was all in fun!" He let the Confederates walk away…with their horses, their guns, their freedom. Had he suddenly lost his marbles? Had he had one too much to drink that day?

I think what happened is the same thing we see unfolding in Jeremiah 49. Grant knew that the job was accomplished. He knew that both sides in the war knew it was over, and so he saw that it was a time for grace and healing. That's what was needed, not smearing someone's face in the ground. So, what happens in Jeremiah? God says, "I'm going to come after you with a sword until you're terminated." (Now, those words really remind me of General Grant.) But, then, immediately after that, God says, "But, after I've clobbered you, I'm going to return you right back to where you were before. I'm going to restore your fortunes." What a surprising turnaround. Maybe Grant had read Jeremiah 49 that morning when he went to meet up with General Lee. I don't know. But it sure gives us hope, doesn't it? No matter how bad our situation, no matter how rebellious we might have been...God says to us, "It's not over till I say it is. And, fortunately for you, I am the God of hope, the God of healing, the God of "Unconditional Grace"...

APRIL 25

> Day/Date   Be sure to remember five things to be grateful for every day.   April 25
>
> Psalm 23:4 Message Even when the way goes through death Valley, I'm not afraid when you walk by my side.
>
> When the widow of Nain in Luke 7 had lost everything, Jesus said to her, "Don't cry." Life can bring great pain and disappointment into our lives, as was the case with this widow. But, if we are walking with God, we don't have to be afraid, and we can be sure that he will bring us safely to heaven.

Cultures often leave me scratching my head... Who in the world knows how in the world everyone in the world got to be so different from everybody else in the world?!? I guess cultural experts could explain it all to me... As an Asian with Western skin, married to a European with American skin...I can tell you about some cultural differences! One big confrontation point we spar over is Truth vs. Grace. In the West, everything is black and white, right or wrong...Truth is everything. In Asia, Grace covers everything, leaving us all living in a gray netherworld...highly frustrating to my European, Dutch, no less, wife. I mean, if we say we're meeting at 4:00:00, why would annnnyone possibly countenance arriving at 4:00:03?? (Oh, brother, sighs this Asian boy...)

Well, you get the point. But, of course, as I relish reminding my wife, I have the Bible on my side. It says so, right there in 1 Corinthians 12&13. Paul carefully goes through all of our differences, how God made us all special, so that we can work together, help each other, live together as one smooth running body. Then he lowers the boom. Yes, all these things are important...but they're all squat compared to Love...Love, in case you didn't realize, is spelled G-R-A-C-E...so, case closed...I was right all along. And Paul backs me up. (Is that a little pride I detect oozing out of myself? Just a rhetorical question...no need to answer!)

Yes, of course we all know Truth is important. Without it, we have nothing. But, without Grace, we are hopeless, lost, goners... Thank God for his grace, his love, his mercy, his compassion. We would all cease to exist without it.

APRIL 26

Day/Date   Be sure to remember five things to be grateful for every day.   April 26

Hebrews 11:26 NCV He thought it was better to suffer for the Christ than to have all the treasures of Egypt, because he was looking for God's reward. This seems like a completely crazy choice, doesn't it! Who would choose misery over the luxurious life of a palace? Yet, wisely, Moses looked at the big picture, the long view, and knew that the rewards of serving God, even accompanied with suffering, were far better and lasting than a few brief moments of pleasure.

As I read Psalm 84, a smile crosses my face and my thoughts go back many years... When we were in elementary school in my hometown of Kwangju, Korea, there were about a dozen of us kids in this quasi private school/home school. We met in the basement of the old Bell Memorial Chapel, named after a venerated missionary, whose descendants were also in the school. Now, one thing that the teachers (who doubled as our parents) made us do every year, was to put on plays, performances, and dances. I'm not quite sure why they made us do those things. In my cynical older years, I'm beginning to wonder if it was strictly for their entertainment and amusement, that they were snickering under their breath at our comical efforts. I mean, it certainly made me proud when my kids performed or accomplished something...but us ragtag scrabble of kids?? I do wonder...

I still remember square dancing...the Virginia Reel, Do-si-doing your partner, and all that kind of stuff. It had to have been amusing to the parents...maybe it was a way for them to get back at us for all the mischief we had created through-out the school year.

What I do know, though, is that it's impossible...yes, impossible - I've tried it...to keep a straight face while you're square dancing. Try as you might, you're just having too much fun, not to break into a smile.

And that's exactly what happens to me when I read Psalm 84...uninitiated, a smile just spreads across my face like a tidal wave. It's like we used to feel in the wee hours of Christmas morn...we would hustle down to the living room to get a good look at all the presents scattered under the tree and around the room (at least to my little eyes, that's what it looked like). When we enter the verses of this psalm, a smile has got to cover our face. God's dwelling place is beautiful... Now, the Louvre Museum in Paris is beautiful, but I don't think that's what it means. You can definitely walk into the Louvre with a straight face. But I just imagine a little child walking into a candy factory (not just a candy shop, mind you, but the whole factory, where it all comes from), and his face lighting up like fireworks. God's dwelling place is beautiful because it's all love and all acceptance. As soon as we walk in, we feel, see, and know, his love. And, even the sparrow...that most lowly of plain, ordinary birds...has a special place there. It's simply a beautiful place to enter and to be in. It's better, in fact, than a thousand days anywhere else. I miss my parents these days...my Dad would have been 100 this year. Sometimes I wish I could just spend five minutes with them. But, it's going to be soooo good in heaven, where God is, that even one day there will be infinitely better than being able to spend a thousand days with anyone else, including my parents. I can't wait for heaven. I hope it's the same for you. I hope we are all preparing for that day right now. Some of us are going to have such big grins on our faces, that our cheeks will probably ache!

APRIL 27

Day/Date   Be sure to remember five things to be grateful for every day.   April 27

Proverbs 3:12 NCV   The Lord disciplines those he loves.

Life can be very hard; sometimes it even seems impossible. But difficult experiences can be useful and helpful in many ways. And God is a master at causing seeming disasters to come out for our good and well being. Many times God allows hard things in our lives because they provide us with opportunities to trust him and to build character, such as patience and perseverance, in us.

There's something about getting a job done and accomplishing a task...a great sense of relief and satisfaction. Shortly before 2000, we were working on opening a Christian bookstore in Moscow, Russia. On one trip to visit our coworkers, I remember spending most of the day, going from one office to another, to another, seemingly accomplishing nothing. We needed to obtain various permits and registrations, and so we set out. One official was busy...come back later. On to the next office. This guy was out to lunch. Come back another time. The next office had moved...go somewhere else. My coworkers kept apologizing for this frustrating, apparently fruitless day. But, I thought, actually, this was a great experience for me. It helped me to understand them, their daily struggles and tasks, the efforts required in getting this shop opened. So I said, "Don't worry...this is a helpful experience for me to go through." Now, I love a little verse in Jeremiah 50 that I don't recall having read before. In verse 25, it says, "The Sovereign Lord Almighty has work to do." Isn't it great to think that even God is working, that he has jobs to do?!? But two things good about what God is doing: one, he is working on eternally good things...everything he's doing is for our good; two, he will accomplish and complete what he is doing...nothing can prevent him from finishing the job; and, three (Did I say two...I meant three things...), unlike all those offices in Moscow, God's door is always open. He's always there waiting to receive us. No matter how busy he is with world affairs...you are more important to him!

APRIL 28

The apostle Paul had passion, that's for sure. When he was speaking to his church members, those he loved so dearly and risked everything for, he swung between love, advice, frustration, knocking their heads together...he wanted so badly to get his message across to them, for them to understand the important aspects of the Gospel. At times, he would go into great detail on subjects that don't seem like such a big deal to us. Other times, he would get steaming angry with them. Then we come to 1 Corinthians 14, and it's as if Paul just throws up his hands, and says, "OK, you blockheads! Forget about everything else. If there is only one thing you should be doing, if you blow it on everything else, at least do this: just do the loving thing. Follow the way of love. Whatever you do, just be loving!"

Such a simple thing...yet so often elusive! How much easier, more peaceful, more blessed would our lives be...if we just did what Paul told us to do: just operate out of love. Lord, help us to do that, to live and be that way. May our lives be colored by, be a reflection of love! Amen! Nuff said.

APRIL 29

> **Day/Date** Be sure to remember five things to be grateful for every day. April 29
>
> Jeremiah 9:24 NCV If some one wants to brag, let him brag that he understands and knows me.
>
> There may be many reasons we can think of to be proud: job, success, family, friends, talent, strength... But all of these things are small and passing compared to the privilege and eternal benefit of knowing God.

If there is one thing God is, it's that he is patient...patient with the world, patient through history, patient with thugs and rogues...patient with me. Paul knew that. After making a career of ruthlessly hunting down Christians and sending them to an early grave, when God captured his heart, Paul described himself as less than the lowest of Christians. He knew he didn't deserve God's patience and long suffering with him. In the 1700s, John Newton joined the British navy. Later, he worked on a slave ship, and even briefly became a slave in Africa himself. Again, following his patient pursuit of this slaver, God captured his heart, prompting Newton to write the words, "Amazing grace, that saved a wretch like me..." It's a beautiful metamorphosis to watch God's patient, persistent pursuit of us bear fruit in individual lives. We get a sense of God's gentle, patient reaching out to us in Psalm 85, which tells us that he shows favor, forgives, restores, gives salvation, demonstrates his unfailing love...all words that, extended to rebellious creatures, reflect God's patient pursuit of us. Where would we be without God's patient extending of his loving arms to us? We would be lost. Paul understood that. John Newton knew that. They were goners until God showed up in patience. And so also with us!

APRIL 30

Day/Date _Be sure to remember five things to be grateful for every day._ April 30

Psalm 143:10 NCV — Teach me to do what you want, because you are my God. Let your good Spirit lead me on level ground.

God has given us the two greatest possible gifts we need in order to know him and obey him: his Word and his Spirit being in us. But we also need to have a willingness and desire to know God better, so this is an important request to pray to God regularly.

In high school, we used to have YFC meetings on Sunday evenings. The boarding school students would squeeze into one of the missionary homes, spreading out across their living room to sing and listen to messages (which I sheepishly admit that I don't remember a single one of...). But I do recall something that happened one evening, 50 years ago, as if it were yesterday. In those post Korean War years, the threat and fear of war still hung in the air. It didn't seem far fetched to imagine that conflict could again break out. In fact, sometimes we kept a suitcase packed...with the possibility in mind that we might have to evacuate with our lives and a single bag of our most valuable belongings, in a moment's notice.

So, on that memorable evening, we were singing our hearts out, probably about "a spark getting a fire going"...when the hostess of the home where we were meeting strode into our room with the most serious of expressions on her face. "Guys, I just heard on the radio that the North Koreans have attacked! Their forces are streaming across the border at this moment. We have to evacuate right now!" My heart started pounding, and the thought came to me: "Will I see my parents again? Will there be time for the four hour train ride back home?

And what will happen then? Will we get out??"

As the lady turned and walked out of the room, our leader, with a grin on his face, said to us, "Actually, that is not true. I just asked her to say that to get our attention. Because this is the point I want to make…" Boy, did he get our attention (even if I don't remember what he told us after that…)!

Now, rumors can certainly seem very real, and can take on a life of their own, as that little tale did, for just a minute or two on that long ago evening…

God reminds us of this in Jeremiah 51, when he tells the people not to listen to rumors. No doubt, all kinds of rumors were swirling around at the time…whispers of Babylon's armies, of destruction, of having to flee for their lives… What does God tell us to do instead? He says, "Don't listen to nonsense. Tell people who I am and what I've done…because, really, that is what's important, that is what matters. Remind people that I am loving, that I deal in righteousness, that my plans will take place, that I will restore you even after calamity, that everything belongs to me, and that includes even the wind and the rain… Don't be afraid. Trust me. And be sure to tell others who I am." That message hasn't changed. And our task of telling others hasn't either…

MONTH 5

Quarantine day 5...

Thoughts from 2 Chronicles, Ezra, Nehemiah, Esther, and Job:

*Whatever success we have comes from God.

*Success gives us an opportunity to honor and praise God. What will we do with it?

*The Perfect and Almighty God...invites us into his presence.

*When people in the Bible encountered God, they fell to their faces in fear. What is our reaction to our Holy God?

*God always loves us...because God is love.

*God is looking for those who will follow and obey him.

*God speaks to us. Are we listening?

*When we follow God, opposition will come.

*God moves the hearts of kings...even ones who do not know him.

*God tells us to trust in him...and get to work obeying him.

*God does not forget us. He loves us.

*God works in the actions of people, for his own purposes.

*There is a lot in this life that we don't understand about how God works.

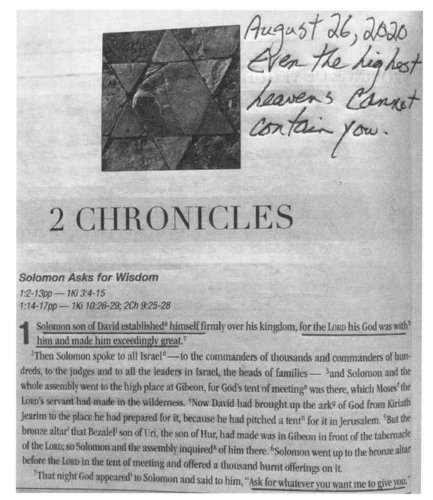

MAY 1

As I think back over my life, I have many good memories, a few bad ones, one or two scary moments, a few experiences which are very memorable…and a handful of times when someone disappointed or let me down. The interesting (and revealing) thing about times I remember when people disappointed me, is that, really, they weren't that big a deal. But, to my shame, I've held on to them, stored them away in my file of memories, allowed them to strain relationships…when, if I were honest, I might have behaved in exactly the same way in a similar situation. Yes, it is revealing of our hearts, how we hold on to small things we don't appreciate about how someone treated us or let us down. But if (when) I have done the same to someone else, it's perfectly sensible, reasonable, understandable, I tell and convince myself.

Then there is God. In Psalm 86, David comes before God and doesn't beat around the bush. David knows who he himself is…"poor and needy"…and he knows who God is…"forgiving, good, abounding in love". David knows that God isn't holding on to every little (and big), petty (and not so petty) moment when David has blown it. He knows that God has dealt with all those times and started over again with clean dishes, fresh paint, a clean slate. It's no wonder that David didn't come running to me for understanding and forgiveness (neither has anyone much else for that matter!). He knew where he could get a fresh start. He knew who would not hold a grudge. He knew who would treat him as a brand new best friend. In our relationship with God, and anytime we approach God, it's always important to remember and recognize these two things: I am needy, and God is loving and forgiving. Such simple truths...even a child can recognize and understand them. But we wrestle with both of these realities all our lives, it seems. Lord God, teach me, show me, that I am spiritually poor and needy. And teach me, also, that you aren't like me. You don't hold onto petty and small disappointments and failures. For with you, we are always welcome; with you, we will always find help in our time of need; from you, we receive an abundance of love and grace and good. Thank you for showing us who you are, through the life of David.

MAY 2

Day/Date   Be sure to remember five things to be grateful for every day.   May 2   1

John 3:16 NCV   God loved the world so much that he gave his one and only Son so that whoever believes in him may not be lost, but have eternal life.

This is the greatest Good News the world has ever heard. God gave his most precious possession for us because he loves us so much. Wouldn't it be a terrible tragedy if some people were not aware of this news? We must tell them!

Over the past 30 years, our family has done a lot of moving. We left behind our beloved home in Tennessee where our four oldest began their young lives, as we headed off on a harebrained wild goose chase in Europe. I remember the heart wrenching pain of watching our home being dismantled before our eyes. It's painful to watch parts of your life being carried out the front door, as folks pick through your furniture, and so on. It's equally painful to realize that those things that you hold dear and are full of memories...are just meaningless second hand bits and pieces to everyone else. Later, after ten years of raising our younger kids in England, we repeated the same process, leaving so much we held dear behind. And, we've done it a few other times as well. Those are hard and painful experiences. But, still, they were our choices, done on our own terms, done more or less how we wanted to do them.

I can't imagine the excruciating process described in Jeremiah 52. In a very faint way, it's kind of like what we experienced. But the similarities quickly end. The Babylonian armies marched up against God's holy city, that sacred place that God rejoiced over, where he promised to dwell among his people, that had been carefully built up over hundreds of years. What a beautiful and glorious place it was, a dear spot that King David had ruled, written, sung, and praised over. Then, the barbarians marched in. First, they humiliated the

MEDITATIONS OF A TRAVELER

people by reducing them to starvation. Then, they hounded and chased down the army of God's people, gouging out the eyes of the king. Finally, they burned down and reduced the majestic city to rubble, dragging off most of the people as captive slaves to Babylon. What a shocking end to the great story that God had started and been building on. How could God have let that happen? I can't imagine the excruciating experience that those people endured. I wonder if many of them may have gone insane simply from the trauma of going through it all. But, do you know what is really interesting, especially since I can, centuries removed from those days, read about these details? The thing that is surprising, greatly encouraging, and more than a bit scary...is that not one iota of God's eternal, good, loving, righteous plan has been thwarted or denied by those terrible events during the waning days of the kings of Israel.

It is surprising...because God put so much effort and attention and affection into that particular place of his people. Then, he just let it all be dismantled, stomped on, and dragged through the gutter.

But, at the same time, it is greatly encouraging to know that bad, terrible, evil events can't and won't deny God's good, eternal plans. The worst things that can possibly happen...won't halt God's lasting designs.

And why is it scary? Well, simply because, being the big time wimp that I am, I really, really don't like pain, suffering, and inconvenience. And it scares me, not a little bit (a lot!), to observe what God allows his own beloved people to go through, to suffer through, to endure...in his good, eternal plans. It's one thing to read about the history, and think, well, I can see that they certainly deserved that. Or, well, it wasn't too bad...it all worked out in the end. But, when I think of any of those things happening to me?!?...then I want to run like Jonah, hide like Elijah, tell God to send Aaron as Moses did... Really, it scares the willies out of me (as we used to say). I just don't want to go there. Please, God, not me!! But, that's when I have to hold on to his goodness, his unfailing love, his wisdom, his care...Lord, do help me, help all of us, focus on who you are, and on your good and eternal plans, when the going gets tough...or even when it gets a little unpleasant.

MAY 3

Distractions can be dangerous...and occasionally, comical. Although Chinese is a very fascinating language, probably the most interesting in the world, I found it impossibly hard, and after two years of banging my head against a wall trying to learn it, I finally, pretty much, gave up. Granted, it's a little hard to learn any new language in your 50s, and even more so, when you are as linguistically AWOL as I am. But, Chinese definitely stands alone in several departments, as far as languages go (having about 50,000 characters, for starters). So, it was not particularly surprising when one of our friends in China, as she was killing time in the airport on her way back to the US, suddenly got really excited. She also had been slaving away at learning the language. As she wandered about the airport, waiting for her flight to depart, she started looking up at all the signs in Chinese above the airport shops...and she got really, really excited...I mean, really, really, really excited. For, you see, suddenly all those crazy, incoherent strokes made sense to her. She could understand what they were saying! Exhilarated, she danced from shop to shop, reading off all the signs and patting herself on the back. Suddenly, all the blood, sweat, and tears of language learning was paying off. She was no longer in a bewildering, incomprehensible world. She could make sense of it all. It was so exciting, in fact, that her over the moon feelings got the best of her...and she forgot, and missed, her flight altogether. Well, I suppose it caused a brief panic when she suddenly realized that the plane had left without her, but it does make a good story to tell her grandkids, and perhaps it even brings a smile to her own face now, as she thinks back on it, years later.

You get the impression, as you read 1 Corinthians 16, that Paul was used to having a few distractions of his own. He held his schedule and plans very loosely, knowing that things could change in a moment's notice. He says, "If it seems like the right thing to do, I'll go there..." "Maybe I'll come visit you..." Not exactly what we would expect CEOs to say...not quite how people with pressing schedules and plans would live their lives. But, I can think of a couple of reasons why that could be a good way to approach life.

If we are truly living for eternity, if we recognize that God wants to save everybody, if we believe that God is guiding our steps and just may bring someone unexpected across our path, then what could be more important than being willing to lay aside our carefully laid plans in order to go after the one lost sheep, or to stop and help the bloke lying in the gutter on the road to Jericho? Paul knew that God might toss into his schedule just such an unexpected interruption, and so he would say, "If it works out, I'll do this..." He knew that his plans were much less important than someone else's eternal destiny.

Secondly, holding our plans loosely can help give us a little bit more of a realistic perspective on ourselves. If I and my plans are so important and inflexible that they can never be interrupted or discombobulated...then I almost certainly have too high a view of my own self importance. Honestly, I'm just not so, so important that my plans can't be disrupted...for the sake of someone else's eternal destiny. It's not about my neat little plans. It's about rescuing people from hell...that's what's really important. Paul knew that...and didn't take his own plans too seriously. I hope we will learn from his example.

MAY 4

Day/Date: Be sure to remember five things to be grateful for every day. May 4

Philippians 1:6 NCV God began doing a good work in you, and I am sure he will continue it until it is finished when Jesus Christ comes again.

When we give our lives to God, he begins working in us to make us the people he wants us to be – righteous and holy. Usually it is long, slow, hard work because we have so much of our own selfishness within us that needs to be changed. But he promises to keep working his good plans in us as we continue to walk with him.

I can still hear my Mom singing out those words: "Glorious things of thee are spoken, Zion, city of our God!" I didn't really understand what they meant, those words sung out to us also in Psalm 87, but my Mom's radiant smile and joyful music told me that it was an exciting and exhilarating experience... whatever it might entail. I had no idea what that involved, and I'm sure I still can't begin to understand it, so far beyond any of our imaginations as it will surely be, on that day we arrive in Zion's city. But, perhaps I did get a teeny, tiny glimpse of it one recent hot summer day, when I did feel great exhilaration and joy.

Now, we hear a lot of stories about growing old, most of them not too great. One characteristic of getting older, is that we can delude ourselves into thinking we are still young. Some time back, a fellow teacher, at a school for North Koreans where we were volunteering, led a group of students in an informal tennis class. Being the tennis wizard that I've always imagined myself to be, I asked him if I could come along with him one day. He was about half my age, so I had to use whatever intimidation I could to get the best of him. I told him that I would kill him on the tennis court. After he had taught the kids a while, I got out there with him and started whacking the ball around. He sent a zinger across the court, and my mind started running after the ball. The problem that presented itself rather quickly and emphatically to me at the moment was that my legs could no longer follow my brain, as they once could. So, my brain followed the ball to where it was...and my legs came tumbling after... I took an embarrassing roll and sheepishly picked myself up off the asphalt. I don't think I've touched a racket again since that day.

Well, back to that hot summer day a short while back...at a weak moment, I listened to a friend extol the wonders that still remained for those who pursued a hike up Chidi San, that mountain we used to climb as children. So, I decided to go up the mountain. I thought, well, at least I can check it out...then, if it is still a great experience, my wife and I can later go up it together. Wisely, my friend offered two of his younger Korean friends to hike with me, no doubt observing the current condition of my physique. We started out...and the trail went up, and up, and up, and up. I wasn't sure it would ever end, and if I would ever make it. But, miracle of miracles, we did finally, eventually, arrive at the top, where the old camp settlement from my childhood memories still exists. For a few moments, there was great exhilaration at having actually made it, of having arrived, of the arduous journey having ended. Hallelujah, I felt like shouting! (And wondered how in the world we ever climbed that mountain in those past days...) But it was truly an elation to have arrived. And we get that sense from those words in Psalm 87. One day, the blood, toil, sweat, and tears of this life will be over. One day we will arrive in Zion's city. One day, all the daily troubles today will be left behind and forgotten. What a day that will be. Let's press on. Every day, we're one day closer to that glorious day that my Mom used to sing about.

MAY 5

Day/Date Be sure to remember five things to be grateful for every day. May 5

John 10:10 Message I came so they can have real and eternal life, more and better life than they ever dreamed of.

Jesus came to give us a great gift, beyond anything we can imagine. But our preoccupation with and distraction by the small cares and responsibilities of life often push us to settle for far less than what God has planned for us. We need to daily focus and decide to seek God's involvement in our lives in order to receive his best.

Ever since I took a class on 2 Corinthians in college, I've loved that book...so much reassurance of God's love, his compassion, his guidance in our lives... And I still remember learning the last two verses of chapter 4, when our Dutch Bible teacher had us memorize them in high school (so thankful he did!). But sometimes, I wish Paul hadn't penned those words. For they speak much of his hardship, suffering, and anguish...and, of course, he wants us to follow his example... (great, Paul, just what I wanted to hear!). He talks about being hard pressed, crushed, persecuted, struck down, wasting away, death working in us...just the kinds of words that give me warm fuzzies...a little too warm, for that matter. But Paul is still excited...because, as bad as life sometimes is, as hard as it is at times to be following Christ, Paul knows that the future is much, much better...so good, in fact, that all these hardships (and, boy, did he have his share) are just light and momentary. So, when the day is dark, when I feel like quitting, I need to remind myself of these words of Paul, written for us. God is allowing us to suffer for his good purposes. Someday, we'll understand it. But, for now, let's remember that these hardships are nothing compared to what is coming ahead in the future. Lord, help us remember that daily!

MAY 6

Day/Date Be sure to remember five things to be grateful for every day. May 6

Titus 3:5 NIV   He saved us because of his mercy.

God is mysterious and in many ways beyond our understanding. Sometimes he can be frustrating or puzzling to us. But the important thing is what we do know about God. He realize he is good and understands us. He is almighty and loves to show us his grace and mercy. That is why he desires to save us from our sin.

Last night we attended a memorial service for a 31 year old young lady that was very sad in several respects. In many ways, she was a person without a country, from the Middle East, but finding herself caught here in the Far East. She had a young daughter, taken care of by someone else, and she was mostly alone in the world. She was found dead by the staff, in a local hotel room. The circumstances were sad, and leave me with a sigh and longing for heaven. Perhaps every year is hard, but it seems that this one is especially so. Well known leaders who have left us, tragic deaths before their time, job struggles, separations, plans disrupted...on and on. The writer of Psalm 88 certainly felt the same way. His words leave you feeling weary and at a loss. He is feeling crushed and abandoned, and ends on this haunting note: "The darkness is my closest friend." Wow...where's the hope and confidence, so common in the psalms? Whatever happened to this guy? Perhaps he is just expressing how we, too, feel on occasion.

As I get older, and approaching retirement, I find myself increasingly weary of this world, ready to cash in my chips and head on out of here. But, appearances to the contrary, the author did understand two things. When he was without hope, when the entire deck was stacked against him, he knew where to turn. He knew that, in his deepest, darkest moment of utter hopelessness, God was the one to turn to. God may not answer him today, God may not give him the response he was hoping for, but, nevertheless, it was God who did hold the key to his hope and his way forward, so he brought his needs to God. Secondly, there seems to be no sign of hope in this psalm...and some pretty strong words of blame against God. But the remarkable thing is that the writer knew he could come, knew he could be brutally honest, and knew he would be received, nonetheless, with open arms. Isn't that truly remarkable? Our God loves us so much, understands us so well, through and through, that we can dish out our worst and lowest thoughts to him...and it will be the same. He will welcome us into his presence with open arms. Is that remarkable, or what? Have we ever heard of any other god that is the same loving, acceptance way? We haven't....because there aren't any... As Jesus said to us: "Come unto me, all you who are weary and heavy laden...and I will give you rest." The offer is still open today.

MAY 7

> **Day/Date** Be sure to remember five things to be grateful for every day. May 7
>
> Psalm 27:1 NCV The Lord protects my life;
> I am afraid of no one.
>
> Although the Lord protects us, we do live in a sinful and dangerous world in which many bad and painful things occur. Even so, we do not have to be afraid because God knows us and knows each day of our lives already. Nothing will happen without his understanding or consent, and he promises to bring his children safely to heaven one day.

When I visited my girlfriend's home in Delaware, during our college days, I entered a world I never knew existed before. That's because they were Dutch, fairly recently off the boat, and their words and habits were sprinkled with quaint, amusing, and on occasion, not so amusing, Dutch customs and language. I learned very quickly that, "If you ain't Dutch, you ain't much!" Some words, they used so freely that even this slow language learner picked them up. They were forever looking for the "doekje" (kitchen towel). And I knew that their home was very special, because no other home I knew was so "gezellig" (cozy). Some words just don't work too well in other languages, in the way that these special words convey the meaning intended. Recently, I had a meeting with some Japanese colleagues, and one of them said a word that instantly joined my list of favorite foreign words. We were discussing finances and what money was available to pay some bills. The Japanese gentleman gave the example of someone who is out of money, in which case, his bank account is "giddy giddy"...nothing left. What a great word! Kind of leaves you giggling, instead of depressed!

There are a couple of words I picked up in China that I enjoy as well. One is the word for "so so"...which is "ma ma hu hu". Now that cheers you up in a hurry, in a way that "so so" just doesn't. Then, there is the word I became famous for at the English school where I taught: "bing geling"...which of course means "ice cream". But contrary to our word, "ice cream", "bing geling" makes you want to rush out right now and get some.

As I read the last couple of chapters of Lamentations, that word "giddy giddy" comes to mind. These are depressing chapters, the people are at the end of their tether...there is "giddy giddy" hope left. But, thankfully, even though you wouldn't know it from these verses, there is hope. God's wrath against our disobedience doesn't last forever, he is a God of restoration, renewal, and a fresh start. It's no wonder that, even in the worst of circumstances, the Bible characters and writers would always keep coming back to him...just as we still are able to do today.

MAY 8

> **Day/Date** Be sure to remember five things to be grateful for every day. May 8
>
> John 6:38 NCV I came down from heaven to do what God wants me to do, not what I want to do.
>
> It required a tremendous love for the Father, and for us, for Jesus to willingly leave his perfect home in heaven and come to earth and suffer terribly for us. In the same way that Jesus did, am I able to say that I want to serve God instead of doing what I want in life? Does how I live my life show this reality?

We've known several people (well, more than several...) who have been amazing examples of grace...extending grace where it is not expected, giving grace where it is not deserved, overdosing grace beyond what is reasonable. There are some big examples, but I'll mention just one rather small one. Once, in college, I was visiting my older brother. I needed a white shirt, perhaps for a somewhat formal event, and he offered me the choice of one of his two white shirts. One was an old fashioned, totally uncool shirt. The other was the most up to date, snazzy fashion it could possibly have been. I don't know if my brother was testing me to confirm the greediness he saw in me, or what... But, not only did he extend grace with the offer...he also followed up my (selfish, of course) decision with a gracious reaction. Talk about heaping burning coals on someone, as it says in Proverbs, he did that to me by the undeserved grace he extended. I have never forgotten that act of grace on his part. And, clearly, it was a deliberate decision on his part to be that way. He didn't have to be that way. No one would have expected him to extend grace like that.

Paul lived his life in very much the same way...under excruciatingly difficult circumstances. He suffered severely, both in terms of things he encountered, and in the way those who he was reaching out to mistreated him. He talks about some of his suffering in 2 Corinthians 5&6. But he always chose the way of grace. He always extended grace to those who harmed him. He responded in grace to those who maligned him. He chose to focus on eternal things, rather than on the things that he could, rightfully, have complained and griped about. Paul chose grace...he chose to live in faith, even though everything visible surrounding him shouted out a different message. We have the same choice. How will we respond to our circumstances today? Will we react in a way we think we deserve...or will we choose to extend, to respond in, grace?

MAY 9

Day/Date Be sure to remember five things to be grateful for every day. May 9

Isaiah 40:11 NCV He takes care of his people like a shepherd. He gathers them like lambs in his arms and carries them close to him.

A shepherd is always watching over and watching out for his sheep. He stays with them, protects them, provides food for them, and will place his own life in danger for the sake of his sheep. He is particularly caring of and protective of the smallest and most helpless sheep. Our heavenly Father cares for us in the same way. Though much of the time we are not even aware of it, God is always watching over and caring for us in more ways than we can imagine.

My first visit to Romania, a country I never imagined I would visit only a few short years before, was in 1992. And, incongruously, it was where I met Mr. Bean. All right, all right, I didn't really meet him in the flesh. But, I do remember hearing two kids hunkered down in front of a video screen, laughing their heads off. I wondered what it was that tickled them so much, and that's when I met Mr. Bean. I guess nearly everyone in the world has met him by now. He tells the amusing story of entering a car parts store in England, waiting for a service guy to help him out. At the same time, another customer started to stare at him, squinting his eyes, and tilting his head, puzzled. Finally, he blurted out, "You know, you look a lot like that Mr. Bean guy!" Mr. Bean turned to him and said, "Well, actually...I am Mr. Bean..." "Hahaha...that's a good one!", the man laughed. "I bet you wish you were him. You could probably make a lot of money acting out the part of Mr. Bean for people!" Try as he might, there was no way Mr. Bean could convince this man that he was in fact the real deal. I have to wonder whether Mr. Bean, in real life, can ever go anywhere without these kinds of encounters happening all the time, all over the place. Poor soul... I guess his false identity is so much a part of his DNA, that he can never shake it.

That's actually the same picture we're given in Psalm 89. The writer describes the love of God that covers those who know God. His love is so pervasive, so all encompassing, so enduring...that we're never able to shake it. It's part of us, part of every aspect of our lives, part of our children's lives, part of all we do... like the old jacket my wife said I always wore, and never took off, in college, we just can't shake it, can't rid ourselves of it. But unlike my jacket or Mr. Bean's acting reputation, God's love is all good, for our own richness and blessing, and is backed and placed upon us by the all loving, all powerful God of the universe, who doesn't and won't change. He will always love us. And there is no better gift and guarantee than that...I don't care how much money someone might be able to make by acting like Mr. Bean...nothing can compare with the love of God, placed into and on our lives, forever. Now, that is truly something to revel in, meditate on, and live daily in...

MAY 10

Day/Date   Be sure to remember five things to be grateful for every day.   May 10

Colossians 3:17 Message   let every detail in your lives — words, actions, whatever — be done in the name of the Master, Jesus, thanking God the Father every step of the way. Really, this is impossible for us todo. Because of our imperfect, sinful nature, there are many times when we would rather go our own selfish way than to honor God in our lives. But we can ask God to help us live for him, and his Spirit in us will work to make us more the way he wants us to be. Then, our lives will begin to look more and more like that of Christ.

Do you remember the movie, "Hacksaw Ridge", about the conscientious objector/medic, Desmond Doss, who became a hero in the Pacific, in World War 2? It was an exciting movie, and soon after seeing it, I discovered that he was buried in the military cemetery in Chattanooga, Tennessee, where we have an apartment, and where our kids attended college. I was so excited about seeing this war hero's grave, that I dragged our son and his roommates away from their all important studies to take a memorial pilgrimage to honor the man's life at his grave. I told my son and his friends that, ten years from now, they wouldn't remember what they were studying, but they would remember this visit. So, somewhat reluctantly, they followed along. It was a pretty special moment, to be there at his grave, and to think about what he had done. The reality of his life was perhaps a little different than what the movie may lead us to imagine. Yes, Desmond Doss did heroically rescue dozens of wounded soldiers at great risk to himself. And rightfully, he received the Medal of Honor. But that's not the whole story. Doss returned to the US, having been wounded himself multiple times. He wanted to become a carpenter, but his severely damaged arm precluded that possibility. Then, he contracted tuberculosis, a souvenir from his time in the Pacific. This led to surgery, with the loss of a lung and five ribs, resulting in 90% disability. Antibiotics prescribed to him led to deafness. Later, Doss tried to raise a family on a small farm on Lookout Mountain, where we also have an apartment. Doss married during the war and had one son, but his wife was killed in a car accident while he was driving. Seemingly, his heroics were rewarded with one tragedy after another. We have to wonder, sometimes, why good people endure so much suffering.

I'm reminded of Doss's life when I begin to read Ezekiel. This prophet was called by God to deliver a harsh message to the Israelites who were captured and exiled in Babylon. As bad as their situation was, Ezekiel came along and made it worse. He bashed them over the head by telling them that God was terribly angry with them and was delivering brutal punishment to them. Talk about being a bearer of glad tidings...Ezekiel would certainly not be in that category. In the worst circumstances, he was given the most odious task by God, which he faithfully carried out for many years...with the result, as God told him would happen at the outset, that the people didn't listen to or heed his message. What a thankless job. It does make one wonder...why does God give such hard tasks to some people...whether it's Desmond Doss or Ezekiel...or perhaps one of us. In both of their cases, Doss and Ezekiel were sent to help and rescue people. Thankfully, God does send people to do that job. And God wants so much to rescue us, the people he loves, that he will even allow someone to suffer in the process of delivering an urgent message to us. And, of course, the ultimate one who was sent to suffer during a rescue operation was God's own Son himself, sent on our behalf, when we were being riddled by and shot to pieces by our own sin. That's something we can remember and be thankful for, when we think of Doss, suffering for the rest of his life, on account of those who had been shot up and who he was sent to rescue. Jesus did the very same for us.

MAY 11

Day/Date   Be sure to remember five things to be grateful for every day.   May 11

John 6:68 Message

Master, to whom would we go? You have the words of real life, eternal life.

Our lives can be bewildering and difficult, and sometimes even God can seem confusing for us. At times we may wonder if it would be easier to live without God. But as Jesus' disciples also realized, if we turn away from God, we are letting go of the true purpose in life, of the truth about who we are and where the world came from, and of our hope of an eternal life of joy with God.

For the past several years, it's been the great privilege of my wife and me to teach English and the Bible to North Korean defectors in Seoul. At first glance, they look just like the South Koreans, but a closer look reveals some differences. In many ways, they are like Holocaust survivors, carrying a variety of scars and pain within them. Frequently, they have lost family members, and the loved ones who remain in North Korea will never be seen again. They land in the South without a country, without much education, without friends or useful skills, very often bearing scars of abuse, trafficking, or trauma, in many ways with the odds of a successful future stacked against them. As we gradually get to know them, and they open up their hearts and lives to us, we try to love and care for them, in a sense to be their parents in this foreign land. One of my students told me his story, which gives us a small glimpse into the world they came from, and their reasons for wanting to come south.

When he was still living in the North, one of his buddies got hold of a pirated DVD from outside of North Korea, a dangerous and risky thing to do. As they put it into the player and began to watch it, they saw that it was the World Cup soccer tournament... No big deal, right? It was to change my student's life forever. From that moment on, he was determined to flee to the South. So, what was it that was so compelling about a soccer game that it would cause him to alter the course of his life? It was seeing the Australian team on the field. So? When he saw the Australian team play, he realized he would never want to raise his children in that North Korean environment, and that he would do whatever was necessary, even at the cost of losing family and country, to get out. For you see, up until that day, he thought everyone in the world spoke Korean, and he had no idea that there were many other countries in the world. Just seeing that team made him realize that everything he had been told by the authorities was a lie, and that he had to get out…and that he would get out. It was certainly eye opening for me to hear his story, as have the many other stories we've heard from our students. Hearing these things, knowing their suffering and pain, and all they've gone through to get here, makes us want to reach out to and love them all the more.

I sense the same longing in Paul in 2 Corinthians 7&8. He is pleading with the recipients, as a parent to a child, wanting to give them guidance and direction. His care for them hovers over them and comes through in his words to them, much as a parent's desire is to guide and care for his own children. And behind Paul's words, of course, we hear the Lord speaking to us with the same passion, care, and love, wanting so much to steer us in the right way, wanting us to receive the full life that he has mapped out for us. Are we listening when God is speaking to us? Paul certainly hoped the Corinthians were listening, and God still wants us to hear his words as well.

MAY 12

> **Day/Date** Be sure to remember five things to be grateful for every day. *May 12*
>
> John 14:15 NCV — *If you love me, you will obey my commands.*
>
> *This is not a forced response or even a threat. Instead, it is the natural behavior we will have if we really do love God. Just as a husband wants to please his wife and show her how he loves her, so we, as a response to our own love for him, will show it by the life we live each day.*

I grew up in Korea with, and attended college with, a couple of people who were related to Billy Graham. During the summers in college, we missionary kids scrambled around for a roof to camp out under, or were shuffled from place to place, as we didn't have our families nearby to return home to. One summer, I spent some time at my grandparents' summer home in the mountains. I had fond memories of that place from having visited as a child, and it even held significant memories for my parents in their younger days. Well, it just so happened that one of my classmates was also spending the summer nearby...except that the roof he happened to be camping out under belonged to Billy Graham. One day, he called me up and invited me over for a visit, so my brother and I drove up the hill to his house. We chatted for a whole about school and other things...when, suddenly, Billy Graham walked in. To say that I was a bit overwhelmed by his presence in our midst might be a slight understatement, but anyway, there he was, and there we were. Now, it can be a little intimidating being in the presence of someone who is fairly well known, but what I remember about those moments was just how ordinary the celebrated preacher was. He chatted with us about this and that, he showed us his German shepherd dog, and it was like we were long, lost friends. What a simple, ordinary, friendly sort of chap this great man is, I thought. He put us utterly at ease.

I can still hear my grandmother (the same one, by the way, whose mountain house we were staying at during that college summer when I encountered Billy Graham) quoting some of the words of Psalm 90, a rare one that was written by Moses. But, what I like and find interesting about this psalm is just how plain and simple this great leader of Israel and man of God sounds in these words of this oldest of psalms. In addition to his great words about the everlasting God, we also hear his sighs, his impatience with God, his weariness with life. Moses knew that the Almighty God invites us into his presence, no holds barred. With open arms, he tells us to come on in, open our hearts to him, that whatever we say, however we feel, we will receive grace, patience, compassion... Isn't that remarkable? Isn't that wonderful? So, that's exactly what Moses did. He reflected on God's greatness, but then also complained about God's behavior and treatment of his people. Amazing, really, when we stop for half a second to consider who Moses was talking to! It's almost like, Moses knows that he is so openly received, that he forgets for a few moments who he is even talking to. It recalls to my mind that brief visit I had with Billy Graham as a teenager. He just invited me in and made me feel like I could say anything I wanted, that whatever I said would be received with grace and acceptance. It was an amazing insight into this great, but simple, man. And, in many ways, it's exactly the same when we come into God's presence. We are approaching the Almighty Sovereign of the whole universe, but he welcomes us like a long lost, best friend, inviting us to unload anything on our minds and hearts, knowing we will be received with grace, with warmth, with love. It's amazing. It's staggering. It's real. He's available to us anywhere, anytime, no appointment necessary. Come into his presence now. What am I waiting for!

MAY 13

Hebrews 12:7, 10 NCV Hold on through your sufferings, because they are like a father's discipline. God disciplines us to help us, so we can become holy as he is. If a child really knows that his father loves him, then the child should be able to get through discipline even when he doesn't fully understand it. God disciplines us, sometimes severely, to make us better. He also dearly loves us. So we should keep holding on and trusting him even when the way is difficult.

Traveling through life, it can often be so random, peculiar, even seemingly meaningless. Why did I lose my pen when I went out yesterday? Why did I misplace my glasses? Why did someone look at me that way? Things can seem pretty perplexing and odd. Of course, then there are much bigger incidents... why did someone have a horrific car accident, why did that family's house burn to the ground, why did he get cancer... Why does God allow someone like Nick Vujicic to be born with no arms and no legs? At the risk of seeming to be incredibly trite and unfeeling, I would like to suggest that God sees the bigger picture, that he invites us to participate in his good plans...that sometimes, even, this participation can include some pretty incredible pain and discomfort. The question is, will we trust God, in the meantime, for what we can't see, don't understand, and really, really, really don't like?

That's exactly where Ezekiel found himself in chapters 4-6 of the narrative of his book that he shares with us. God is in dialogue, you might say, with the people of Israel, his select followers, and he's doing so in full living color, with graphic illustrations, and with dire consequences. And poor Ezekiel gets squeezed into this whole unfolding dynamic as exhibit one of the painful way that God uses people for his purposes. God says to him, "OK, Zeke, you ready? Hold onto your shirt...we're in for a ride, a rather bumpy one, at that! First I want you to draw a picture. (That's the really easy part.) Then I want you to lie on your left side for 390 days. Yes, you heard me right. For a whole year and change, lie there...in rain, snow, bugs, ants, and all...just lay there. And, really, I'm not quite sure how to put this for your delicate ears...but I want you to cook your food that whole time, all year long, using your own crap to keep the fire going!" Remarkably, Ezekiel was still there, listening to God. Jonah and I would have been long gone, I'm sure. Anyway, the point is, God uses some pretty strange, weird, unpleasant, painful, unfair, costly, excruciating means of getting people's attention, of speaking his message to a lost world. And he invites us to have the privilege (well, kind of a privilege, anyway) of participating with him in that. So, how will we respond? Will we run like heck, as Jonah and I would probably do...or will we trust God and his wisdom and goodness, even at the cost of great pain, like Ezekiel and Joseph did, knowing that he knows and carries out what is best? That's the question, the situation, the challenge, the cards, we are presented with everyday. Lord, help us to trust you. In our weakness, fear, selfishness, humanity...help us to trust you in your love and goodness.

MAY 14

Day/Date Be sure to remember five things to be grateful for every day. May 14

Acts 8:31 NCV How can I understand unless someone explains it to me?

We have the great and rich privilege of having had someone explain God's love to us — either by a person directly, or perhaps through God's Word. But what if someone hasn't heard or doesn't understand? We should do all we can to tell people who haven't heard about God's love for them.

Back in the good old days, growing up in post-Korean War days, we had precious few diversions or special events. There was a US military base not too far from the mission community where we lived, and every so often, they would invite the missionaries en masse to come watch a Disney or cowboy movie. That had to have been the all time highlight of our entertainment experiences. Never mind that we had to crowd in on the floor (I didn't know better and just assumed that all movies were watched, sitting on the floor.), and no popcorn or drinks were served. It was an evening to remember! Life could not get better than that. Well, one day, I thought life was, in fact, actually about to get better. My Dad and I met a young foreigner, whom I didn't know and hadn't seen before. In the course of their conversation, the man invited us (yes, me included!) to go hunting with him...on the coming Sunday. I held my breath as I turned toward my father, willing him to say yes. My Dad politely replied that we were unable to join him, as we went to church on Sunday. "Come on, Dad," I thought, "what can missing church on one Sunday hurt, if we're able to go hunting?!?" He was polite, but firm. And that was that. It was a big disappointment...and a lesson I never forgot. The commitment his life demonstrated, as a follower of God, impacted me profoundly. He was the greatest influence in my life...and it was largely because of consistent, day in and day out, decisions and actions like this. A seemingly small, inconsequential choice...but which colored and guided his whole life. That is what I saw...that is what stayed with me.

Paul saw the same thing in 2 Corinthians 9 & 10. He commended the Corinthian Christians for their example of generosity...then carried right on into a long, theological sermon, as he was so often wont to do...but, the point is, their generosity was noticed and was an example to many...including to us, still today. One of my greatest motivators as a father of nine is thinking often: Now, how will this decision affect my kids? What will they see, what will they learn...by whether I read my Bible, by whether I go to church...and really, any number of other ordinary and mundane choices I make all the time? I think that is partly what Paul was talking about to the Corinthians. Everything I do, every choice I make, every action I take...is an example to someone, will be seen by somebody...not the very least, by God himself. Am I giving that any thought in my daily life? In the decisions I make all the time? Whether we like it or not, whether or not we ask for it, all that we do becomes who we are, becomes the legacy we leave behind. What about you? What about me? What legacy are we leaving behind? What do others see in us?

MAY 15

Day/Date Be sure to remember five things to be grateful for every day. May 15

Psalm 37:3-4 NCV — Trust the Lord and do good. Enjoy serving the Lord, and he will give you what you want.

There is an element of faith and uncertainty in following God. He tells us to obey him and how he wants us to live. And we don't always know the outcome of doing this. Will we lose what we have? Will life become harder for us? Interestingly, because God made us to love and have a relationship with him, when we do live that way, we discover that we increasingly want what he wants, and our desires become exactly what he wants to give us.

I've always loved Psalm 91, probably because it was read at my baptism, but also, of course, very much because of the message that God expresses to us through the words. I remember my grandmother, Nai Nai, quoting these words with a wonderful smile lighting up her face. She knew the words were true, she knew they were true for her, and she wanted to share that excitement with others she met.

At first glance, the words sound a little like a fairytale or like pie in the sky. Come on, we all know these words aren't true, aren't serious. I mean: no fear, no plague, no terror, no harm, no disaster? All of us have seen or experienced these words too many times to believe that they never happen. So what do they mean? What is God really saying to us through these words? Well, for starters, Nai Nai certainly had her fill of terror and fear. More than once, in China 100 years ago, she had to flee for her life, was threatened by bandits, thought she had lost her husband, and more. If these things don't strike fear in a person's heart, probably not much will. So, why was Nai Nai so fixated on these words? What did she find in them that brought radiance to her face and joy to her heart? As with King David, who had more than his fill of terror, fear, enemies, and opposition, Nai Nai knew, and we can know, that God is right there with us through all of these experiences. The psalmist says that we will find refuge when we need it, that God will be with us in our troubles, that he will deliver us. Paul certainly would have confirmed those words, and, of course, Jesus would have as well. But both of them lived as brief pilgrims on this earth, their lives filled with trouble, hardship, and terror. So, in what way could they trust in these words? They had confidence because they knew in a very real way, along with Nai Nai, that God was right there with them through all these experiences. His presence meant that they didn't have to be afraid. Just like I wasn't afraid, as a young child, when I was with my father, in his presence. Yes, scary things could still happen to us, but I was safe with him. The picture of being "under his wings" is the exact same image we get from the Chinese "yi" character, of our sins being covered by the Lamb of God. That is what keeps us safe. That is what gives us confidence. Our position before, with, and under God, is safe. Our destiny is secure. Our eternity is untouchable. And that is where our true security lies. I don't doubt that when David was on the run, when my grandparents were fleeing in China, this is what they knew and held onto. Their relationship with God was unchangeable. They could rest under his wings. And so can we.

MAY 16

Ezekiel 7-9 paints a very scary, terrible picture for us. God has had enough of the people's dallying, messing around, nonsense, their complete scorn for God. Finally, God says, "That's it! That's enough. This is the end! You're terminated." That's a scary thing to hear. It's one thing to hear it as a threat in a cowboy movie. But there is a terrible, terrible finality about it when coming from the mouth of God, when it's what he has decreed. There is nowhere else to turn. No second chances. It's all over. As I was just reading these passages, and thinking to myself, "Man, I would be happy not to ever read these verses again!", it came to me, almost as a new revelation, that, in fact, these words are describing all the horrible, horrific, unimaginable punishment and abuse...that God poured out on Jesus...instead of on us, who deserved it. These words are directed toward our sin and disobedience. But the punishment that God did indeed mete out...landed on Jesus, instead of on us. Whew! That puts reading through these terrible verses in a whole new light. These terrible statements of doom and gloom, decreed because of God's perfect justice and holiness, were caught by Jesus when he stepped forward and stood in my place. All the guns of God's justice were pointed at me. Then his Son stepped up and took the whole blistering attack on himself. Is that love, or what? Does that demonstrate the value of a single individual in God's sight, or what? If that's the incredible, awesome, unbelievable Great News that God gives to us...wow, I hope I'm sharing it with a few other people as well! Am I? Are you? What a privilege God has given us...in addition to this fact of his unbelievable grace and mercy.

MAY 17

Day/Date — Be sure to remember five things to be grateful for every day. May 17

Jeremiah 15:16 NCV Your words came to me, and I listened carefully to them. Your words made me very happy.

God's instructions and truth come to us mainly through the Bible. When we follow God's messages, we find that they are good and loving, even if they are not always easy or exactly what we want to hear. And when we obey God's Word, it brings us joy.

When I was young in Korea, there were not many indications of Christianity around the country. From my limited perspective, the church seemed weak and marginalized. More than 50 years later, you get a very different picture in Korea today. Everywhere you go, you see church steeples and crosses raised high. More likely than not, as you pass through crowded shopping areas in the capital city, someone will reach out and hand you a tract or leaflet, or a church group will be out on the sidewalk, singing hymns or preaching. My, how things have changed!

But there are some worries for the church on the horizon. Probably the biggest is that few young people attend church. Along with the hasty growth of the church in recent decades has come a parallel growth in prosperity and materialism, which no doubt has become a great distraction for the younger generation. Few of them see much need for attending or being part of a church. They already have everything that they need. (Never mind that suicide is also at an all time high...and about the highest in the world.) Something else troubles me about much of the Korean church. It's the divisiveness that is so much a part of it. Someone told me once that just among Presbyterians, there are over 200 separate denominations, or distinct church groups. I don't know how accurate that is, but a quick online check comes up with over 100 Presbyterian groups in

Korea, at any rate. There is nothing wrong with that, per se. But it is a symptom of a malady which seems to be part of the Korean Christian culture. And that is divisiveness, territorialism, the idea that I have a corner on the truth, and I'm not going to share it with anyone else.

In the last few chapters of 2 Corinthians, Paul addresses divisiveness, false teaching, and the dangers of being distracted or led astray by the wrong focus. He pleads with the readers, with us, with the Korean church, to focus on what is really important. And what is that? It's laying down our lives for others, for the Gospel, for God. Territorialism does just the opposite. I exalt myself, my views, my rights...at the expense of others, at the expense, really, of the Gospel. It's the same danger we see everywhere, not just in the Korean church, and, no doubt, that is why Paul speaks about it. These days, the Internet seems to have heightened and sharpened the rhetoric of many voices around the world, frequently in a harsh and unloving tone. That's a little bit like what some of the church voices can sound like...a harshness toward others. I pray, let's pray together, that God will save you and me, the Korean church, all of us, from an unloving message to the world by the way we live and communicate.

MAY 18

Day/Date   Be sure to remember five things to be grateful for every day.   May 18

Psalm 106:7 NCV   Our ancestors in Egypt did not learn from your miracles. They did not remember all your kindnesses.

Perhaps the hardest thing parents endure is teaching their children to be wise and to avoid certain things that are harmful... only to later watch their children grow up and get entangled in the very things their parents warned them about. That is what Samson did after being warned by his parents. And that is what the Israelites did after being warned by God. God tells us their stories as a warning to us as we go through life.

A few years back, I was visiting Bangladesh, where my father toiled in his latter years (up until age 79, in fact...). As the years passed, we children grew increasingly vocal, imploring our dear old Dad to hang up his stethoscope and come back home. He would smile gently and say something to the effect that he still had work to do there. Indeed, he did.

When I had my brief visit back to Dhaka, where my Dad had worked in two medical clinics, I found glimpses and evidences of his work, still there, after he had long departed. I was on a bus one day, headed out to an appointment, when a man hopped on and sat down next to me. He told me that he had worked with my father. He just shook his head as he reflected on Dad's years spent there, hardly finding the words or images to describe a life of service for the Lord. I wish I had asked him more questions about his experiences with Dad, but after a short distance, he got down off the bus and was gone. Another time (I think probably on an earlier visit), I walked into a church courtyard, and there stood a man with a table of books and Bibles that he was selling. We got to chatting, and excitedly, after realizing who I was, he told me, "Your Dad got me started in distributing Christian books and Bibles!" Here and there, pictures of a life of sacrifice, of sharing the Good News with those who were most needy and down-trodden in society.

I think of my father when I read the words of Psalm 92: "They will still bear fruit in old age." And, "It is good to proclaim your love." My mind also goes back to my father's example, as my wife and I begin to hear those same words I myself spoke not too many years ago: "It's time to come home. You've done enough. Hang up your books and traveling shoes, and come home." But I want to follow in my father's footsteps. He knew that there was joy in sharing God's love with the lost…that is what keeps us "fresh and green", as the psalmist says, that helps fulfill the purpose God has given us during our brief stay on earth. I hope each one of us will discover that same joy.

MAY 19

During our years in Korea, we made an unlikely friend...unlikely, because we come from different worlds, we were both just passing through Korea briefly, and "chance" brought our paths together. This lady seemed like a simple, uncomplicated person at first. But as we got to know her gradually, we discovered more complex layers of beauty, talent, passion, heart, strength, courage, and zeal for righteousness...much more there than had first appeared on the surface following our initial meeting...an amazing person who we were not able to fully grasp upon first meeting her. I thought of her when I just read the words of Ezekiel 10&11. The prophet receives some unclear, hard to understand pictures or visions from God. What is going on here? What is God doing? What does he have in mind? In the middle of these images, it's not entirely clear. But, then, toward the end of chapter 11, God's magnificent plan becomes clear...and it's all about restoration, fulfillment, compassion, grace, patience, persistence...somewhat like the friend we met in Korea. There is much more depth and good in God's plan unfolding in the world than first meets the eye. Can we wait on him until he makes himself clear? I expect there is more to our friend than we even already know about...more good things happening than we realize or have yet discovered. But we will patiently wait and watch...and see how her life and plans unfold. And that's a picture of what our life with God is, also. We don't see it fully yet...but there is more good and blessing and grace to come, if we wait patiently on him, as we keep waiting on him...

MAY 20

Day/Date Be sure to remember five things to be grateful for every day. May 20

Psalm 67:1-3 NCV God, have mercy on us and bless us so the world will learn your ways, and learn that you can save. God, all people should praise you. Children always ask their parents for things that give them instant gratification. But parents especially enjoy giving to their children things they know will be good for them. God also delights to give good gifts to his children. How he must rejoice, then, when we offer up this prayer to him — that he will bless us for the benefit of others, and not simply for our own pleasure.

Aside from Jesus, Peter and Paul were probably the two most important people in the New Testament, and especially in the early years of the church. They could not have been more different, and certainly the normal course of events would not have brought them together to be the close friends they came to be. Peter was a simple, uneducated fisherman from the shores of the Sea of Galilee. He was impulsive and curious, an unlikely candidate to be one of Jesus' closest friends, and later one of the main leaders of the church. Paul was also an unlikely follower of Jesus, but for very different reasons. He was highly educated and privileged, one of the highest Jewish leaders of his day. But he had a supernatural encounter with Jesus that caused him to throw his background, his education, and all of his advantages to the wind...and follow Jesus at all costs. In fact, that is how he describes his life in Galatians 2, when he says (speaking to Peter and some other Christians), "I'm not really even living anymore. I gave up my own life, and this life that you see belongs completely to Christ and to following him." Paul was so focused on following Christ that his own life, goals, plans, desires...all were irrelevant to him. What an amazing and challenging example to us. Peter and Paul were able to serve and challenge and be an example to each other, just as, often, the unexpected friends that God brings to us do in our lives as well.

A couple of years ago, my wife and I were at a public meeting in Seoul that was highlighting the needs of the North Koreans. As we sat in the middle of a crowd of people we didn't know, I turned around and met the Korean pastor sitting behind me. It was just a polite greeting, and I never expected to see him again. After the meeting, we walked back to the subway to catch a ride home. In the subway station, we bumped into this same Pastor Kim again, and, wondering what these elderly foreigners were doing in Seoul, he asked us why we were here. I explained about our teaching, and then we went on our way. Some time later, he messaged me and invited me out for lunch. Well, that was nice, I thought. The next month, he invited me out again. The following month, the same. The one after, the same thing. We've been getting together regularly for the past two years...two unlikely people, who enjoy each other's friendship and company. Mr. Kim has certainly been one of God's blessings to me during our time in Korea. When we spend our lives following Jesus, he brings into our lives unexpected friendships that are a real blessing and encouragement to us.

MAY 21

> **Day/Date** Be sure to remember five things to be grateful for every day. May 21
>
> Isaiah 55:11 NCV The words I speak will not return to me empty. They make the things happen that I want to happen, and they succeed in doing what I send them to do. This promise is a very great comfort to us. As a parent, I want my children to listen to what I tell them and to learn from my instruction. Sometimes, though, children choose not to listen or learn, and I am powerless to force them. But we can have great confidence in God's Word because it is not just words, it is his Word, his Truth, and it will accomplish what he plans for it to do.

As we come to the end of the infamous year 2020, no doubt most of us will leave it behind without too much regret or sorrow over its passing. During this year, plans have been disrupted, goals have not been realized, people have been stranded, money has been expended or lost, loved ones have unexpectedly and tragically departed, businesses and ministries have been hammered and crushed and abandoned. Perhaps it is somewhat like a year during World War 2, or any other war, that we thankfully and wearily say goodbye to. Throughout the year, it has been my privilege to meet with the other leaders of our organization and to share, hear, and walk through together a variety of experiences and stories of challenge, loss, difficulty, and sorrow. All of us ourselves have, or know others who have, walked through the valley of hardship during this year. But, at the same time, we have all held onto, and continue to hold onto, the truths we're reminded of again in the short and simple…and powerful…words of Psalm 93. These brief five verses seem to be rarely referred to or noted…but, actually, they are precisely the treatment, or medication, if you will, for all that has infected us or that ails us, as we trudge, battered, through this year. So, what does it speak to us?

"The Lord reigns." That's it; that's enough. That reality covers everything. Even as things seem to slip out of our grasp or control (whether plans, goals, investments, whatever...), God is over everything. There is nothing outside of his control. Nothing has caught him off guard. Nothing can even come close to thwarting his good and perfect plans. Obviously, we don't see everything clearly, because from where we stand, things do indeed seem pretty slippery, pretty wobbly, pretty chaotic, and very uncertain. But God reigns. That is one truth that is sure.

Additionally, "The Lord is robed in majesty." Well, so what, we may think... That speaks of God's greatness, his perfection, his inability to be touched or contaminated by evil and all that has happened this year. God is not like some bruised and battered boxer who has just barely managed to get through this horrible year. No, he is still majestic, still in control, still unbound by evil, still victorious in all his ways...or, in other words, he is majestic! That is truly something to celebrate, if we are on his side, in his family, following him.

"He is armed with strength." Pandemics are scary. Tsunamis are frightening. Wars strike fear into us. Death devastates us. But God is greater. He holds all these things in his hands, under his control. We are not alone. We don't have to somehow conjure up the strength to survive. Strength is in God's hands. He is working out his plans. We are part of his plans, as we trust and walk with him. Don't be afraid!

"The world is firmly established." No matter how much shaking, rattling, destruction, devastation, or tumult, God controls what happens. He's got the whole world in his hands. No part of it has slipped out of his hands. Everything happens according to his good plans. Let's trust him for what we can't see or understand or control.

"Your statutes are firm." God's holy, perfect, and complete Word, that he has placed in our hands...has been given to us to guide, direct, show, lead, and speak to us. Let's hold on to it. Let's feed on it daily, as he tells us to do. With his Word, and by the leading of his Spirit, we can get through, we can succeed, we can continue on in life's seemingly, to us anyway, uncertain journey. It's all in his hands. He reigns. We have nothing to fear.

MAY 22

Isaiah 45:22 NCV   All people everywhere, follow me and be saved.

Such a simple statement — but with profound consequences that last forever! The way to a fulfilled life is so simple, and God offers it to everyone, without preference. In addition to a full life, God offers us a secure and joy-filled future — if we will only make the choice to follow him.

Being an exile sounds like a terrible thing. When I left Korea in 1974, to head off to the exciting adventure of college in America, I didn't give much thought to the fact that I was really saying goodbye to the only home I had ever known. Though I've returned to Korea from time to time, and been here longer now, it is no longer my home as it once was. In a very real sense, I have lost my home forever. I also remember, when my parents left Korea after living here for 25 years, my mother's comment that she was tired of having to live out of a suitcase. That surprised me, because Korea had always been my permanent home. But in a very real sense, while she was living overseas, she was in exile from her own home. And, when I left Korea, I felt like I was in exile in America, because it wasn't really my home either! It's a painful thing to live away from what is comfortable, familiar, and important to us. In many ways, during our past 30 years serving with a literature mission, we have been in exile. Moving around from place to place, we have often being living out of a suitcase, not really firmly rooted in our own place. That's hard. And that's what Ezekiel is talking about in chapters 12 & 13 of his book. They were forced into exile, and it was a painful experience being away from all that was familiar and important to them. But, being in exile can also be a good thing. Even though it has a painful aspect to it, I have always felt that not living rooted to this world has actually been a good thing. It has kept us from becoming too firmly attached to this world. It has helped us be less distracted by the things of this world. It has caused and helped us to cling more tightly to what does last and what does stay with us...eternal things, our relationship to God, focusing on God himself. That is a wonderful thing. So, when we feel at times adrift in this world, let's use that experience to cling more closely to God, to what lasts, to what cannot be taken away from us.

MAY 23

During the current year, the pandemic and subsequent quarantine reality have disrupted many things. It has meant that our previous means of staying in Korea is no longer feasible...we have to find another way to live here long term. So, this requires us to head back to the US in order to apply for a new visa from there. As we approach the Christmas season, the schools will close down for a long winter break, and we can be away without too much difficulty. Thus, this is a good time to depart for a while. During the past week or two, we have been meeting with as many of our friends as we can to have one last visit together before we leave. Today was no different. We met a friend, enjoyed a nice lunch together, then decided to take a leisurely walk along the footpath that snakes next to the Han River, which splits the city in two. As we were walking along, we saw a little baby duck in the water. We were discussing the differences between ducks and geese, and their names in English and Korean. Just then, a huge wedge of geese went flying by right over us. The weather is due to turn sharply colder here in the next couple of days, and the geese must have been monitoring the weather report because they seemed in quite a hurry to hightail it out of here. Then another pack of geese flew by overhead, then another, then another, then another. There must have been hundreds of them, all flying in neat formation. It was amazing and beautiful to watch them fly in perfect order, doing so, apparently, with no verbal communication and no planning meetings ahead of time. Somehow they each knew what to do, who was to fly in the lead position, how they were to fly. It was a beautiful demonstration of working together in perfect harmony.

That seems to be what Paul was trying to accomplish in his letter to the Galatians, in chapters 4&5. Paul wanted the people to work together toward the same goals, and he was expressing frustration at their lack of cooperation. Finally, he said, "Look guys, just do what I do. Follow my example. Become like me." In a way, that seems like a slightly arrogant statement for him to tell the people to do. But Paul knew that he had laid down his life for God, for the Gospel, for others. He knew that his own life was not really important to him. And that's what he wanted the people to also do. He was having a hard time explaining it to them, so he just said, "Serve other people. Lay down your life for others. Do everything in love. Let your life be the picture of love. And what should that look like? Your life will be an example of love, patience, kindness, goodness, gentleness..."

Now, what if we all started doing that? What if, suddenly, we all were laying down our lives for others, putting others first, thinking of others as better than ourselves, focusing on others instead of what we want for ourselves. What would we look like? I think it would be a beautiful sight. We would all be living the same way, all following the examples of everyone else, all moving beautifully in the same direction. It would be an impressive sight for all to see. In short, we would probably look like a giant pack of geese, flying south. Maybe, a few folks would even stop and take notice and wonder what it was all about. What do you think? Shall we try it? I will if you will! Let's do it!

MAY 24

> Day/Date Be sure to remember five things to be grateful for every day May 24
>
> Acts 17:28 NIV In him we live and move and have our being.
>
> This is an eloquent statement which is also very profound. It sounds poetic, but it is much more than that. Quite literally, everything that exists is held together and operates only because God gives it the power to do so. And additionally, as God's children, our full and renewed life is only possible because he gives it to us.

Prayers can be very dangerous things. About 20 years ago, for several years, I prayed that God would have his way in my life. I wanted so much to be the person God wanted me to be...that I asked him to have his way with me, whatever that might mean. What happened then? How did God answer my prayers?

I remember as a boy watching Korean women pound grain, until it gradually turned into flour. Using a short beam, held in both hands, they would raise it high, and then bring it down hard on the grain that was sitting in a stone bowl. After some minutes, there would be no grain left...just the powdery flour that they were looking for from their efforts. When I remember the past prayers of mine during those several years, I think of those ladies pounding the grain. That is how God answered my prayers. What happened in the ensuing years after my prayers? We had to close our Christian bookstore, due to the increasing competitiveness of successful operations like Amazon and Barnes & Noble. That was painful because I had enjoyed and loved the bookstore we owned in Tennessee so much, and had hoped it could carry on even after we went overseas to work. Then, I sunk into a decades long dance with depression. Not exactly a dance, of course, but in a way it was, as it clung to me and followed me, step for step. Later, we had a shooting by a Muslim fanatic in our bookstore in Karachi, Pakistan, which was under my supervision...a very traumatic and serious occurrence, especially as we were located in the heart of the Taliban section of the city. Then, my boss, who was the International Director of our mission, and with whom I worked closely, fell to his death, leaving me to keep things going in the office. After that, my parents both died in quick and unexpected succession. And, for the final crushing blow, God allowed my wife to get cancer, which the doctor told us, she would not survive. We had nine children, and the youngest was only three. Probably the best way I could describe myself at that moment was feeling like the crushed and pounded grain in the stone basin, after a few minutes of intense pounding by the Korean ladies in the old days. I had asked God to have his way with me...and he did...he crushed me. Now, why in the world would God do that? Probably because most of us are like rough and unusable raw grain. God looks at us and sees what might be, sees our potential, sees what he wants us to be. And so, he starts to work on us, usually in painful ways.

That's why, when I read the opening verse of Psalm 94, I am stopped in my tracks, so to speak, by these words: "O God, shine forth." It's a prayer, asking God to display himself in our lives, to have his way in our lives, to do what needs to be done, so that we will be useful to him, so that we will become what he made us to be. A few verses later, it says, "Blessed is the man you discipline, O Lord." It sure doesn't at all feel like a blessing, but God says it is. Later, we read about God's consolation and about him being our refuge. Those are true as well. And I can, many years later, see how God has slowly and methodically been working in and on my life. Nearly always, it's painful, nearly always, it is not my chosen path. But God wants us to be better, more loving, more effective, stronger, more mature. And this usually requires a good bit of pounding. I still don't enjoy God's way of working...but, now, as much as ever, I want him to keep working...because I know it's what he wants...and, ultimately, it's what I know (with fear and trembling) that I need. So, Lord, I will continue to pray that dangerous prayer: Have your way with me. Shine forth in my life.

MAY 25

Day/Date   Be sure to remember five things to be grateful for every day.   May 25

Leviticus 8:19-21 NCV   Moses cut the male sheep into pieces. He washed the inner organs and burned the whole sheep on the altar. Its smell was pleasing to the Lord.

Moses was the leader of a great nation of people. Yet he spent much time offering sacrifices to God that perhaps other people could have done. He was demonstrating the importance of obeying God and of spending his life serving God, and also was showing the people that God is holy and is to be revered.

I love a good, true life mystery, and among the best are those of the Israeli secret forces methodically, and for decades, hunting down some of the Nazi leaders on the run, at the end of World War 2. The lengths they will take, the attention to the slightest detail, hanging on and not letting go even as the trail goes cold...it makes for fascinating reading. And you almost begin to feel sorry for the poor Nazis, because you know their days are numbered, you know that the agents hounding them won't give up the chase, you know that eventually they will be caught and brought to justice. That's the same picture we get in Ezekiel 14&15. The Israelites had turned away from God. They had chosen to disobey him, and God declared that they would be brought to justice..."and then they would know that he is the Lord." It would happen. It was a done deal. No use running. No use hiding. The last chapter had already been written, even if we hadn't read it yet. God is a God of justice, of holiness, of perfection. He doesn't just shrug his shoulders at disobedience that seems like it's not such a big deal. His divine nature won't allow him to ignore "little sins". He just doesn't work that way...he can't work that way. So, if I fool myself into imagining that this little slight of hand will slip by his notice...well, it's a bit silly (and tragic), because, in the end, I am only fooling myself. God can't be fooled. He won't be overturned or outmaneuvered. He will have his day. Our lives will get settled. Justice will be done. Poor Nazis...poor us, if we are not covered by Christ's righteousness on our behalf...

MAY 26

Day/Date   Be sure to remember five things to be grateful for every day.   May 26

Psalm 124:8 NCV   Our help comes from the Lord, who made heaven and earth.

This is a powerful statement of truth, and of worship to God. We may have talent, money, strength, and good fortune. But ultimately God is behind and directing all that happens in our lives, including any help that we get. Even the things that we have are because he gave them to us, so it is very wise to thank him for them.

From his writings, it's very apparent that the apostle Paul was well educated and very knowledgeable with languages. And as he grew in his knowledge and understanding of God and living in a relationship with God, Paul expressed and characterized this relationship with superlatives. He just could not quite seem to be able to express fully how magnificent God...and a relationship with God... was. But he sure gave it his best shot as he explained and described who God is. In his letter to the Ephesian church, Paul declares that God has given us every spiritual blessing, and that God has lavished his grace on us. Then he mentions that Christ has been put over everything...for the church. I'm not entirely sure what Paul is saying here (and as his friend, the apostle Peter, reminds us, sometimes Paul is hard to understand...), but what is emphatically clear is that, the church is very, very important to God. Paul's description and words regarding the church remind me of a picture of the church that our pastor shared with me once. He said that whenever we are tempted to criticize someone else in the church, it is like God taps us on the shoulder and says to us, "Just a minute there! Hold on...you're talking about my bride! You do realize that, don't you??" The point is, God loves the church. The church is very precious to him. Given all the bad press we hear about the church coming from every corner today, that can seem surprising to us. I mean, what is it that God sees in the church? What makes it so special? Why does he unload all his blessings on the church? Well, as my pastor reminded me, these are the folks Jesus came to die for. You can bet that they are very precious in his sight. Somehow, we imagine that those in the church are supposed to be perfect. So it's very easy for us to be critical. But God doesn't love us because we're perfect. (Otherwise, he would have no one to love.) He loves us just because he's decided to love us...lavishly, as Paul says. Let's remember that, the next time we are feeling critical of everyone out there. God loves the church. These are his precious people. These are the sheep of his pasture. He doesn't take kindly to people messing with them.

MAY 27

Day/Date Be sure to remember five things to be grateful for every day. May 27

Acts 20:23-24 NCV In every city the Holy Spirit tells me that troubles and even jail wait for me. I don't care about my own life. The most important thing is that I complete the work that Jesus gave me – to tell people the Good News.

What an amazing declaration of faith and focus Paul makes on this occasion. Already he has suffered greatly for sharing the Good News to people. And God tells him that he will continue to suffer. But whatever the cost to him, Paul was determined to keep on telling people God's Message so that they could be saved from being separated from God.

"It's cancer." Simple words...chilling words. Words that change your life forever. In 2003, my wife discovered a worrying lump, that we then had tested. For several anxious days, we awaited the results. The entries in my diary from those days express our anxiety. Following a full day that included giving four training sessions in another city, I returned home in time for our evening appointment with our cancer doctor. He sat us down, brought a nurse in with him, and gave us those words, that, no doubt, he had needed to give to others many times before us. I can still hear those sharp words he enunciated, coming from his mouth. Instantly, the energy went out of my wife's body, and she collapsed next to me. She broke down in tears. Our life would never be the same. A years long battle began, and we did not know what awaited us, did not realize all that would be involved in the fight, did not know how it would affect us, and did not know the outcome. The future was uncertain, the prognosis was very grim at best.

So, what do you do in a situation like that? How do you face it? How can you prepare yourself for a fight for your life? Psalm 95 gives us the answer. This ages ago statement is the best medicine for a life changing cancer moment that has ever been given us. We are told to come to God with thanksgiving. Just as medieval warriors went into battle with quivers full of arrows, we are to approach cancer (or any alarming situation) with a load of thanksgiving. How does giving thanks help us? What does it have to do with a struggle, potentially, to the death?

Compiling a deliberate list of things we are thankful for prepares us for what is ahead. It gives us a healthy, positive, proper attitude. And it gives us a plan of action. All of us have things we can be thankful for. When life is hanging in the balance, being thankful gives us strength and the best attitude to have as we enter the battle. Fear will not help us. Self pity? No. Bitterness, anger, panic? No, no, and no. But thankfulness gives us balance, perspective, calm...and strength. It reminds us that God is in the picture as well. He knows what is happening, and he is walking the journey with us. That gives us strength. It reminds us that we're not alone. It gives us a positive attitude instead of one of fear and panic. Being thankful also affects those around us. My attitude affects my family and friends. It sets the tone for how I face life. It determines the legacy that my life will leave behind, especially to those surrounding me. Preparing a list of what we are thankful for is not only a good idea for a cancer or any other battle we may be faced with. It's also the way we should approach coming into God's presence...whether for my personal devotions and prayers, or for entering a church service or meeting. How would it affect the worship time at church if we all arrived with a thankful attitude? I hope I will do that...I hope we will all do that.

MAY 28

Day/Date Be sure to remember five things to be grateful for every day. May 28

Psalm 19:1 NCV The heavens tell the glory of God, and the skies announce what his hands have made.

Where we live in China, we enjoy some of the most spectacular displays when the sun rises and sets – beautiful colors, shadows, and clouds. Again and again when I watch these heavenly performances I am reminded of God's creative power and greatness at putting all these things in place so we could enjoy them and so he would be glorified by them.

God came knocking again to Ezekiel in chapter 16. I wonder if the prophet was thinking, "Oh boy, what's God going to hammer us with now? How many more different ways can he tell us that we've blown it?" And, yes, that's exactly what God did. He gave a rundown, for the umpteenth time, of all the times Israel had messed up, gone astray, disappointed him. How bad the people were…and with how much fury God was going to deal with them, punish them, set them right. It can make for wearying reading…and frightening reading, as we observe the levels that God's anger and temperature can rise to. But there's something that we can overlook, if we only skim over these words with a sigh. It's the feelings and commitment that are behind the words. God comes once again with a message to Israel…why? Because they are wayward children? Yes, for that reason. But more than that…because he cares deeply about them. If he didn't, then he wouldn't bother going to such repeated lengths to try to get their attention, to get his message across, to shake them up. What he's really communicating is his deep, enduring, long lasting, never ending, pursuing love and grace for his people. That's why he keeps coming back.

This morning I received a message from one of our sons. "Dad, I left you a voice message…" It didn't particularly surprise me. He's good and intentional about connecting with people, about sharing his heart, about speaking messages into other people's lives. This one was no different. Many kind words, thoughtful words, words of thankfulness and grace...just the usual stuff. But what his words really conveyed to me was a secondary message behind the actual words themselves...in the same way that God's messages to Ezekiel and the people conveyed his love and care that were what motivated his words to spill out in the first place. My son's words were the same. They were filled, oozing really, with grace, with thankfulness, with his entire attitude and approach to life...smiling at who God is in his life...and sharing that smile of gladness with others. What a wonderful way to approach life, to respond to life, to communicate what's important in life to others. Sometimes (frequently, really), I wonder what kind of legacy we will leave behind us after our life is finished. I'm pretty sure what my son will leave...a message of thankfulness, of grace, of the blessing of living in God's smile on us. God repeatedly leaves us with that message as well. Even when he chases us in anger...it's really a message of love. He's pursuing us because he cares deeply for us. What kind of message are we leaving for other people through our words, our actions, our attitudes...by our life? Are we leaving a message of anger? Selfishness? Of concern only for the things of this world? I hope we will pause and consider this question. All across the Bible, we find in hundreds of messages, interactions, and lives, a picture of God's grace, his pursuing love, his preoccupation with what is important, with what lasts. Lord, may our lives leave the same message behind us, after our days are all over and spent.

MAY 29

What began as something of a stopgap, short term solution, turned into a 30 year journey, when we decided to take on homeschooling as a temporary tool for a year or two with our oldest child. As it turned out, we somehow ended up with nine children...they just seemed to keep showing up at our door, and it was hard to turn them away. From kindergarten through high school meant that we taught each child for 13 years...which came to a total of over 100 years of schooling, when all the individual school years are added together. My wife was made for teaching, I suppose, with her organization, thoroughness, attention to detail, consistency, enthusiasm... She especially got excited when one of the kids had a science project that demonstrated how something was affected, influenced, or changed by a series of ingredients or variables. Having majored in science, she understood well the factors and dynamics at work, and her enthusiasm would spill over to the kids as she explained or described how and why various reactions were happening, and the results that came about.

If he hadn't become a theologian and missionary, I suppose Paul would have made a good scientist as well. His excitement comes through in Ephesians 2 & 3, as he explains the results of Jesus' death and resurrection, the outcome as it affects us. Listen to the words Paul uses in describing God's "experiment ", if you will.

"God is so rich in mercy, and he loved us so much."

"The incredible wealth of his grace and kindness."

"We are God's masterpiece."

"Our hostility towards each other was put to death."

"We are carefully joined together, becoming a holy temple."

"May you understand how long, how high, and how deep his love is."

"God is able to accomplish infinitely more than we might ask or think."

It's no wonder Paul got excited about what Jesus did. This was no experiment to show something. Jesus actually accomplished what we most needed. He made us alive again after we were dead because of sin. That is how much God loves us. That is what he did for us. That reality is what God wants us to live with, and by, and for. It is what makes all the difference. Thanks be to God for his indescribable gift!

MAY 30

Acts 21:13 NCV   Why are you crying and making me sad? I am not only ready to be tied up in Jerusalem, I am ready to die for the Lord Jesus!

Following the Lord is not easy and can be quite costly to us. Paul's friends knew that he was likely heading to certain death when he left them, so naturally they were weeping. But Paul told them not to cry. Why? Because he was focused on the long term, the end result of his efforts, which would be that many more would learn the Good News and be saved from a life of darkness. With that goal before him, he was ready to face any difficulty.

There's one name that always brings a smile to the memories of my siblings and me...the "Little Elder". I never knew the name of this old man who was perhaps four feet eight inches tall. We just called him by his nickname. Even as a boy, I remember him seeming to be awfully short. But when I picture him in my mind, Teddy Roosevelt's grinning face is the image I see. He just always seemed to be full of joy. I don't know what his real job was, where he lived, anything about his family. But, for some reason, he loved coming to visit Dad, to spend time with him, to pray with him. You might have thought he was coming into God's presence, he was so excited to see Dad. And whenever we caught a glimpse of him pushing his old bike up the hill toward our house, we kids got excited, too, running to each other and shouting, "The Little Elder is coming! The Little Elder is coming!" We were excited to see him, and for some reason, he was excited to come see us. We were excited because he always brought us a wrapped up scarf full of the biggest chestnuts we had ever laid eyes on, or the juiciest, plumpest persimmons ever to be had anywhere. And if that made him happy, well, we certainly weren't going to deny him the privilege of bringing them to us.

I think of the Little Elder when I read the verses of Psalm 96. There is enthusiasm and excitement in these words, just like we saw in the face of that sweet man, so many years ago. This psalm invites us to come into God's presence in a number of different ways: singing, proclaiming his Good News, publishing his Word (which is what our literature mission has been doing for many decades), telling others, bringing offerings...

Apparently, God loves to welcome us in any variety of different ways...they're all good with him, all welcomed by him. The Little Elder came, pedaling his bike and bringing gifts...and I'm sure that his offering was pleasing to God (not that we complained, either). God delights for us to come in any number of ways. We don't have to all be Billy Grahams...we can be Little Elders just as well. How about you? How about me? How do we come to God? He is waiting to welcome and receive us...just as we are, with whatever offering we bring...he just loves to receive us...and no doubt his angels scramble to him, telling God, "So and so is coming! So and so is coming!" I don't know what the angels get out of our visit, but I'm sure they get excited, knowing that our Heavenly Father is also very excited. So, what are we waiting for?!? Let's go into his presence.

MAY 31

The summer we were on furlough, when I was in ninth grade, we stayed with my grandparents at their summer cottage in North Carolina. My good buddy from my hometown in Korea was there at the same time, so we were able to enjoy palling around together. That meant curling up on a bed, straining and listening to the Atlanta Braves getting clobbered once again, making the rounds to all the nearby Coke machines, checking for stray quarters…I mean, what kind of paradise was this, where free money was just there for the taking?? And occasionally, we got into other mischief. One day, as we were walking by the big old auditorium building, there stood a small apple tree loaded down with fruit. A few of the apples had fallen off the tree, making for the perfect baseball practice. Over near the auditorium stood an old stone water fountain, the perfect target to hurl our baseball apples at. I let a pitch fly…high, as it turned out, and it sailed right through the glass pane window which was situated just above and behind the water fountain. The apple disappeared with a smash, and instinctively, without a thought, we both took off running. Eventually, I got back home…and started feeling guilty. I confessed to my parents what I had done, hoping they might smooth it over and tell me not to worry. Nope, didn't happen. They told me I had to go myself to visit the austere old man in charge of the auditorium and surroundings, and confess my misdeed to him. So,

I headed off, and approached his office with fear and trembling, again hoping (how careless of me...) for mercy and a wave of the hand that would set right whatever problem I might have created. Again, no. This was a real problem we had before us. I had broken a window pane, someone had to pay to have it fixed, and obviously, that someone was me. So, I paid the ten dollars, as I remember it, and turned and left, feeling a bit chastised.

That was an important lesson for me, which, clearly, I have never forgotten. The lesson is this: the one who sins in the one who will be punished. It's the exact message we are given in Ezekiel 17&18...an important truth we all have to learn as we navigate life. My parents won't always be there to bail me out, I can't shuffle off the responsibility for my actions on someone else. I am the one who will answer for my actions. God tells us this...and the sooner in life we learn it, more than likely, the less painful it will be for us as we take the lesson on board. How sad it is, to see at times, someone who still, as an adult, has not learned this lesson, who still imagines that he can offload his responsibility on someone else. God made us to live, to live fully...and that includes making choices, being creative, receiving his blessings...and being responsible for our actions. The sooner we learn and accept that, the better.

MONTH 6

Quarantine day 6…

Thoughts from Psalms and Proverbs:

*Immersing ourselves in God's Word is like putting on armor.

*Following God will not be easy…but he will be with us.

*When we follow God, we are his treasured possessions.

*God delights for us to come into his presence.

*God engulfs us in love.

*God's greatness is visible…can we see it?

*God does what is right...but often what he does is not the way we would do it.

*God sees every single person on earth.

*Keep our focus on God.

*The Almighty God hears and listens to us. He loves to rescue us.

*The universe shouts about its Maker.

*God's Word is perfect and gives us wisdom, joy, warning, enlightenment, and meaning.

*Trust God even when we can't see why we should.

*God loves us and can be trusted...at the same time, we still have to live in this fallen, broken, troubled world.

*God makes us safe...not our circumstances.

*God covers our sins...but we still live with our sinful nature, in this sinful world.

*God has good plans for us.

*God's eternal plans will come to pass.

*God is always with us.

*God wants our gifts and our thanks...not because he needs them...but because they are pleasing offerings to him.

*Confess to God, not because he doesn't know already, but because we need to confess.

*God rescues us in our troubles, not necessarily from them.

*God is all powerful...and all loving.

*God delights to care for us and save us.

*God holds us...even when we aren't aware of it.

*In spite of all he does for us, we choose to rebel against God.

*Tithe to show God that you love him.

*God disciplines us because he loves us.

August 27, 2020
The Lord is my
Shepherd.

PSALMS

BOOK I

Psalms 1–41

Psalm 1

[1] Blessed is the one
    who does not walk[a] in step with the wicked
or stand in the way that sinners take
    or sit[b] in the company of mockers,
[2] but whose delight[c] is in the law of the LORD,[d]
    and who meditates[e] on his law day and night.
[3] That person is like a tree[f] planted by streams of water,[g]
    which yields its fruit[h] in season

1:1 [a] Pr 4:14 [b] Ps 26:4;
Jer 15:17
1:2 [c] Ps 119:16,35
[d] Ps 119:1 [e] Jos 1:8
1:3 [f] Ps 128:3 [g] Jer 17:8
[h] Eze 47:12

JUNE 1

Day/Date *Be sure to remember five things to be grateful for every day.* June 1

Deuteronomy 10:12-13 NCV Serve the Lord your God with your whole being, and obey the Lord's commands and laws that I am giving you today for your own good.

In the same way that we give rules and guidelines to our own children, God also gives us laws to protect us, to provide justice and righteousness in our relationships, and so that we can show our trust in God by obeying them. Because he is good and his laws are good, we will also be more happy and content as we follow God's regulations.

I have to admit I was proud of my wife (fiancée at the time) when we graduated from college. With a 4.0 and a double major in two sciences, I knew she was going places. She had her eye set on medical school, which certainly made her father very happy. Unfortunately, though, at just the wrong time, I came along and messed up the best laid plans and completely upset the apple cart. We decided to get married instead. We both wanted to have children, and she realized that for her, being both a Mom and a doctor would be too much for her. Both would require 100% of her time. And so she chose to be a Mom. That was over 40 years ago. My wife reminds me of what the apostle Paul says to us in Ephesians 4. He had been explaining to the believers in Ephesus, in his wordy sort of way, about all the amazing privileges and blessings and rewards we have as Christians, using all the greatest superlatives he can muster in his discourse. Paul, of anyone in the Bible, was a real scholar, highly educated and trained, privileged as a leader of the Jews. In a very real sense, he had the best that life could offer. And then he met Jesus, and his whole apple cart got turned upside down, too. Not only did he throw it all to the wind, he didn't even care to take on the rightfully due status he deserved as being the major leader of the early church. No, he just called himself a slave of God. Serving God, belonging to him, giving up everything for the Gospel...all that was so much better than any status or position, that he would rather call himself a slave and serve Christ, than anything else. That was far better, far more worthwhile, far more desirable, than anything else he could possibly imagine. Everything else, in comparison, was just rubbish. And that's where the comparison with my wife comes in. She loves science. She loves the discovery and research involved in it. She loves serving people. It all fits her just as well as Cinderella's glass slipper fit her. She would have been a great doctor. But, my wife threw it all away. Compared to being a Mom...well, there was no comparison. Being a Mom was also what she was made for. Nearly 40 years after our first child showed up on the scene, she's still 100% a Mom. That's what she thrives in, that's what brings her joy, all else is rubbish by comparison. What an amazing lady!

JUNE 2

Day/Date   Be sure to remember five things to be grateful for every day: June 2

Romans 1:5 NCV   God gave me the special work to lead people of all nations to believe and obey.

Jesus gave us the privilege and task of sharing God's Good News with those who have not heard it. Although it is what all of God's children should be involved in, Paul, as single-minded as he was, considered it his own special privilege and responsibility. And so also should we.

The Himalayas are truly stunning mountains, the greatest in the world. They soar right up into the skies, with snow covering their tops... For seven years, in Dali, China, we were privileged to live nestled against their feet. During the summer months, it was the rainy season, which kept that time of year pleasantly cool. Clouds would start to spill over the mountains, which were to our west, in June, and they would just keep pouring over until they covered the whole landscape. Then the mountains would disappear from view for much of the next several months. During the winter months, the skies were clear and bright blue, and the mountains sparkled under the intense, high elevation sun. They were dazzling, and I never tired of sitting in our living room, gazing out the picture window, looking up at that magnificent creation. It's interesting how, during the stormy summer, you could almost forget that the mountains were even there. All you saw were the clouds, the rain, the storms. When the clouds eventually lifted and scurried away till next year, they left behind the spectacular mountains once again...which of course were there all along. Psalm 97 reminds us of the same phenomenon with God. During intense times of trouble, testing, pain, and hardship, God seems to become obscured from view. We wonder where he is, why he isn't with us. But, then, when we regain our balance and our equilibrium, we realize that God is still with us, that he has been right there all along, that he never left us after all. And this psalm tells us the same message: that God is here, he is ruling, he has control over the whole world. So, even when our view becomes hazy or shortened, we don't need to worry. He's still there, he's still on the throne, he still knows what's happening...and one day we will again see him more clearly.

JUNE 3

Day/Date   Be sure to remember five things to be grateful for every day.   June 3

Psalm 32:10 NCV   The Lord's love surrounds those who trust him.

This is a picture of a parent carefully holding and protecting and surrounding his child with his loving arms, which provide the safest place that the child can be. God tells us that he also surrounds us with his loving and protective arms.

Have you ever observed an autopsy? I don't suppose many of us have. One of the perks, if you will, of growing up in a Third World country where your Dad was the Director of a Christian hospital...was that you got to see and participate in some pretty interesting things. I remember, as a teenager, watching two surgeries, in particular. One was of a lung cancer, the other was stomach cancer. During the lung cancer surgery, I was a bit startled at how barbaric the whole thing seemed to be, to one untrained and unused to such a thing, as I certainly was not. The doctors seemed to be joking around as if they were sitting around a table playing cards. They used some big spreader contraction thing (which no doubt has some sophisticated scientific name, but to me looked like it had just been carried in from the garage) to pull apart two ribs so they could get a closer look at the lungs. One of the ribs cracked in the process. (Now, I'm really not saying all this in any way to be critical of the medical profession. I'm sure they know what they're doing, what they need to do, and what the limits to their joking and so on are, as well. Probably pilots, policemen, firemen, and others joke around to maintain their sanity from time to time also.) Then, they took one look at the lungs, saw cancer everywhere, and realized there was no hope...so they went ahead and just stitched him back up. Later, I saw the same man in the recovery room as he began to come to...and thought of the terrible news of no hope that he would soon be greeted with. The stomach cancer surgery also looked rather barbaric to my utterly uneducated eye. At one point, the doctor reached in and pulled out a long strand of the intestines. Goodness, I thought! I started to get lightheaded, and they barked at me to go lean against the wall so they wouldn't have to tend to me instead of their real patient. Needless to say, that was not only my first experience at watching these kinds of surgeries, it was also my last. Whew...I never wanted to be a doctor! It certainly is remarkable how different we look on the outside...compared to how we look on the inside of our bodies!

Now, Israel had the same infliction of blindness that we perhaps have as well. In Ezekiel 19&20, God is declaring to the people that they had seriously sinned against him. They thought they were all fine and dandy, just like a cancer patient may look on the outside. But they had a serious spiritual cancer that was affecting them, and they were in denial. For their own sakes, for the saving of their eternal destinies, God had to be straight with them. He had to deliver the bad news...which, of course, he followed with good, hopeful, restorative news. It was not the end of the world, there was hope...but they did have to take their cancer seriously, they did have to accept the needed treatment for their ailment. And, of course, it's the same with us. One thing that's a little hard about growing old is that, instead of arriving at a point where you no longer sin or make bad decisions (as if that were possible), instead, it seems that you only become more and more aware of your sinfulness and of all the places you fall short...a little like waking up from a surgery, only to discover that the outlook is worse than you had assumed just a few hours before. So, who can deliver us from the mess we're in? Thank God...he loves us and has already provided the solution, the cure, for all our diseases.

JUNE 4

> **Day/Date** Be sure to remember five things to be grateful for every day. June 4
>
> Romans 3:24 NCV — All need to be made right with God by his grace, which is a free gift.
>
> Because God is completely holy and pure, he can only accept and have a relationship with those who are also pure. All of us humans have been contaminated and stained by sin, so we are incapable of coming to God on our own. But since he loves us so much, he provided the way for us to come to him by sacrificing his own Son on our behalf, as only he was adequate to take the punishment for our disobedience.

As a teenager, I used to love watching, and keeping up with, major league baseball. It was a big part of my life at the time. Occasionally, on special family days or other events, the kids of the players would show up on the field, decked out to look just like their Dads. Man, how lucky they were, I thought. Look who their Dad is! And they look just like him. But, of course, the similarity stopped right there. While the Dad could hit home runs and snag impossible fly balls, the kids were just as silly and fragile looking as any other kid on the block. We definitely look the same way as those little kids if we are ever compared with God. I mean, how could we possibly be confused with, compared with, even mentioned in the same breath with, the Almighty God of the universe? Well, as crazy as it sounds, apparently, God thinks we can be. In Ephesians 5, God tells us: "I want you to be just like me! I've filled you with love, I gave you my Son as a sacrifice and as an example…now, I want you to be just like me!" Well, in addition to being pretty crazy, these words are spoken in great love to us. It's like those little kids on the baseball fields. They were nothing like their Dads. But the Dads wanted their sons to be just like them…to look like them, to copy them, to grow up in their footsteps. Now, I'm pretty sure God doesn't need glasses. And, knowing me inside and out, as he does, I know that he knows that

I'm dead in the water, nothing like him. I don't care how much wishful thinking he might have...I'll never be like him. So, really, the only explanation for his statement for us to be like him...is love. God loves us so much that he tells us, "Come along! Follow me. Copy my example. Just be like me. I love you so much...I know you can do it!" Remarkable...that's the only way I know to describe it. God's love for me...for you...is remarkable.

JUNE 5

My grandmother, Nai Nai, lived to the very ripe old age of 97. She was a very strong woman, having lived and thrived through the decades of turmoil, up-heaval, evacuation, and loss in China in the early 1900s. But, as the years passed, it became increasingly difficult for her to live so long. Her daughter, my Mom, tenderly cared for her in this latter years, but, still, all her seven siblings had predeceased her, all her contemporaries had passed, she had no friends left. Fi-nally, at the end, she firmly told my mother to just let her go, to not hold on to her so tightly to this earth. I remember being rather surprised that she would want so much to die. I have now lived about two thirds as long as she did, and increasingly, I can understand the feelings of my Nai Nai in her last years. More and more, I'm getting weary of this old world, and I feel ready to move on to my heavenly, my real, home. It sometimes seems that every direction we turn, we see sadness and tragedy. Here are a few examples I've seen only recently:

I met a 19 year old US soldier in the Seoul airport the other day, stationed in Korea, but heading home after receiving, just the day before, the news that her older sister, who had four small children, was shot and killed by her partner.

I read the story of a nine year old, who recently lost both her arms, following a car accident.

A friend of ours, with three kids, dropped dead after a routine run. He was 41.

On my Facebook page this week, the story of a six year old girl came up. She spends her days in the sweltering tropical sun, along with her mother, pounding bricks into pieces for less than a dollar daily.

An article about prostitutes, written by a photographer who documented their lives, shared that, in South Asia, they would earn about $1-5 per client...until their usefulness had worn them out.

And the stories and heartbreaks go on. All of these make me feel ready to leave this earth, sooner rather than later. I wonder if the Israelites, controlled and beat down by the Romans in Jesus' day, felt the same way...looking for a way out, looking for someone to rescue them. Jesus appeared, saying he was their Savior, but disappointingly, he didn't release them from the Romans. Interestingly, when we look at Psalm 98, we read the words that God has already won the victory. His righteousness has been revealed. That sounds like a prophecy of what Jesus, in fact, did accomplish. He came and conquered evil. So, a thousand years before Jesus arrived, God already knew and revealed to us through these words, what Jesus would achieve...it was already a done deal, and the psalmist knew it, as well. This truth, that God has already won the victory over evil, can give us hope in these sometimes dark and evil days that seem to contain tragedy in every direction we turn. Yes, we are still very much living with the residual effects of evil in the world...and those effects are not to be discounted. They are terrible. But, God has already triumphed over evil, and we can hope for the day, as my Nai Nai did, when it will become fully evidenced in all of our lives. Amen! Come, Lord Jesus!

JUNE 6

Some years ago, I read about a Christian lady who decided to send her son out of the house (as in, sent him packing), because he just would not cooperate or follow the family guidelines...he was becoming too unruly to be part of the family any longer. It startled me that she would take such a drastic step toward her own son. Was it right for a Christian to banish her own son? Could I ever do that? Thankfully, I never had to take that step. All nine of my kids were such jewels...(well, at least occasionally they were...). I do sometimes wonder, though, whether I could bring myself to take that step. Could I actually ever come to a point where I would turn my back on my own child? It seems so cruel, so final, so judgmental... But I knew that lady well enough to know that her action was not done out of cruelty or hate. In fact, it was done for the opposite reason. It was done out of a deep love for her son, a love that demanded that she apply seemingly severe and harsh treatment to the situation. She had to get her son's attention. He had to be made to realize that he was headed down the wrong path. He had to be stopped in his tracks and turned around. And this required a painful treatment plan.

Sometimes I've heard skeptics say that the God of the Old Testament is a cruel, mean, hateful tyrant, who goes around punishing and hurting people. A superficial glance can bring us to that conclusion. And that's what we can think is happening in Ezekiel 21&22, where God says, "I'm your enemy, and I'm coming after you with a sword!" Is that really the true picture here? God makes it abundantly clear, over and over and over again, what he really thinks of us. "I have loved you with an everlasting love," he says. "My love for you stretches as far as the east is from the west." In other words, his love is too profound, too great, to be measured. And, I have no doubt at all, that was the same thing that mother was doing with her son. Her love was so deep, that she was willing to prescribe the excruciating treatment that was required in that situation. It was painful for her son, it was painful for her. But she knew that it was what he needed. It was required to rescue his life. It's the same way God dealt with folks in the Old Testament...it's the same way he deals with us today. Our sin and rebellion demands harsh treatment. It's the only way he can save us from the destructive path we've chosen. What appears on the surface to be a mean-spirited action, is actually God reaching out to us in love. What is God doing in my life today? In your life? When painful things come my way, what is he teaching me? In what way, and for what reason, is he working to get my attention? (And doing, out of love...) Lord, open our eyes to your love, to your working in our lives. Help us to be in tune with what you are doing. Amen.

JUNE 7

The letters of Paul to the Ephesians and Philippians were written to encourage his audiences (including us, 2,000 years later!), and they were both written at about the same time, while he was in prison in Rome. He mentions his situation in his letters, but what he says may surprise us...and almost certainly is not what we would write, if we were in the same situation. One verse in particular, Ephesians 6:5, can sound shocking to our ears, and I'm sure it has many times been used to justify immoral behavior. Paul says, "Slaves, obey your masters." Did you hear that? It looks like Paul takes it for granted that slavery is OK; after all, he doesn't condemn it. He only commands the persecuted to obey their persecutors. Wow! That sounds crazy. But, Paul's point is not what it may first appear to be saying. A little further down in the chapter, and continuing over into Philippians 1, Paul says that his own imprisonment (which clearly he believed was unjustified) served a good purpose. As he obeyed God, God used his unpleasant and wrongful circumstances for the carrying out of his good plans. So, Paul was willing to lay aside his own comfort, even to ignore justice for himself...so that God's eternal, good plans could be carried out in other people's lives. And when he tells slaves to obey their masters, it's for the same reason...not because slavery is right in any way, but so that God's good purposes can come to pass, even in bad circumstances. It's amazing the length to which Paul was willing to go, the extent to which he laid down his life, for the sake of others' eternal destinies. Could I say the same? Would I be willing to give up things that are rightfully mine...for the sake of someone else's good? That's a challenging question...but it sounds like what Paul is telling us to do. Lord, help us to seek your ways before our own, the eternal good of others before what is rightfully my own.

JUNE 8

Day/Date Be sure to remember five things to be grateful for every day. June 8

Philippians 1:21 NCV To me the only important thing about living is Christ.

Of course Paul cared deeply for his family and friends, his books, his work, and other things as well. But compared to these things that pass away, living for Christ was the only real, lasting, and important thing in his life. Paul knew that living for Christ would make an eternal difference in many lives and would be the only thing in his own life that was permanent.

When we come across Ezekiel 23, its words are hard to read. We wish, perhaps, that we could just erase it from the Bible. In terms too graphic to repeat, it describes the worst depravity of a prostitute...two, actually. But, there it is, in God's holy book. This chapter lays out for us the horrible betrayal of God's people as they turned away from him to follow other gods, other idols. In God's eyes, their behavior and actions are like that of a prostitute, but not just any prostitute who sells herself...rather, like a deranged prostitute who pursues her trade with eagerness and relish, looking for people to turn herself over to. An awful picture. On occasion, I've passed a prostitute by the side of the road. Even as a boy in Korea, once or twice I recall finding myself on the wrong street, and seeing young ladies hanging about, calling and cackling at passersby, and especially at these unsuspecting kids who happened down the wrong lane. When I encounter someone like this, I can't help but wonder what happened to them. How did they get to this point in life? What brought them to this destination? Where was their family when they needed it? Why was no one around looking out for and protecting them? It's bad enough when someone has no one to protect them and then falls through society's cracks. But, it's something else indeed, when a person knows what they're doing, and with eyes open, marches down such a path. And that's what Israel did, as it's described in Ezekiel. They knew God, they had experienced his protection...and they turned and decided to walk in the other direction. So, God, in this chapter, lays out their deprived behavior, and states that their day of reckoning had arrived. They were in for real trouble now.

When something like this happens in the world, I wonder how excruciating it must be for the parents, if they are around and aware of what's happening. How agonizing it must be for them to watch their child travel down this awful path. God made us for blessing. He made us for a relationship with him. He wanted us to be fulfilled in the greatest meaning of the word. But many of us choose to turn and walk away. How that must hurt his father heart. How that must grieve and pain him. Yes, he punishes such behavior. But, it's not with any relish that he does so. It's with grief and sorrow at what might have been, at having to punish his very own creation. What an awful picture, what an awful scenario. How much better, far better, infinitely better, if we would all just choose to walk the path of grace and joy and love that God desires for us all along! Let's keep telling folks of this possibility, this reality...especially to those who seem to have fallen through the cracks.

JUNE 9

I'm not sure why, but the words of Psalm 100 take me back nearly 50 years. It was the summer of 1973, Bangladesh was a new country, recently broken away from West Pakistan. The needs were very great there, and my medical doctor father wanted to investigate the situation, as he felt that his 25 years in Korea were coming to a close. I was the last child at home, so he let me tag along as he scouted out the needs there, on our way to a summer in the US, as my oldest brother was getting married. Bangladesh was utterly different from Korea, being in the tropics, maintaining a hint of the British empire, with many educated people speaking English. Following their war for independence, the people were still struggling to get on their feet. We found the quaint little Shalamar Hotel to stay at, with its seven guest rooms, in the capital city, then known as Dacca (now Dhaka). As he was roaming around the city, my father encountered an Australian missionary, and this kind man invited us to come spend a night at his home in the north of the country, in Mymensingh. So, we hopped aboard his Land Rover jeep and headed north through the jungles. There seemed to be people everywhere in this small, crowded country, even out in the jungle, where you wouldn't expect to see much sign of life. Finally, we arrived at our host's home, a welcoming oasis after the journey. I stepped outside to look around...and a curious sight met my eyes. On top of a nearby house, men were working to repair the flat roof. But what was interesting was the man standing next to the men. Our host told us that the roofers wouldn't work without this all important man, and that he was paid a good bit more than they were. Standing out in the blazing tropical sun, this tall man wearing a long lungi (which appears to be something like a skirt to the uninitiated eye) was holding a large black umbrella...and singing. I can still hear his tune and words today, 50 years later. He was the workers' accompanying singer (I don't know what they called him, officially.), and they would pound and toil along with his music. They would join in on something like a refrain. Without him, they wouldn't work. What an interesting sight, a strange world to me, still fresh in my memory.

Psalm 100 also talks about singing, coming into God's presence singing. Why should we sing? What do we have to sing about? Singing conveys or expresses our heart joy and thanks that is rather unique. And these few verses tell us to sing before God because he cares for us like a shepherd, he never stops loving us, he is always faithful to us. Perhaps, as well, when we come to him singing, we are better prepared for the work he has for us to do, as were those laborers I observed in far off Mymensingh.

JUNE 10

Day/Date Be sure to remember five things to be grateful for every day. June 10

1 Timothy 6:6 NCV Serving God does make us very rich.

In the world's eyes, my father was a relatively simple man who was unremarkable in terms of his lifestyle and wealth. However, he considered himself rich because he belonged to God and had the great privilege of sharing God's love with so many. And truly he was a contented and wealthy man in terms of God's spiritual blessings, which were heaped upon him as he spent his life serving God.

It's interesting watching animals work...I mean wild animals, not something like cows plowing or horses carrying burdens. Especially creatures like birds, bees, ants, or chipmunks...they can be fascinating to observe. Two things I notice about many of them: they are very, very busy and hardworking; and, oddly, perhaps, they appear to be content. They don't seem to take many coffee breaks, and you don't hear them grumbling too often...perhaps that's what separates them from us!

Paul, in his letters, talks about athletes and soldiers...we need to be like them. I don't know why he didn't use the example of animals (unless he did, and I'm just forgetting...). They actually seem like the perfect fit for what Paul was talking about at the end of Philippians and the beginning of Colossians. He says that we have all we need in Philippians 4...in other words, what's to complain about? If we have everything we need, do we need to complain? Should we be complaining? And if we have everything we need, well, then, there's nothing to do, right? We can just sit back and relax. Strangely, though, after telling us he has all he needs (and stating that we also do), Paul begins Colossians by telling us that he's busy as...well, a bee or an ant (except that he forgets to use those examples, so I'm providing them for him). He has all he needs...but he stays as busy as possible, working as hard as he can. Does that seem like a contradiction? Maybe. But Paul tells us that just like the wild animals around us, we have all that we need (and have nothing to complain about), but at the same time, we have a job that should keep us busy from sunup to sundown. So, what is that all important job that we have to do? Well, now that I have your curiosity piqued...you'll just have to check it out for yourself...it's right there in the last two verses of Colossians 1...on page 2030 in my study Bible, if that's a help to you. Better check it out. Paul says it's urgent!

JUNE 11

2 Corinthians 4:8 NCV We have troubles all around us, but we are not defeated.

This statement reminds me of the military general who, when surrounded by the enemy, considered it an opportunity to attack in any direction. Indeed, this life does bring us many troubles, as Paul certainly experienced. But he knew that his work would last, and that final victory is ours— and we also can know that with certainty.

One of my favorite books is Billy Graham's autobiography, "Just as I am." I'm not quite sure what we might expect from a world renowned leader of the church, but one thing he isn't, is "high and mighty", too lofty to relate to us common-ers... He writes as if you are sitting across from him in the living room of his log cabin in the North Carolina mountains, reminiscing about this person and that, one encounter and experience after another. Never mind that he met and rubbed shoulders with the greatest leaders and figures of his day, he never managed to shed the common country boy (in a good sense!) way of chatting with anyone. And he didn't mind making himself look a little silly. He recounted the story of once returning home from an appointment filled day. Exhausted, he curled up, fast asleep, in the back of the car that was being driven by a friend. They stopped for fuel along the way, and as the car stopped humming along, Billy woke up and got out to use the restroom. When he returned to the car...it was gone! His driver buddy had taken off with Billy still sound asleep in the back, or so he thought. Billy had to then ask the shop attendant to use his phone, as he explained what happened to the man. The funny thing is, the man at the counter would not believe him that he was really Billy Graham...a somewhat comical encounter that perhaps more than a few celebrities have experienced along the way. Another story he told that I also enjoyed was when he was involved in the development of the Lausanne Conference, held in Amsterdam (if my memory serves me right), for the encouragement of third world pastors from around the globe. In addition to serving them with various ministry opportunities, the event also provided a clothing room for those that it could be a help to. Mr. Graham came by the room one day to see how things were going. While there, he encountered a man from a country in Africa, and struck up a conversation with him. Thinking that the man probably had never had the privilege of a good education, Billy asked him if he had had any schooling. The man replied, "Uh, yes, I received my graduate degree from Oxford..." Talk about feeling chastised and receiving the lesson of not judging a book by its cover, Billy Graham felt very chastised by that encounter...and was happy to share it with us for a good laugh at his own expense.

But there was another thing that I remember and that really impressed me about what Billy shared. At the same time as he was rising in prominence, quite a few other religious voices were also gaining visibility and recognition, due to the new medium of television. Tragically, a number of these leaders fell badly, due to a lack of integrity or accountability. But, Billy, in his book, said, and I will never forget this, that any time he had an important decision to make (like, probably every day!), he would contact at least five trusted friends and acquaintances to get their feedback and advice on the issue at hand. With as many people fawning all over you all the time, as he must have had, it would be a huge temptation, in that position, to begin to believe that you were great enough to "handle things", that you really didn't need to get other folks' advice, that you really knew better anyway. And that is exactly the temptation that many others fell into. But Billy Graham always knew his own fallibility. He knew he couldn't trust himself to always be right or wise or sensible. He needed others speaking truth into his life as well. And, in large measure due to that understanding and practice, his ministry maintained its integrity. He was able to continue, throughout his life, to speak truth into millions of people's lives.

Although he later stumbled badly himself, King David in Psalm 101 expresses the same sentiment. He says that he will surround himself with faithful companions, those who will hold him to account. What a wise decision for any of us to make. Who we spend time with, surround ourselves with, commit ourselves to...these are the folks who will color and shape our lives. They, to a large degree, will become the influences that determine the kind of life we live and the legacy we leave behind. That is something that is well worth each of us giving

serious thought to...

JUNE 12

Day/Date Be sure to remember five things to be grateful for every day. June 12

Ephesians 1:17-18 NCV Asking the Father to give you wisdom to know him better. I pray that you will know the hope to which he has called us and how rich and glorious are the blessings God has promised his holy people. What a wonderful prayer and a great example to us of how we should ask God to bless, build, and mature others so they will become more like Christ. Let's pray for each other, that God will work in us to become the people he wants us to be.

The other day, I had a bit of a heated discussion with one of our sons about the conditions some people have to live in...and what needs to be done about it... This always seems to be a major issue in politics, in society, in education... Our experiences and our perspective certainly do temper and color how we feel about these things. I made the exaggerated point to my son that if I drive a Cadillac, and am moaning and groaning about having to drive it because all my neighbors are cruising in Lamborghinis...well, I still do own a Cadillac, after all! And, those of us in the industrialized West are a little bit like that. We have a friend whose relatives in Africa struggle to survive...to live without electricity and running water, to have enough daily food to eat...and, compared to them, I, at the very least, am driving a Cadillac (even if my car tells me it's really a Honda)... Sometimes when I talk to assembled groups, I will refer to the parable of the talents, where Jesus not only says that God (for whatever reason, known only to him) entrusts us each with different amounts of talents (or gifts, advantages, strengths, or money)....he also has a day scheduled when we will report to him about how we made use of those talents he placed in our hands...and we will be rewarded (or otherwise), accordingly. That's a very sobering truth to ponder...and I shudder to think about how we sometimes make use of these talents that God has placed in our hands.

Ezekiel 27&28 is addressing the very same question. The magnificent city of

Tyre (between modern day Beirut and the Sea of Galilee, but over on the Mediterranean coast) had been lavished with the greatest gifts and advantages from God. I expect that God loves beauty and creativity, and that sometimes he just pours these things out onto different people and places. At any rate, Tyre received more than it's fair share. But, sadly, the great seaport did the same thing many of us perhaps do...let it all go to their head. They began to believe that their greatness lay in themselves...rather than in what God had bestowed on them. They turned far away from God, and their appointed day of accounting was about to come due. In our day, when I talk to groups, I tell them that compared to the one, five, or ten talents that most people have been given, we have had 100 talents placed in our hands. How can that be, you may ask, as you drive by in your Honda? Well, because no other generation in the history of humanity has had such an abundance of God's Word at its fingertips, in the way that we have. Most previous generations didn't even have access to all of God's Word. I have dozens of Bibles of every stripe and color on my bookshelves. In addition, we have all sorts of phenomenal products at our fingertips (Thank you, Amazon!), unimagined transportation possibilities (I'm still struggling with jet lag now, because we just flew from Korea to the US in a dozen plus hours, an incomprehensible possibility only a couple of generations ago), the ability to reach and touch the whole world in a way never imagined before. Talk about talents entrusted to us...we are able to share God's Message with countless people around the world today by means that were impossible not so long ago. The real question is, what are we doing about it? With it? God apparently saw in us the quality of being able to participate in his great plans of reaching the world...because he placed all these talents into our laps like he's never done before, with anyone else, ever! Now, before we let that great privilege all go to our already expanded craniums...let's remember daily...God is a savvy investor...and he will be expecting a return on his investments. I have to say, that does scare me at times...what am I doing with what he has put in my hands?

JUNE 13

Day/Date Be sure to remember five things to be grateful for every day June 13

2 Corinthians 4:17 NCV We have small troubles for a while now, but they are helping us gain an eternal glory that is much greater than the troubles.

It is impressive to observe the punishment that professional athletes put themselves through for the possible hope of winning an event and receiving fleeting satisfaction and recognition. How much smaller are our difficulties when we consider the sure promise of a much greater reward that will last forever.

For being the simple frontier rail splitter that he was, Abraham Lincoln turned out to be an amazing and unexpected President. Arriving on the scene at the absolutely worst possible time in the nation's history, when our hinges were coming unglued, still, this simple, plain man was able to see clearly the issues at hand, hold onto what was critically important, and see the fight through to the end while the world was crumbling down around him. What was perhaps equally remarkable was that this supreme leader of the land didn't see himself as any better or even an inch above anyone else. He was the true public servant in that he saw himself as living to be a servant to everyone, not in any way taking on board for himself many of the privileges that I certainly would have in his position. And to that end, he did something truly extraordinary. He held office hours for the common folk. Ordinary citizens could walk into his office at 1600 Pennsylvania Avenue and unburden themselves of the seemingly little troubles they were grappling with. Sometimes, at the end of the day, after he had battled Congress, moved armies, and done whatever else a President needs to do, Lincoln would think to himself, "Well, at least I listened to and hopefully helped that one lady who came to my door with her burdens." Truly a remarkable and unusual gift to the nation at our moment of greatest need. It's interesting to me that, wherever I travel in the world, people know who Abraham Lincoln is. Most other American Presidents, they have never heard of. But they all know Abraham Lincoln.

Now, I don't know how many average citizens Lincoln listened to in his four years in office. Hundreds? Thousands? More? It was really remarkable, at any rate. There's only one person I know of who matched what our 16th President did in terms of listening to anyone, everyone. We meet him in Psalm 102. He also is the Supreme leader, but, of course, a few notches ahead of Lincoln. The Almighty God of the universe looks down from heaven and hears our cries, our groans, our distresses, our worries, our troubles. He holds court as Lincoln did...and his office is always open. He's always "in", always waiting for us, always here to serve us. Considering who he is, that's truly amazing! Have you met with him recently?

JUNE 14

As we have grown older, we have noticed something changing about our bodies as well. Silently, they tell us that they are tired and older, also. We wish at times that we could return to the days when we could physically do much more than we are now able to do. My wife seems to think that it's still possible for us to reclaim those days of old. (I'm not so sure...) This year she has taken it upon herself to carry us back to our former years. Like it or not, she pulls me along with her. So, this year, she has begun walking (marching, if truth be told), and just the other day, she passed the 1,000 mile marker since she began in seriousness...which comes to an average of four miles walking a day. Whew, makes me tired, thinking back on it all. One thing we like to do, though, whether in Korea or the US, is to meander through a variety of neighborhoods, uphill and down, along this road and that, to observe life that is taking place around us. It's fun to watch things change along our route. Several months ago, we kept passing an old house that had certainly once seen better days. It appeared to be abandoned, a tired, old looking house that once was someone's home. Then, one day, as we passed by, several tractors were there on the property, causing total havoc and upset to the quiet little corner. A day or two later, when we walked by, there was nothing left...just a flat, leveled off scrape of dirt. All signs of the house were completely erased. We began to wonder what was going to appear there next. Everyday, as we rounded the corner to that spot, we looked to see what would be there...and it remained silent and empty. For many days, nothing changed. Finally, finally, another tractor appeared. I was curious to see what was going to happen now. The next day, huge boulders had appeared. It began to look like they were constructing some sort of large boundary to a new house that would shortly start to take shape. It was fascinating watching this metamorphosis (especially since someone else was doing all the sweat associated with it!).

In a way, we see the very same thing happening in Ezekiel 29-31. God shows up on the scene, looks around, and declares, "All right, this nonsense has gone on long enough! You all have made a right mess of things, and I'm going to have to set things right. To begin with, we have to clear away the debris that you've created with your life. It can't be fixed, so I'm going to have to level it, sweep it all away. But that's not the end. I'm going to come back, start all over, and restore and revive what was once there. We're going to make things right. Things will be good again. You just wait and see." That is what God does...and that is what he does with each of us. There is a lot of tearing down and destruction in the Bible. But it's not because God likes to destroy things. It hurts him to tear down the beautiful things he has created and built. But he also can't leave things to become derelict. And more than anything, that includes us, his greatest creation. So, when it looks like God is coming at us with a wrecking ball, let's remember that this is not his final statement. He has good plans to restore and rebuild each of us. Let's hang on and see what he will do. God doesn't like to leave messes, even if things get a bit messy along the way... Better and more beautiful days lie ahead.

JUNE 15

Day/Date Be sure to remember five things to be grateful for every day. June 15

2 Corinthians 5:14 NCV — The love of Christ controls us, because we know that One died for all.

God's amazing love for us, described particularly well in Psalm 103, will grab us like nothing else if we can catch only a glimpse of it. When we really begin to see, understand, and accept it more fully, it will surely captivate and dominate our lives.

When we have been on furloughs back in the US, in between serving overseas in various places, we have tried to visit as many of our friends and supporters as possible, to give them an update, as well as to thank them for their partnership with us. A few years ago, we visited my brother's "church" (You'll understand why I put that in quotes in just a moment...), which has been a faithful supporter for several decades, and it's always great to be able to see some of the kin at the same time. That Sunday morning, we rushed off to an early service, where I spoke briefly. Then, rather abruptly, my brother hustled me out of the sanctuary, pushed me into his car, and off we drove to another church. I spoke there as well, and then the same thing happened. We rushed out, drove across town, and arrived at a third church. Same thing, repeated. At that point, it was time for a much appreciated lunch. Then after lunch...you guessed it...on to one more church. At the same time as I was running from congregation to congregation, my wife was speaking to two ladies' groups. So, my brother's church turned out to entail half the county, and we spoke to six different groups by the time the last hymn was sung. My brother is six years older than I am, and I wondered how in the world he kept up this merry go round every Sunday, as he approached 70 years of age. It pretty well tuckered me out doing it only once. I had to wonder whether my brother had recently read Colossians 4. Paul tells us to "make the most of every opportunity". OK, I get it, do what we can, whenever we are able. But cover half the county?? That seemed to me to be carrying every opportunity a few miles too far. Anyway, I appreciate my brother's zeal for taking Paul at his word. Perhaps we should do likewise. (It's been a while since I've visited my brother again, I have to say.)

JUNE 16

Day/Date   Be sure to remember five things to be grateful for every day.   June 16

James 1:2 NCV   When you have many kinds of troubles, you should be full of joy.

If we think back over our lives, many of the most important lessons we've learned have been during or as a result of difficulty. In our spiritual walk with God, we learn the same way. So we should actually be grateful when we are struggling — because we can be sure that God will use the experience to make us more like him.

What legacy are we leaving behind, as we go through life? That is a terribly important and sobering question, something that is frequently on my mind. We can look at some people's lives, and it is very apparent what they are living for, or what they will be remembered for. Two obvious examples come to mind...Thomas Jackson and Rowan Atkinson. Who, some people may ask? Of course, they are better known as Stonewall Jackson and Mr. Bean, and those legacies are permanently stamped on their lives. I don't know if it was her deliberate intention, but Nai Nai, my grandmother, left a legacy, at least in my mind, that has never left me, and has directly affected me ever since I was a child. To confirm it, at least to myself, I just asked my wife a question: "Do you know which book of the Bible I like the best?" "The Psalms!", she said with a smile. Yes, exactly, and that fact is surely due mostly to Nai Nai. I still picture her, hunched over her black, weathered King James Bible, sitting by the window in her summer cabin, most certainly poring over a psalm. She even had descriptions for different psalms, the two I remember the best were the most beautiful psalm (103), and the most wonderful psalm (139). Her exuberant facial expression when she talked about the psalms she loved will never leave me. Her face would just light up when she shared about the joy and blessing contained in their words. One of her favorites was Psalm 103, and it would be right at the top of my short list of favorite ones as well. Listen to these magnificent words from this psalm:

"He forgives all my sins."

"He crowns me with love and tender mercies."

"The Lord is filled with unfailing love."

"His unfailing love is as great as the height of the heavens."

"He has removed our sins as far from us as the east is from the west."

"The Lord is like a father, tender and compassionate."

"The love of the Lord remains forever."

You can just feel God's love for his people wash over us in waves as you read through those words. And that's what I love so much about the Psalms...they teach us about God, about how to talk to God, about how to have a relationship with him. What a marvelous legacy for Nai Nai to leave behind...better than all the jewels in Solomon's palace!

JUNE 17

Marriage is such a disruptive institution, isn't it? What was going on in God's mind when he devised it, I have to wonder... Shortly after my wife and I were married, I approached my Mom, who by this time had the wisdom of 40 years experience under her belt, with a rather serious and important question. "What do you do," I asked her, "when you want the toilet paper turned one way, and your wife wants it coming off the wall the other way??" My Mom just laughed. "Don't worry," she said, "there will be much more important things to deal with as you go along!" Great, I thought, that was very helpful and encouraging! But, she was certainly right, oh, was she right. If toilet paper was all we had to worry about, marriage would all be pretty smooth sailing. One thing that really makes me go ballistic, my wife will confirm, is when she walks by and lifts one of my pens from its precise resting place on my desk. Now, that can really bend my day out of joint. I mean, really, why can't she just get her own pen, without having to contaminate mine? And so it goes, at every turn, something else challenging, puzzling, yes, disruptive. But there is something I've very gradually come to see and understand. (Granted, I'm a slow learner; I'm sure most people have figured this out much faster than I have.) And that is, that all the disruption does serve a purpose. It's not all bad, it can be a good thing. Uncomfortable, yes, but not necessarily bad. Being married, in addition to irritating me on the odd occasion (numerous times a day), has taught me many good things, and hopefully, thanks to my wife's patience and God's grace, has initiated some changes in me for the better. It certainly can be useful for our pruning and refining. I like to tell younger folks that marriage is primarily for our sanctification, not for our own happiness. I really believe that…and I expect life will be easier for us, the quicker we realize and accept that.

God kind of addresses the same issue in Ezekiel 32&33. He's not talking about marriage, but he does say that he will "disturb" us…as in, unsettle us, make us uncomfortable, or disrupt our lives, just as marriage does. Why does God do that? Does he just enjoy a good laugh with the angels at our expense? No, because later in the passage, he tells us, "Look, I don't enjoy making life uncomfortable for you. But I do want you to live. I want you to live fully, as I planned for you all along. But that's going to entail some pruning, some pulling, some stretching…some uncomfortable things, initially. But, it's all for your good. It's all for your blessing. It's all so that you can live the life that I have always wanted for you since the moment I created you. So, will you trust me as I work on you and in you? Will you trust me as I stretch you and throw some unsettling things your way? Trust me! It's all for your good!" So…will we listen? Will we trust him? I hope we will do a better job at listening and trusting and obeying than the Israelites did in Ezekiel's day…

JUNE 18

Day/Date Be sure to remember five things to be grateful for every day. June 18

James 1:4 NCV Let your patience show itself perfectly in what you do.

If I begin to understand how much I've been forgiven by God, it should give me much greater patience for the very small incidents when I feel like I've been wronged. Patience is something we all need and is a sure sign that God is working in your life.

We've lived in a number of places over the years, and I've been privileged to visit quite a few countries in the course of my work. But as I have aged, the excitement of traveling has diminished, and I have become happier with just simple, quiet, mundane, daily life. After living for several years in the dead center of Seoul, Korea, one of the largest urban areas in the world, it's nice to be able to retreat to the calm, slow pace of a small town such as Lookout Mountain, Tennessee. Where we lived in Seoul was perfect for what we were doing, teaching part time at, and commuting between, several schools, and regularly skating around the city, visiting this friend or that student. But I did miss watching a sunset, being able to see trees, instead of high rises, when we looked outside, walking along quiet neighborhood roads. So, when we return to the US from time to time, it's very refreshing to simply walk along and look up at the leaves of a variety of trees, to see squirrels hopping from tree to tree with acorns in their mouths, to watch children playing outside as we walk by. Out of curiosity, I looked up the best known natural wonders of the world...and was very surprised to discover that I had never even heard of most of them, let alone, visited them. I mean, really, who has ever seen Semuc Champey, Guatemala (number one on the list); Great Blue Hole, Belize (yes, number two); Tunnel of Love, Ukraine; and on it goes... I think I had heard of only two of the first 20 listed. Now, these are only natural wonders that we humans have discovered and are aware of. Have you ever thought about what we may never have even set eyes upon yet? What about in the far reaches of outer space, in a desolate corner of the Sahara Desert, or in an incredibly deep point in one of the oceans? I'm always surprised to hear that someone has again discovered a never before known species of plant or animal...I mean, where have they been hiding all these zillions of years? You begin to catch a glimpse of the staggering greatness, majesty, creativity, and wonder of the God of the universe. I get impressed with the colors of the few trees or flowers I see as I walk along the road. But there must be millions of living things (and non living) all across the universe...that no one will ever even set eyes on. That certainly makes us realize that the universe is a bigger place than we are aware of. God has made oodles of things...just for his own creative pleasure...human eyes will probably never even see them. God opens a little window into his magnificent creation in Psalm 104, when he tells us that:

"He stretched out the starry curtain."

"He placed the world on its foundation."

"He makes springs pour water out, so that animals can drink."

"He causes grass to grow."

"With his wisdom, God created a world full of diverse variety."

"They all depend on God for their food, and he richly satisfies them."

Next time you're out for a walk, thank God for his creative beauty, for giving us the senses to enjoy his creation, for his care in providing for all that he made, for his magnificent greatness, that we have barely even scratched the surface of...

JUNE 19

There weren't many pets in Korea when I was a boy. Not many years had passed since the Korean War, which followed on the heels of World War 2, and there just wasn't a lot of extra food to go around, much less to waste on a pet dog. Occasionally, you might see a shop advertising dog meat for sale, even more occasionally, you might actually see a pet dog running around. In most cases, it was the foreigners who were able to afford pets. My, times have changed. Today, in Seoul, not only will you see pets for sale, there are also pet food stores, and even pet clothing boutiques. I expect that if a pet clothing store had opened up on the high street 50 years ago, it would have drawn quite a crowd of on-lookers...not that there were any pets around, and, certainly no pets needing a new suit of clothes. No, people would have gathered for the sheer novelty of a shop like that, and probably to get a good chuckle at the thought of some wild beast actually needing to get dressed up. I can just see all the roughly dressed farmers of that day, drawing up to the store window with their buddies, to get a good howl out of the far-fetched notion of an animal getting all dressed up in the morning. What a laugh! Well, what a change a generation or two can make. I'm old enough that I still smile to myself when I pass a pet clothing store on the street. But, I haven't seen a single other person break into a laugh or a grin at such a store...everyone else just marches past as if the pet store is just another 7-Eleven or Dunkin' Donuts, not giving it a second thought. And, then, sometimes we'll come up to a young person pushing a stroller, and peek in as we walk past...only to see a little poodle or puppy staring up at us from within. It must have seemed funny the first time I saw it...it's so common now, that I hardly even remember the first reaction I had. It seems like it's more unusual to pass a stroller and to see a baby in it, these days.

In some ways, I suppose, the current generation may better understand Ezekiel 34 than my generation would have. God is fawning all over his people, telling them they are his sheep, that as their shepherd, he gives them everything they need, that he looks after and provides for all their wants. What is he talking about, older folks may wonder? Sure, I understand beating, prodding, or poking a wayward sheep...but, caring for it like it's a baby, lavishing it with everything it needs? Come on...a bit over the top, isn't it? Today's young people would understand that perfectly. They do the same with their animals...baby them, feed them the finest, dress them in miniature knitted slippers, cover them in cute little coats...goodness! But that's how God describes us in this passage. He cares for us, looks over us, pours his love on us. As if we're his little pet lamb, he dotes on us, protects us, he loves us. Isn't it amazing that, that is how God describes his love and care for us?? Wow! What a loving heavenly Shepherd we do have!

JUNE 20

James 1:5 NCV   But if any of you needs wisdom, you should ask God for it. He is generous and enjoys giving to all people.

God gives us many things, but his is not foolish or without understanding. He gives wisdom as we seek him and follow him. It is unlikely that he will answer our prayers for wisdom if we haven't been walking with him and obeying his Word. So the offer to answer our prayers comes with the understanding that our hearts will be open to God and that we are honoring him in our lives.

On one of my early trips to Pakistan, my boss and I were traveling together, and at one point, I had to answer a call of nature. I walked into the said room...and looked around. That's odd, I thought, where's the toilet paper...as the call of nature knocked with greater urgency. I quickly came back out and said to my boss, "Where's the toilet paper??" "Oh, I forgot to tell you...they don't use toilet paper here!", he replied, with a bit of a mischievous grin on his face and a twinkle in his eye. Great, I thought, now you tell me, as I hustled back in. (You'll have to private message me if you want the end of the story...) At any rate, it was enlightening, sometimes amusing, and occasionally, uncomfortable, when you visited different places and discovered how people did things differently in various cultures and societies. One thing I found very interesting and educational was how people pray across the globe. It seems that their heart cries very much reflect the local urgencies, priorities, and issues they live with daily. For example, in Pakistan, attending small church gatherings, where we sat on the floor, men on one side of the room, women on the other, and kids crawling all over, their prayers seemed to focus, at least more than in other places, on persecution, personal safety, and so forth...certainly reflecting the pressure and marginalization they felt in that overwhelmingly Muslim society. On the other hand, in England, where we lived for ten years, there were many more prayers about care for our planet and the things that had been entrusted to us, than I was used to hearing. In Korea, many prayers focus on the issues and concern for the people of North Korea. So, what do our prayers in America focus on? I'm afraid, at least to my limited ears and understanding, that the things we pray about are not quite so lofty as saving the planet, religious persecution, or freeing the captives. What is it that we pray about? We pray about our ill aunt, our neighbor with the upset stomach, someone going for a job interview...in short, our worldly comforts and concerns. Sometimes, as I listen to people praying in different places, I almost wonder if we really all believe the same things. We also experienced childbirth in three very different cultural settings over the years, and it was surprising how different having a baby can be in different places. I mean, how different can it be? There's basically only one way for a baby to be born, right?!? Oh no, think again...or if you really want to know...have your babies born in several distinct societies. You will discover all kinds of differences! It can all be a bit of a fuddle...such a diverse world we live in.

In fact, David tells us, in the words he wrote in Psalm 105, where our priorities should lie, what our focus ought to be, what our hearts should be set on. Listen to what he says here:

"Proclaim God's greatness."

"Tell everyone about his wonderful deeds."

"Search for the Lord...continually seek him."

"Remember the wonders he has performed."

"Follow his decrees...obey his instructions."

Would our lives be changed if we followed David's admonitions? Would our prayers sound unlike they do today? What would happen to us, if just for one week, or even one day, we spent all our time and energy telling others about God's greatness, seeking him moment by moment, obeying how he tells us to pattern our lives? Shall we try an experiment...and then gather back together next week to share our experiences in these things?? I'm game, if you are!

JUNE 21

Day/Date   Be sure to remember five things to be grateful for every day.   June 21

2 Corinthians 12:10 NCV   I am happy when I have weaknesses, insults, hard times, sufferings, and all kinds of troubles for Christ. Because when I am weak, then I am strong.

Before Paul became a follower of Christ, he was understandably proud of his education, accomplishments, and standing in society. But when his eyes were opened to his true bankrupt position before God, he was grateful for the privilege of enduring hardship for Christ, and he was thankful for his weaknesses that reminded him that on his own he was without hope before God.

When my childhood friend in Korea started to draw pictures from her childhood over 50 years ago, she was also bringing my early years back to life. We grew up next to each other, so everything she remembered and recorded was also what I remembered (or in some cases, had long forgotten). It is remarkable to see a childlike "book" of your long ago years, after so many decades have gone by. She remembers the games we played, the snow we rollicked in, caves we ventured into, our pets, gardens, eating watermelon, the cemetery where my brother is buried, her home and our home, trees we played in, and many, many other things. One thing she remembers is a legacy, if you will, of my father...something that probably everyone who knew him back in those years also remembers. My father was a fully engaged hospital administrator during those busy days, pouring his energy into the lives of those battling deadly diseases, and doing so in the toughest and roughest of circumstances. But at the same time, he had a routine, so mundane that I never gave it a second thought, that he squeezed into his already busy and demanding days. Before we gathered as a family for breakfast and devotions, he would mount his trusty old bicycle, add a stash of John's Gospels to his basket, and pedal off down the dirt path into town, to pass out God's Message to anyone he encountered. It was such a part of his regular day, that I never thought anything of it. But, my childhood friend remembered...and drew her recollection of those moments, even including the prominent, Western nose attached to my father's head. So, one legacy my father left behind was the importance of sharing God's Good News with people.

Ezekiel, in chapters 36&37, is told to do exactly the same thing. God tells him, "Give this message to my people." He even tells Ezekiel to share his message with the mountains surrounding Jerusalem. Now, perhaps some theologian can clarify to me exactly what that means. I don't really know. But one thing is clear: God's Message is important, so important, in fact, that everyone and everything needs to hear it and know it…including the mountains. That Message, actually, hasn't changed. All these years later, it's still the same all important, life message that we need to know, that those around us need to know. Are we sharing it? Are our bikes loaded up and ready for us to pedal off down the road on? Maybe they need to be. Maybe we need to be about that business. The world's needs don't seem to have diminished too much since Ezekiel's day.

JUNE 22

> **Day/Date** Be sure to remember five things to be grateful for every day. June 22
>
> James 1:19 NCV — Always be willing to listen and slow to speak.
>
> As much as we want to share the Good News with people, sometimes we may need to just listen to them first to learn what their situation is, what their needs are, and to be able to show them compassion by being willing to share in their lives. Then we will be in a better position to speak into their lives if that is what is needed.

I've been a parent a long time...maybe as long as Moses was, I'm not sure... If I add up the ages of my nine kids as of this moment (38+36+34+32+29+27+25+23+21)...it comes to a cumulative total of 265 years...and counting. Man, talk about feeling old! You would think I could write the definitive book on parenting by now. But, it's strange...it seems that my knowledge of parenting is inversely proportional to how long I've been a parent. I clearly remember knowing all there was to know about parenting when I was in my 20s and 30s. I don't know what happened in the interim, but somewhere along the line, I must have lost a screw or two. Today, I was sitting with my wife enjoying Sunday dinner together on a beautiful autumn day. Most of the meal, I was just staring off into space, feeling confused, befuddled, baffled. I just couldn't make sense of things, parenting-wise...and we don't even have any kids at home anymore! I wonder if my parents felt the same way in their day. I must say, they did seem a little checked out at times. I can't say for sure whether they had lost a screw or two along the way, but they did kind of seem like they would shuffle along with a nod or a smile, at times, and not much more. Maybe they were feeling befuddled as well. When your kids grow up-...you've changed over the years...and they begin to change, too. They are not the little six year olds that they once were. And maybe that's where some of the befuddlement comes along. One thing is for sure, though, and that doesn't change. Appearances aside, I do still love my kids just like I loved them when I rolled around on the floor with them at age 2, 3, or 4. The underlying love for my kids is still there, whatever else may have changed.

In his first letter to his fellow believer and friend, Timothy, Paul seems to be trying to convey this very same idea to him. I don't know if Timothy was forgetful (probably not), but Paul seems to hammer the reality home every way that he can. It's so important for Timothy to know, as well as to pass on, that Paul stresses how important God's love for us is. Listen to what he says...

"How generous and gracious our Lord was!"

"God our Savior wants everyone to be saved."

"He gave his life to purchase freedom for everyone."

So, God loves us lavishly. He wants to spend eternity with all of us so badly that he paid for our bail out of hell...for all of us.

Then Paul really goes over the top. He tells Timothy, "Pray for all people." Now, granted, there weren't seven billion people in the world back then. But that's still a lot of people to pray for...and, presumably, to tell about God's love. And, of course, Paul was talking to us, too. Goodness, I guess we have our work cut out for us. We have a lot, I mean, a lot, of praying and talking to do. We better get busy right away. No more time to lose! (So much for those retirement plans..I guess I'll be busy till I reach the age of Moses...)

JUNE 23

Day/Date Be sure to remember five things to be grateful for every day. June 23

Revelation 21:4 NCV He will wipe away every tear from their eyes, and there will be no more death, sadness, crying, or pain, because all the old ways are gone.

What an amazing hope and future we have! I would despair of all my wrong doings, selfishness, and sinful disobedience if there was no way to erase and cleanse them. But thank the Lord, he has made it certain that all these stains and wrong doings will one day be forgotten.

In his later years, well into his 70s, my Dad, who by this time had left Korea and was now serving at medical clinics in Bangladesh, would travel back and forth through London, on his way between Dhaka and my parents' home in the US. We were living in Sheffield, England, at the time, so when he had an overnight in London between his two long flights, I would pack all the kids into our rattle-trap red Ford Transit van and head to Heathrow Airport to meet him. We would drive him to his hotel for the night, enjoy a brief visit, then I would show the kids a bit of London, before heading back up the motorway for home. On one of those visits, we were on the London tube, as the subway is called, and we were pulling into a station. "This is our stop!", I told the kids. As soon as we pulled up, Julie hopped off. Right at that moment, I realized it was actually the next stop that we should be getting off at. "Wait", I said, "Not here!" At that moment, the doors slammed shut...leaving Julie, about aged 12, standing on the platform alone. I was frantic, as was she, and tried to motion for her to wait where she was, so we could come back to pick her up. Thannnnkfully, the doors then slid back open, as apparently the subway operator has seen this gal alone outside. Whew, I can't tell you how relieved I was. Another time (Was it on the same trip...I don't remember?!?), we were by the Queen Victoria Memorial, outside of the majestic Buckingham Palace, home of Britain's longest reigning monarch, Queen Elizabeth. It was a drizzly day, not entirely rare thereabouts, and so only a few tourists were sprinkled around, here and there. The Palace had been recently opened to visitors, and I happened to notice that the line of people waiting to go in was unusually short, not the normal serpent of people, curled up around the memorial. So, on the spur of the moment, we joined the queue and went in. What an amazing place. Thrones, crowns, storied paintings, royal furniture...it was all too much for the senses to try to absorb...and to imagine that right here was where the royals had made their abode for generations. It was a once in a lifetime experience.

When I read the opening verses of Psalm 106, my mind goes back to that visit in London. It says: "Who can list the glorious miracles of the Lord?" There are certainly regal glories in Buckingham Palace. But in this psalm, we are given a glimpse of God's glory and majesty. And we realize that his actions and his being place him in an entirely separate category from the human royals who inhabit the earth. God commanded seas, controlled the actions of nations, directed the course of nature and the events of the world. Suddenly, we realize that this God of the universe is the one who is truly awesome, totally majestic, beyond our comprehension and understanding. He is the one who truly should capture our attention, our wonder, our worship!

JUNE 24

I love libraries, and there are some pretty amazing ones in the world, which I know, not from having visited them, but from observing their incredible pictures. Some of them look like they are holy ground, almost too sacred to walk into, certainly too special to wander noisily and carelessly into. Some look so enormous that I wonder if they hold all the knowledge of the world within their walls...well, probably not the whole world, but definitely more than I hold between the walls of my brain. It's also fascinating when we read a story about some long lost treasure...a letter from a president or monarch, or a famous painting...that has been discovered tucked away on a dusty shelf of a library somewhere. Amazing, when that happens...and makes us wonder what other treasures might be waiting to be uncovered somewhere in the world.

Although he may not have fully realized it at the time, Ezekiel received in his hands some priceless treasures as well. In chapters 38&39 of his lengthy chronicle, he speaks of again (Is that weariness we detect in his voice??) receiving a message from God. How could he not have been over the moon with excitement about a word from the Almighty Sovereign of the universe?? Well, just perhaps, if we were in Ezekiel's dusty sandals, we may not have been totally excited either. Some of the messages he received were not entirely the greatest news he hoped to receive. Nevertheless, hearing from God really is priceless, and though he can approach us with a frown, he always ends in a loving embrace when we respond to him. Truly, there are treasures in his messages to us...vastly more than in all the greatest libraries of the world. And we have all his messages in our hands today...not just the sober ones Ezekiel received. So, what are we waiting for? Let's pull one of his messages off the shelf and dive in!

JUNE 25

Day/Date Be sure to remember five things to be grateful for every day. June 25

Matthew 6:21 NCV Your heart will be where your treasure is.

It is very important for us to set our hearts on following and honoring God in our lives. If we do not set our hearts on serving God, then they will turn to and settle on other things – success, money, or popularity. These things will then become what we value, and our hearts will not treasure serving God.

I'll never be a good piano player. I'll never be a good basketball player. I always thought I was pretty decent at tennis...but as I watch the big boys play in championship highlights, I come to the painful conclusion that I'm really not much good at tennis either. Could I ever have been really good at it? Truthfully, I doubt it. I just don't think I would have the drive, the discipline, the passion needed to practice my backhand or my serve 6-8 hours a day. That's what I would need to do if I truly wanted to be a "big boy" in that area...or in piano or basketball, for that matter.

Paul takes to lecturing his younger brother in the faith, Timothy, in 1 Timothy 4-6. He drives him like a pro sports coach, but, of course, he's talking about something entirely different. Along the lines of what Paul is talking about, I remember hearing that a Korean pastor in Seoul reads his Bible all the way through, 8-10 times a year. Whew! A little closer to home, I recall two serious readers when I was a boy. My mother used to read her Bible through four times a year...and that was in addition to taking care of a houseful of kids, including schooling us. Then, there was another missionary, a small man, but a giant in the faith, who used to annually read his Bible through twice a year...as well as twice a year in Korean. Now, I expect that's the kind of feat that would grow hair on the chest of any missionary! My wife and I have taken to reading our Bibles regularly, for the past several decades, as well...but it seems pretty wimpy compared with my Mom. I follow a yearly plan that I enjoy very much, which has me reading through the Old Testament once, and then through Psalms and the New Testament twice. Would I pass Paul's rigorous standards? I'm not real sure. Listen to his words to Timothy, about how we should live as Christians:

"Be committed to the faith."

"Train yourself to be godly."

"Work hard and continue to struggle."

"Keep a close watch on how you live."

"Stay true to what is right."

"A widow should pray day and night." Wow...better pray that your husband doesn't die prematurely!)

"Be content."

"Fight the good fight."

"Be rich on good works."

"Always be ready to share."

Now, Paul knew as well as we do that we're saved by grace, and that God loves us greatly. So, in a sense, we're not going to score points by doing all these things. But, at the same time, we can hear Paul's urgency. What he's talking about is important, terribly important. So, as with an athlete, we need to take our spiritual walk seriously. There certainly are plenty of distractions in this life that can derail or sidetrack us. So, let's buckle down as the good saint told us to; let's focus on and commit ourselves to what's important.

JUNE 26

Day/Date   Be sure to remember five things to be grateful for every day.   June 26

James 1:21 NCV   In gentleness accept God's teaching that is planted in your hearts, which can save you.

Because of our sinful human nature, our natural tendency is to think and do for ourselves. God's ways are in direct opposition to our natural desires. So unless God's Spirit changes our hearts and works in our lives, we will not be able to accept God's ways in our lives. But when we open our hearts to the Spirit's work in us, we will be able to receive God's instructions and work in our lives.

Ti... 77

On so many fronts, on so many levels, the years around the time of World War 2 brought destruction and death, everywhere we look back at it. No wonder there was celebration and spontaneous dancing in the streets when it finally came to an end. It was heartbreaking for soldiers to return to their home-towns...and to find that their homes no longer existed. Others were separated from family members that they never located again. One man I interviewed in China lived in Nanjing before the war. His father owned a hotel there. As Japan-ese forces advanced on the city, his mother took him, as a small child, and fled to her brother's home in Beijing. After the dust had settled, his mother returned to Nanjing to look for her husband. There was no sign of him or their hotel at all. This caused her to become deranged, so the man I was interviewing was raised by his uncle. He was never to see either of his parents again. Then, there were those who spent years, slowing dying in concentration camps. As death was daily all around them, surely many of them gave up all hope of rescue. One day, though, as the end of the war neared, in some cases, Allied soldiers appeared out of nowhere and rescued them. The amazed joy at being rescued can be seen on their faces in photos that exist from those days.

Psalm 107 speaks of a similar day. It tells of people being rescued from exile...those close to death being saved...those imprisoned in darkness and gloom being given a new lease on life...prison gates being broken down. Of course, these verses are not talking about China or World War 2, but the image is similar...people being rescued from long enslavement in darkness and sin. The psalm talks about exiles being brought home from the east and west, the north and south. As I look around our world today, and see so much lostness and pain, it gives me great encouragement and hope to realize that God's rescue plan is already underway. We can't see all that he's doing yet, but he is working, and good things are happening. Additionally, God invites us in on his rescue plans. Can you imagine the privilege it was for those soldiers to drive up to the gates of a concentration camp and to tell the emaciated creatures inside the barbed wire that their days of suffering were over? What an amazing privilege. God gives us that same privilege spiritually. He's given us the joyful task of pronouncing to slaves that their days of spiritual darkness have ended!

JUNE 27

> **Day/Date** Be sure to remember five things to be grateful for every day. **June 27**
>
> **Genesis 41:52 NKJV** God has caused me to be fruitful in the land of my affliction.
>
> It is a puzzling irony to humans, but God uses and blesses us most richly and allows us to be the greatest blessing to others, when we are suffering or going through trials. For it is in these situations of weakness that God's work in us is most evident and when he can speak most clearly through us into other people's lives.

One day in your life that you never forget is the day you graduate. Such exhilaration, such a sense of accomplishment… For one day, at least, you feel on top of the world (until reality sets in the day after, and you realize you are jobless and need to figure out what to do next). All the sweat and labor, finally ended. And, now, at least for a moment, the stage is yours, and everything you poured into that program is being acknowledged. But, what if you invested all that time and money and energy into getting that degree…and then did nothing with it…just laid it aside and forgot it. Of course, there are many occasions when someone earns a degree and then decides to move in another direction or do something different with their life. That is certainly fine and understandable. But, usually, you pursue a degree, hoping to use it, to do something with it, to allow it to contribute to what you want to do with our life.

In Ezekiel 40, God calls on the prophet again with a very specific and important message…kind of like bestowing a degree on him, so that he can use it for it's intended purpose. In this case, God wants Ezekiel to pass on to others what he has learned in God's crash course. This must have been a very important message, because you sense the urgency in how the story is described. He says that God "took hold of him". Then God picked him up and set him down on top of a high mountain. That's a pretty impressive way to give a message to anyone. Then,

God told Ezekiel that he had many things to tell him, and that the prophet was to pass on everything God was about to tell him, to all of God's people. And, still today, thousands of years later, we have that same message that has been passed down to us. But, what if Ezekiel had not been bothered to pass it on to the people, and to us? What if God's whole message of truth, love, and salvation had not been passed down to us? What a tragedy that would have been. And we see, sometimes, in the Old Testament, what happened when people didn't bother passing the message along as they were supposed to...a new generation grew up with no knowledge of it. Not only did they not know about it...but, they were lost and in darkness without that vital message. Today, again, we have the message that's been entrusted from God into our hands. What will we do with it? What are we doing about it? Let's be as intentional as Ezekiel was, shall we, and pass on the message that God wants all people everywhere to know. Let's not leave the world in darkness, without having graduated, so to speak, and missing out on the exhilaration of knowing what God has intended for them.

JUNE 28

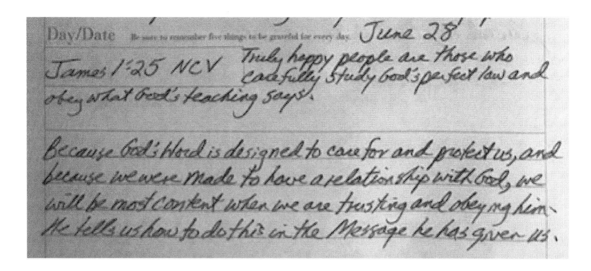

Day/Date — Be sure to remember five things to be grateful for every day. June 28

James 1:25 NCV — Truly happy people are those who carefully study God's perfect law and obey what God's teaching says.

Because God's Word is designed to care for and protect us, and because we were made to have a relationship with God, we will be most content when we are trusting and obeying him. He tells us how to do this in the Message he has given us.

We are very fortunate in that we have the accumulated knowledge and wisdom and writings of all the thinkers and teachers who have gone before us. Timothy, in the first century after Jesus, was also the recipient of the apostle Paul's accumulated wisdom and experience. The second letter of Paul to Timothy is especially precious, because Paul was shackled in a Roman dungeon, his appeals had run their course, and he knew his days were numbered. So, he was sending off this one last letter to his close friend, to pass on to Timothy has last will and testament, so to speak. So, what would Paul say to him is his very final communication? It's been wonderful to know you and work with you?? Well, I'm sure he felt that way, and he certainly included words to that effect. But Paul was so captured and enraptured by the message he had been entrusted with, that, with all the passion and energy and force within him, he urgently stressed the essential task of carrying on, of passing on, this treasure that God had revealed to him, that has also been revealed to us.

I'm so thankful for all the wise teachers from past generations who have weighed in on Paul's words here. Paul had a critical message, and I love the way the great preacher Charles Spurgeon, for example, comments on what Paul has written. Listen to what Paul said:

"Night and day I constantly remember you in my prayers."

"Fan into flames the spiritual gift God gave you."

"Never be ashamed to tell others about our Lord."

"I'm in prison for him. Be ready to suffer for the sake of the Good News."

"God chose me to be a teacher of this Good News. That is why I am suffering in this prison."

"Carefully guard this precious truth."

"The word of God cannot be chained. So I am willing to endure anything if it will bring salvation..."

"God's truth stands firm."

"All Scripture is inspired by God."

Now, listen to Spurgeon's take on Paul's words:

"Every living saint has his charge to keep. The Gospel truths are a revelation from God, omnipotence is in them. It is not possible that the omnipotent Word can be bound. The Holy Spirit's being with the Gospel is the reason for its great power."

So, Spurgeon confirms Paul's message and urgency...and the certainty of why we should pass on the message Paul is talking about. It brings life to people, and because God's Spirit brings it to life, it will bring about God's intended good plans in people's lives. As much work as it may entail, as hard as it may be (even landing us in jail on occasion), we can't fail in this endeavor. So, let's join Paul, and Timothy, and Charles in this task! Our success is sure.

JUNE 29

> **1 Peter 1:6-7 NIV** In this you rejoice, though for a little while you have had to suffer trials. These have come so your faith may be proved genuine and result in honor when Jesus is revealed.

While going through difficulties, the pain and discomfort can grab our whole attention to the extent that it seems unending and insurmountable. But when we remember how precious we are to God, and the great reward that is waiting for us, and the value that suffering can often have in our or other people's lives, then, with God's help, we can endure it and overcome it.

I never expected to live in Europe, but when Eastern Europe opened up to the Gospel in the 1990s, we spent 13 years in that part of the world as we sought to make God's Word available to those who had not freely had it before. Coming from the US, where our history is very limited, I loved the longer and deeper stories and experiences we discovered in those countries. I particularly liked that the countries were all so close to each other. This allowed these crazy Americans to drive all over the continent as if we were taking a Sunday drive in the countryside. One day, we piled all the kids in the car and drove from southern France to Interlaken, Switzerland, and back, in the same day. Another time, again with kids in tow, we drove to Barcelona, Spain, and back. Ireland, Romania, Italy, Czechoslovakia, Austria, Scotland, Liechtenstein...I must confess I was a little crazy...but who could resist this alphabet soup of nations, all staring in our windows, waiting for us to discover them... I don't know how much of those trips our kids remember, but I sure recall them all with great fondness. Since my wife's parents immigrated to the US, from Holland, after the Second World War, she still had kin and cousins there, who we could also now visit with relative ease. On one such trip, we stopped in Haarlem, the Netherlands, to visit the home, now museum, of Corrie ten Boom, whose family gained great notoriety by hiding Jews from the Nazis during the war. It was quite amazing to be able to walk through the clock repair shop of Corrie's father, to climb the winding staircase of their quaint Dutch home to the upper room, that had a wall, behind which, a small space held the Jews, who were on the run for their lives. Corrie's family knew full well that their lives were in danger for what they were doing, which was all the more remarkable, considering that they were Christians, putting their lives at stake for these Jewish people, who they knew that God loved. Her father was unshakable and outspoken in his faith in God, even though they were discovered and trucked off to prison, where, except for Corrie, they all perished. Corrie, too, remained resolute in her confidence in God, and for the rest of her days, she tramped the globe, as she described it, sharing with people about the Lord she loved.

Corrie ten Boom's steadfast commitment to God is similar to what we hear shared in the words of Psalm 108. David, also, like the ten Booms, had more than his fill of tumult, opposition, and suffering. We wouldn't blame him for running the other way. But, whatever he went through, however badly he stumbled at times, David always returned to God. He knew that his Savior could be trusted, so that's where his confidence lay, just as with the ten Boom family, even in their darkest hours. I hope we will take comfort from and follow the examples of these great saints who have gone before us, and have shown us how to cling to God, even in our most desperate days.

JUNE 30

June 30

James 2:18, 26 NCV   I will show you my faith by what I do. Faith that does nothing is dead!

What kind of husband would I be if, because I was legally married, I decided it was unnecessary to show through my actions that I was married? I would be a husband in name only. Showing my wife that I love her doesn't make me married, but it does demonstrate that I am married. In the same way, if my life has no sign of God in it, then it is very questionable whether I have ever placed my trust in him at all.

When my parents passed away in quick succession many years ago, thankfully, they had pared down their belongings over the years, and really didn't have much left for us kids to dispose of. Still, I found it hard, almost painful, to have to think about throwing any of their things away. It just felt too much like we were, in a sense, throwing their lives away, when we did that. I almost couldn't do it...in fact, some of their things are probably still sitting around somewhere. Now, with our kids, that won't be a problem at all. We trained them so well to focus on the eternal...that they don't want any of our stuff (which in itself is a bit painful!). But, there it is...new generation, new values. And, it certainly is not a bad thing that they don't want to hold onto everything like we tended to do. I suppose we grew up with parents who had lived through the Great Depression and World War 2, times when there was very little extra to be had, so everything was held tightly, "just in case". That's how we grew up... which means that now I have all kinds of things I've held onto from a trip to Russia, a conference in Kyrgyzstan, or a council in England. Boy, oh boy, what to do with it all?? (I know what my kids will do, as soon as they get their hands on it!) Really, though, even though all these things hold some memories or sentiment for me, in and of themselves, they are pretty useless...(Did I just say that??)

Obviously, some things are more important to hold onto than other things. No one will notice or remember anything I now have, once it's taken to Goodwill (or worse). But some things are, in fact, essential to hold onto.

Ezekiel, during another one of his visits from God, was reminded of this very thing. In chapters 41-43, God is describing how we should worship him. Some of it is hard to understand, and I'm sure there is disagreement as to exactly what God was intending. But, some things are pretty clear. Worship of God is a very serious thing. God is holy and must be approached (and followed) with that in mind. And, we are to hold onto, and also to pass onto those who come after us, these important truths. They do not wear out, get useless, or become something we can toss out. God's message came with terrific glory, noise, and shaking. Ezekiel even fell down on his face as he encountered God. So, this was not just a casual message. God gave his message to the prophet, then God told him to pass it on carefully to the people...so that they would study it. In other words, read it, meditate on it, discuss it...make it a part of their lives. Does that sound like a Bible study to you? It really does! So, we better get busy doing it, making God's message an important part of our lives. When was the last time you read Ezekiel??

MONTH 7

Quarantine day 7...

Thoughts from Ecclesiastes, Song of Solomon, and Isaiah:

*Been there...done that...it's all been tried before. Will we learn from the people who have gone before us?

*All humans know that there is more to life than what we see with our eyes.

*What lasts are the things that God does.

*Be content...even though there is much we don't understand.

*Marriage is based on a committed decision...as is our choice to follow Christ.

*Turning away from God brings trouble and loss.

*There is hope in God!

*God will receive honor on earth.

*God punishes disobedience.

*Am I available to God?

*Trust in God...he is working out his good plans.

*God will accomplish his plans.

*God wants to show us his love.

*There is Great News for the world!

*God holds us close...if we will allow him to!

*When we trust God, he tells us not to be afraid.

*God is calling out to us.

*God loves us...and his love will triumph.

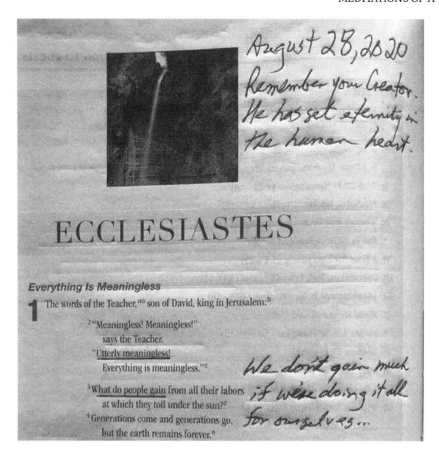

August 28, 2020
Remember your Creator.
He has set eternity in
the human heart.

ECCLESIASTES

Everything Is Meaningless

1 The words of the Teacher,[a] son of David, king in Jerusalem:[b]

² "Meaningless! Meaningless!"
   says the Teacher.
  "Utterly meaningless!
   Everything is meaningless."[c]

³ What do people gain from all their labors
   at which they toil under the sun?[d]
⁴ Generations come and generations go,
   but the earth remains forever.[e]

We don't gain much
if we're doing it all
for ourselves...

JULY 1

My parents used to always say that, of all the grandkids, I was the most like my Grandpa, Lewis Lancaster, who, appropriately, I was also named after. I wasn't entirely sure if that fact was meant to be a good thing or a bad thing, but there it is... Certainly, in three ways I can think of, I am indeed like him. He was very quiet, apparently thinking that talking, in most situations anyway, was unnecessary. That's pretty close to how I am, most of the time, as well. He also seemed to be good at saving money, and, as far as I know, they were never hungry, though, as a missionary to China nearly 100 years ago, I don't expect that they had an over abundance either. He was so frugal that he managed to keep the same apartment, in his retirement, for many years, the entire time, paying only $30 a month, well into the 1970s. And, finally, he liked water, lots and lots of it. A funny story was told about when he lived in China. He was visiting another missionary family one day, and as he came up the walkway, one of the family's kids saw him. Spinning instantly around, the young boy ran for the house, yelling, "Hurry! Quick! Get the pitcher of water! Mr. Lancaster is coming!!" One of our children seems to also have inherited all three of those same Lancaster traits; apparently, he received the entire DNA package. I don't quite understand it, but I can watch others spend money with pleasure and glee... while, for me, the pleasure comes mostly in the saving. For whatever reason, I just enjoy seeing cash stack up (not that I've really had that much experience in that situation, mind you). However, there is one circumstance when it seems that I just don't mind spending money. If we're going on a vacation, for example, and I'm carrying $100 cash in my pocket, I guess I kind of think of it as already spent, since it's previously been allocated to the vacation, and so, I can happily expend what, to my mind, anyway, is already gone. I don't know if that makes sense, but that's kind of how I feel in a case like that.

Now, Paul, in his second letter to Timothy, shortly before he was to leave this world, said a truly remarkable statement. He said that he was not afraid to suffer or to die, because, "My life has already been poured out like an offering to God." So, Paul wasn't afraid to expend his life, throw it away, if you will, because, in his mind, he had already done that, kind of like me with my vacation money. He had already handed his life over to God. He talked about himself being a slave to God, so, he didn't even think of his life as being his anymore. He could spend it, use it up, because, to him, it was already used up. That's an amazing thought, isn't it. When we're at work, in a very real sense, our life belongs to the company. When we get married, our life, to a large extent, belongs to our spouse, and certainly it belongs to the marriage we've committed ourselves to. Now, imagine what our life would look like if, 24-7, we literally thought of it as belonging to God. How would that impact our thoughts? The books we read? The way we used our free time? How we spent our money? It would potentially be pretty radical, wouldn't you say? (Unless, of course, you are miles ahead of me, and are already living like this.) I wonder what would happen to the world, to society, to our culture...if, suddenly, every Christian did this. What do you think? Paul seemed to think this is how we were all meant to live. Lord, help us in this, what seems to us to be a monumental, endeavor. Help us to be the people you always planned for us to be. Amen!

JULY 2

Day/Date — Be sure to remember five things to be grateful for every day. July 2

John 15:7 NIV

Remain in me, and my words remain in you.

Jesus promised that when we live with him and follow him, he would answer our prayers. Perhaps just as important, if we live with and for him, he will be able to use us for his glory and to mold us into the people he desires.

As I completed school and took my first real job, I suppose it was important in those early days that I felt recognized and validated for who I was. One time, something happened that affected my area of responsibility, that I really felt was just not right, and I complained about it to someone above me. Later, the issue was discussed in a staff meeting, and my point of view was discussed and rejected. But there was a single voice that voted for me, and he later came to me and told me that he had stood up for my perspective. Although I didn't receive the verdict I had hoped for, somehow, knowing that this friend had stood with me, affirmed me, and represented me publicly meant a whole lot to me. He gave me the recognition and validation that I needed in those early days. So, rather than thinking that I had been voted down 6-1, or some such lopsided number, I felt mostly OK about it, because I had been heard and supported by this loyal friend.

David shows us in Psalm 109 that it is the same for us when we come into God's presence. God already knows everything, knows our needs, even knows the wrongs that are at times committed against us. But he invites us to come into his presence and open our hearts, our pain, our longings, and our struggles to him. He loves us, accepts us, hears us. I'm sure David still struggled and was wronged in the future, but at this moment he came to God with his grievances, knowing that God would listen and understand. Just as my friend listened to me, and confirmed that with his lone vote on my behalf. Somehow, that was enough for David, just as it was enough for me, knowing that my friend understood me and my hurts. We can still do the same thing today that David did when he recorded his words for us. We can lay open our hearts, and God promises to hear us, heal us, and love us. What a great privilege we have to be able to do this!

JULY 3

Day/Date *Be sure to remember five things to be grateful for every day.* **July 3**

Exodus 33:14 NLT / I will personally go with you, and I will give you rest - everything will be fine for you.

What a stunning promise from the almighty God! If a friend or parent is with us, we usually feel safe. But the God of the universe promises to go with us as we travel with him through life. This world is full of many uncertainties; how wonderful to know that God promises to go through it with us.

It's impressive to observe how societies treat and view monarchs and royalty. In Bible times, a king's wealth or greatness might be measured by how many wives he had. In the book of Esther, you could lose your life if you even approached the king without being formally recognized and invited by him. Some monarchs have multiple palaces they live in and visit. It seems that in our modern world, the greatness of kings and queens has become something of the past. Some of the European countries still have monarchs, but they may be seen pedaling their bikes around town just like the rest of us. Probably no one puts on a royal display like the British do, with all the pomp and ceremony befitting the greatest of any monarch. They have the protocol down to a right perfect science. Occasionally, I'll observe (on televising or in a movie, of course!) some royal ceremony, with all the honor and deference shown to the revered king or queen...and I'll think, it's actually kind of amusing to see how people behave before, treat, and bow to someone else who is a mere mortal exactly as we are. What a curious species we seem to be!

And then, of course, there is the Almighty God of the universe...the one true monarch, in every sense of the meaning of that word, who really does hold the power, the honor, the prestige, the greatness that an actual king holds. We get a picture of who he is in Ezekiel 44&45. In explaining how the temple was to be built, we are told there was a gate that, once God passed through it, was never to be opened again. That truly demonstrated God's greatness and separateness beyond who we are. Then, as God was explaining these things to Ezekiel, God's glory filled the Temple, and this caused Ezekiel to fall down on his face. Even the presence of God near him affected him profoundly. Nearly always, I forget that this is the very same Almighty God who I am praying to, whose words I am reading, who I am living for. I become so familiar with the thought of him being with me...that I tend to just shrug my shoulders or yawn. Lord, help me to get a glimpse of you as Ezekiel did, to see and understand you for who you really are, to live for and honor you as your greatness truly deserves. Open my eyes to you, Lord!

JULY 4

For about ten years before we began serving overseas, during the 1980s, I had a Christian bookstore in Tennessee. It was a time of energy and growth in the Christian book industry, and it looked like the sky was the limit. So, when we decided to go overseas in 1990, I figured that I would get a manager, and hang onto the shop, and perhaps, I thought, it could continue to contribute to our support overseas. On one of our first trips back home for a furlough, I walked into a huge Books-a-Million Bookstore, as I always loved poking around all kinds of bookstores to look at the latest titles and whatever else interesting they might have. Just inside the front door, they had a large display that immediately caught my eye as I walked in. It contained all the current bestsellers... being offered at 40% off. Now, that is great news for anyone...except for a small, struggling, private bookstore like mine. Included in the bestsellers on that display were the top Christian bestsellers as well. I knew instantly that there was no way I could match their discounts, and only one thought went through my mind right then: "We're dead..." Sure enough, not too much longer after that, our sales were slipping, and quickly we could no longer cover our bills. As hard as it was for me to have to close my well-loved bookstore, I knew I had no other choice. Initially, my manager had wanted to buy it from me. But as the months passed, she also realized that she would not be able to turn a profit, and so she backed out of the takeover plan. My only recourse at that point was to just shut it down altogether. Somehow, I heard about a Christian book discounter, who would buy out the leftover stock from shops that were closing, and then sell the stock in his large warehouse. I realized that this was about the only option I had left. So, we agreed that he would come, take over the whole thing as is, for a set price. It was a very painful day for me, but there was nothing else I could do except move on from the business I had loved so much. A number of years later, we decided to move from Europe to China, where again we saw a great need for God's Word, that we hoped to fill in some small way. After initial investigations, we realized that it would probably be impossible for a foreigner to open a Christian bookstore in that country. So, we reverted to plan "B", which was to accumulate a large sized English library in our own home in China, and then to invite students and others to come to our home and make use of the books (as well as to hopefully study the Bible with us). Because of our work in the Christian book industry, we had good contacts with many of the publishers. I wrote to a number of them to tell them of our plans, and to invite them to join us in putting together our library. We were greatly encouraged by a good many books that were donated to us in this way. I don't really remember if I wrote to him or not, but the man who owned the discount warehouse and had bought me out some years ago, also heard about our China plans. He invited me over for a chat, and we sat down together. "You can walk through my warehouse and take whatever you want for China!" I was stunned. "Let me get this straight," I said. "What if I walk through here and take everything you have??" He said, "Take whatever you want." To say that I felt like a kid in a candy shop probably wouldn't do it justice. I think I felt more like I was walking through Santa's global warehouse, just before Christmas! At any rate, I hope I didn't go overboard in taking advantage of his huge generosity... I do seem to remember carting out several boxes of books and Bibles for China after canvassing his whole place.

The memory of what happened to me that day comes to mind when I read the words that Paul wrote to Philemon in his short letter to him. "You lost Onesimus for a little while, so that you could have him back forever." Philemon's slave had fled, run away. So, he had lost something of great value to himself. But, in God's timing and plans, Onesimus was returned to him...and more. He would now be his Christian brother forever. God knows all about our lives. He controls all that happens. Sometimes he allows us to lose something...because he has another thing in mind that is even better for us. As much as I was saddened to have to shut down my bookstore, it was the only way forward at the time, and the discounter helped me out in that hard moment. But then, later, God brought him back into my life to bless me even more, in a way I could never have for foreseen. God's ways are really surprising and amazing. Let's trust him and see what he does...(which may include losing a few things along the way, because he has something better in mind for us.).

JULY 5

Day/Date   Be sure to remember five things to be grateful for every day.   July 5

Exodus 33:15 NIV   If your presence does not go with us, do not send us up from here.

When God told Moses to go into the land God had promises to him, Moses was wise enough to say, "I'm not going unless you go with me." We will be wise to recognize that we can't and shouldn't go through life on our own without God's help and presence. Thankfully, this is exactly what he desires to do.

My first visit to Pakistan was quite an eye opener. The crowds, the heat, the prominence of Islam which was something new to me, the scents of mysterious spices, the crowded and narrow alleyways. We walked into one bank and were met right in front by a "Complaints Desk". I thought, well, that's very considerate customer service, to seek out the comments and reactions of their clients. Behind the desk sat a sober soldier...with his hand on a double barreled shotgun. I came to the reflective conclusion that I just was unable to think of a single thing to complain about on that particular day. Maybe tomorrow, yes, but definitely not today. Later, our bookstore coworker took us weaving and dodging through crowded and fascinating alleyways with all kinds of sellers and hawkers...which I found mildly unsettling, as eyes zeroed in on these gringoes, in this hotbed where the Taliban happened to have made their residence in Karachi. But, our coworker cheerfully led us on, plowing through the crowds without a care in Karachi. As long as he was in charge, and I was reasonably sure he knew what he was doing, I felt remarkably safe. (Though my two back pockets had been slit by razor blades, I discovered, when we returned to our hotel room. Thankfully, I was not in the habit of carrying my wallet in my back pocket...)

When I read David's words in Psalm 110, I am reminded of those alleyways on that day in Pakistan. Not especially a place I would want to venture into alone, I really did feel secure as long as our friend was with us. What David talks about is light years more sure and certain than any fleeting security I may have grasped at on that hot March day in Asia. David makes allusion to the Messiah, to our Savior, that certainly he did not fully understand himself. The psalm says: "The Lord has taken an oath. You are a priest forever. The Lord stands at your right hand to protect you." God is truth...it is outside of his character to be untruthful. So, really, God never needs to make an oath. His word is already far more certain than any oath we could possibly conceive of. But when the passage says that God takes an oath, God is emphasizing to us emphatically, without a breath of doubt, that this will happen. It's so certain, it's as if it was already done yesterday and can't be changed. It's already happened and accomplished. What is God talking about here? He's talking about what Jesus did as our priest, as our Redeemer, in securing our salvation. Once he's done it, it can't be undone or reversed. Additionally, he stands with us to protect us. At our "right hand" is the most important place for him to be. So, when we trust in him for our salvation, Jesus has already accomplished it, it's fixed in concrete, it can't be changed, and he's standing with us, moment by moment, to watch over us. No crooked alleyways to worry about, no uncertainties to contend with, no worries that he may not know where he's leading us. Now, that is security we can stand on. Thank you, God!

JULY 6

The summer I turned 14, my family headed from our home in Korea to a furlough in Atlanta, Georgia, where I was to meet my passion for some years to come, the Atlanta Braves baseball team. But, on the way, we stopped off in Osaka, Japan, to take in the World's Fair, better known as, Expo 70. It was my first experience encountering something rather exotic and global in scale, so I was very excited. Especially, since there were loads of country pavilions (a new word I learned there), where I could feast on postage stamps from the world over, my particular passion at the time. My cousins, whose family were missionaries there in Japan, thought I was completely nuts to be spending all my carefully saved pennies on stamps, of all things. There were some pretty cool country displays. Australia's was an open air stadium, and they had a groovy rock band that played everyday. I really enjoyed returning to New Zealand's repeatedly. They had the most delicious lamb burgers I had ever tasted (the only ones I'd ever tasted, actually). But the two that were most popular and most sought after, perhaps not surprisingly, were the USSR and the USA. The Russian pavilion was a white, grand edifice that swept up to the sky, mounted by a hammer and sickle. Oddly, the US pavilion was more like a flying saucer, as low to the ground as any country's there, and with all its displays below ground level.

Both had long lines of patient (and impatient) people waiting to get in. I sighed and figured we would miss out on both of them. But, good fortune was on our side. One day it rained, and we noticed that the USSR line was very sparse. Seizing the opportunity, we jumped in, and I still remember today, the wonderful pleasure I received from all the Russian stamps that I picked up that day (and still have, tucked away somewhere). Then, good fortune visited us again. It just so happened that my cousins knew someone who was working at the US pavilion. One day we met their friend at a side door, not open to the normal common people, and we walked right in, skirting all the riffraff masses waiting in the hot sun. That was pretty fun, too, especially as important as it made me feel to waltz right past all the lowly folks. I already had plenty of American stamps, so their selection wasn't overly impressive to me.

What is interesting about all this, at least to me, is the subject of Ezekiel 46-48. It goes on and on about the details of the Temple, the protocol for approaching it, the area surrounding it, and so forth. There are certain doors, not open to the common people (I'm afraid in this case, that means you and me.), that only the royalty may enter through…kind of like that side door to the US pavilion, that made us feel like celebrities for a few moments. But the really cool thing about those special doors to the Temple is just this: when Jesus hung on that terrible cross for you and for me, he blew open those exclusive Temple doors and invited us straight into the king's presence. Isn't that grand! And not only does it not require a special invitation, we don't have to wait for a rainy day. We are invited into God's presence, any time, any day. What are we waiting for?? This is way better than Russian postage stamps!

JULY 7

Whenever we're in Asia, I remind my European wife that, in Asia, it's the thought that counts. OK, so we don't need one more set of mugs that someone brings us...but they are expressing their care for and thankfulness to us through the gesture, so that's really what's important...and we can be grateful for the expression given by this gift, even if our mugs are already spilling out of our cupboards. My good friend, Mr. Kim, contacted me shortly before we left Korea to return to the US, this last time. Generally, once a month, we'll have lunch together just to catch up and enjoy each other's company. Several months ago, the wives tagged along as well, and that was fun, too. But, the last time we met together, he picked me up in his car, which was unusual, since we normally travel by subway to meet at a park or shopping area that has restaurants or coffee shops to choose from. We drove and drove, and I wasn't sure where he was taking me. Then, we started climbing up a wooded hill, a rarity in this bustling metropolis, and my curiosity rose a few more notches. What was going on here? We turned onto a road that only recently had been opened to the public. We passed a few foreign embassies, and my friend casually mentioned that this was a pretty expensive, exclusive area. Then we passed the "Blue House", not to be confused with the White House, this is the residence of the Korean President. Finally, when we could climb no more, we pulled into a restaurant valet parking area, and headed inside. We were directed into a roomy, quiet corner, and sat down. Several spiffily dressed waiters and waitresses came hovering around to take care of us. Gradually, dishes began to arrive. The first was delicious and filling. Another arrived, then another, and another. Although I grew up in Korea, these were quite special dishes that I didn't even recognize the names of. They were, each one, so delicious…I wish I knew how to describe the tastes, but, trust me, they were exquisite. I tried to help pay for the meal, and Mr. Kim said, "Next time…next time." (It seems to be one of his favorite lines. I haven't quite figured out yet how to get around it.) As we departed from those very special moments spent together, I got to thinking…you know, he wanted to give me a gesture. He wanted me to taste the depth and sweetness of our friendship through this special dinner together. I was touched by his gesture, as well as by the wonderful gourmet meal.

Hebrews 2 says something powerful, in verse 9, that sends us a powerful message, as well. It says that, "by God's grace, Jesus tastes death for everyone". Later, in chapter 4, it talks about us being able to find rest because of what Jesus did for us, because of God's undeserved love for us. But, Jesus wasn't just executed in our place, by hanging or by a firing squad. He tasted death in our place. He experienced the full taste for us, just as I received the full taste of Mr. Kim's friendship during our meal together. Jesus suffered the full, deep, painful, excruciating, dark death that we deserved, both to pay the penalty for the punishment we deserved, but also as a sign of God's love for us. He tasted what we should have tasted, what I should have tasted, and it reminds me of the friendship I also tasted through that delicious meal that day.

JULY 8

Day/Date Be sure to remember five things to be grateful for every day. July 8

Proverbs 18:20 NCV People will be rewarded for what they say; they will be rewarded by how they speak.

Does it matter what we say and how we live? If God has saved us, should it matter what we do after that? Yes, it is important. How we speak and live each day honors God, draws others to him, and makes us more like he wants us to be ~ or else it does not do these things.

When we landed in England, on a warm July 4th day in 1995, we knew almost no one, and as we nervously landed on the shores of this nation that ours had broken away from two centuries before, on this exact same day, we weren't sure what to expect, as the Immigration officials snapped up our passports and marched me away. But, instead of a lecture about our naughty predecessors, the Customs officials gave us a chunk of the White Cliffs of Dover that we had just crossed, and told us: "Welcome to England!" To complicate matters a bit, our seventh child was born less than a month later. That was a hard time for my wife...alone, no friends, no Mom for herself, or grandmother for our kids... I encouraged her to join a ladies Bible study at the church we began attending to get some of the support she was needing at that moment...and it was there where she encountered Grace. Grace was an "older lady", a step or two ahead of us in life, with five mostly grown kids of her own, while our seven still had a lot of their growing up to do. Grace was everything my wife needed at that moment...a Mom, friend, confidante, grandmother to our kids, encourager...of all the people we've ever known, her name probably described the best who she was. She just exuded grace. My wife would be busily cleaning up the lunch dishes from the table (while I was off changing the world!), the kids would be scattering in every direction, and the doorbell would ring. There stood Grace, a smile on her face, a bouquet of tulips in her hands. How did she know that my

Dutch wife loved tulips?? She would come in, sit at the kitchen table, and my wife would have a good "natter", while Grace just quietly listened as my wife unburdened herself of the cares of her busy world. How did she do this? How did she find the time, with her completely engaged involvement at church, with her busy surgeon husband who headed up a Christian literature organization, among other things? How did they have time to host us, visit us, pull us into their family, love us? I'm not sure she did find the time...it was just who and what Grace was. She couldn't help herself.

That's the same thing we find in Psalm 111. We are given a picture of who God is: a doer of amazing, glorious, and majestic deeds; a God of wonder, righteousness, grace, and mercy; the Sovereign who gives generously, is always faithful, and always good; the One who is holy, trustworthy, and who has paid our debt. What a God we have...the Almighty who just can't help himself...because that is who he is. He's not able to be different than his character...just like our dear friend Grace. What a great God we have!

JULY 9

As long as I've known her, my wife has worn glasses. As she got older, her right eye became slightly cloudy, and her eye doctor could no longer correct her vision with a new pair of glasses. So, he recommended cataract surgery. Her eyesight is amazing now. No longer needing glasses, she can read, see at a distance, and drive...all without glasses. It was as if someone had waved a magic wand over her face, and suddenly, her eyesight was perfect. But I know better. Because, you see, quite surprisingly to me, the doctor invited me to observe her cataract surgery, and so I did. It was an amazing experience. She lay there on the table, and the operation began. I won't go into all the details for the faint of heart, but, suffice it to say that I watched with great interest as the doctor skillfully cut away her impaired lens, pulled it out, and then inserted a new one. It was all very quick, smooth, and tidy. I found it so interesting, in fact, that I thought, I should do this, too, so that my wife can watch me get this surgery as well. Being the scientist that she is, I knew that she would find the whole procedure quite fascinating.

Actually, my wife's cataract surgery reminds me of the story of Daniel. In chapters 1&2, we are told repeatedly that God did this, allowed that, caused the other thing to happen. It's abundantly clear to us that God is behind the events that are happening. Not just behind them, as if in hiding, but, he's actually, deliberately orchestrating all the events. In many ways, Esther and Daniel are very similar stories. Both take place in the foreign empires that had dominated Israel. And in both, you can clearly see God at work behind the scenes of the events. The one big difference, though, is that, in Daniel, we're told explicitly that God did this and that. In Esther, we are left to sense that God is working behind the scenes, because the account doesn't specifically tell us that, that was what was happening. For any friend of ours who saw my wife after her surgery, they would know it had been done, even though they had not observed it. For me, it was like reading the book of Daniel. I not only saw the result of the surgery, I observed it happening...just like we see God working in Daniel. Life is like that, isn't it. Sometimes we see God working in dramatic ways. Other times, we are pretty sure God is working behind the scenes, but we can't see it definitively. That's the Esther perspective. But either way, in both cases, God is at work. Thank God, that he is on our side (assuming we're on his side, that is!), always there, always with us, always faithful, always working out his (and our) good plans. Thank you, Lord!

JULY 10

Day/Date Be sure to remember five things to be grateful for every day July 10

James 4:12 NCV God is the only Lawmaker and Judge. So it is not right for you to judge your neighbor.

At times we may be treated unfairly. At other times, we may see people living unrighteously. But in either case, God is the holy and righteous One, and considering how much he has forgiven us, we are in no position to judge others who are also sinners.

The US Civil War makes for an interesting study in personalities, on both sides of the conflict. Lincoln mostly clashed with his own generals, until, finally, US Grant showed up on the scene and showed that he could fight. That was all Lincoln needed, so he let Grant and his buddy, Sherman, get on with the business at hand. On the other side, Robert E. Lee was blessed with a whole boatload on good generals. One in particular, Stonewall Jackson, he leaned heavily on to carry out his plans. Both men were from historic Virginia, from old school military traditions. Knowing they were outmanned and outgunned by the North, both men realized they had to fight hard, hit unexpectedly, and hightail it as soon as they ran out of bullets. That was their strategy, and they understood each other intuitively. General Lee knew that no matter what happened, whatever unexpected or dangerous situation arose, Jackson would be there to respond and arise to the specific occasion. Lee knew that Jackson would meet the circumstances in the same way Lee would have, and that if anyone could pull through, it was Jackson that would make it happen.

Hebrews 5-7 talks about the same kind of person that we can count on implicitly. It this case, however, the stakes are even higher than they were when the Civil War armies collided. Hebrews is talking about who we have to count on to fill in the gap for us spiritually, redemptively, eternally. In our spiritually bankrupt condition, we required a Savior we could be sure of, one who would show up and meet the specific needs that our condition required. In this passage, God tells us that he deliberately chose Jesus because he knew, with more certainty than Lee did with Jackson, that Jesus was the precise solution to our need, once and for all, but also, that he still, daily, stands in our behalf, and brings our needs before his Father, God Almighty. Jesus filled in for us, met our needs, and is still here with us, daily, and always. With more certainty than General Jackson ever could do.

JULY 11

> 1 Peter 1:2 NCV God planned long ago to choose you by making you his holy people, which is the Spirit's work. God wanted you to obey him and to be made clean by the blood of the death of Jesus Christ. When we trust Jesus for his salvation on our behalf, we are counted as being clean from sin because of what Jesus did for us. But the reality is that we still have sin and disobedience within us. As we open our lives to the work of the Spirit in us, he makes us into people who are closer to how God wants us to be.

It frequently surprises me, when I am visiting Bangladesh or Korea, where my father spent all of his working years, how often I will encounter someone who knew my Dad or had run across him in the hospital in Korea or the clinics in Bangladesh. He left Korea in 1974, Bangladesh in 1999...yet, still I run into people who knew him or knew of him. He was one small individual in a little known corner of far off Korea, and an older doctor toiling in medical clinics in the slums of Bangladesh. I just recall seeing him march off to work every day in Korea, or, in later years, receiving his letters from Bangladesh, telling about his work there. So, it's remarkable to me that some people still remember him being around. Even my memory of him is fading these days, and I suppose others will gradually forget him, too. How fleeting life seems to be. What we do today seems so important. Then, one day, it's over, and a few people remember us. Gradually, the memory of us fades altogether. I think about that sometimes as I walk through a cemetery...all the lives represented there...does anyone remember them?

But there is one thing that is remembered, that does last. Psalm 112 tells us about it, with great excitement, as if the writer has uncovered a before unknown treasure. He says this to us:

"Their children will be successful everywhere."

"An entire generation will be blessed."

"Their good deeds will last forever."

That sounds pretty amazing. They will never be forgotten. So, who are these people who will be successful in this way? The psalmist tells us. It is those "who fear the Lord", those who reverence and have confidence in him. The writer goes on about these same people, telling us that they "trust in the Lord". This psalm tells us that those who belong to God will not be forgotten, that when we trust God, he remembers us and preserves us. That our spiritual lives that belong to God will endure. There are many things we can do in this life, in this world. But, as we look way back through history, we realize that very little is remembered...most things are long forgotten. But what we do for Christ will last...our relationship to God will endure forever. The famous British cricketer and missionary, C.T. Studd expresses it well in the lines of his poem:

Two little lines I heard one day,

Traveling along life's busy way;

Bringing conviction to my heart,

And from my mind would not depart;

Only one life, 'twill soon be past,

Only what's done for Christ will last.

JULY 12

> Day/Date Be sure to remember five things to be grateful for every day. July 12
>
> James 4:14-15 NCV "You do not Know what will happen tomorrow! So you should say, "If the Lord wants, we will do this or that."
>
> It is wise and correct to realize that although we make plans and preparations for many things, we still are dependent on how God is working in our lives and how he is guiding events. Let's not be so proud or mistaken to think that everything depends on our own plans and decisions.

After a tiring day of teaching and traveling around Seoul to the schools where we volunteer, there is nothing we enjoy more, some evenings, than to settle into our bed, with dinner on a tray in our laps, and then to switch on a movie to relax in front of. One kind of movie we enjoy is a tale that has a twist, a mystery that pulls you along, leaving you guessing at how it's going to be resolved, who is really the hero and the villain, when the dust and the bullets finally settle. Sometimes we don't know right till the end how the puzzle will be solved, and someone who certainly appeared suspect along the way turns out to be pretty innocent. You would think that, after watching a few dozen of such stories, we would be able to fairly easily figure out what is happening. But, they seem to surprise us most of the time.

I'm sure someone who is clever and imaginative could turn the book of Daniel into one, or several, mysterious shows with some interesting twists and unexpected turns in it as well. Daniel is a wonderfully encouraging book in that it lets us in on what's happening behind the scenes of the apparent story. We see events happening, with all the drama and suspense of any James Bond movie, but then we are also given a glimpse of how God is working behind the scenes, how he is actually calling the shots and determining the flow of things in the way that he chooses. When we think about our lives, about our world, when we see events that look out of control or beyond mending...let's remind ourselves of the book of Daniel. Chapters 3&4 show us events that are crazy and desperate...but then we are shown what's happening behind the first images, and we realize that, actually, all appearances to the contrary, it is going to work out OK. God's in charge, it will all work for good. It most likely will be a wild and rough ride at times, as Daniel and his buddies discovered, perhaps a little too close for comfort. But, thankfully, they held onto God, they trusted him, when there seemed to be no reason to do so...and he didn't let them down. He promises to do the same for us, as well.

JULY 13

Blood really is pretty thick. We didn't have very much to do with who our family is, but all through life it's hard to escape it. I was attending a conference in Australia some time ago, and slipped into a meeting a few minutes late. I had come into this session because I knew the name of the speaker, and so I was interested to hear what he had to say. As the gathering came to an end, he asked my name, since I had arrived too late to introduce myself at the beginning. As soon as I mentioned my name, his whole face broke into a smile, and he started talking about memories he had of my family from 50 years earlier. I had hardly met him before...perhaps a time or two in passing...but, because of the family connection, the name, he responded as if I was a long lost friend who meant everything to him. That's what family does for you. For good, or occasionally for bad, we are linked all our lives, it seems, to the blood that we come from.

The book of Hebrews talks a lot about blood. About the sacrifice Jesus made on our behalf. We are connected permanently to him because of the blood he spilled for us. And his task was totally fulfilled. Jesus completed the payment for our disobedience to God in full...and then sat down, signifying that his work was done. But then, we are told that he continues to minister on our behalf. He still brings our needs before the Father, daily, moment by moment, because we are now connected to him by his blood, by being adopted into his family forever. That is beautiful. That is wonderful. That is permanent, and can't be taken away from us. Thank the Lord!

JULY 14

Perhaps my siblings can correct me here if my memory is getting a little carried away, but I seem to remember my mother telling me that, when we were paid each month in Korea, when I was a boy, my father would divide the wad of local currency in half. He would give half to Mom, so we could eat, and he would pocket the other half, to distribute to needy people he encountered along the way. I'm sure we might be shocked at how little their wage was back in those days, but still, in the Korean money, it was a pretty good sized stack of money. Now, my father would not be accused of being the most astute with finances, with planning, with administration...well, perhaps with most anything that had to do with running a medical facility. He seemed to allow his heart to dictate his decisions...whether it had to do with his time, his money, how he lived...I mean, why would he save for a rainy day when those around him were trying to eat on a sunny day? So, that was how he lived. His heart was focused on the poor and needy...those without food, those requiring help medically, those heading down the wrong road spiritually... He just seemed to use up what he had...why else would he have been given it, if it wasn't to help the needy with? That seemed to be his logic. I remember, in 1973, as he and I landed in Baltimore, where his elderly mother lived, after we had visited Bangladesh and come halfway around the world, we got out of our taxi upon arrival from the airport...and he had about 25 cents left in his pocket. You couldn't accuse him of not using what he had, that's for sure. I'm sure he could have been correctly accused of careless planning...but, truthfully, he life spoke loudly to me of using what God had given him...to help those that had not been so blessed.

I can't help thinking about my father's life when I read the words of Psalm 113: "He stoops to look down. He lifts the poor from the dust and the needy from the garbage dump." We can spend a lot of time and energy discussing, defining, and planning finances and the wise use of them. And I wouldn't disagree with doing that. But the question I have to ask myself is, am I lifting the needy from the garbage dump? Could anyone accuse me of doing that? Of doing it too much? Too recklessly? (You don't have to answer that question!) Perhaps it's a question we all need to reflect on. It is, after all, the heart of God.

JULY 15

> **Day/Date** Be sure to remember five things to be grateful for every day. *July 15*
>
> **1 Peter 2:9 NCV** You were chosen to tell about the wonderful acts of God, who called you out of darkness into his wonderful light.
>
> It is a very wonderful thing to recognize the darkness of our sin and lostness, and then to experience the forgiveness, joy, and new life that comes with salvation. As wonderful as it is, God plans for us to announce this great news to others who aren't aware of it. This is what God wants us to do.

It seems that the more we know of life, the more mysterious it is. Perhaps the best conclusion we can come to is that God is mysterious...and, thankfully, good. I'm reminded of the English poet and hymn writer, William Cowper, who lived a tortured and pained life, during which, he wrote these well known words:

"God moves in a mysterious way,

    His wonders to perform;

He plants his footsteps in the sea,

    And rides upon the storm.

Deep in unfathomable mines

    Of never failing skill;

He treasures up his bright designs,

    And works His sovereign will.

Ye fearful saints fresh courage take,

    The clouds ye so much dread

Are big with mercy, and shall break

In blessings on your head.

Judge not the Lord by feeble sense,

But trust him for his grace;

Behind a frowning providence,

He hides a smiling face.

His purposes will ripen fast,

Unfolding ev'ry hour;

The bud may have a bitter taste,

But sweet will be the flow'r.

Blind unbelief is sure to err,

And scan his work in vain;

God is his own interpreter,

And he will make it plain."

Cowper was born into a pastor's family, but his mother died in childbirth when William was six. He and his younger brother were the only two, out of seven children, to survive beyond infancy. So, it's not surprising that he struggled all his life with depression, self doubt, and suicidal thoughts. It's hard to understand or make sense of his life. However, God, in his goodness, allowed Cowper to be a blessing to the converted slave trader, pastor, and hymn writer, John Newton...and, of course his hymns have been used to bless us as well.

We see God at work in powerful, mysterious, and good ways, in Daniel 5&6. The Babylonian king, Belshazzar, learned the hard way, that it's dangerous to mess around with God. He knew from the previous king, Nebuchadnezzar, that God was the Almighty Sovereign of the universe. But, Belshazzar had ignored that truth and flaunted what he knew of God. God responded by appearing in a mysterious and terrifying way, with the famous handwriting on the wall, to bring about righteousness. Later, when King Darius came along, Daniel was greatly punished and allowed to suffer for his commitment to God. It's a puzzle, mysterious again, why God would allow Daniel to suffer so severely for being a faithful follower of God. As with William Cowper, we don't fully understand it; but, we can see how God used it for good, and brought good out of evil circumstances. Perhaps neither Cowper nor Daniel understood fully what God was doing...but, thankfully, in the midst of the mystery, they clung to God's goodness...and we are still being blessed, even now, by both of their examples. When things seem to be a puzzling mystery to us today, let's remember the examples of these two men. What God is doing is frequently difficult for us to comprehend at this moment. He does allow us to suffer, as he brings about his good purposes. And, his good plans and righteousness will prevail. That, we can be thankful for!

JULY 16

One of the Bible teachers we studied under in college was well liked for the down to earth, friendly manner he conveyed to everyone. He joined in on pick up basketball games between classes, and had some pretty slick moves, considering he seemed to be rather ancient, compared to us young kids. And, he had one chapel message, given over and over each year, which became legendary. He would pack out the auditorium whenever he gave his three lettered message: "Sex". Teaching us Christian doctrine, what our beliefs are all about, he was famous for talking about the "now, but not yet". It was during the semester we took doctrine that I began to get to know a certain Dutch girl. When he talked about the now, but not yet, he was referring to the salvation that Christ accomplished for us, fully completed…but, which we don't fully realize while we still live in this sin-filled, sin-ravaged world. Hebrews 10 talks about a similar concept, except that it refers to the animal sacrifices in the Old Testament, which were a shadow or a picture of the once and for all sacrifice that Jesus made for us. During Old Testament times, they could anticipate and have an idea of Jesus' death and resurrection, but they hadn't experienced it fully. Both the ancient sacrifices, as well as the now, but not yet situation we are living in today, are perhaps illustrated by a couple of paintings produced for us by student friends in Korea. As the paintings were underway, we got a few glimpses of them. It was very apparent what they were developing into, but at the same time, it was clear that they were not yet completed. So, we had to look forward to and anticipate the finished portraits. Hebrews 10 talks about "a shadow, a dim preview of the good things to come, not the good things themselves". All these images and shadows of the final product made me eagerly look forward to what is to come, what one day will be the reality...when there will be no more brokenness, sadness, pain, or loss. Yes, Lord, bring it on, and soon!

JULY 17

1 Peter 2:12 NCV   Live good lives that will give glory to God on the day when Christ comes again.

All my life as a parent, I've been motivated by the knowledge that my life would, for better or worse, have a significant impact on my children. How much more important it is for us, spiritually, to live lives that honor God, knowing that our manner of living will have eternal consequences.

For seven years, we lived in a small, dusty outback, a little town that until recently had been unknown to the rest of the world. But it included a large university, and that is what attracted us to it. The school included many students from nearby surrounding countries, and so it provided an important possibility for reaching a broad spectrum of young people. Unbeknownst to me as we relocated there, a major highway had not long before been laid from the provincial capital, all the way to that town, and suddenly this spot of Dali became a sought after destination, for its spectacular Himalayan setting, its ideal weather, and its unique tribal minority culture. A handful of foreigners were also attracted to Dali...for it's culture, it's language opportunities, its medical needs, its outdoor activities... Occasionally, we would encounter some of the "weiguoren", the foreigners, but many days could also pass without seeing a one. Then, for special events, Thanksgiving, Christmas, or something else, a group of us would come together to celebrate. Even though we were a motley, hodgepodge clump of folks, still, our weiguoren status drew us together to swap stories and experiences. The very last time we met for such a gathering was for the 40th birthday celebration of one of the guys. I was surprised at the turnout...just about every non-Chinese in the whole district showed up. I guess not much other entertainment was available. The wife and mother who put on this big event for her mildly sheepish husband poured our lavish accolades on her wonderful, marvelous, amazing husband...certainly, all very true. Perhaps I was a touch envious, I don't know. But, obviously he deserved every bit of it.

We actually see a similar thing going on in Psalm 114, a brief, little known, never quoted series of verses referring to the majestic works of God in delivering the Israelites from centuries of slavery in Egypt. Considering the stunning, earth shattering methods that God demonstrated in carrying out his rescue operation, he clearly deserved (and still deserves) something more along the lines of that great birthday celebration in Dali, rather than the skimpy eight verses reserved in his memory. Shall we pause a moment and reflect on what God did then? The same God is active today, carrying out his same dramatic rescue operations. And he won't be denied. I can't wait, one day, when the scales fall from my eyes, to discover what he's been doing all along, in places around the world that I've been praying for. I'm sure we'll be dazzled, even more than by the loving wife's words in Dali, when we hear fully what all he's been doing. What a great God we have, as these few verses also acknowledge.

JULY 18

July 18

James 5:10-11 NCV   The prophets suffered many hard things, but they were patient. You have heard about Job's patience, and you know the Lord's purpose for him in the end. You know the Lord is full of mercy and is kind.

Paul suffered greatly but was confident that there was an important purpose in all that happened to him ~ even though he may not have known immediately the reason behind each incident. No doubt God has reasons and good plans for the hard things we experience ~ a bad job, a difficult marriage, or a painful illness. God can use them all for his glory.

All through our married life, we have encountered interesting people. In our early years, we would invite Japanese engineers and businessmen into our home in Tennessee, welcoming these foreigners in our strange land. They were fascinated by the freedom, openness, and easygoing lifestyle they discovered here. Some even expressed the sentiment of not wanting to return to Japan, where, on the job, one would never dream of leaving the office before 8:00 p.m., before the boss finally closed up shop. Then, it was expected, more like required, to go out drinking with the group, before one could stagger home in the dark, late at night. They couldn't believe how easy we had it here. We hoped to reach some of these folks that we encountered, with the Gospel, which they had never heard. Some returned to us repeatedly, a few expressed spiritual interest, others didn't return at all. It was the same in China. We invited scads of students and others we came across along the way, into our home...for English study, tea and cake, and hopefully, spiritual conversations and Bible study. But, there were some, here and there, who expressed no interest, who didn't return, who, on occasion, even expressed hostility. We wanted so much to share with them some Great News...sadly, some didn't want to hear it.

I expect it's the same with God. He wants so much to give us his Message, to develop a relationship with us, to save us from the mess we find ourselves in, throughout this lost and broken world. Sometimes, that sounds great. Other times, we are too busy or distracted to want to listen. Still other times, perhaps we're just too frightened to want to contemplate other worlds or ideas than what we've neatly constructed around ourselves. We find in chapters 7&8 of Daniel, that God broke into his world with a message...in a most terrifying and baffling way. Daniel could have run or closed his ears, but he didn't. He sat up in bed and listened to the vision that God sent him...which is remarkable, considering how scary the whole event was for him. Daniel tells us that: "I saw terrifying and dreadful things. My face was pale with fear. I became so terrified that I fell with my face to the ground. I fainted and lay there with my face to the ground. I could not understand it." I guess, after all that, if anyone had a right to run, it was Daniel. God was speaking into his life, and he was scared out of his wits...and he had no idea what was going on. Charles Spurgeon has wise and comforting words relating to this passage. He says: "Nothing will happen to us that God has not foreseen. He stands in a position from which he can look down on the whole past, present, and future at a single glance. All the future is foreseen by him and fixed by him." Daniel must have understood this because, even though he was scared out of his wits by God's Message, he didn't run or hide. He listened. I think of all those folks we encountered along the way, those who turned away, who didn't want to listen, when I think of Daniel. God speaks into each of our lives as well...sometimes in scary or unpleasant ways. Will we listen anyway? Will we hear him when he comes to us in ways that are uncomfortable or that might rock our world? God's plans are good. They are fixed, as Spurgeon reminds us. But they are also quite unsettling at times, as Daniel recounts. Let's hold onto him anyway. One day our eyes will be opened fully, and we will then see the greatness, the beauty, the magnificence, the goodness, the pure love, of all that God has been doing. Let's hold onto that...and listen, rather than turning away, as some tragically have done.

JULY 19

Day/Date *Be sure to remember five things to be grateful for every day* July 19

1 Peter 2:13,16 NCV For the Lord's sake, yield. Do not use your freedom as an excuse to do evil. Live as servants of God.

Jesus died so that we would be freed from all of sin's consequences. Real freedom is found in God's forgiveness. But we can be careless in thinking that this means we can live any way we like. We are free so that we can live in honor to God and to serve and encourage others - not so that we can live wickedly.

Our little boy is in a far corner of Africa I have never been to before, likely will never visit. It's a place where there are about the fewest number of doctors, per person, of any place on the planet, where over 80% of the folks will most likely never see a doctor in their lifetime. It's called Mwanza, Tanzania, not that the name probably rings too many bells for most of us. So, how in the world did our little boy end up in such a far off place? Well, to begin with, our little boy is actually 21 years old, about to finish college, before he hopes to head off for further studies in public health. But, I still see him running around the house as a three year old, scurrying to hide from his father, with the ever present camera in tow. It's a little unsettling having your youngest fly the nest, all full of confidence...especially when you know that there are a lot of unexpected, uncomfortable, wish-we-could-forget-them, encounters and people out there in the big wide world. At 20, you're confident you can handle anything that comes your way. By the time you reach my age, if anything, you're surprised you've managed to survive this long. My wife and I both had a few sleepless moments, the night after our boy departed on this far off journey. So, how do you get through an experience like this? I guess I'll tell you if I survive to tell the tale...and if our son makes it back in one piece.

But, actually, we are given the formula on how to make in through, in Hebrews

11:27, where it gives us a riddle, a conundrum, and a contradiction, if you will, but which, at the same time, is the dead on truth. It says, as it talks about the great heroes of the faith from Biblical days, Moses in particular: "He kept his eyes on the One who is invisible". Now, Moses had every reason to be fearful, as in, full of fear. He had grown up in Pharaoh's palace, and he knew firsthand that the king was not to be trifled with. Just a wrong expression, and your head could roll. But this Invisible One, that it talks to us about in Hebrews, gave Moses some marching orders. And, although Moses couldn't see his invisible God, he proceeded with confidence (still probably fearful, mind you), as if God was walking visibly next to him, along with his legions of angels. Moses was so certain of God's presence with him, that he could step out on his terribly challenging and mine strewn path, knowing that God was right there with him. It hasn't gotten easier with time. God, still today, calls us to step out in faith... faith in the one we can't see...to follow his lead, to live the life he's called us to, perhaps even to head off to a far corner of Africa...(or worse, to watch your little boy head off alone to Africa)...because he is the same God that showed himself to be faithful, trustworthy, to Moses, to all those ancient heroes. He's still with us today. This Invisible One can still be trusted. Let's keep our eyes on the One we can't see.

JULY 20

> **Day/Date** Be sure to remember five things to be grateful for every day. July 20
>
> James 5:16 NCV
>
> Confess your sins to each other and pray for each other so God can heal you.
>
> God desires for believers to be a united body in living for and serving him. Part of this includes not keeping or holding on to sin but dealing with it as we become aware of it, as well as praying for each other. When we are living in this way, we experience God's healing in many different ways!

I have to say...I'm beginning to wonder if one of those high tech companies (or is it the Democrats...OK, OK, bad joke!) has somehow slipped one of those computer chips into my brain when I wasn't aware of it. What makes me wonder about it is that I've been starting to get all these videos appearing on my Facebook page. How do they know what I like? How do they know all this stuff about me?? It does make me wonder. I can handle the tennis championships, and the baseball is OK. When the boxing matches start showing up, that's stretching it a bit. Recently, all these soupy singers from the 1960s and 70s have been appearing. Maybe they're mixing me up with one of my roommates, I don't know, because I never listened to music in high school and college. Of course, I had roommates from age 12-21, so it's possible that the chip is confusing me for someone else. Anyway, all of a sudden, all these drippy oldies are showing up...Neil Diamond, the Carpenters, The Who, the Mamas and the Papas...even Elvis has resurrected a time or two... Good grief, where are all these things coming from? I have to say, though, it does take me back...man, it takes me back. To those days of roller coaster, raging hormones...those moments when one glance by a certain girl could make your whole day...or a perceived snub could set you down in the dumpy doldrums for days. What crazy days. And those songs bring it all back. All those folks sing with passion about love lost, love missed, love shipwrecked...my, those trying teenage days! It's a miracle any of us survived. But, on hindsight (so far hind that I can hardly see it...), I wonder why we let all that stuff tug at us so much. Why did we chase all that music, all those whiffs of smoke that dissipated in an instant?

Because there is something better...oh, so much better, so much more secure, reliable, certain, and able to be trusted. Psalm 115 tells us about it. The writer (and he may have been a singer, I don't know...) assures us that God's love and faithfulness are always with us, they are unfailing. We can trust him; he wants to protect, help, and bless us. I mean, why would we chase after all those illusions, when we can have something that is secure, more satisfying, much more likely to give us joy? I don't know. But not much has changed. The same, or similar, distractions try to grab my attention and my heart today, just like in those old days. (OK, probably Elvis won't distract me too seriously, but...other things can.) Will I learn this time around? Will I remember that all those other things vanish like the mist...that God delivers on what he promises? I hope so...and I hope that will be the reality for all of us, as well.

JULY 21

Day/Date Be sure to remember five things to be grateful for every day. July 21

Daniel 3:28 NCV They were willing to die rather than serve or worship any god other than their own.

During Daniel's day, there was tremendous pressure, even including the threat of death for disobedience, to bow before the ruler of the empire. No doubt some bowed out of fear, against their true beliefs. But Daniel and his friends knew that God was who he said he was; and they were willing to hold to their beliefs, knowing that it would send them to their deaths. They could not imagine betraying their God and King.

As we've lived in multiple places in the US and around the world, we've attended and joined many good churches and fellowships...Anglican, Evangelical Free, non-denominational, Presbyterian, government, underground, above ground, and probably one or two others. Many good folks, good pastors, good preachers, good music...we've been blessed multiple times over. The one or two pastors who really stand out to me, personally, are the ones who bring us into an understanding that we are coming, undeservingly, into the presence of a great and holy God. Different pastors have a variety of gifts and strengths, but for me, anyway, the ones I most appreciate are the ones who help me gain a picture of who God is...and who I am.

I suppose we would all like to sit under Daniel's preaching...can you imagine him recounting to us how he bunked down in the dark with a pack of starving lions, and lived to tell the tale, seeing God's handwriting on the wall, or dramatic dreams he was able to understand and interpret? Wow, what an amazing experience that would be. We gain a large picture of what Daniel experienced, as he encountered...and discovered...who God is, in Daniel 9&10. There are so many lessons in those 38 verses...we would probably do well to read them every day for a week, or longer. Someone who's a good theologian could probably write a compelling book simply on those two chapters. Let me just mention a few interesting points:

1) Daniel says he learned from reading God's Word. I find it remarkable that someone who heard and saw God speak and act in the amazing, supernatural ways that he did...learned from reading the Bible. And, he only had bits of the Old Testament at his disposal. We have a feast today in the whole Bible we have in our hands, compared to what Daniel held. Am I reading to learn what God is waiting to teach me today? Am I digging into it every day?

2) He pleaded and confessed to God, acknowledging Israel's many sins. Additionally, even though he heard God dramatically, it was not at all unnecessary for him to ask for forgiveness and pardon for himself and his people. Granted, I'm rather a cynic and a pessimist, but as I look around me, I have to wonder whether we are not in the same place today...a place of needing to repent before God. Now, Daniel was living as a captive exile, a position none of us would ever want to be in. So, how did he pray? God, get us out of here?!? No, he prayed for mercy for their sins. This disastrous year of 2020 (which thankfully is nearly over!), I've heard a lot of prayers asking God to get us out of this mess. But am I praying that other kind of prayer, as Daniel did...Lord, have mercy on our grievous sins, personally, and those of our nation and society? Is that what God is waiting for us to do? It seems to me that there is a lot we could and should be praying about in that department.

3) Even though we don't deserve it, God is merciful and forgiving to us. Am I thanking him daily for that? Daniel did, repeatedly.

4) God is not past scaring the living daylights out of us (never mind exile and slavery), to get his message across to us. When an angel showed up, Daniel, who we would expect would be used to these sorts of encounters, was so scared that he fell down comatose and unable to speak. And, of course, don't forget the lion's den and other things that God brought his way. God will work out his good plans...even when it means scaring us to death or giving us quite a ride in the process. (I have to admit, that frightens me!)

5) Amazing...the angel Gabriel told Daniel: "The instant you started to mouth a prayer, I was commanded to come to you with a message!" How often do you and I pray? Do I realize that when I start talking to God, big things start happening? Not because I'm great or spiritual...but, because God loves us, hears us, and loves to answer us. Imagine, if every time I opened my mouth, the President or

the Queen jumped into action in response to my words, with all the power and resources at their disposal. Now, imagine if the Almighty God of the universe did that? Guess what...he does.

6) God told Daniel three times in these verses: "You are precious to me. Don't be afraid." It's hard for me, in my little weak self, to reconcile these words with the lion's den or the fiery furnace. How does God put someone so precious to him...through such agony? But it's remarkable, and, I think, shows us the depth and distance God will go to carry out his wonderful plans, that he, at times, allows his precious children to suffer. I would never want any of my own children to suffer...so, if I did allow them to suffer, it would have to be for something terribly, terribly important. I would never do it casually. What that tells me is that, when we are suffering, God is allowing us to participate in something very, very important, just as he did with his own son. (Of course, I'm not talking about suffering for my own stupidity or sinfulness...that's another thing altogether.) But, the point is, we are very precious to God. And, going through suffering does not mean that he doesn't treasure us.

(Goodness, I almost did write a book...I'm sure there's a lot more there, but that's what jumped out at me in the first round.)

JULY 22

James 5:16 NCV — When a believing person prays, great things happen.

God does not answer our prayers because of our great faith. Rather, our weak and small faith in the almighty God is rewarded by God because of his love and goodness. Our strength is nothing to God — but we serve a great God who loves to hear us call to him.

Most of my life growing up, I was the youngest in the family. All my older siblings will tell you, emphatically, that I was hardly disciplined at all, at least compared to them. I don't know if that's true or not, though I do remember being disciplined, sometimes painfully...both at home and at school. We ourselves have nine kids, and it's the same story with them. It seems that the higher up in the pecking order you are, the more certain you are that you were disciplined the most, that the younger ones got off easy. Again, I don't know if that's true or not. I sure felt like we disciplined them all the same. But, did we mellow and ease up in our advanced parenting years? Or, maybe, it was just that we had the routine down by the time number nine rolled around, so it looked more effortless and easy, both on him and on us. (I wonder if there are any child psychologists around who could answer these questions.) But, back to me. I do remember being disciplined, and thinking it wasn't fair. (I mean, I was an angel. What could I possibly have done wrong??) And, I'm sure that even the awareness of the possibility of discipline kept me from doing more bad things than the three times in my childhood when I actually did something bad. It's interesting, though, looking at our society today from the viewpoint of an also ran, how the perspective on discipline has changed. It seems to have become an off limits topic, something we just don't talk about in polite society, kind of like our weight, or the question of divorce. The Bible does seem to touch on these questions, most often on the topic of discipline.

So, what does the Bible say about it? Well, Hebrews 12&13 talks about it...and not in some sensitive, off limits, kind of way, but just in an ordinary, everyday discussion, sort of way. Here's what we read:

1) Following Jesus is tough, and it requires discipline...the kind of discipline that an athlete undertakes. As Christians, we can't set our life on cruise control and just coast along. We are fallen, selfish humans, living in an evil, broken world. There are a lot of things pushing and pulling against us, and it takes intentional, hard work...or as Eugene Peterson likes to call it, "A long obedience in the same direction", if we are going to reach the finish line. That's the hard news.

2) The troublesome news is that: Jesus was disciplined. How could the perfect Son of God, God himself, be disciplined? Only because he loves you and me so much that he willingly suffered excruciating discipline in our place.

3) God disciplines those he loves...us. I disciplined my kids only because I loved them. (OK, OK, probably once or twice I blew my top and disciplined our oldest out of exasperation.) I wanted so, so much for them to learn to be wise, to teach them what was important in life...and part of that process was through discipline. God disciplines us for the very same reason. That's the "Rats!" news.

4) Even though it's not pleasant, we are told to endure it willingly. Sometimes I thought my parents were wrong or unfair. Today, many decades later, I know they disciplined me with wisdom, and out of love. We are faced with the same scenario today. Sometimes it just doesn't seem fair. Job comes to mind. And, still, to this day, we don't entirely know why God allowed it. So, we have to trust God for what we don't understand, even for what seems very unfair. That's the "tough it out" news.

5) it's good for us. (Great...just what I wanted to hear!) That's the scary news! It builds us into the (good) people God wants us, designed us, to be.

6) Moses, in a sense, was disciplined...and it terrified him. Probably, it terrified Job, too, and Jesus, for that matter. That's the even more scary news! God doesn't always tell us (more likely, almost never tells us) ahead of time what he's doing. Lord, help us in our weakness, when we are faint. Help us to trust you for all that we don't understand.

7) Find, and focus on, our contentment in our relationship to God and in eternal

things, not on whether or not we're comfortable here on earth. Life sure throws a lot of unexpected things at you through the years, that's for sure. In plenty of ways, it's an uncomfortable ride. Lower expectations means lower disappointment, I say. (That's the unsolicited news...)

8)Ultimately, we're living for God, not for ourselves. That's the true reality. That's the real news...(not the fake news!).

So, shall we get on with it?

JULY 23

Have you ever seen a cuckoo bird? If you have to think about it, then you almost certainly haven't. I never knew what they were...until I heard them in southern China, where we lived for seven years. About one or two months out of the year, they would move into the neighborhood. I don't know where they went, the rest of the year, or where they came back from. The minute they came back, I knew they were there. Sometimes, I'll see a bird, and think, now, is that a hawk or an eagle. And someone will be sure to correct me: "No, you dummy...that's a raven!" Not so, with the cuckoo birds. They are unmistakable, probably the most unique bird I've ever encountered. Why? Because they make the incredibly distinct call: "Cuckoo! Cuckoo!" They sound exactly the way we say their name. It's remarkable. Until I heard one, I thought it was just some odd name someone had given to an obscure bird. But they were so clear and distinct, that as soon as I heard them again, after a long absence, I would go to the window and look out, or go outside, looking for them. I just never could quite get enough of them.

I don't know if you've ever been called "cuckoo", but, what is truly amazing to reflect on is that, God thinks about us, in the same way I used to respond to those cuckoo birds in China. When we start our call, just like those birds...(except that our call sounds more like, "Help! Help!")...he drops everything, turns, and with a smile on his face, listens to our voice. Isn't that astounding! God loves your unique voice so much...that it stops him in his tracks when he hears your voice calling him. What's even more amazing...when we come to him in trouble (Don't we always!), he loves that, too, and is so excited to hear from us. Perhaps the closest example of that we can think of is when our little child comes to us with some big problem...like tying his shoelace...we just love to hear his voice, to stoop down, and to help him out, so thankful that he thought to come to us for help. Psalm 116 paints the very same picture for us. It says: "I love the Lord because he hears my voice. He bends down to listen. I saw only trouble and sorrow. I called: 'Please, Lord, save me!' How kind the Lord is! How good he is! So merciful, this God of ours! And so I walk in the Lord's presence." Sometimes, we may wonder if God hears us at all...after all, he only has a few billion people to listen to. But your voice is unique...just like the cuckoo bird. And as soon as you start calling, he turns to listen. Your voice gets his attention. What is equally amazing is that he delights to hear all our troubles and sorrows. He knows we are coming with a list of troubles that we can't sort out...and he loves to hear it. But, of course, to him, our problems are like fixing our child's shoelace...they're like, well, like child's play. He can sort things with a flick of his wrist or a nod. The tricky part for us is, listening to and taking on board his medicine or remedy. My three year old may not like my instruction: "Practice tying your shoe 20 times!" He may think, forget it. That's too much trouble. So, am I listening to God? Am I listening to him...as much as he is listening to me? Our Heavenly Father loves to hear us call, anytime, with any message. So, let's keep calling...and let's also be listening to what he tells us in response, in his Word...

JULY 24

James 5:20 NCV   Anyone who brings a sinner back from the wrong way will save that sinner's soul from death and will cause many sins to be forgiven.

What a wonderful and amazing joy it is for us to watch and experience the new life in someone who turns away from a life of sin to be saved by God. And we are told that the angels in heaven rejoice when this happens. Yet God gives this privilege of sharing his Good News to us — even when the right to do so if fully his.

Have you ever read the US Constitution? (Or, has anyone, I might ask??) I don't know how many people actually read these documents that, rightly, most of us are proud of and, perhaps, will even defend with our lives. I confess, I don't recall having ever read our Constitution, but I do have a copy of it, and that must count for something. Just reading the first sentence or two provides some monumental concepts that can give us goosebumps, as we reflect on them. Now, we know that the reality in our country, in any country, has many times not matched the rhetoric. But, still, the ideas are beautiful, lofty, worth struggling to attain. Listen to a few of these words: "…to form a more perfect union, to establish justice, ensure domestic tranquillity, promote the general welfare, secure the blessings of liberty…" And, on it goes. Still magnificent, still treasured…and still to be strived for, because we haven't, after 200+ years, arrived there yet. But, even if we haven't read it all, just reading a few of those phrases gives us a lot to think about, reflect on, live for, perhaps, even die for. You don't have to read the entire document to grasp the greatness and beauty of the ideas in it.

And, you know, it's exactly (but on a far more grand and great scale) the same with the message of the Bible. I'm wading through Daniel right now…some great stories, great truths... Then I reach the final chapters 11&12, and I'm stopped in my tracks. It starts out: "Now then, I will reveal the truth to you." Then, it goes off on all these rabbit trails about this kingdom and that, this king of the north, and that king of the south (I don't think it's talking about the Civil War here...), about tax collectors and coastlands, this vision, that onslaught, alliances, armies, plunder, gold, silver... It will give any sci-fi movie a run for its money. Honestly, I have no idea about most of what it's talking about. But, you know what? It really doesn't matter. And, why not, I am hoping you will ask... Because, just like with the Constitution, which has plenty right there in the first sentence or two to blow us away and to keep us pondering and reflecting for years to come, the Bible has more than enough for us to meditate on, even if we don't understand every single detail. God is a mysterious God, way beyond our understanding...but we know enough about him to have a relationship with him and to worship him. And that's enough. We don't need to understand everything about God in order to know him. Not that we shouldn't seek more, not that we shouldn't seek to understand more fully, books like Daniel. But, there's plenty, already, that we do understand and can take on board. So, let's start out by focusing on what we do know and understand, such as:

1) God loves us dearly, more than we'll ever comprehend.

2) We have a serious problem on our hands...our pride and prejudice, as Jane Austen helped us see, so well.

3) God has the cure for our problem...if we are willing to take it.

4) God also wants us to live well, as he meant for us to, all along. (But, his idea of "well" may differ a good bit from our notion of it.)

5) So, really, ultimately, it comes down to, will we trust him? Whether we take our car to the garage, or get into the dentist's chair, it involves trust, and maybe more work and expense than we would wish, but there it is...

I say, let's trust him! What have we got to lose?!? (Everything, actually, if we don't decide to trust him.)

JULY 25

2 Corinthians 5:21 NCV   Christ had no sin, but God made him become sin so that in Christ we could become right with God.

From eternity Jesus was perfect, enjoyed a full relationship with the Father, and had never experienced sin. Yet, because God loved us so much, he willingly took all our sins in the world on himself as Jesus in an unimaginably horrible event ~ so that we could be saved from this same wrath.

It's interesting what you learn as an adult...and especially as a parent of older kids. When they were young, our kids were all sweet, little angels. (Good thing I have selective and forgetful memory...) As they've gotten older, every now and then, an innocent little story will slip out about something that happened 10 or 20 or more years ago...and with a bit of fear and shock rising within us, it suddenly dawns on us that the little tykes weren't such angels after all. Like when a certain teenager snuck out his window late at night to join some friends for some "good, clean" fun, who knows where, or what, or with whom. Or, when another child smuggled her peas off the table and out the door...as well as any-one snuck anything past the Nazis' eyes in the "Great Escape"...so that the said person would not have to eat them. Or, worse, when they figured the hot air vents on the floor would work just fine in place of the throne in the bathroom... Goodness, how naive and unsuspecting we parents were back in those days. We sure won't let the grands get away with the same shenanigans. And why is it, we may ask in a reflective moment, that children will go to those great lengths to create such misery and mayhem for their parents? Well, I think it's probably for the same reasons that we do a lot of the things we do. We really, really don't like being uncomfortable. I mean, who wants to be in pain, who wants to miss out on fun with their friends, who wants to have to wolf down something nasty by the shovelful...and on it goes? I know that, at least for me, my motto is, go where it is most comfortable, the way with the least resistance. Just give me smooth sailing (with a little money in the bank), and I'll be happy. There's just one ittsy, bitsy problem with that philosophy of life. It is in contradistinction (Is that a word?? I mean, it flies in the face of...) with what God wants, with his idea of what is best for us. And, somewhat painfully and uncomfortably for us, God usually has his way. Sometimes, he will patiently allow us to first get ourselves into a real pickle before we are finally hanging from the end of our tether and are ready to listen...but, generally speaking, God's going to have the last word, no matter how clever, sneaky, or whatever else we may be.

James, in his short, practical letter, talks about this exact thing. He basically says that God tells us that we should get excited when we're uncomfortable, rejoice when we are feeling pressed, be happy when we are having trials. This is a curious little letter, but actually very practical and very enlightening. Just like with many things...trees battered by strong winds, iron hammered by the blacksmith, muscles aching from exercise...all these things are for the purpose of making things stronger and tougher. James 1 tells us that trials, hard times, make us stronger. So, we should accept them, welcome them, even, as opportunities for good, for growth, for blessing. I don't find that easy. For my neighbor...sure, I can see that he needs to be tempered and sharpened. But, me? I'm pretty fine, just where I am; really, God, I'm OK. (I don't think God is buying it...) God loves us too much, cares about us too much, is too concerned about our health and well being, just to let us vegetate. He wants something better for us. He wants us to be better, more joyful, closer to him, more like he made us to be. So, Lord, next time I'm feeling squeezed or under pressure...remind me that this is for my good, that you haven't abandoned me, that you bring beauty out of calamity. Help me to trust in you as I hang on during the roller coaster. Amen!

JULY 26

Day/Date Be sure to remember five things to be grateful for every day. July 26

Hosea 2:19 NIV   I will betroth you to me forever.
I will betroth you in righteousness
and justice, in love and compassion.

Just saving us from sin and then moving on to something else
was not enough. God wanted to save us and then to have
a perfect relationship with us, symbolized by a marriage.
He gave himself fully to us, and one day we will be rid of
our sinful human nature and know him fully.

We heard a funny story once; I don't remember if one of our friends was recounting it, or if we read it in a book. Someone said that all their life, they would cut their Thanksgiving turkey in half before putting it into the oven. It's how their mother always did it, so they learned by her example, that this was how you cooked the Thanksgiving turkey. It was just how you had to cook the turkey in order for it to come out right. It was only many years later that they finally put two and two together and understood why their mom had done this. It was simply because her oven was too small...the whole turkey wouldn't fit into it, so she had to cut it in half! That sounds like something I would have done. I tend, not like my wife, to just do things without asking questions, just assuming that, that's how things have to be done. We may even go through life doing some things...because it's always been done that way, because "that's just the way it is". Sometimes it's helpful and wise to ask and to discover why we actually are doing our activities the way we do.

In Psalm 117, we are given the answer to two very big and important life questions, contained in these two little verses, for any Christian to ponder and meditate on. These are the two questions:

1) What is it we should be doing?

2) Why should we be doing this?

Verse 1 tells us that all the nations should be praising God. Not just the Jews, not just Christians, not just the believers I know...but, everyone. So, the real question is, what am I doing about it? What am I doing toward the end goal of having everyone, the whole world, praise our God? There are many people in the world who still do not know the One they are to be praising. Is there something I need to be doing about that, more than I may already be doing?

So, why should we be telling others to give honor, praise, and worship to God? Because he loves us and is faithful to us forever. Not just because he happens to be diligent or focused. It's because he is, by his nature and character, the essence and epitome of love and faithfulness. That is who he is. He loves us because he can't be any other way. And that means that he is also faithful to us. He stays with us. He will never abandon us. That is who he is. That is why we believe in and worship him. That is the Message we need to be communicating to the world.

JULY 27

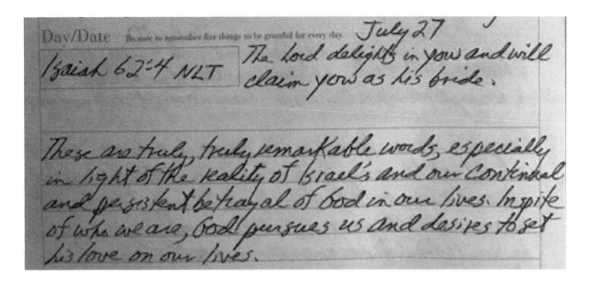

Day/Date Be sure to remember five things to be grateful for every day. July 27

Isaiah 62:4 NLT

The Lord delights in you and will claim you as his bride.

These are truly, truly remarkable words, especially in light of the reality of Israel's and our continual and persistent betrayal of God in our lives. Inspite of who we are, God pursues us and desires to set his love on our lives.

Sometimes I give a sigh of relief that I don't live in a former generation. Many of the stories we read, the pictures we see, reveal to us that not a few of the bygone cultures and ages have been pretty merciless and unforgiving, scary places to survive or travel through life in. Maybe today, though, we've carried it too far in the other direction. Whereas, in former days, you might have been tossed into a dungeon or placed in stocks for the slightest infringement, today, it seems, you are in danger of getting into trouble for even suggesting or insinuating that a person is in the wrong. While, I guess, it's human nature to suppose that we are innocent and have been wronged, certainly not deserving the punishment we're receiving, there are, surely, plausible reasons for handing down punishment in certain situations.

I guess we could debate or argue over whether it was really punishment or not, but Hosea 2 provides us with some insight into what and why God operates...in a way that we probably often perceive as either harsh treatment or unfair retaliation. God approaches the prophet Hosea with his grievances about the way Israel has abandoned God and chased after idols and other gods. But, in verse 14, God tells Hosea what he's going to do about Israel's behavior (and we can put ourselves in the place of Israel in this narrative, because the same applies to us today), and then, dropping down to verse 20, we see why God is operating in this way. God says he's going to take Israel out into the desert. Reminds me of hearing about "woodshed treatment" in the old days. A desert is not a pleasant place. Peaceful, maybe...but not somewhere you would normally want to be caught in for long. Desert conjures up the picture of harsh, desolate, desperate, dangerous... And God says, "This is where I'm going to take you." He takes us to desert locations to get our attention. Places where there will be few distractions. A place, even, where he can talk to and deal tenderly with us. Why does he take us to such a place? Why a desert, in particular? Because he has our full attention there. He's made us uncomfortable enough that we look up and listen. Then, he gives us his message: He loves us and wants something better for us. He wants to make us into the beautiful creation that he has planned for us all along. But that means changing us. Pruning us. Cutting us. Squeezing us. Ouch, ouch, and ouch. Is that how Israel understood it when swarms of armies, from time to time, descended on Jerusalem...God's means of getting their attention? I wonder... But the path they were going down was serious enough, dangerous enough, that God had to apply some serious treatment to resolve it. I hope they paid attention and returned to him. God operates in the same way today. Am I feeling squeezed? Pressured? Attacked? Am I suffering? What is it that God's trying to get my attention about? Maybe, instead of putting all my efforts and energy into trying to escape my uncomfortable circumstances, I need to stop, pause, look around, and listen. What is God telling me today? What have I been missing? God, give us ears to hear you...and the desire to follow you and live for you.

JULY 28

Isaiah 38:17 NIV — You have put all my sins behind your back.

How terribly and tenaciously do we sometimes hold on to wrongs done against us, rather than forgiving them, even though they are so minor. Yet, as terribly as we betray and turn away from God, he completely puts our sins behind him and treats us as if we had never sinned when we turn to him for forgiveness.

Maybe it's this way in every generation, but it's stunning to think about all the changes that have taken place in our world, just in the last couple of lifetimes. When my parents were young, cars and airplanes were only beginning to be developed, understood, and used. Some bacteria and viruses, and many other diseases and their causes, really were starting to be recognized and dealt with only in the past several generations. Electricity was harnessed and put to use. Space age, the whole computer world, and all the technology that has been exploding around us...most of these are advances that not too distant societies could not have even imagined. It's amusing to pick up an old science, medicine, or other book from bygone years, and to listen in on the discussions of those days. So much today that they weren't at all aware of! But, one reason I know that the Bible is true and is God's Word, is that, even after thousands of years, it reads like it was written yesterday. It's not like some outdated science book from 50 years ago. The message it delivers is clearly, perfectly relevant for then, for now, and for a million years from now, if need be. Listen to these thoughts from James' letter. With all the advances we've made throughout the generations, it still is quite apparent that some things haven't changed...primarily, I would say, the heart of mankind. And that's what James is addressing in his letter. In chapters 3&4, he's talking about being wise. He says that God's wisdom is "peace loving, always gentle, willing to give in to others, full of mercy and good deeds. God favors the humble." Such simple, yet, mind blowing ideas. What would happen in our world, if all the presidents and leaders who met together for conferences, summits, and congresses, had these simple attitudes? I can tell you, wars would probably tail off pretty quickly. We might start to scratch our heads and wonder why we have built up such heavy duty arsenals of fire power. We might suddenly find that we could balance our budgets a bit easier, once we realized that we really didn't, after all, need the latest technological weapon. These words in James are so simple, aren't they...yet, at the same time, they are out of our reach...because of the basic human condition...which all the clever and sophisticated and amazing advances have not touched. After all these generations of advances and wonders...man's basic problem, as well as the remedy, remain the same. Charles Spurgeon understood that as well, in the comments he made on James 4:14...unless we understand the future, eternal world, we won't be able to make much sense of this present world that we are living in.

JULY 29

Day/Date Be sure to remember five things to be grateful for every day. July 29

Micah 7:18-19 NLT Where is another God like you, who pardons the guilt, overlooking the sins of his special people? You will not stay angry forever, because you delight in showing unfailing love. You trample our sins and throw them into the ocean!

As parents we can at times see past the disobedience and failing of our children because of our deep love for them. God is the same way with us when we come to him. He sees us as lost children who he loves, and he doesn't hold our sins against us because of his love for us.

One of the first conversations I had with my future father in law, Wilhelmus Johan Schaffers, I knew I was in over my head. For a boy not long in America since arriving from, at that time, primitive Korea, I couldn't keep up with all his carrying on about the mechanics and engineering of his car, how it had run on his drive down to Georgia from Delaware, what he might need to work on to keep it in perfect running order. As I got to know him further (He was part of the package that came with being attracted to his daughter, I was to discover.), I learned that he meant what he said, said what he meant, and once was enough. He didn't have to say things twice. I also learned that he could be counted on. When he said something, you might as well have considered it done, because it was going to happen. In his later years, he invested in an atomic watch (What in the world is that, I wondered...), a finely tuned instrument that could be relied on to stay on course to the degree that it was within a second correct within any given year, according to Greenwich Mean Time. After serving as a mechanical engineer at DuPont de Nemours for 35 years, he closed out his career by teaching mathematics at Covenant College for another 15. Perhaps one of his most enduring lessons to (some of) his students was when he would lock the classroom door at 8:00:00 a.m. for his early morning class. I dare say that his students learned quickly the meaning of "8:00 o'clock". I think of my wife's "Dear Old Dad", as she refers to him with fondness, as I read through the verses on Psalm 118, which we read aloud together at our wedding. It hammers home to us with such regularity that it reminds me of an atomic watch, that God's love for us is enduring and doesn't quit. He always loves us, always can be counted on. Like my wife's father, even more so, God's faithful love for us doesn't change, always stays with us. Now that news, I must say, is far less intimidating than my first encounter with W.J. Schaffers.

JULY 30

There's a reason why some of us are scientists, and some are not. My wife falls in the former category, I, decidedly, in the second. She is tenacious, focused, determined..."quit" is not a word she seems to have learned. I, on the other hand, just want to get on with something, move along to what's easier, not get fussed or bogged down in the details (a disastrous combination for any scientist or engineer, I'm sure...). It's wonderful living with a scientist (most of the time), because nothing is ever broken or messed up for long. I don't have to worry about new technology, because I know that she'll be able to figure it out, sooner or later. One of the problems, however, is what happens when something breaks. My wife is, of course, too stubborn to understand the word, b-r-o-k-e-n, so it will be fixed, repaired, made to work again, no matter what the cost, no matter how long the procedure, no matter how disruptive the process. It's very tempting for me, after about 30 seconds of trying, to just let it go, to move on to something else, to just smooth things over.

I have to say, though, that in Hosea 6, the way God is described as working on, in, and at us, sounds an awful lot like my wife. Shamefully, I have to admit that how Israel had been behaving sounds a lot more like how I operate. Israel had been disobeying God, God sent his messenger to get their attention, and their response was, "Ah, yes, I see. Sorry about that. OK, we'll try to do better. Shall we move on?" And God replies, "Hold on a minute. You don't seem to understand. You're broken. I'm going to have to completely take you apart in order to fix your problem. A Mickey Mouse bandaid will not do it. This is going to take radical heart surgery. It's going to be messy, drawn out, painful, uncomfortable. But, I'm going to do it...because you're too precious for me to just leave you there, decaying in your long term rot. I'm going to clean out the mess, then we'll start over again." Now, I don't know about you, but I find that to be an uncomfortable message...uncomfortable, well, because it's uncomfortable. It jars me out of my lethargy, it rattles me out of my slumber, it messes up my coziness. But, I have to keep reminding myself, this is for my good. It's because God loves me...not because he enjoys punishing me, which he doesn't. Lord, help us to trust you, to trust your ways, to trust your work in our lives. Hold on to us, in your mercy, as you perform the radical and painful surgery that we so desperately need. Amen.

JULY 31

How do we teach our children...to be wise, to be kind, to learn what is right? When our kids were young, impressionable, and growing up, I wanted so badly for them to do the right things, to learn how to navigate through life, to avoid making costly mistakes. To say that my wife, who was holding down the fortress at home while I only had to work at a 9-5 job, had her hands full would probably be a mild understatement. With nine offspring of every age imaginable...well, I remember on one or two occasions her getting frighteningly close to tossing in the surrender towel. But, we wanted so much for them to navigate life well, to avoid dangerous pitfalls... I can still hear myself lecture them sternly: "Your job is to make Mom's job easier!" Or, she would blurt out, "Look at Mommy's eyes! Obey Mommy!" Whew...somehow, we all made it through, more or less in nine pieces... But, the question and puzzle still remains: how do we get across to our kids the tools to life that we believe are so, so important and necessary?

It would seem that God faces the same task toward us, though, I should quickly point out, he has several billion people to try to work on, while most of us only have a few little people to deal with. We get the real sense, though, as we wade through the verses and verses and verses of Psalm 119 (nearly 200 of them... more than making up for the two small verses in Psalm 117), that God is feeling and expressing the same urgency to us that we felt toward our children when they were little. He states, over and over, how important his Word is, how we have to make it part of our lives, how dangerous it is for us if we forget about it. Listen to a few of these statements: "Joyful are those who obey his laws. You have charged us to keep your commandments carefully. Open my eyes to see the wonderful truths in your instructions." Again and again, God lectures us, warns us, teaches us, that his Word is critical to our lives, that it is the tool we must have in order to successfully sail through life. So, will we listen? Will we hear and take on board what he is trying to tell us? Or, will we be stubborn and not happily cooperative, so that he has to declare to us, as I on occasion had to tell my kids: "You can do it the easy way, or the hard way. But, either way, you will obey me!" The choice is ours...

MONTH 8

Quarantine day 8...

Thoughts from Jeremiah, Lamentations, and Ezekiel:

*God wants to have a relationship with us...but he is also a holy God who must punish disobedience.

*Like a parent, God wonders why we turn away from him.

*God can't imagine not having a relationship with us...he pursues and pursues and pursues us.

*The Jews were looking for an earthly, military Messiah to save them...so many of them missed Jesus.

*God is everywhere...he knows everything.

*Sometimes God uses wicked people to carry out his good plans. All people are in his hands...under his control.

*God has already made plans for us for our good. Will we follow him so that we can see how his plans will unfold?

*There is always redemption with God...always the hope of forgiveness.

*A day of rich blessing from God is coming.

*God does not abandon his people.

*Serving God is hard, disappointing, and painful. We don't always see what God is doing or accomplishing.

*God can do anything.

*God gives us the task of communicating his Message...but we're all called by him in different ways.

*One day God will restore all things to the way he had planned.

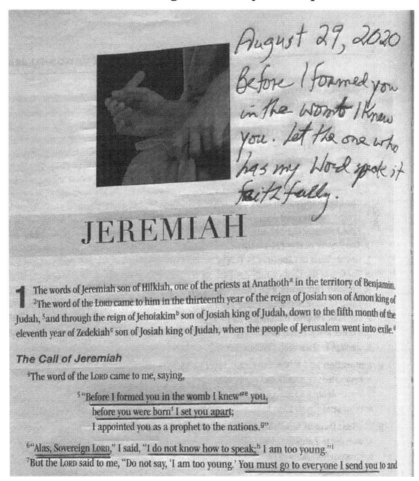

August 29, 2020
Before I formed you in the womb I knew you. Let the one who has my Word speak it faithfully.

JEREMIAH

1 The words of Jeremiah son of Hilkiah, one of the priests at Anathoth[a] in the territory of Benjamin. [2]The word of the LORD came to him in the thirteenth year of the reign of Josiah son of Amon king of Judah, [3]and through the reign of Jehoiakim[b] son of Josiah king of Judah, down to the fifth month of the eleventh year of Zedekiah[c] son of Josiah king of Judah, when the people of Jerusalem went into exile.[d]

The Call of Jeremiah

[4]The word of the LORD came to me, saying,

[5]"Before I formed you in the womb I knew[e] you,
before you were born[f] I set you apart;
I appointed you as a prophet to the nations.[g]"

[6]"Alas, Sovereign LORD," I said, "I do not know how to speak;[h] I am too young."[i]
[7]But the LORD said to me, "Do not say, 'I am too young.' You must go to everyone I send you to and

AUGUST 1

I'll never forget, in 1965, when I was a little boy and our family was on furlough in the US, walking into a 5&10 cent store in Wilmington, North Carolina, something equivalent to a Dollar General today. The grand glass doors slid open with ease, and as I stepped into the store, I really thought I had arrived in heaven. The whiff of freshness, cleanness, sweet perfume (or so it seemed to me)…it all brought a smile to my face. This, truly, was paradise. Then, as I wandered, with eyes the size of Kennedy half dollars, up and down the aisles, all the treasures I could possibly have imagined…and truly, along with the Queen of Sheba, less than the half had been told me…lay glistening before me. Anything I wanted, just there for the taking. There was a kindly, grandfatherly, sort of gentleman, who took my quarters with a smile at the checkout counter, as if I had made his day, just by coming into his store. Many months later, as we were stuffing our suitcases and barrels to head back across the ocean for Korea, this same man gave our family a whole bag full of candies and treats to take with us. Truly, I had arrived in paradise…even the Queen of Sheba would have been dazzled. Back in those days, in the US in the 60s, a family might have a small 12 inch black and white TV, they might own one used car, just maybe they would have one or two rooms with an air conditioning unit that rattled and hummed and struggled to keep the temperature below 80, almost certainly they would own a muscle pushed lawn mower, with a clothes line out back to hang the wash, the only books or clothes or appliances we had access to were what were available at the dusty corner shop on Main Street, two lane paved roads were the way we travelled to Nashville, Miami, or even San Francisco… And, computers, the internet, Amazon, iPhones, jet travel that is affordable and accessible to any corner of the world, central AC, painless dental visits, interstate highways that are as smooth as silk (and before I hear anyone crying foul, try some of the gravelly, potholed, dangerous roads found in many places across the globe)…during those distant days we never could have even dreamed of such marvels. Truly, truly, the world has utterly been transformed in our lifetime.

Now, I know, by saying this, I sound like an old fogie (but I am one, so what do you expect??), but I catch my breath when I read the sobering words of judgment that God speaks to Israel (and to the US today?) in Hosea 10. I wonder if they were written precisely with us in mind in our day. God describes the Israel of that day by saying: "How prosperous Israel is - a luxuriant vine loaded with fruit. But the richer the people get, the more pagan altars they build. The hearts of the people are fickle." And, remember, as much as Israel had been blessed by God, they still didn't have electricity, cars, AC, personal libraries, TV, internet, phones, ice cream…I mean, how could they survive, really?? Was God just teasing them when he said they were prosperous? No, he wasn't. And, today, we've been blessed a thousand times more…and have responded precisely, on cue, as the Israelites of old did… with ungratefulness, forgetting God, grumbling, bored, mean spirited… I have to wonder what God is thinking when he looks down from heaven on our exceedingly blessed land. When will his patience with us run out? When will he crush us…as he did to Israel…and take all these blessings from us? It's scary to think about. But, maybe, it would be for the best…because, clearly, all our blessings have not made us better people, they have not turned our attention to God or made us thankful. We may be in for some corrective pain and surgery one of these days… That seems to be how God operates, with the people he loves the most.

AUGUST 2

Day/Date	Be sure to remember five things to be grateful for every day. August 2
1 Timothy 6:17 NLT	Trust in God, who really gives us all we need for our enjoyment.

God is rich, generous, and full of love for us. But all too often we decide that we want to have crumbs and scraps instead of the nourishing and tasty spiritual feast that God has prepared for us. Let's daily ask God to help us focus on his feast and to keep us from being distracted by the unsatisfying garbage that surrounds us.

I hope this isn't too much of a shock, because I'm sure no one else has had these same kinds of experiences...but on occasion, just every now and then, my wife and I spar. On rare moments, the temperature may even rise a tad. The conversations go something like this:

"I have to work all the time, day and night."

"But, I have to earn all the money."

"Yeah, but I'm the one expending all the energy."

"You should try trudging to work in the rain, day after day, having to go work in a gloomy office, like I do, while you get to kick back with a hot cup of tea, listening to your favorite music."

And so it goes...just on occasion, like I said, nothing to worry too much about.

One sure way to get started in on a discussion like this, if you've never had the opportunity, is to read 1 Peter 3 together. I seems like it was written, just to get us enflamed. Peter starts the ball rolling by saying: "Ladies, hey, you wives... submit to your husbands." Now, if you want to get your wife's knickers tied up in knots, that will pretty well guarantee it. You really don't need to read past verse one. Of course, every wife has. Because they immediately come back with, "Yeah, but read on. Listen to what Peter says next... He says to honor your wife. You do know what that means, right!?! It means you give her honor, you lay down your life for her, you treat her like Christ treated us, dying to yourself!" By this time, fireworks have been lit, sabers have been rattled...even one or two grenades may have been launched. Maybe, it's better just to avoid 1 Peter 3. So, why did Peter work to get us so riled up? Maybe he was just having a bad day...or maybe he had himself had a run in with his wife, and that put a little fire into his thoughts and words. But, the truth is, if we will look a little past some of the seemingly inflammatory words, step back, and cool down, we'll probably be able to see more clearly what he was trying to express. Peter tells us to love each other, consider each other as equals, be tenderhearted, be humble... Honestly, it's hard, downright nigh impossible, in fact, to get all wound up and upset if we are exhibiting these things that Peter tells us. How, really, can I get upset or bossy with my wife...if, at the same time, I am treating her as my equal, being kind and humble? Peter gives us enough to work in, for a lifetime, and it has nothing to do with demanding my rights or being bossy. It really is about laying down my life. So, will I follow that path in my marriage? The choice is mine. The consequences go beyond me.

I like what Charles Spurgeon shared, when he offered this observation:

"Marriage is not all sugar, but grace in the heart will keep away most sours."

AUGUST 3

"Lewis, Julie is in heaven…" I can still hear my father's words in my ears, as if it were yesterday. Not long married, my wife and I were spending Christmas at her parents' home in Delaware. Her father mentioned that my father had called from North Carolina, and that I should call him back. I didn't think anything of it. It was Christmas, after all, and he was calling in his usual way to wish us a Merry Christmas. So, there was no big rush or urgency about it. I went back to my book, from off my father in law's shelf. But my wife's father mentioned again that I should call Dad back. Two or three times. It still didn't occur to me to be anything out of the ordinary, but finally, to get this bothersome father in law off my back, I picked up the phone and dialed my family. That's when I heard those words from my father. My older sister was a nurse, and the night before, she had been driving home following a late night shift at the hospital. A drunk driver, coming down the wrong side of the interstate highway, crushed into her, head on, and they were both killed instantly. I still think of my sister, 40 years later, every time I drive by that same spot in the highway where the accident happened. A few days later, my wife and I left her family's home in Delaware, to return to visit my family. My father had visited the family of the drunk driver, to offer his condolences to them, on losing their son. Billy and Ruth Graham (whom my mother had grown up in China with) also came by to visit my parents. It took me most of two years to get myself back to feeling somewhat normal after losing my sister. Initially, I remember thinking, "I want the world to stop, so I can get off." And, my parents? How did they cope, upon losing the second of their children, following the loss of their youngest son, 13 years earlier? Remarkably well, that's all I can say, remarkably well. I'm reminded of them as I read the verses in Psalm 119. Verse 25 says: "I lie in the dust; revive me by your Word." No doubt, that's how they must have been feeling. But they knew where their hope, their confidence, lay. Later on, we read: "Encourage me by your Word. Expand my understanding. Make me walk along the path of your commands, for that is where my happiness is found." That is what I observed in the lives of my parents during those days of excruciating loss and pain. They believed God's Word; they knew that their hope was in him. They knew that by living, by walking, according to God's Word, their hope would be restored, their equilibrium maintained, life would continue to have meaning…that literally, all would be right with the world, because of Who was guiding and directing the events across the globe.

AUGUST 4

August 4

Day/Date Be sure to remember five things to be grateful for every day.

Philippians 4:19 NIV My God will meet all your needs according to his glorious riches in Christ Jesus.

God tells us that all the treasures of wisdom and knowledge are found in Christ. He holds greater spiritual wealth than we will ever need, and he is happy to meet our needs according to his glory and what honors him. All we need to do is to come to him for help.

As a little boy in Korea, I had a gang of buddies (PAN, BPB, RLM, GWY...maybe one or two others that my fuzzy brain is forgetting), most of who were a year younger than me, so we hung out together (and I bossed them any chance I had, I'm sure they can confirm...). One blustery and cold winter day, a group of builders were working on putting up a new house in the missionary community. As they worked on various projects in our neighborhood, if we were lucky, they might carve a wooden sword for us out of their scraps of leftover planks. That was great, if we found someone willing to create a treasure like that for us. For the rest of their unused bits of lumber, they would build a little fire to burn up the scraps. So, on that chilly winter day, one of my buddies and I crowded around and hovered over the small fire they had lit on the ground, to pull in whatever warmth we could. I can still feel the lovely warmth of that fire. As we stood there, suddenly, my friend turned and tore off, screaming in terror, across the grass. What on earth was going on, I wondered?? Far down, across the yard, one of the workers ran after, caught up with, and tackled my friend. The man rolled my friend around, then picked him up in his arms. As we had been huddled together near the fire, the wind blown flames had hopped onto my buddy's pant leg, and rapidly ate their way upwards. My friend screamed in pain, and tried to outrun the flames. Thankfully, one of the workmen responded out of reflex, and brought my friend down to the ground, surely saving him from a worse injury than he otherwise would have endured. Long after, I still remember the large scarred area he had on his lower leg.

The incident, and the fast reaction and dramatic takedown by that worker, come back to me as I read the account related to us in the book of Joel. Israel was being their usual naughty selves, they were suffering and in pain, and God decided that he had to respond by taking them down. They were headed in the wrong direction, the flames (if you want to depict their condition that way) were burning them alive, and God had to bring them down and stop them in their tracks...in this case, by sending a blanket of man eating, at least that is how they appeared, locusts...critters that buzzed through any and everything as effectively as the sharpest chain saw could ever do. They swept across the land, leaving behind, as the account tells us, cattle howling in hunger, because the locusts had eaten everything within sight (and apparently, they could see quite well). I'm sure, by this time, the Israelites were howling right along with the cows. "God, do something! Get us out of this mess. Fix this problem. You created it...you fix it!" That's pretty much how we all respond, isn't it, when anything doesn't go our way. So, why in the Sam Hill would God let something like this happen to his own special people...especially if he's good, all powerful, and controls everything. It just doesn't make any sense. What kind of a God is he, anyway? Well...the passage tells us why he takes the people down. And it's for the exact reason that the worker I observed, as a boy, took down my friend. If my friend had been fine, it would have been shocking to watch what the worker did to him...tackling him, smashing him into the dirt...I mean, what kind of a crazy person was he, anyway?? But, thank God, the worker was there. He saw, not only a boy running across the lawn. He saw a little one, in danger for his life, and pounced in to save him. God did to the Israelites, and on occasion does the same with us, what was needed in their desperate plight. Like us, many times, the Israelites had no clue that they even had a problem. I know it seems like the contrary at times, but really, God does not enjoy taking us down. He doesn't enjoy seeing us howl and squirm. But, he will do that to us if he needs to. If we need an emergency heart transplant, he will do what is necessary for us...because-he-loves-us. That is what he says. He doesn't change. He works the same way in our lives today...stops us in our tracks, takes us down, crushes us...because we don't realize that we're on fire...and because he loves us. That's the kind of intervening, going all the way, God who loves us dearly, that we have. It might be easier on him...and on us...if we just choose the wise path and follow his paths from the beginning...and avoid the take down.

AUGUST 5

> **Day/Date** Be sure to remember five things to be grateful for every day. **August 5**
>
> Proverbs 10:22 NLT — The blessing of the Lord makes a person rich.
>
> At the end of his life, it was very apparent to me that my father was blessed and rich in many ways. A casual glance at his life may have suggested otherwise. He was not great or wealthy according to how this world counts them. But he had lived a long, satisfying, peaceful life without regrets and left behind a long legacy of goodness and blessing that touched many lives.

One of our relatives used to be a Navy Seal. (I don't need to tell you what a Navy Seal is, do I??) They are so storied and intimidating that...well, let's just say that I felt a trifle on edge whenever he was in our presence. On one such visit, he did something that caught us all off guard. He pulled out his official Navy Seal pocket knife and offered it to whoever wanted it, among the rest of us. Naturally, all of my well brought up kids politely declined the offer. Not me, though. I jumped at the unique opportunity and stuck my hand right out...and smiled to myself, all the way home! Now, I don't know what your experience is with knives, but that one is what I call a "real knife". It makes all the other knives I've ever seen seem like flimsy counterfeits. I don't know if it is titanium, or what, but it is clearly in a whole separate category from any other toy knives. (Regrettably, one of my sons quickly relieved me of the knife, once they discovered that they really didn't need to be so polite as all that. And, sadly, I can't even get it back, because, with five sons, I don't even remember which one of them left our home with said knife.) The Navy Seals really are something special. Do you remember the movie, "Lone Survivor"? It was a touch bloody and gory, but somehow, your heart feels tugged by any folks who seem like the underdogs, and you want to cheer them on. Those handful of guys, though, appeared invincible. Wounded multiple times, falling over cliffs, chased and hunted by scads of warriors, they just kept coming back, taking down oodles of their attackers...and nearly managed to make it through...nearly. It does, though, make you come away feeling like Navy Seals are invincible. I really don't know how they do it. I've seen some movies about the Vietnam War, and some of those local fighters would go into battle with flip flops, straw hats, loin cloths, and not much else. Clearly, they were not Navy Seals. The Seals carry everything with them, except, perhaps, for the USS Ticonderoga, to meet any conceivable eventuality that may come their way. Their legs, backs, arms, shoulders...everything is bulging with ammunition, equipment, weapons, that Navy Seal knife, and anything else they might possibly need. It's no wonder that they are nearly invincible and can deal with anything that might show up at their tent flap. I'm sure even Goliath would break out in a sweat in their presence.

Do you know what I really find amazing, though? You and I are Super Seals. You surely know what those are, right?? He explains it for us right there in 2 Peter, the first chapter. The apostle Peter utters the most incredible words we could possibly hear. He says: "God has given us everything we need for living a godly life. He has given us great and precious promises. These promises enable you to share his divine nature." Then, in chapter 2, he adds, "The Lord knows how to rescue godly people from their trials." Our Heavenly Father, who himself is overwhelmingly invincible, has given us all we need (including the Ticonderoga, if we need it) for this life, as we walk spiritually in step with him. A promise by God Almighty is quite a promise. So, when he gives us "great" and "precious" promises, you know that they are great...his promises to be with us, to rescue us, to love us, to comfort us... Then, Peter says something that perhaps even he didn't fully understand. We "share in God's divine nature". Along with Peter, I don't quite know what that means, either. But, it does set us apart. It is what makes us Super Seals. We are God's special ambassadors on earth, given his most supreme task of working so that "no one is destroyed", as Peter reminds us in chapter 3. God has equipped us, given us the mission...now there's just one thing left... As with the highly equipped Navy Seals, they're only as good as if and when they apply and put to use all their equipment. And, so it is with us. We have the mission, we are equipped...now, let's go do it!

AUGUST 6

One of my sweetest memories as a child was when packages would arrive from the promised land of America at Christmastime. Our grandparents, no doubt guided by letters from our mother, would send us just the right toys and new clothes, dazzling our little eyes as we tore the wrappings off as early on Christmas morn as possible...once Dad got done droning on and on and on with our, apparently, much needed devotional at the breakfast table. Those spiritual lessons could go on for at least as long of some of Moses' grand and lengthy sermons, at least it seemed so to my squirmy little legs, which were just wiggling to be let loose from the table, to make the fast dash into the living room, where the best of Christmas gifts were waiting impatiently for us to release them from their wrappings. The odd thing, as I think back about it, is that I hardly remember very many of the toys we received. What does stand out to me, though, is that the packages, at least the ones that got through the Customs officials and managed to find their way under our Christmas tree, were stuffed with living color comic pages from the Sunday newspapers in America. The comic papers were what really got us excited. Once a year...once a year only...we got to see with our own eyes and devour the comic strips that were delivered weekly to all the families back home. Those papers were every bit as treasured by us as, I'm sure, the gold, frankincense, and myrrh that dazzled Joseph and Mary back on that first Christmas day. My, my, how I do still remember those comic pages...long after I've forgotten the gifts that they enfolded.

As magnificent as those comic strips were to us kids back on those early Christmas mornings, we have something even better today. Are we even aware of it? Or are we so eager to unwrap what's inside, that we miss the treasures that are staring right up at us? Psalm 119:57 shouts out to us: "Lord, you are mine!" Other verses tell us: "Your promise is my only hope. It comforts me in all my troubles. O Lord, your unfailing love fills the earth." Verse 57 reminds me of what Paul tells us in Colossians 2: "In Christ are hidden all the treasures of wisdom and knowledge." And, he is ours, as Paul and the psalmist remind us. Now, those are some serious treasures...all our troubles...covered. All the wisdom we need...given to us. It's close, I know, but I'd say that these gifts even edge out the gold mine contained in those comics of the old days. Forget about any Christmas treasures you may see in shop windows these days. What we've already been given, what we have in our hands in God's Word, his promise to be with us in all our troubles...these are the real treasures. Let's get excited about what God has already given us!

AUGUST 7

August 7

Day/Date Be sure to remember five things to be grateful for every day.

John 17:11 NCV

Holy Father, Keep them safe by the power of your name, so that they will be one, just as you and I are one.

God has given us a job and a purpose in this life. Although a privilege, it can include hardship and disappointment. But he does not send us out and leave us on our own. In fact, his Spirit lives in us and helps us, and Jesus himself is also praying on our behalf for our safety and blessing.

I guess it shows how programmed we are without even realizing it, but it's strange how one small image, picture, word, or sound can strike fear into the toughest or most courageous of the lot of us. What scares the willies out of you? I'll tell you what does it for me. Every year, in the spring, after dutifully filing my taxes (Well, OK, my son does it for me, but the government doesn't know that... They don't, do they??), the anxious waiting for the days to tick by, wondering if maybe, just maybe, they will find a comma or colon out of place on the tax form and drag me off to the dungeon at Fort Knox for the rest of my earthly days. Yes, for me, that's it. The fear that one cheerful sunny day, I'll go out to the mailbox, reach in, and retrieve a stiff, white, legal size envelope with the letters, I-R-S in the upper left hand corner. The day that happens...well, it will be curtains for me. I'm sure they will unearth all the sins of my youth, as well as everything bad I've even wondered about doing since then. I'll be like the hapless rogue, hung up in stocks in the public square in Jamestown, for the whole world to see and snicker at, as they pass by. And, then, can you imagine, after trudging halfway across Europe, how the Jewish roundups must have felt, when they finally, bone tired, arrived at the gates of Auschwitz, and were greeted by the sign, high above the entrance, that proclaimed to them, "Work Makes Free"... I can't think of too many things more scary than those two scenarios.

But, actually, there is just one other...that matches those two, and more. A little known shepherd on the hillsides of Judea shares that frightening message with us. His name was Amos, and he was given a terrifying warning to pass on. The message, unfolding in the first several chapters of his book, was simple, really: "The people have sinned again and again, and I will not let them go unpunished! The Sovereign Lord has sworn by his holiness: the time will come when you will be led away." The scary thing for us, in a very real sense, is that God is holy. What that means is that it's part of his DNA (which, I'm sure I don't need to remind you, stands for Divine Nature Absolutely)...in other words, it's set for eternity and can't be changed. His can't go against who he is, his nature, his DNA. So, when he says he's holy, he's telling us that our selfish disobedience has to be paid for. Thankfully, we already know it has been paid for, though not by us. The question is, with all those selfish things we've piled up, have we taken on board the payment made on our behalf? As harrowing and hellish as it is to see the Auschwitz inmates identified by their dirty striped pajamas, in the opposite way, we can be identified by outfitting ourselves in the righteous, clean clothing of Christ, tailor made for us. Have we put them on yet? Are we covered and protected by those clothes?

AUGUST 8

Day/Date Be sure to remember five things to be grateful for every day. August 8

1 Peter 2:23 NCV People insulted Christ. Christ suffered. He let God, the One who judges rightly, take care of him.

Though he was perfect, Jesus suffered. He could have demanded fair treatment, but instead he left his life in God's hands. Jesus knew that God is fair, that bringing the Good News involves suffering, and that his behavior was the example he was leaving for us to follow.

During the years we lived in Europe, we visited a number of churches, and were able to latch on to two, which proved to be great blessings to us. You really shouldn't tell stories about other people, I'm sure it says that somewhere, but there is one story I just have to tell you about…that had to do with one of the pastors we had along the way. The church we attended at this particular juncture was a dynamic fellowship that was just what we needed at that stage. It provided good programs for a variety of needs and situations, that proved to be a blessing to many folks. One lady in the community, not a church attender, as far as I know, took note of our church, as well. Now, I only heard this story second or third hand, so I can't entirely pledge my life on it, but I'm pretty sure it's true. The lady in the neighborhood approached our pastor one day, and said, "You know, I've been observing what you folks have been doing at the church, and honestly, I like what I'm seeing. I like what you're doing in the community. So, I'd like to help you out just a bit. I'd like to offer you $1,000,000 (yes, that's six zeros), to do as you wish to help your church along." Goodness, when I heard that story, I could feel the juices start to move around in my mouth, practically tasting already all the wonderful things that I could do for the church, if I had been the one that lady was talking to that day. "Why, thank you very much for thinking of us. Honestly, though, we have all we need. Perhaps, you can find some other more needy cause to contribute your generous gift to." Can you believe it?? That was our pastor's response! Had he lost his marbles? Why in the world hadn't I been with him that day, to add some clarity to his foggy mind? My, oh my, what an opportunity...gone. I mean, when God offers us something, shouldn't we cheerfully receive it, just as cheerfully as the one offering it to us? So, what in the world happened that day? (I still grind my teeth, thinking about that missed opportunity when I remember that encounter today.)

Well, I think what happened, is that our pastor knew (obviously much better than I did) what it was that the church really needed, what was most import-ant for us. And, it wasn't a new roof, not new pews, not new landscaping. It was something money will not cover. He knew, and had the clarity to avoid being derailed, that all we simply needed was the message of the Gospel. We needed to know God's love, to live his love, to communicate his love. Cash in the bank was not going to help that. (I still think a bit of a landscaping facelift might have helped...)

I expect the apostle John, the one who was called, "the one whom Jesus loved most dearly", had the same clear focus. And he wanted just as badly for his congregation to understand what was important, just as our pastor did, back there in Europe. In his first letter, in the first few chapters, John's thoughts come through to us very clearly and passionately. "God has given us his total love. And, all he wants us to do is to love others in the very same way...just love others fully, as Jesus showed us how to do by his life and his example." I am so thankful that our pastor deflected that whopper of a temptation, that he kept focused on what was important. Showing, by doing so, his love and commit-ment, both for his Heavenly Father, and also for us, his flock. (But, a few extra bushes might have been nice...)

AUGUST 9

Day/Date Be sure to remember five things to be grateful for every day. August 9

Philippians 1:27 NCV Only one thing concerns me: Be sure that you live in a way that brings honor to the Good News of Christ.

Life is complex, and sometimes it is not easy or straightforward to know what to do or how to respond in a given situation. But rather than weighing how something will affect or impact us, the most important response is: how will my life and actions bring honor to God.

I was having an ordinary, quiet day in my little Christian Book Nook, in Alcoa, Tennessee, back in the 1980s, when a man in a three piece, dark suit walked in. Unannounced, unpresuming, without a word, he entered my little world, walked around among the bookshelves...and changed by business forever. Waiting till no one else was in the shop (which didn't take too long in my 800 square foot universe), the man came up to the counter, and with a warm smile, said, "I'd like to give you something." He handed me a beautiful, genuine leather (i.e. expensive) study Bible, one I was not yet familiar with, but knew immediately I could sell for a good price, and caught me, from that moment on, in his salesman's net. I was dead fish from that point on. Whenever he came around in the future, I would buy as much as I could from him. (He must have made a bundle off me, over the years.) What I remember about this remarkable gentleman, who I later discovered was the most successful Bible salesman in America at the time, is that he always entered my world, seemingly so glad to see me...as if he'd been waiting for months to see me, as if just laying eyes on me had truly made his day. He always had good deals for me, his generosity toward his customers, I'm sure, must have reaped many benefits to him, because, if I was like any of the other little book dealers scattered here and yon, we sure gave him the business. I just knew that this man, with the slicked back black hair, who came cruising up in his black Cadillac, was bringing good things to me. He really did.

And, quite interestingly, decades later, my son became acquainted with him as well, as, in his retirement, he and my son attended the same church.

My pleasant memories of this gentleman come back to me as I read some of the verses in Psalm 119. Listen to these words from verses 65 & 68: "You have done many good things for me, Lord, just as you promised. You are good and do only good." Now, if that salesman, back in my book dealing days, would bring a smile to my face, which he did, without fail, how much more should the truths in these verses being a daily smile to our faces. God brings us good things, he always has, and his good things are given generously, extravagantly, with no tangible return benefit to God, and he's going to keep right on doing that as long as he knows us. What an amazing, unexpected, remarkable bit of good news that is to us today! Let's give it a big smile, shall we!

AUGUST 10

> **Day/Date** Be sure to remember five things to be grateful for every day. August 10
>
> 1 Peter 2:24 NCV   Christ carried our sins so we ~~should~~ stop living for sin and start living for what is right.
>
> Jesus saved us from sin and evil, but he also saved us to something. Part of our salvation includes living daily to honor God in all we do. If we are really God's children, we should not be using our lives to live selfishly or in ways that dishonor God.

The French politician Marshal Foch, as the Versailles Treaty was being signed in 1918, stated quite prophetically, "This is not peace; it is an armistice for 20 years." Exactly 20 years and a few months later, the world was launched into an even far more damaging and costly conflict than the "war to end all wars" had been in 1914-1918. We could still debate and discuss why that agreement at the end of World War 1 failed so badly. At any rate, we humans don't appear to be too adept at securing lasting peace. Whether it's one on one (with a spouse or friend), in a family, a community, a state or province, nation, whatever...we continue, since time long forgotten, to grapple, without success, to find, secure, hold onto, make happen...something that seems so simple as peace...just getting along. (It's not really for public consumption, but even after over 40 years of marriage, I find the issue of peace within my own four walls to be a daily struggle...) What in the world is our problem, really, seriously??

Actually, we discover the problem in the little book of Amos, tucked in your Bible near the end of the Old Testament. And it's bad news. Worse than we might have imagined. Now, I'm a pretty honest, upstanding, humble, kind, (and I'm sure a few other good adjectives could be thrown in) person...but there's one little bitty verse, chapter 5:12, which totally blows out of the water and utterly refutes any of those nice warm fuzzies that I think about myself. So, if you're like me and think you're not really such a bad guy or gal, you may want to sit down before I break the pretty depressing, a bit too close to the knuckles, news that I am about to unload on you as well as the best of the B-52 bombers would have done in past wars. Here it is...you ready? God, who is nothing if not just and truthful and honest, tells us this: "I know the vast number of your sins." What?? Come on, God, I'm too busy reading in my room, minding my own business, to have done anything seriously wrong... What in the world are you talking about?? It's just this...something that I forget every day. God is perfect...holy. Not only does he not like sin and disobedience, not only is he allergic to it...he can't even live with it, be with it, coexist with it. So, every little, itsy bitsy, small selfish thing I do that is if no consequence...he knows about and can't accept. He will exterminate it...which means, I'm terminated. Really, there is only one thing that can and will save me from my own shortcomings and sin...and that one thing is every bit as good, no, better, than that baddest of bad news that we just heard. The good news is: God has the fix for our vast sins. Not only is he aware of the cure...he is the one who paid for it. Not only that, he loves us so, so badly, that, even though we are worse than we could imagine, he shouts to us: "Run! Run! Run to me, so I can save you! Right here, with me, is where you will find the cure for your sin, the solution to that illusive peace that you can't seem to locate. It's right here. I am going to give it to you. Just come to me. That's it! What are you waiting for?"

AUGUST 11

Day/Date Be sure to remember five things to be grateful for every day.

August 11

Psalm 119:11 NLT I have hidden your Word in my heart, that I might not sin against you.

We will always have sin in us as long as we live. But what we fill our lives with — our eyes, minds, hearts — will affect, set the tone for, and determine who we are. If we fill ourselves with God's Word, it will shape us in such a way that we will live increasingly for God and less for sin and selfishness.

August 12

Don't you love it when your wife or husband snores at night? (You think I'm kidding, but I'm not.) When my wife snores (Now, she really doesn't snore very loudly, mind you, hardly at all, really...), it makes me happy, because then I know she's resting well, might just be a trifle easier to live with, come morning, might just make for a happier world. But, the truth is, this is a pretty scary world we live in, and there's a lot on our plates to worry about. We got over a dozen kids and their spouses, more than a dozen grandkids, an apartment that might start leaking at any moment, a car with nearly a quarter million miles on it (practically toast already), bodies that ache, all my books to worry about, the IRS that I'm sure has someone posted outside our door just waiting for us to slip up, my upcoming appointment with the doctor that may not bring good news...and I'm sure there must be one or two other things that I'm forgetting... We really do have a lot to worry about, don't we? It's pretty close to a full time job, really, just making sure I do worry sufficiently about all the things that need my brain attending to them about... When I'm laying there in bed and I don't hear my wife snoring...then I start worrying because I know she's awake worrying about all the things we have to worry about...and so, we both just lay there worrying. Snoring, really, is much better.

But, maybe, there's something even better than snoring. 1 John is a wonderful book, and he delivers the good news that God loves us in a beautiful way...then, of course, encouraging us to do the same toward other people (once we got all our worrying out of the way, that is). But, between all those verses talking about love, John tells us something else...and it just might even be good snoring medicine...helping us snore even more, I mean. He says, in chapter 4, "But you belong to God, my dear children." It's almost as if he's reminding us that, in the same way kids sleep soundly, knowing their parents are watching over them, because they care for them...in that same way, we belong to God, he's looking out for us, he's watching over us. Then, not more than a moment later, John says, "The Spirit who lives in you is greater than the spirit who lives in the world." So, we're covered. Nothing can touch us, really, in terms of separating us from God's love. Then, with a twinkle in his eyes, as it were, John adds one more time, "But we belong to God." He's telling us: no worries, quit worrying, don't even think about it...just get on with your snoring.

AUGUST 12

Day/Date Be sure to remember five things to be grateful for every day. August 12

1 Peter 3:4 NCV Beauty should come from within you — a gentle and quiet spirit is very precious to God.

Our senses tend to cause us to focus on what we can see and experience in the world around us. It is easy for us to spend an excessive amount of time and attention, then, on things that are external. But God tells us that what is really important, and what he is most concerned about, is the condition of our heart and character, on the inside. That is where our greatest focus should be.

I never knew, as a little boy, that my world would one day change forever. But it did. The first crack in my neat little world was when I left my home for boarding school, at the age of 12. My home was still there, but it wasn't quite the same, since I was no longer residing there during most of the year. Later, I left Korea, to go to the US for college, and when I returned to my childhood home some years later, it was as if I was on the outside, looking in, on what used to be my home, but clearly no longer was. As the economy and the church both grew dramatically in Korea during the late 1900s, it seemed that the whole country changed and became unrecognizable. Health care improved beyond imagination, education was more accessible, the church was more dynamic...and suddenly, it looked like the foreign missionaries had worked themselves out of a job. Few are left today, and the mission community that I called home as a child is no longer there, save for a few remaining buildings or landmarks. In fact, the whole city I grew up in is gone, the dusty mud huts having been replaced by towering skyscrapers. The one high church spire I remember that is still in existence, which used to pierce the sky, can hardly be seen any longer, as it's all but buried in surrounding apartment buildings. Whenever I have the chance to return to my childhood hometown, I search for anything that I can recognize, that looks familiar. Only a handful of things remain, most notably the large mountain of Mudungsan, though, in my day it kept watch, overlooking and high above the city. Today you can only catch glimpses of it as it tries its best to peek around all the tall buildings that nearly obliterate it. But the most significant landmark for me, which hasn't changed, is the missionary cemetery, where my little brother's remains still lay buried. Anytime I'm in my home-town, for whatever reason, I feel compelled to return there, to stand by my brother's stone, with the words from John 10 cut into it, and which we brought home from atop Mudungsan, and reflect on my childhood, and the things that haven't changed in my memory.

I think of this, too, as I read verses from Psalm 119. These truths tell us that God's Word is eternal, it stands firm, God's faithfulness remains with us, gener-ation after generation, and he and his Word are what carry us through life, give us life, in fact, and teach us about life, and how to navigate through it. Many things change, and come and go, and pass away, as we travel through life. But, just as there are a few things that remain from my childhood days, so, God's Word remains unchanged, it is still the compass and the guide by which I find my direction, my stability, my life. I've found that it can be trusted...it remains the same, whenever I return to it.

AUGUST 13

Do you wonder what it will be like on the day we arrive in heaven? We hear, on occasion, stories of people who came close to heaven, perhaps nearly dying, and then recovering or returning to their previous life on earth. It's hard to know what to make of those accounts. Many of these such stories suggest great joy and delight on the part of the one approaching heaven. Maybe there is a look of peace on their face. Perhaps their arms are outstretched as if someone is welcoming them home. It does make us wonder. In the meantime, we look around our world today, and we view a whole lot of mess, confusion, evil, chaos, bewilderment. What to make of it all? I expect we will be surprised, delighted really, even blown away, on that day when our Lord calls us home. On the one hand, we see crazy things happening on every side. But, then, looking underneath or behind the surface events, we may also see hints and glimpses of what God is probably really doing. And, on that day when we arrive in heaven, I expect that we will be truly amazed to discover and see clearly what God has been orchestrating all along, right under our noses, but just beyond our view.

As we skip across the pages of the brief Minor Prophets, tucked away at the end of the Old Testament, we catch snippets of what God may be doing beneath the surface, out of our sight, but which one day will all come to light. On that day, which I can't wait for, our eyes will be opened to how God's good and perfect plans have indeed being carried out all this time, while we weren't even fully aware of it. In chapter 8 of Amos, God says that our sorrow at being punished for our disobedience will be so painful that it will feel as if we have lost our only child. Does that sound cruel to you? It does to me. But as soon as I read it, my thoughts go back to that day when Jesus encountered a poor widow in the exact same situation. Her only son had died, and she was utterly distraught. And Jesus' response? He wept in sorrow at her loss. It hits me powerfully that God is not, ever, happy to see us suffer or be punished. It hurts him, just like it hurts us. But...he willingly allows us to suffer, because he loves us, to get our attention, for our good. We flip over a page to Amos 9, and we are given the picture of God shaking the people to wake them up, like we might shake a fruit or nut tree. But, then it says that, even after all this shaking, not one single true kernel that belongs to God, as in, those who have trusted God, will be lost. Good will prevail. Obadiah's story comes next, and after the usual litany of destruction, suffering, and captivity, we are left with the assurance that the exiles, those in captivity, will be rescued and brought home. Again, rescue out of chaos. On to the well known story of Jonah, who I can relate to, because he ran at the first sign of discomfort... But, again, we see hints of God bringing good out of apparent tragedy and loss. When Jonah was on the run from God, was he out of the picture and useless at that point? Maybe not. In a moment of clarity, when Jonah acknowledged that the disaster that had befallen the crew and the boat he was on, was actually due to his own disobedience, he told the crew to toss him overboard into the raging seas, and that all would be right with the world once again, if they would only get rid of him. A crazy notion, but in their desperation, the crew did what Jonah instructed and jettisoned him into the frothy ocean. What happened? Instantly, it all got quiet. I don't know if they forgot about Jonah at that point, or what, but, at any rate, he was no longer anywhere to be seen. But they didn't forget his God. They started worshiping him and committed themselves to following him. No doubt these were hard bitten and toughened seamen. Perhaps they were beyond the reach of ordinary preachers trying to give them the Good News. So, maybe God decided to do something radical...and he used his disobedient prophet to be the vehicle of their rescue. Now, isn't that a story you just love. God must delight in a happy ending. He's not past having a little excitement along the way, even at our uncomfortable expense (which, most likely we deserve and have asked for, like our hero, Jonah), but God still loves to weave a good climax and finale out of it all. And I imagine that those folks who catch early glimpses of heaven seem excited because it's finally dawning on them that God was working out a whole lot more good things than we could have ever imagined, given our limited, fuzzy eyesight on this planet. So, let's hang on...a happy ending is on its way!

AUGUST 14

> Psalm 119:50 NLT Your promise revives me; it comforts me in all my troubles.

> God promises to love us, to save us, and to stay with us. The cares and difficulties of life can surely get us down, but when we remind ourselves of these promises, and that God helps us in and through our troubles, it will give us courage and hope to keep going.

Have you ever wondered what it would be like to always be on the go…to never really have a place you could call home? I remember reading about a lady, widowed, and with grown and gone kids, who boarded a cruise ship…and never left. She enjoyed traveling, had visited well over 100 countries, liked the cruise atmosphere, and so she just stayed. And the crew of the ship more or less became her family…no house repairs, bills to pay, shopping or meals to cook. I think I would find it very stifling after a while, to have no place to go beyond the ship's rails, but I guess if you enjoy moving around and not having to cut grass…well, then, perhaps she found the right solution. There are definitely advantages to not having to keep up with all the worries that go with having a house or a car, but where would I put all my books, that's what I'd like to know.

There are a couple of curious verses in 3 John, which I don't recall having noticed before, and I am really not sure what to make of them. John says to his readers: "Take care of those traveling teachers, the ones who are traveling for the Lord." Do you think they had cruise ships back then? Were there some teachers who were permanently on the go?? Who knows, maybe some innovator once read these verses and thought, "Eureka! That's it! I'll make a boat that people can just keep sailing around on, and I'll make a ton of money off them at the same time." If so, then he can thank the apostle John for the inspiration.

But, in truth, I kind of doubt that these were cruise ship travelers. For one thing, John is specifically reminding his audience to help take care of these folks. So, more than likely, they probably were not quite in the cruise ship economic level. But, truthfully, in a very real sense, whether we have ever been on a cruise or not, we're all traveling teachers...at least, those of us who love the Lord and want to teach others about him. In a way similar to how Jesus and Paul moved around, looking for people to share God's Message with, that is also our task. And because we know already that this is not our permanent home, that we really are just passing through it...in that sense, anyone who is living for God is a traveling teacher...whatever our profession here on earth may be. We're here temporarily, without a permanent home, we're teaching people about God's love...it's almost like we are permanent cruise ship residents. We're moving on to the next destination, which, ultimately, is heaven.

AUGUST 15

> **Day/Date** Be sure to remember five things to be grateful for every day. **August 15**
>
> Psalm 8:3-4 NLT   When I look at the night sky and see the work of your fingers — the moon and the stars you set in place — what are people that you should think about them, mere mortals that you should care for them? The complexity, size, and beauty of the universe are staggering to our minds and understanding. They show us how great and beyond our ability to comprehend God is. His greatness makes it all the more astounding that God loves each of us so much and paid such a costly price to save us.

I was the most enthusiastic of parents...when we had only one or two kids. I'm afraid I got a bit overloaded by the time numbers 8&9 came along. When our oldest was a young lad, I excitedly got involved in our church's Pioneer Boys club, and later, the Boys' Brigade club. We would listen to stories, play games, help them work toward earning badges to sew onto their vests. I loved Charles Swindoll at the time. He kept coming out with loads of books, and he was the most wonderful storyteller that I knew. So, I would pass on his stories to the assembled kids. The one I remember the best was the tale of Youssuf the Terrible Turk. The story goes that he came to America, was a sensational wrestler, and won a ton of money. Being a suspicious sort of person, unused to trustworthy banks, he demanded all his winnings in gold, which he carried on him in pouches inside his wide leather belt. Tragically, on his return trip to Europe, his ship collided with another, and sunk. Many passengers perished, including Youssuf the Super Swimmer, pulled under by the weight of his gold. There was definitely a great spiritual lesson in that story, which I'm sure all those kids took to heart and must remember to this day.

Something else I recall easily from those club meetings was when one of the other leaders taught the boys, using hand motions, "Your Word is a lamp to my feet and a light to my path." I don't know if the boys got that, but I sure did, and can still picture my friend repeating those words to the kids, to this day.

That statement actually comes directly from Psalm 119:105, and I'm sure I will never forget it, thanks to the boys' club. And I hope those boys from back then remember it as well, for God instructs us repeatedly to pass on his Word and his truth to the next generation. It doesn't happen automatically, without our efforts. And we see the tragic reality of that when God's own people forgot to teach their children about God. Are we passing God's truths to those coming after us? It is one of our most critical responsibilities.

AUGUST 16

There's a reason why introverts should stay home. We are so socially inept, that we can get ourselves all tangled up into endless troubles, anytime we venture out. I learned a long time ago that it's way safer for me just to stay home with my books. Like a loyal pet dog, my books stay faithful and uncomplaining, no matter how I treat them. But, one time, I got careless and ventured out. In fact, on that occasion, I travelled a long way to attend a conference. During the conference, two young gals stood up and performed some beautiful music for us. Something about the way they sang and swayed with the music, however, tickled my funny bone...and I started to giggle. I giggled and laughed through the whole thing, while they stood before us, singing their hearts out. I expect I scarred them for life after that incident, and, at any rate, I don't recall ever being invited back. I really should have just stayed home and saved us all a lot of discomfort.

Now, I don't know if Jonah was an introvert or not...but, I'm guessing he was. He said and packed in so many comical, and embarrassing, really, things in the four short chapters that bear his name, that he's given as bad a reputation to introverts as any of my biggest blunders ever have. The book is written as if it's serious prose, but Jonah can't fool me. I mean, listen to some of this stuff he spits out, with a straight face. We all know that a giant fish came along and swallowed Jonah, probably a one of a kind beast that God made especially for that occasion. Like any of us in that unspeakable panic, Jonah tells us, "I called out to God from the land of the dead." He was nearly dead, true, but then, he wasn't exactly on land, was he! Then he says that God snatched him from the jaws of death. Really? I thought the jaws of death just snatched you, Jonah?!? He goes on in this humorous mode: "I'll offer sacrifices to you." Considering who he was praying to, the Almighty God of the universe, does anyone else start to giggle, as I do, at the thought of Jonah saying with a straight face that he's going to light up a sacrifice in the whale's pit? To top it all off, Jonah becomes furious when God decides to forgive some honestly repentant folks. I mean, that must border on blasphemy for Jonah to respond that way. But God, in his compassionate way, once Jonah escaped from the whale's jaws, arranged for a nice leafy bush to provide shade for the overheated Jonah. Then, to continue the comedy, God requisitioned an energetic and famished worm to come along and eat up Jonah's now favorite shade tree. (I really didn't make that part up. It's in there!) Jonah fumes at God, in a huff...and the story ends. What a crazy, goofy story? Did Jonah get included in there with the rest of the prophets, by mistake, I have to wonder? Actually, I do believe there is a sane explanation in all of this insane narrative. You know what it is? It's this: God includes this true tale (I know it's true...it's too far fetched to have been concocted.) in his holy book so that we can know for sure that he looks down at us with such a feeling of warmth and love and preciousness, that he allows and invites us, even those of us who are inept introverts, to participate in his eternal plan...just like he invited Jonah to participate in his plan to reach the people of Nineveh. The invitation is still open. God still wants us to tag along as part of his grand plan for the world. How about it? Shall we join him? (Personally, I think I'll go along, rather than risk an unpleasant meeting with some jaws or a worm.)

AUGUST 17

August 17

Deuteronomy 33:27 NLT — The eternal God is your refuge, and his everlasting arms are under you.

The Bible uses many word pictures to describe God's attributes and characteristics to us. Though God is a Spirit without a body such as we have, in this passage we find one of the most beautiful descriptions of God. He cares for us and protects us, and he surrounds us with his security as a mother hen covers and protects her baby chicks.

When we were young parents, we had a pastor who was very missions-minded, had served the Lord for many years in Japan, and had started a Christian college there. I used to love listening to his passion for God's Word, as he shared it with us. As he finally was ready to retire, I remember him giving his last sermon before the congregation. What would this great man of God share with us? What great words of wisdom, what profound spiritual truths, what secret keys to the Gospel message would he impart, I wondered. When he unfolded his message, it was actually, refreshingly simple and profound. His parting instruction to us was this: trust and obey. Just as the simple song tells us to do, he recounted how, all through his illustrious life, he had learned that the simple secret was to trust God and to obey him. For the simpleton that I am, it was actually a relief to discover that the secret to life, to the Bible, to following God, was that straightforward. This, I could handle, understand, take on board.

As I begin to read the final Bible book of Revelation, which I arrive at near the end of every calendar year, I am also comforted and encouraged by its simple opening words (before it gets into all the complicated, mysterious stuff). John reminds us that God is giving us grace and peace. That is exactly the medicine we need in life, isn't it...grace and peace. At the same time, although when God appeared to him, John was completely blown away by his dazzling presence,

God assured him: "Don't be afraid. I am here forever. And I have all the answers to life, so there's nothing for you to worry about." All we have to do, God seems to be telling us, is to trust and obey. It's that simple. That's all there is to it. Now, if I can just remember that again tomorrow...

AUGUST 18

When you reach a certain age, you can really get taken in by people who tell you how young you look, how fit you are... During our recent ten years in Asia, we heard that a lot. Now, most unsuspecting Westerners would probably be taken in by those kinds of comments, failing to understand that it's just part of the gracious Asian culture, where they are forever trying to tell you what they think you want to hear...never mind if it strains reality just a tad (which it definitely did when they told me how young and fit I looked). Having grown up in Asia, and knowing well this aspect of the culture, I used to respond to them, jokingly (but truthfully), "I don't believe you! I never believe an Asian when they tell me I look young, because they all tell me that...and because I know I stopped looking young about 30 years ago!" Nevertheless, when I taught at a private English school in China for a number of years, I have to confess that it was a trifle flattering when many of the Chinese teachers in their 20s and 30s (especially the female ones) would tell me these things. Maybe they were hoping I would respond by buying them ice cream, I don't know, because they did all know that I was a nut for bingjieling (ice cream). After eating our usual fiery, spicy lunch together, I couldn't run down the steps and out into the streets quick enough to search for an ice cream vendor to tamp down the flames licking the back of my throat. They all found it pretty amusing. The school I taught at (for the purpose of obtaining a visa), was large, in fact more than likely the largest in the province, or even beyond, among all the scattered small private language schools, now that the whole world had decided that English was the ticket to a bright future. The school where I taught, which took me about an hour of walking and bus riding to get to, with my heavy book bag in tow, had about 7,000-8,000 primary school students, all, little busy bundles of energy, curious about this waiguoren (foreigner) in their midst. There were also about 100 or so Chinese teachers, laboring to teach the students English, plus one or two foreign, native English teachers, like me, who roved around from class to class, giving the kids a taste of first language English pronunciation. Truthfully, my job was the easiest there. Not only was I paid more than the Chinese teachers, who were slaving diligently, but, because I moved from class to class, I didn't have to give (or grade, more importantly) tests or homework. I just sauntered into the classroom, spun some silly tales, then walked out at the end, with a spring in my step, knowing that I didn't have all the heavy work at home to do, like all the other teachers. (I should have felt guilty for being paid more for doing less, but, for some reason, I never felt too guilty about it. After all, I did have the extra expense of having to buy ice cream everyday, and none of the Chinese teachers had that added burden.) In addition to the students, every Friday afternoon, I taught the Chinese teachers English. They were a very sweet, patient lot, and I'm sure they knew English grammar better than I did...but the speaking and the pronunciation did need a little work to be done to bring them up to snuff. We had built up quite an English library in our home (which we offered as a source for students wanting to learn English), and so, every Friday, my book bag (or two) would be really bulging with excess English books that I offered as prizes to the teachers after they had given a presentation or recitation in English, in front of the class. That really motivated them to want to stand up in front of the other teachers. One day, one of the teachers gave the usual presentation, and afterwards, she selected one of the books I had spread out before them on my desk. I glanced at her selection and noticed it was a "New York Times Bestseller" title. I'm not sure what prompted me, but I grabbed the book out of her hand, held it up in front of the class, and asked them: "Do you know what it means when a book has this printed across the top of it?" They didn't. I continued, "If I were to write a book, and it had this printed on it, then I would really have arrived. I would be a celebrated author who would be able to pay his bills. But there's one book that, every year, outsells any of the New York Times Bestseller books...yet, it never appears on the list. Any idea what that book might be?" Silence… Finally, one timid, brave soul raised her hand, and questioningly, said, "Uhhh…Harry Potter??" "Not!", I replied, or something to that effect. As they all listened, and the headmaster of the school was on the front row, not six feet away from me, I held up one copy of the stack of Bibles I had also brought along that day, and I declared to them: "If you really want to learn English, if you want to understand Western civilization, culture, our laws, our idioms, our names, our traditions…you need to read this book." At the end of class, the teachers all surged forward and cleaned my stash out. I was stunned as I watched this happen before my eyes. I was in China, right, I thought to myself?? If I had tried this foolery in a school in America, someone would have howled in protest. But, here, in the bastion of atheism, no one gave a peep of protest. I was amazed at the freedom we experienced here.

I wanted so much for those teachers to know of God's love and truth. They were my dear friends and colleagues, and I would do anything to share with them my most treasured possession: God's Word. That day returns to my thoughts as I read these verses near the end of Psalm 119: "Your laws are perfect and completely trustworthy…that is why I love them so much. Your laws are always right." What a privilege is ours to be able to share God's precious treasure with others!

AUGUST 19

In 1995, our family crossed the Channel from France, to arrive in England, with six kids and another due imminently. Because we didn't know for sure how long we would be living in Europe, I thought it would be wiser to rent an apartment, rather than trying to buy some kind of housing. So, we began searching for and checking out a number of places which were available for rent. Perhaps not surprisingly, nearly all the places we found had space for one or two, or at a stretch, three people. We came to the eventual conclusion that purchasing a home was our only option, whether we liked it or not. England is not the cheapest real estate market, even in the best of times...but, thankfully for us, the market was submerged at close to rock bottom, just as we walked in. After a good bit of further looking, we settled on an old Victorian home, built nearly 100 years earlier, with stone walls several feet think, and with a few quirky laws still attached to it. We learned, for instance, that it was against the law, at least in our neighborhood, to slaughter cows in our basement. Noted. The house still was covered by its original Welsh slate tiles, still had lead water pipes, and was so solid, it was sure to last a few hundred more years. Although we apparently got a good deal on the house, it did have a few "rough edges", and it got to be that every year, we would have one or two major projects to undertake, in order to bring it more up to date. So, we got to work (or at least our friendly builder did), and by the time we were ready to sell it, ten years later, we had replaced carpeting, windows, fireplace, kitchen counters, oven, pipes, and probably a few other things as well. When we finally sold our home, it was just about where we wanted it to be, a beautiful, updated residence, which, thankfully, was selling for a good price, now that the market had caught fire. A family with a number of children was very interested in our house, and we really wanted to pass it on to someone who would appreciate all the nice updates we had spent ten years putting into place. It was looking very much like they could purchase it, but at the last moment, they were unable to get the financing together, and they had to back out of the deal. Not to worry, another buyer, a young single guy, came along and offered us our asking price. We were grateful to have a buyer, though we were a little sorry that the family had been unable to get it together, so they could enjoy it for years to come. As soon as we closed on the sale and pocketed our cash, we watched as the buyer promptly tore out our new fireplace, carpeting, updated kitchen...basically, he destroyed our entire home...because, of course, he wanted to really bring it up to date, and then turn around and sell it again for an even better price. Clever idea, but we felt just a little sad that all our renovations had seemingly been for naught.

When I read the first few chapters of Micah, I'm reminded of our home back there in Sheffield. We knew we had it just perfect, exactly the way it needed to be, precisely the way we had it all planned out. Then a new guy came along and gutted all our beautiful appointments. Apparently, that's what happened to the Israelites living in Jerusalem (and also does with us, on occasion) at the time God spoke to the prophet Micah. They thought they had their lives perfectly neat and tidy, just how they wanted them to be...but they were blind to what God saw, to what needed to change, to the better plans God had for them (namely, following him, rather than chasing after all kinds of misguided idols). So, God came in with a new floor plan, trashed the place, and started all over again. It must have been a terrible shock and disappointment for them. But, God knew what he was doing (as he does with us, of course), and he had to tear out and tear down the rot before he could start to build something strong and new and good. Are you facing what looks and feels like a lot of tearing down and destruction in your life today? It can certainly happen at times. Remember, God has good plans for you. He sees the bigger picture. Trust him and hang on...things will one day become more clear, and you will understand better, why God has allowed some of these unsettling and uncomfortable things to visit your life.

AUGUST 20

Day/Date   Be sure to remember five things to be grateful for every day.   August 20

2 Timothy 2:19 NLT   God's truth stands firm like a foundation stone with this inscription: "The Lord knows those who are his," and "All who belong to the Lord must turn away from evil."

A building is set and secure when it is supported by an immovable foundation stone. God's Word is like that: it doesn't change, and we can have confidence in what it tells us about God and about ourselves. When we belong to God, we have a new life, and this involves choosing to turn away from selfishness to a life of serving God.

During the years we lived in China, God brought someone into my life, who was just what I needed at that particular juncture. We were an odd match, really. I was a generation older than he was, nearly old enough to be his father. We came from different church backgrounds, our family makeups were not the same, and we had differing personalities and interests. But at that stage in both our lives, we were experiencing similar things, both navigating a foreign country that was at times perplexing, each attempting to serve people in a variety of ways. Both our families lived outside the old city of Dali, whose ancient stone walls formed a square, which were about a mile in each direction. Once a month, my friend and I would meet early in the morning at the southwest corner of the city, and from there, enjoy a prayer walk around the city walls. Following the walk, we often stopped in at a familiar restaurant or bakery for some breakfast. Those were precious times, I think, for both of us. Because we were living through the same experiences, wrestling with many of the same challenges and problems, we could understand each other and nod agreeably to each other as the conversation moved back and forth between us. Those were special moments shared together. It is wonderful to be with someone who understands you fully, someone you feel free to unburden yourself with.

In the opening chapters of Revelation, God sends personal messages to each of the early churches in Asia Minor at the time. These were messages of encouragement and admonition. A number of the fellowships were struggling, and God was keen to set them back on the right path. What is interesting and comforting to me about these messages is that God tells them: "I know everything about you. I understand your situation. I can see when you are struggling or suffering. Don't be afraid. Hang on and stay faithful. I am with you." So, whatever their particular situation or dynamic at the moment, God saw it, understood it, and could relate to what they were going through. I am sure that those messages, written 2,000 years ago, were also written to us. They apply and are appropriate to us, just as they were to each of the early recipients. God knows us, loves us, understands what we're wrestling with, promises to stay with us. He does sometimes allow us to struggle and suffer, but we don't need to be afraid. Just as it was a great comfort to me that my friend understood me, so, also, does God. He knows us. He understands us. He loves us. He is with us. That is enough. That is sufficient. Lord, help me to remember these truths, remind me, when I am fretful and anxious, that you are indeed with me, and you are watching over me. Amen.

AUGUST 21

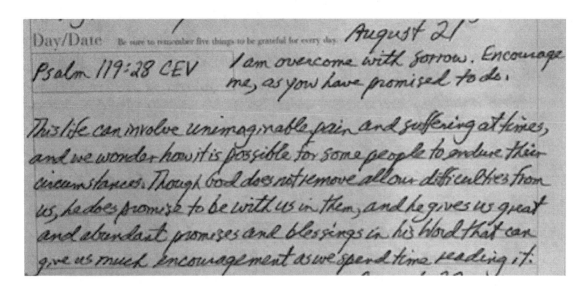

Day/Date Be sure to remember five things to be grateful for every day. *August 21*

Psalm 119:28 CEV *I am overcome with sorrow. Encourage me, as you have promised to do.*

This life can involve unimaginable pain and suffering at times, and we wonder how it is possible for some people to endure their circumstances. Though God does not remove all our difficulties from us, he does promise to be with us in them, and he gives us great and abundant promises and blessings in his Word that can give us much encouragement as we spend time reading it.

Goodness...there are so many things that make you feel old...

Achy joints...yes, car joints, but I'm talking about joints even closer to home than that.

Walking into a room to get something...seeing something else that gets your attention, then five minutes later, remembering that there was some other completely different reason why you first came into the room.

Forgetting where you parked your car at Walmart. (And what's even more scary, is finding your car, starting to climb in, then seeing someone else in the passenger seat and discovering that it's really not your car at all. Now, that's enough to startle and scare both of you!)

Forgetting how many grandkids you have...is this number 14 or 15?? (Never mind remembering their middle names and birthdays, like my wife does...good grief!)

I'll tell you what is a pure delight, though...it's when those same grandkids (and, perhaps even our kids, every once in a while...) come running up to you, all excited to tell you about their latest lego contraption, their newest outfit, a doll they treasure, or a picture book they've been enjoying. I really need to confess that it's not so much that I'm ecstatic about legos...but, just that fact that they notice me and want to share something with me at all...that's what makes this old man excited.

I reflect on all these things as I read the opening verse of Psalm 120. In verse one it says that, "I brought my troubles to the Lord." In one sense, we don't need to do that. God knows everything about us already. I don't need to tell him my problems. He knows them all, backwards and forwards. He already knows all the solutions, how they will be played out...everything. So, what's the point of telling it all to God, then, we may ask. Just this...in exactly the same way that I delight to have my grandkids come running up to me with excitement written all over their faces, to show me what is so critically important to them...God also responds to us when we come to him. As a Heavenly Father who loves us dearly, he just loves to see us come running to him and unloading all our burdens on him. He loves us so much, that it delights him when we come into his presence, troubles and problems, all in tow. He just loves it! Shall we make God's day today? Shall we bring him joy by coming into his presence now? Let's do it!

AUGUST 22

Day/Date · Be sure to remember five things to be grateful for every day · August 22

1 Peter 4:12-13 NCV My friends, do not be surprised at the terrible trouble which now comes to test you. Do not think that something strange is happening to you. But be happy that you are sharing in Christ's sufferings.

When we understand the true nature of our sinfulness and what Christ gave to pay for its punishment, we can be overcome with gratefulness, joy, and peace that we have not previously experienced. It can come as a shock, then, when life continues to be difficult, and when people are opposed to us. But our life in Christ stands against many of the values of this world. We are privileged to share in some of his sufferings on our behalf.

In some ways, this year of 2020 has been very nostalgic. Not that a pandemic is winsome in any way, or that we will some day look back with longing to return to this year. I rather doubt it. But, someone in some studio somewhere seems to have dug up a gold mine of old gems. I guess because so many things have been shut down this year, folks in studios where nothing is happening have more time on their hands to dig for hidden treasures...or, because so many events have been cancelled, that the entertainment business is scrambling to fill the time slots with anything, even if they have to reach back half a century to find something. All of a sudden, I'm seeing highlights of old baseball games from the 1970s and 80s being rolled out. Even more entertaining, and what brings back long forgotten memories from even further back, is to see ancient music groups and celebrities, being pulled out of the history books...folks I hardly remembered even existed...Elvis Presley, the Beach Boys, John Denver, Neil Diamond, the Mamas and the Papas... Did we really listen to that music, once upon a time? And when they show videos of these groups, it's funny to see the odd and outlandish clothing they wore, the way they clapped, whistled, or did other things that apparently were entertaining 50 years ago. My, my, how time has moved on. (I wonder what people listen to today...can't say that I would really know.) Occasionally, I will check online to find out whatever happened to this or that entertainer. Tragically, all too often, it seems that their lives were cut short…ended too early due to reckless or careless living…or their lives were marked by multiple broken marriages or sadness in some other way. It can make for depressing reading.

Perhaps God was looking ahead to our day when he gave his message to the prophet Micah to pass on to the people. A lot of crazy things were happening back then as well. Chaos. Upheaval. Distress. Trouble. Exploitation. Uncertainty. So, what did God tell the people in response? He said, just as he tells us today: "Return to me. Follow my ways. I love you and will restore you. Live rightly, and trust in and honor me. I will save you. I will forgive you and have compassion on you." It's actually the very same message we need in our day. Not much has changed in all these intervening years. OK, they didn't have Neil Diamond back then, but they did have gold, and they still got very messed up. They needed to turn back to God. We need the very same medicine today. Lord, help us to turn our eyes and our hearts back to you today.

AUGUST 23

We have been enjoying watching "The Crown", a Netflix series that follows British Queen Elizabeth, from her youth, all the way through her reign as the monarch. It's a fascinating look into how the royal family functions, the many details requiring the proper protocol, and the centuries standing traditions that dictate how things are done specifically and correctly. Hundreds of staff have precise tasks for every condition imaginable, and there is always the correct manner of operating in every situation. It would be impossible for someone like me to ever imagine having an audience with the Queen. All this...for someone who, truth be told, is a mere mortal, like you and me.

Then, there is the true Monarch of the universe, God Almighty. We are given a glimpse of this profound, infinite Being in Revelation 4-6. Listen to how he is described. He is glowing like glittering gemstones. Thunder and lightning come out of him. In heaven, every living being worships him, day and night. In his presence, the sun turns black in darkness, the sky collapses, mountains are shaken. How could any one of us imagine ever being, and surviving, in his presence? But, do you know what is really amazing about this infinite, all powerful Monarch, who rules the whole universe? Just this...in his presence are golden bowls...which are filled with your prayers and mine! Can you imagine that?? God so values us, so values us coming into his presence, that he greatly treasures and collects our conversations with him! Unbelievable, really. Just that one image provided for us in Revelation tells us how precious each one of us is to him...and how loving, faithful, and compassionate he is toward us. Let's come before him today...he waits to hear from us!

AUGUST 24

> Day/Date Be sure to remember five things to be grateful for every day. August 24
>
> Genesis 28:15 NIV I am with you and will watch over you wherever you go. I will not leave you until I have done what I have promised you.
>
> Life takes us to places and puts before us tasks and circumstances that greatly test our character and our personal resources. But in each of these places, God promises to be with us. We are not alone, we do not have to journey through life alone, and God promises to be with us and to bring us safely to heaven

When we were little and visiting my grandparents, anytime we were about to start off on a trip, we could be sure that my NaiNai, our grandmother, would pull out her Bible, and read to us (or, more like, quite from memory), Psalm 121. She called it the traveler's psalm. She had been through, had seen, an awful lot in her lifetime. Losses, deaths, illnesses, tragedies...plenty of hardship. But, she always went back to this psalm. Its words are beautiful, the images it paints for us are wonderful. The God who made the universe helps us. He is always watching over us, never falls asleep at the wheel. He keeps watch over us as we go out (like on a trip), and as we come back. So, what is this psalm telling us? Will we never have a car accident? My sister was killed in one. Will we never get sick? I think we all know that's not the case. Will we never drown? My brother did. Will we never be taken advantage of or lose what we have? My parents and grandparents had to flee in wartime and lost everything. Well, if it's not giving us protection from any of these things, then what is it saying? What's the point of even referring to it or going back to it, if it offers no protection. Just this...these words remind us to look to God. They remind us that he's in charge. They tell us that nothing is out of his control. We know that he's a good God, and that he loves us. He reminds us in these words that he's watching over us and taking care of us. That is a wonderful truth and gives us security and peace.

Does that mean, nothing bad will ever happen to us? Clearly not. We all know (or will discover soon enough) that this is a pretty messed up, broken world. Bad things happen, people get hurt, tragedies take place. But, God is watching over and guiding us. Sometimes we need something (that we would consider bad or unpleasant) to wake us up or to get our attention. So, God may send something "bad" our way because it's the medicine or discipline we need at the moment. But he hasn't forgotten us. He hasn't walked away. He's still working, still guiding, still in charge. And, that's a good reminder, wherever we may be heading today.

AUGUST 25

Day/Date *Be sure to remember five things to be grateful for every day.* August 25

Deuteronomy 31:6 NLT So be strong and courageous! Do not be afraid and do not panic before them. For the Lord your God will personally go ahead of you. He will neither fail you nor abandon you. Much of the time, we are able to see only what is observable around us. And many times, what we see frightens or overwhelms us. But if we are able and willing to see beyond the obvious and to accept what God has told us and promised us, it completely changes the circumstances we are in and reminds us that we are not alone and that God is more than adequate to meet whatever need we may have.

I have always enjoyed history and have sometimes thought it would be fun to go back to school and study the subject just for the pleasure of it. My love of history played a hand in two, probably careless, recent investments that I entered into. Not many people would argue that I am short of books and need just a few more. But I couldn't resist buying two additional volumes, one of which is 827 pages, the other a mere 704 pages. It's a very good bet that I'll never read through either of them. So, why in the world did I purchase them, you might ask? Well, aside from the price (Both were selling for 75 cents at my favorite used bookstore.), they are filled with interesting and obscure historical trivia and possibilities. One provides oodles of bits of useless history that makes for entertaining reading...such as the bumpy early days of Harvard University (if what the story says can really be believed). The other book is full of fascinating, imagined, different directions history might have taken if only one or two little things hadn't happened the way they did...if a soldier hadn't lost his army's battle plans and the enemy hadn't then discovered them; if a decade in Europe hadn't been unusually wet and thus preventing the Ottoman Empire's fleet from reaching and conquering some of Europe, rather than being delayed by the weather; if Pontius Pilate had pardoned instead of crucified Jesus; and so on. (You can probably understand why I fell for these two books!) It's also interesting to read about all the complicated chess moves that different governments and countries make...along with the resulting fallout from these decisions, the ramifications of which may not come to light until many years later. For example, I have to say, I've wondered sometimes (with not a little suspicion), why Russia just happened to declare war on Japan three weeks before Japan's surrender, right at the tail end of World War 2. Did it have anything to do with something called the "victor's spoils"?? There certainly is plenty of room for speculation...and entertainment...and 75 cents does make it pretty affordable...

There is one thing, though, that does seem pretty clear to me about history...and that is the profound importance of staying on God's good side. Probably one of the scariest verses in all the Bible is Nahum 2:13. It's so scary that I doubt if I have to even remind you of what it says. But, I'll refresh your memory, anyway. Here it is: "'I am your enemy!', says the Lord of Heaven's Armies." So, who was God addressing in this verse? Do you remember when Jonah went to Nineveh...and, quite surprisingly and unexpectedly, they listened and turned to God? Well, apparently, it didn't last long. By the time Nahum came along, a few generations later, Nineveh was right back to their usual bad ways...and this time, God said enough was enough. Although he is a patient and forgiving God, there is a limit...and Assyria had reached that point. God called himself their enemy...and 50 years later, it was all over for them. Their empire collapsed. I get scared, at times, reading these passages and thinking about our own country. How close are we to the point where God will tell us, that's it! Enough, and no more. Let's pray for a turning back to God, shall we? Wouldn't it be wonderful if there was a great turning to God all across the globe! Shall we pray together toward that end?

AUGUST 26

Day/Date   Be sure to remember five things to be grateful for every day.

2 Timothy 4:16-17 NLT *The first time I was brought before the judge, no one came with me. Everyone abandoned me. But the Lord stood with me and gave me strength so that I might preach the Good News, and rescued me from death. Even the great apostle Paul felt fearful and alone on occasion. How heartbreaking it must have been, after pouring himself into others' lives, to see many turn away from him. But his trials had a purpose, and they are an encouragement to us as we see how he received help from God in his time of need, just as we also can.*

We watched another episode of "The Crown" last night, and it included a rather cute and amusing incident, which was, at least partly, based on an actual encounter. Shortly after her husband, King George VI, passed away, and her young daughter, Queen Elizabeth, ascended the throne of the empire, the Queen Mother decided, in 1952, that she needed to get away from the continual intrigue and stresses in London, that accompanied such a position. And she did...escaping all the way to the very northern tip of Scotland. While there, she stayed with some friends, and one day they were out for a walk near the coast, in the blustery and chilly Scottish weather. As they were strolling along, the couple pointed out an ancient castle in the distance, which they said, after hundreds of centuries of use, was to be torn down, as the current owner could not afford the upkeep of such a massive place. The Queen Mother was intrigued, and on a whim, decided to march over, knock on the door, and inquire about its status. She did so, and as the front door was opened by an elderly man, standing before him was a middle aged English lady in a raincoat and floppy rain hat...or at least that's who he assumed it was. He invited her in, and she asked about his house (the castle). Her interest increased, and she asked about the possibility of purchasing it. He really couldn't bring himself to sell it to her for any sum, due to the massive repairs he knew were necessary, and the ongoing upkeep required. Finally, he agreed to sell it for £100 (about £2500 today), knowing that she would have to sink another £10,000+ into it, just to get it livable. At this stage, it didn't even have electricity or running water. During their conversation, the elderly man was puzzled...he was sure he knew this lady from somewhere; it was right on the tip of his tongue, in fact, but he just couldn't quite place her. Were they old friends? Was she a famous actress? Who was she?? No, no, the Queen Mother assured him. We've never met before. At the same time as this was all taking place in Scotland, a member of the royal staff at Buckingham Palace was sent on an urgent mission to fetch the Queen Mother, and escort her back to London, due to a pressing need that had arisen. So, in the middle of one of her conversations with this elderly Scottish gentleman, the royal emissary burst onto the scene, and declared, "Your Majesty, you are urgently requested to return to London at once!" Suddenly, the old man was speechless, as it dawned on him who he had been having a friendly chat with! "Why didn't you tell me?", he asked. "It was so nice just having an ordinary conversation with you!", the Queen Mother replied, with a little smile. That was certainly one encounter that the man could enjoy repeating endlessly to all his grandkids and anyone else within earshot of the coast of Scotland. It must have been something like the two guys who, unknowingly, encountered Jesus, as they headed toward Emmaus, after his resurrection, but without realizing who they were talking with. When it finally dawned on them, they also were unable to contain their excitement. Imagine what it would be like if you or I bumped into someone as celebrated as the Queen, but without realizing it! Wouldn't that be incredible! Actually, we have, and probably do, every day. How so? Well, how important would someone have to be, for the Almighty God of the universe to stop what he was doing, and to turn his head and listen, whenever that person spoke? How important would a person have to be, if whenever he or she prayed, their prayers were brought directly to the King over all of heaven's armies, the most powerful force on earth? There is someone that important. That person is you. That is how God treats you and me, we are told in Revelation 9, when we come into his presence to chat. If that is how God and the angels treat us, how should we be treating each other?

AUGUST 27

Day/Date   Be sure to remember five things to be grateful for every day.   August 27

1 Peter 4:10 NLT   God has given each of you a gift from his great variety of spiritual gifts. Use them well to serve one another.

Often we don't know what spiritual gift we have nor how to use it effectively. But God tells us that he has given us gifts to use as we live for him. So how do we discover them? One good way is to look around us and see what needs to be done as a service to God and others. As we involve ourselves in serving God, we will see and understand how God has equipped us to live for him.

When we first joined a literature organization to work overseas, we had belonged to a church fellowship in the US for about ten years, and had been greatly blessed by the many aspects of the church life that we were involved in. So, naturally, we wanted to find a good fellowship that we could become engaged with as we headed to France...then England...then China...then Korea. In each place we lived, we found very different groups to plug into...large, small, formal, informal, denominational, nondenominational, pastor driven, fellowship driven...and many other varying aspects. But, in each place, no matter the color, the makeup, the language, or the structure, we became committed to a group that was eager to worship God, fellowship together, and reach out to those around us. The differences didn't matter, they were not what stood out to us. It was what united us and brought us together and held us together, that was important. These groups, in each place, were essential to our spiritual health and well-being. We found that each group was what we needed as a family, for our children, as followers of God. They had a big part to play in how we thrived and stayed healthy in each place.

I think back on the blessing that each group was to us, and the warm fellowship we shared in each place, when I read the beautiful opening verse of Psalm 122: "I was glad when they said to me, 'Let us go to the house of the Lord.'" This brief psalm was written by King David for folks to sing as they came into the ancient city of Jerusalem. You can almost hear their excitement as they near the city and anticipate gathering with God's people. That's how it's meant to be. That's how it should be for us. As we think about going to church today, do we look forward to coming into the presence of Almighty God? Are we coming to worship him together with his people? Are we anticipating hearing his Message to us today? Are we pondering how we can reach out to and serve others, both within and outside of the fellowship? That is how God meant for it to be. That is why he has provided for us the gathering of his people together. Am I deliberately seeking out what God has provided for us, that he tells us is essential for our life? If God knows us and loves us and tells us that we need to be invested in his people...shouldn't we agree with him?

AUGUST 28

Day/Date — Be sure to remember five things to be grateful for every day. August 28

Psalm 73:26 NLT — My health may fail, and my spirit may grow weak, but God remains the strength of my heart; he is mine forever.

What is important is not how strong I am, but who God is and what he has done for me. I may wear down, wear out, get discouraged or feel like giving up. But God stays the same, and we can have confidence in his promises and presence with us.

Of course, we won't mention any names here, but when I was in seventh grade, I remember as if it were yesterday (It was actually closer to 100 years ago, than it was to yesterday.), seeing our boarding school principal running laps around the football field with one of the older students (who was popular, but let's just say that he had a bit more flair about him than I ever dared to have). Now, they weren't just out for an afternoon fun run together, that was emphatically clear. I could nearly see the steam coming out of the principal's ears, as he heatedly lectured the particular student about something that must have been terribly, terribly important. Although I wasn't close enough to them to hear the content of the discussion, I recall wincing to myself at the gravity of the situation. (After all, I was still very new to boarding school and probably had never realized before that these sorts of intense confrontations and tête-à-têtes ever even took place.) Whatever it was that the student had done must have been extremely serious for it to warrant this kind of attention. Why couldn't he just have behaved correctly the first time? Why did he have to do something so grave that it required this trip to the woodshed (or more like, the cow pasture, in this case)? I guess sometimes we just don't learn...at least not the first, or second, or third time...

History does repeats itself, when we choose not to learn from an experience, the first time around. If there's one thing you learn about history, if there's one thing that cynics agree upon, if there's one thing you learn by the time you get old...it's that we don't learn very well from other people's past mistakes. We all seem to believe that it's our God ordained right to make the same disastrous mistakes that our parents or friends or someone else made long ago. We just have to experience and learn it again in our own way, on our own terms, going through all the pain ourselves, thank you. Maybe that's why Revelation was written hundreds of years after the Old Testament prophets were written...because the people apparently hadn't learned from history, so they had to receive the very same message again. Since it's the same message that many of the prophets delivered, it probably doesn't really need to be repeated. But, in case it's been a while since we've studied through Obadiah or Zephaniah, I suppose we could review a couple of the key lessons. Here they are:

1) God doesn't change. He is working out his eternal and good plans. More than likely, he's not going to change them, just because I don't happen to like the way they appear to be unfolding.

2) God is mysterious. I may think I do, but I don't actually have the right to know, and it's not part of God's job description, to tell me exactly why and how he's doing something, even if I really, really think I need to know.

3) God is loving and good. Even more than the most loving parent adores their child, God loves each of us. His love means that, in some cases, he will allow us to suffer, either because it might be good for us in some way...or, perhaps, because it will be used to bring about good in someone else's life, even if I never understand why, this side of heaven.

4) God doesn't shrug his shoulders at bad stuff. He has the (sometimes seemingly irritating) habit of always, always dealing with disobedience and wrong doing. And don't fool yourself (I'm really talking to myself here.) into imagining that you can slip something past God, or that he won't notice something nasty that I decide to do. He knows my thought even before I do...who, really, am I kidding?

So, rather than risking a trip to the shed or the cow pasture, shall we just all agree together that the consequences of sin (as they are laid out for us in painful, living color in God's Word) are really not worth it...and avoid them like the plague... or the virus? Maybe, just maybe, we can be the first generation to discover that history does not have to repeat itself after all...

AUGUST 29

Matthew 25:34 NCV Come, my Father has given you his blessing. Receive the Kingdom God has prepared for you since the world was made.

One day, if we are trusting Jesus as our Savior, we will hear these wonderful words as God welcomes us into his presence in heaven. From that moment on, we will have no more pain, sadness, or hardship. All we have to do now is to accept God's gift of salvation for us.

It was one summer in the early 1960s, that it happened. I must have been about five or six. After some relaxing days at the beach in Korea, our family was driving home in an old Isuzu bus. This was in the days, long before seat belts, so us six kids, along with our parents and our Korean cook, were jumbled all over the place, mixed in with our suitcases, kitchen ware, and whatever else we were carrying. The journey couldn't have been more than about 100 miles, hardly worth mentioning in today's terms. But 50+ years ago, it was an utterly different world. The road from the beach to home were entirely rough, rutted, hard packed dirt and pebbles...which meant you bounced along in clouds of dust at something like 30 miles an hour, in addition to, as part of the journey, waiting interminably at a river for a smoke belching ferry to approach and carry you across. Deep in the rice paddy strewn countryside, at one point, my father guided us around a tight left bend in the road. At precisely that moment, we bounced across a gully that straddled the road, and were sent catapulting through the air, our momentum carrying us to the right...and ever the edge of the road, down an embankment, and with a splat, right into a soft, muddy rice field below. As we came to our senses, we untangled ourselves from the strewn suitcases, and crawled out of the windows and doors of the van, which lay on its side, in the field. As we staggered out, my older sister, who had been barefoot in the vehicle, placed her feet on the exposed exhaust pipe, while lowering herself to the ground. She received large burn blisters on the underside of both her feet as she did that. The family in the farmer's nearby mud hut invited us in to recover, as my father scratched his head and pondered how to get the van upright and back on the road, now six feet above us. Providentially, save for my sister, none of us was injured, in what could have been a much more dangerous accident. Thankfully, several friendly farmers materialized with shovels, and they got to work, along with Dad, to dig us out of the paddy. They had to carve a rough car path from the field up to the road, so that we could drive and push the vehicle back up onto the road. The bus also had to be heaved upright from its side, and dug out of the muddy and watery rice field, which, given its very gooey consistency, had no doubt saved us from what could have been a much more serious catastrophe. As the men dug and sweated, I remember wandering out of the little hut where we were resting, to watch the men labor to extricate the car. At one point, my Dad reached down, ripped off his useless sandal, and flung it into the back of the bus. He carried on laboring in the thick mud, in his bare feet. Eventually the task was completed, Dad gratefully thanked the local men who helped us, and with a wave to the gathered onlookers, we again headed down the road toward home, perhaps a bit more cautiously this time. We were a muddy, smelly, exhausted bunch, when, at last, we arrived back at our home in Kwangju. I'm sure my parents lifted their eyes toward heaven, and thanked God for, traumatic and memorable though it was, a journey that saw us safely home, instead of what could have been a much more tragic ending.

The sketchy details of that day come back to me as I reflect on the verses of Psalm 123. The writer says, "I lift my eyes to you, O God, enthroned in heaven." Perhaps, this is a reminder to us of two ways to approach life. We can focus on the mud and mess around us, and sink into despair...or, we can lift our eyes to the One who is enthroned above the earth, to the One who is in control, watching over us, guiding us, and walking with us, along our bumpy journey. He saved us from catastrophe on that day long ago, no doubt he continues to do so, most of the time, when we're not even aware of it.

AUGUST 30

> Day/Date _Be sure to remember five things to be grateful for every day._ August 30
>
> I Corinthians 9:25 NLT All athletes are disciplined in their training. They do it to win a prize that will fade away, but we do it for an eternal prize.
>
> Some people start from childhood training many hours, day after day, for the possibility of competing in the Olympics. They may dedicate their entire lives to winning a reward that is very brief. When we live for Christ, though, we are living for a goal that has eternal significance and results.

I was ready, that day, over 40 years ago. I had doggedly studied and sweated for a whole week, I now took my seat, and my MBA Marketing Research exam was handed to me. It was several stapled pages in length. I scanned the first page, flipped it over, and glanced down page 2...and the next, and the next. Panic awakened in my belly and began to rear its visible head. I didn't know a thing. Following a week of thorough study and review of my notes and the textbook, I... Somehow, I wrote what I could, answered as best as I was able, and, with quaking and shaking, handed my exam paper back to the professor. As I headed for the door, my friend, Tom, asked me how I did. "I think I blew it. I didn't know a thing." "Me, too!", he responded. "Let's go talk to the professor about it." "All right, let's go," I said, not knowing what else we could do. We approached the professor's office with fear and trembling, and he invited us to sit down. We explained our situation, hoping to get him to understand that, the reason why we had been destroyed by his test was not because we hadn't studied or because we were delinquent. As we made our case, he sat quietly, and patiently listened, not saying a word. After we had made our appeal, and said what we had to say, the PhD professor responded, gently, "Well, let's wait and see what happens." It wasn't much, but it was at least a sliver of hope we could hold on to. That was all we had. Hope for a better outcome than we were afraid was coming. (Somehow, I managed to squeak through that class. I hope Tom did, too...)

The book of Zephaniah presents us with the exact same scenario as I experienced on that nerve wracking day, back in my early 20s. God came to Israel and told them, "You're finished. I'm going to slaughter you, sweep you away, your money and armies won't be able to save you." I expect the people must have been shaking in their boots, by this time. It was all over...or was it? Just as the frightening book comes to a close, in the final words, God ends with what he is famous for...he extends to them a sliver of hope...a big sliver, actually. He says, "You're due for punishment, yes. But, that's not the end of the story. I'm going to restore you, bring you back home, make things right again." And, that is exactly the God we have. When things are bleak, when we flip the pages of our life and see no answers...don't forget God. Don't count him out. He's the one ace, the wild card, so to speak. With God, there is always hope. Because he is the God of hope.

AUGUST 31

Day/Date · Be sure to remember five things to be grateful for every day. · August 31

Psalm 13:1 NLT

O Lord, how long will you forget me? Forever? How long will you look the other way?

Psalms is a wonderful book for us because it contains so many expressions and prayers of how we feel and what we experience as humans. God has promised to always be with us and to never forget us. But this psalm expresses how we sometimes feel — even when we know that God is with us. And God invites us to come to him and express to him how we feel, just as David did in this psalm.

Politics is a complicated profession, and, honestly, I don't know how the elected officials juggle and balance so many complex, differing issues, that are frequently at odds with each other. What do you do, if your country is dependent on another's vital resources, but, at the same time, that other country is operating, dealing, or coercing in ways that are internationally unacceptable? I really don't know what I would do in some of those situations. I do know that it's a whole lot easier to just sit back and criticize the officials...so that is what I tend to do, even though the complexities of many of the issues are pretty well beyond being able to get my head around. I suppose, at times, leaders just have to weigh the cost and become unfriendly or hostile with others that they are unable to agree or continue on good terms with. Wouldn't it be nice if we could just all agree and get along with each other? On occasion, the bad blood runs so deep, that it continues for generations and for multiple regimes or administrations. Perhaps, some are just unmendable, unfixable...

That is one way in which God is radically different from us. There are some people who probably I would almost be unable to mend fences with, due to some sort of long, unfortunate history between us. But God doesn't operate that way. Even though he knows every single thing there is to know about us (which in itself is pretty frightening), still, if we want to mend fences with him, if we want to have a relationship with him, he utterly wipes the past slate clean. Never mind what I may have done in the past. With God, it's over and done with. It's as if it never happened. We can begin with a whole new start. In Zechariah 1, God tells us to return to him...and then, he'll return to us. In other words, if I turn toward him, he will turn back toward me, as well. That's it...no extra negotiating, no additional terms...just turn to him. Now, that is wonderful, I have to say. In fact, without that truth, I would be sunk, lost in the deepest bottom of the darkest, sharkest ocean.

MONTH 9

Quarantine day 9...

Thoughts from Daniel, Hosea, Joel, Amos, Obadiah, Jonah, Micah, Nahum, Habakkuk, Zephaniah, Haggai, Zechariah, Malachi, and Matthew...

*God directs and controls all things.

*God can do anything he pleases.

*God looks for those who are faithful to him.

*God knows the future...and has unchangeable plans for it.

*We are incapable of handling God's overwhelming presence.

*God loves us so much that he goes to extreme ends to have a relationship with us.

*Sometimes we go through the motions of spirituality when our hearts are in fact far from God.

*No matter how far we have strayed, God pursues us relentlessly.

*A day of reckoning is coming...as well as a day of restoration.

*God provides blessing and testing...because he loves us.

*God has hopeful plans of restoration and redemption that will come.

*God loves to forgive us! Will we come to him?

*One day the world will know him!

*Jesus fulfilled all that was talked about in the Old Testament.

*Jesus poured his life out for everyone.

*Our salvation is wholly dependent on God's mercy and grace.

*Jesus chose the most unlikely people to carry the Good News to the world.

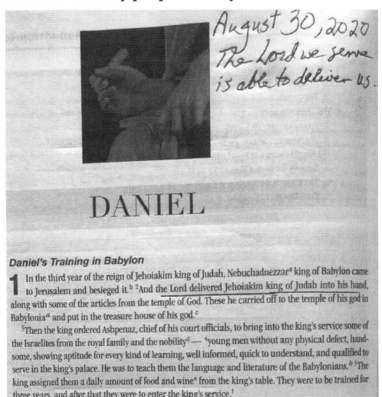

August 30, 2020
The Lord we serve
is able to deliver us.

DANIEL

Daniel's Training in Babylon

1 In the third year of the reign of Jehoiakim king of Judah, Nebuchadnezzar[a] king of Babylon came to Jerusalem and besieged it.[b] [2]And the Lord delivered Jehoiakim king of Judah into his hand, along with some of the articles from the temple of God. These he carried off to the temple of his god in Babylonia[c] and put in the treasure house of his god.[c]

[3]Then the king ordered Ashpenaz, chief of his court officials, to bring into the king's service some of the Israelites from the royal family and the nobility[d] — [4]young men without any physical defect, handsome, showing aptitude for every kind of learning, well informed, quick to understand, and qualified to serve in the king's palace. He was to teach them the language and literature of the Babylonians.[b] [5]The king assigned them a daily amount of food and wine[e] from the king's table. They were to be trained for three years, and after that they were to enter the king's service.[f]

SEPTEMBER 1

> Day/Date Be sure to remember five things to be grateful for every day **September 1**
>
> Psalm 19:14 CEV Let my words and my thoughts be pleasing to you, Lord, because you are my mighty rock and my protector.
>
> This is a wonderful prayer to offer to God at the beginning of each day. If we belong to God and want to live for him, we should offer each day, including all that we think, say, and do, as an offering to God for his honor.

Some years ago, when I was working at the international headquarters of our mission organization, my boss, the International Director, died in a tragic hiking accident. To complicate the unfortunate situation, his whole family was overseas at that exact moment, so the police came to me, as the closest one around, to convey the heartbreaking news. After that, I was requested to travel to the park where he had passed away, in order to identify his body. I wasn't sure what to expect, but because we had worked together so closely, and for so long, it was a traumatic task for me to even think about doing. I remember driving up to the mortuary, where his body lay, and walking in, to view his body. Following the long drive from home, I first ducked into the boy's room, just at the last moment. As I stood there, I couldn't stop my legs from shaking. I was so anxious and upset about the task to come, that I couldn't stop shaking. I don't know how they do it, but I am thankful that there are skilled and willing folks available to handle the details and logistics in such cases. Some things in life are just almost too disturbing for us to deal with, and we can be grateful, in those cases, that others are willing and able to step in and handle whatever may need to be done.

I expect the same is true with God. So often, we want to understand why God does this or that, why he lets things happen, why he doesn't just tell us what's going on. Why does he so often leave us in the dark? Well, we may get a clue to God's behavior in Revelation 20, and the surrounding chapters, near the end of the book. As the apostle John heard and saw these things that were being revealed to him, it was almost too much for him to contain, so frightening and beyond his comprehension everything was. Just seeing God, his brilliance, his greatness, his overwhelming presence, nearly did John in. It was all just too much and too powerful for an ordinary mortal to deal with. So, why doesn't God tell us more of what he's up to, more of his strategy and game plan, more of what's going on? We know he's a good, loving, and compassionate God. And, I'm sure there are things he just doesn't tell us because it would scare us nearly to death. Just like, at times, we don't tell our three year old everything…precisely because we care about them…so, I'm sure, it's the same with God. One day, we will know and understand…but, for now, he doesn't tell us everything…because he loves us and cares for us. Can we live with that for now?

SEPTEMBER 2

Day/Date   Be sure to remember five things to be grateful for every day.   September 2

2 Corinthians 6:10 NCV We have much sadness, but we are always rejoicing. We are poor, but we are making many people rich in faith. We have nothing, but really we have everything.

Very often life seems full of ironies, paradoxes, and conflicting purposes. Following Jesus can also be that way. Our comfort and happiness in this life are not God's greatest concern, since he is focused on eternal things. So, while there are many blessings in following Christ, we are also affected by the suffering of the world and are usually not rich, materially or in other ways.

When I was a boy, in Korea, we might as well have been living on another planet, we were so far from home in the US. Once a year, on Christmas, Dad would place a telephone call to his mother, back in the US. He had to place the call through a switchboard operator, long before the phone call actually took place. Eventually, she would call us back, and patch the connection through the cables, all the way around the globe. For two or three minutes, Dad would ask his mother how she was, and assure her that we were all fine. These calls were expensive, but they provided a slim connection with home, for my Dad. When I was nine, we returned to the US for a furlough. For the first time in my memory, I met this lady, who was the mother of my father. Boy, were they happy to see each other. I'm not quite sure I understood what all the fuss was about, but when she saw me, her whole face lit up, she bent down, and enfolded me in her arms. I don't remember for sure, but I expect that I squirmed away from her warm, and slightly moist, embrace as quick as I could. They say that what goes around, comes around, and I think, in this case, they are right. Now, I'm a wobbly, slobbery old geezer, and I do exactly the same thing as my grandmother used to do, when I see my grandkids today. My face lights up like a Christmas tree, I bend down, and enfold them in my arms, giving them as many smooches as I can, before they can squirm out of my arms. I want to hold on to them and snuggle them and never let them go.

Perhaps that's one of the best images we have of how God loves us. Psalm 125 says: "As the mountains surround Jerusalem, so the Lord surrounds his people, from this time forth and forevermore." God surrounds us, and wraps us up in his love. He never wants to let us go. Like a loving parent, he wants to hold on to us, keep and protect us in his protective arms. Isn't that a beautiful picture, a wonderful image, the best reality? That's the all loving, Heavenly Father that we have...

SEPTEMBER 3

> Day/Date   Be sure to remember five things to be grateful for every day.   September 3
>
> John 11:6 NCV   But when he heard that Lazarus was sick, he stayed where he was for two more days.
>
> This is one of the most curious verses in the Bible. A close friend of Jesus was seriously ill, and his family hoped that Jesus would come and heal him, as Jesus had done to others many times before. Instead, Jesus delayed, and his friend died. Then, finally, Jesus came and did something amazing. He brought Lazarus to life after he had died. God's plans are greater than we imagine, and his apparent lack of concern may be because he is working on something unknown to us. We just need to trust him!

When our youngest was small, he probably got lost, on occasion, in the shuffle of all the other kids. One day, when I did happen to notice him, I realized that, as the kids were together watching a cartoon or some kids video, our youngest was camped out about six inches in front of the screen, squinting his eyes out, trying to catch what was going on in front of him. Oh my, I thought, clearly the boy has a vision problem that we didn't know about till then. Later, at age five, he was fitted with glasses, one of the first of the kids to get them. Suddenly, his whole world changed...including his plans for his life, for, from then on, he knew what he wanted to do with his entire future. I don't know where the idea got lodged into his head, but after that moment when his vision became sharper, whenever someone sweetly asked him what he wanted to be when he grew up, his answer was always the same. "I'm going to be an eye surgeon!", he would proclaim, with unflinching self confidence. Well, the jury, it seems, is still deliberating about that possibility, so we will see... On a trip to a country in Africa, recently, between college semesters, this same son again had his vision adjusted. He had learned and picked up bits and pieces about what life was like in Africa, how the people were, what the culture looks like, during his early years. But being there, experiencing and tasting things first hand, in living color, was like getting his vision adjusted, brought into sharp focus. He got a whole new understanding and appreciation for what this corner of Africa was actually like.

In Zechariah 6, we also get a sharper picture of what life will one day be like for us, in heaven. My vision is very limited to my own small world today, as I experience it. Everything I imagine is based on the little that I know about. I think of all the people in the world who still have not heard that God loves them. I wonder how they will hear, how they will be able to find their way to heaven. But verse 15 tells us that people will come together from "far off", to help build God's kingdom. Apparently, God has bigger plans going on, and unfolding, than I can imagine. No doubt, we will all be surprised, one day, when we arrive at heaven's gates, to discover that God has been hard at work at many more things, in many more ways, with many more people, than we could possibly have imagined, just as our son's eyes were opened when he put on his first pair of glasses, as well as when he landed in Africa, only to discover a whole new world, than he was previously aware of. I look forward, one day, to putting on my heavenly glasses, and discovering a whole new world, from God's perspective, as he sees things.

SEPTEMBER 4

Day/Date Be sure to remember five things to be grateful for every day September 4

Psalm 138:8 NLT The Lord will work out his plans for my life — for your faithful love, O Lord, endures forever. Don't abandon me, for you made me.
One of the richest promises in the Bible, it is also one that we very much have to accept on faith. We don't often see how God's plans are working out in our lives. Sometimes we feel like he has abandoned us. But we have his certain promises that he is working things out for his good purposes — so we need to have confidence in him.

Don't you love it when you hear some, unexpected, super great news?!? Like, as you walk into the classroom to take your final exam, the teacher announces, "I've decided that you were such a good class that I'm just going to give you all 'A's', we're going to skip the exam, and, instead, we're going to have a fun party together!" I don't know if anything like that has actually happened before, but it's fun to dream or imagine that something like that could happen. That never happened to me...I guess I was never part of such a good class like that. But, it is nice, when you're in a meeting, for example, and right at the end, your boss announces some great, unexpected news. When I walked in for an initial meeting with my boss, as I began my first real job, at the end of all my studies, I was greeted with some exciting, unanticipated news. My new employer told me that I would be starting at a higher wage than we had previously agreed upon. That was great to hear! Never mind that the amount wasn't much in actual dollars...it was the surprise and positive element of the news that made me excited.

As we close out Revelation, in chapters 21&22, we also receive some unexpected, good news. In other places in the Bible, we hear about one day being in heaven with God. Though short on details, we do get the impression that it will be a good thing. Then, just as the Bible closes out its final few pages, we get an overload of good news. We are given a glimpse into life in heaven...no more sadness, no more problems, no pain, no conflict, only joy and happiness. Then it closes out with these final words: "Hurry up and get here, Jesus! Come back, and take us to heaven!" I expect there is a lot more good news that could be included, but I think John was so excited (and probably figured we wouldn't understand it all, anyway), that he just closed it out, and said, "Hurry up, Jesus! Bring on the great news!!" Let's get excited. Let's share this exciting news with everyone!

SEPTEMBER 5

Day/Date Be sure to remember five things to be grateful for every day. September 5

Proverbs 18:10 NLT The name of the Lord is a strong fortress; the godly run to him and are safe.

All through the Bible, we read stories of people who were in difficult situations, who called out to God, and who were dramatically saved by God as a result. What is perhaps most surprising is that even after amazing rescues by God, people still turn away from him or forget him. But God doesn't forget us, and he repeatedly reminds us to come to him for safety.

My grandmother used to talk about the sweltering hot summers in China. Of course, she was referring to a time before air conditioning, when the foreigners, both men and women, dressed to the nines, even in the most uncomfortable conditions. It's not surprising that, during those muggy summer days, they searched for any escape from the heat that they could find. Some foreigners discovered a little hideaway in the mountains, west of Shanghai, that became a sought after destination during the most sultry days. They even came up with a Chinese sounding sort of name for it, which also sounded suspiciously English: Kuling. I imagine the name itself drew plenty of Western people to it, throughout those summer months. During our years in China, we did enjoy the luxury of occasional AC, of clothing that didn't smother us, of refrigeration and ice cream…things that the early brave travelers never could have dreamed of. But I still remembered those stories of the mysterious Kuling…and wondered what it would have been like to visit it back in its heyday. Although I figured out where Kuling (with its new name) is located today on a current map of the country, I never took the opportunity to visit it during our years in China. But I still hope that maybe one day I can go see it. It won't be the same, of course, as I could never restore it to how it once was, but it would be fun to walk the same ground where my grandparents walked, and dream of those former days.

So much has passed, has been lost throughout history, of things that once were...times, places, events, and people that can never be restored. Many things, we can only faintly guess at or imagine. God does talk about a time of restoration that will one day take place, in Psalm 126. He is able to restore the important things, the things that really matter. As Israel declined from its past splendor under Kings David and Solomon, the nation was invaded, plundered and destroyed, repeatedly. No doubt, the people despaired and lost all hope of restoring anything of its former greatness. But, God says he can and will restore what is important. And what is it, that is so important? Both for Israel in its past, as well as with us today, God is talking about restoring a relationship with him. We may lose significant pieces of our lives along the way, as the years go by, but God promises that he can restore our oneness with him, and the purpose he meant for us to have, when we look to him and seek him. That restoration will be far greater, more important, and longer lasting, than any return we could possibly have to former physical things that we once knew.

SEPTEMBER 6

Day/Date — Be sure to remember five things to be grateful for every day. September 6

Colossians 2:10 NLT — So you also are complete through your union with Christ, who is the head over every ruler and authority.

We were made by God to have a relationship with him. That is why, down through the ages, every generation has been curious, puzzled, seeking, and longing to know God. Our disobedience has broken the relationship with God, and he has made a way to restore the relationship. But very often we don't accept God's way — and so we continue in our restless journey through life.

We lived just across the street from a wonderful park in England, for ten years, perfect for our young family. It was long and skinny, bounded by a creek on one side, and one of the busiest streets in Sheffield, on the other side. If you walked the length of the entire park, depending on the time of year, you might encounter a game of lawn bowling, gentlemen at play in a cricket match, a busy kids' playground, or even some out of place Yankees throwing a baseball or trying to get a softball game underway. There was something for most anyone, who enjoyed wandering around or just getting out and stretching their legs. The tricky thing, though, was the road. To get to the park, we had to cross the heavily trafficked road, with plenty of cars sailing by. I'm not entirely sure how she did it, but between dodging, hollering, dashing, and pushing and pulling, my wife somehow managed to get all the kids safely across that road, all those years of heading down there, for some fresh air and exercise. Only once, do I remember hearing about a near miss. Our youngest little boy, all eager and excited, started to dart across the road, without a care or thought or a glance, knowing that, with his Mom next to him, his world was safe. Except, just at that moment, a car came rocketing down the road. In an instant, an arm reached out, and grabbed the little boy, back to safety. Our son always felt secure. What he didn't realize though, was that he was safe because his mother was looking out for him...not because the road wasn't dangerous, or because he was fast enough, or for any other reason...except that his mother was providing an invisible shield around his life.

Zechariah 9 offers us the same beautiful image. It says that God "has an eye on mankind". Isn't that a wonderful thought. It gives us many examples of how God is watching over us...providing us with rain, fighting for us, caring for us, providing us with salvation. It's the perfect picture of a loving parent, reaching out to his child and protecting him, many times, when he's not even aware of it. We may discover, when we arrive in heaven one day, that there were numerous instances when God watched over us and saved us, when we weren't even aware of it. But, the most important way that he watches over us, is by providing us with the costly price that is necessary for our salvation. His greatest rescue operation for us is to offer us this salvation. Let's take his protection on board, and then, also, remind those around us that God offers this protection to them as well.

SEPTEMBER 7

Day/Date Be sure to remember five things to be grateful for every day. September 7

2 Peter 1:3 NCV   Jesus has the power of God, by which he has given us everything we need to live and to serve God.

When we chose to disobey God, our lives became terribly incomplete and unbalanced. Most people spend much of their lives trying to fill them with success, money, power, friends, or hobbies. But God has told us that we will only be fully complete through a relationship with Jesus, which is offered to us freely.

I didn't realize it when we first decided to move there, but the far off corner of China where we used to live was one of the prettiest spots we could have chosen. Next to a lake, with the Himalayan mountains rising behind us, it was indeed a beautiful location...if that's what you were looking for. We weren't. In fact, it was really an inconvenient place for us to live. My work meant that, not too infrequently, I had to travel to other parts of Asia, or beyond. But it wasn't an easy airplane hop to get out of the country to some other destination. Just going from our town, meant taking a bus into the bigger nearby city, then from there, taking another 4-5 hour bus or train to the capital city of our province, where we could then fly to a coastal city, to spend the night. After an entire day and night, the next day we would be ready to actually leave China, and fly to wherever we were going. It was a tiring journey, even if it came nowhere near David Livingstone's or Henry Stanley's treks across Africa. On one such day, after purchasing my ticket, I climbed aboard the bus, found my seat, and plopped down, for the 4+ hour journey that awaited me. "Are you British?", the young Chinese gal sitting next to me asked. That was how we embarked on a nonstop conversation, that lasted the whole trip. She was from the provincial city we were heading to, but had just been to our town for a little sightseeing getaway. While she was wandering the streets of our town, she stumbled into a historic church, located on our busiest shopping street. It had originally been founded by some folks connected to the missionary, Hudson Taylor. This Chinese girl had heard the Gospel ten years earlier, while in college, from some foreign missionary. At that point in her life, she was not really interested in spiritual things, and shelved the conversation somewhere in the back of her mind. But, in the intervening years, through some misfortunes, she began to think more seriously about spiritual things, and that reminded her of the conversation she had, ten years earlier, in college. Perhaps, that was what nudged her to enter the church. Anyway, after a peek around, she moved on, and now she was returning home. And as it happened, this foreigner sat down next to her, with a sigh. Thankfully, she knew English well...otherwise, our conversation would have lasted about 30 seconds. But we got into a deep discussion about the meaning of life, the Bible, and God's Good News. By the time we reached our destination, she was ready to turn her life over to God. I was heading on to the next leg of my journey, but we weren't quite ready to say goodbye, after our fairly intense conversation. I still had a little time, so we ducked into a cafe, so that we could continue our chat. We sat down and ordered coffee. Just across the way, at a nearby table, sat a foreign couple. My curiosity got the best of me, and I asked them where they were from. They had arrived from Chile, he was a medical doctor, and he was planning to study Chinese medicine. She knew of our CLC bookstores in Chile, and she was a Christian. I was, by now, running out of time, and had to move on. So, I asked the lady to pray with our new Chinese friend, so that she could receive Christ into her life. She did, and we still keep up with our Chinese friend, many years later. What an unexpected privilege that day was!

The Gospel of Matthew starts out with a pretty hefty genealogy, which may leave you wondering what the point of it all is. But, Matthew does, at least, give us a hint, near the end of chapter 1. It says: "All this took place to fulfill what the Lord had spoken." I think back on that day, meeting that young Chinese lady. She had heard the Gospel ten years earlier, and a seed was planted. She hit some turbulence in life, wandered into a church, then had this strange looking foreigner sit down next to her. Further, we stumbled on a cafe, where a newly arrived couple from Chile sat, she, who was a believer. And "all this took place..." One say, I expect, we will arrive in heaven, and we'll discover that many such incidents took place as part of God's eternal plan. I can't wait to meet the lady who first shared the Gospel with our Chinese friend, so she can hear the rest of the story. What stories do you imagine that you might one day hear about?

SEPTEMBER 8

Psalm 25:4-5 NLT Show me the right path, O Lord; point out the road for me to follow. Lead me by your truth and teach me, for you are the God who saves me. All day long I put my hope in you.

Why is this a good prayer? Because it reflects and acknowledges several key truths. The answers to life, and truth itself, rest in God. As we follow God in our lives, we need to look to him for help. And following God is not only a one time event. It is something we must pursue all day, every day.

When we lived in England, I really enjoyed picking my way through church cemeteries. That sounds a bit macabre, but in the old days, they used to, in poetry or prose, express a significant piece of a person's life story right on their stone. Just before we entered our church building in England, on the left, was a gravestone, in the churchyard, that told the tragic tale of its owner. On a New Year's Day (if my memory serves me…though it seems like an awfully cold time to be out, now that I think about it…), this young boy was out swimming with his friends. One of the girls found herself in trouble, and struggling to stay afloat. This young boy went after her, saved her life, but lost his, in the process. What a tragic reminder, every time we walked by that stone, and yet, what a precious reminder, also, of a life given, to save another. Some time ago, while our wives were energetically undertaking their daily constitutional in a cemetery, here in Tennessee, my friend and I were undertaking a more important activity. We wandered up and down the hills, under the giant oak trees, looking for interesting epitaphs on the gravestones, scattered all around. I guess the stones in America just aren't old enough to hold the fascinating stories that the ones in England do. There wasn't much exciting to read about. Every now and then, we would come across a 20 foot tower to someone's memory, and I would tease my friend that this was the stone he needed to copy for his own. Actually, in this same cemetery, my wife and I have already purchased a stone for ourselves. Now, I now that sounds very weird to some ears, but my wife remembers the emotional trauma of having to go through the process of choosing her Dad's stone, and thinking of what to write on it, right as he passed away. So, we thought we would spare our own kids the same experience. We also wanted to highlight, a little, some of our own story...where we were born (a bit unusual), some of what we did (also kind of strange), and especially listing the names of all our kids (necessitating a rather large stone, mind you), who have most certainly been one of the most important legacies that we hope to leave behind. We wanted to include Psalm 127:3 on our stone, as well, reminding us that children are a blessing from God. Now, I have no idea why God gives some people nine kids, and others none. Personally, I thought 4-5 would be plenty, but, apparently, when we got in line for kids, we picked a ticket that had a big "9" on it, because that's what we got, in spite of a few halfhearted efforts to the contrary. But, in addition to affirming the gift of kids, Psalm 127:1 says that we're kaput, unless God is in the equation...not only in the equation, but unless he's the builder, the driver, the director, of the home, it's a lost cause. How are we building our homes on a foundation with God? How well do our kids know what's important in life? It is one of the saddest and most sobering statements in the Bible, when it says, "A new generation grew up who did not know God." Let's be sure that our own children do not grow up to be that generation. Let's build our homes and families on the foundation of God.

SEPTEMBER 9

> **Day/Date** Be sure to remember five things to be grateful for every day. September 9
>
> Matthew 16:26 NLT — And what do you benefit if you gain the whole world but lose your own soul?
>
> Wouldn't it be a foolish waste to spend all my life's efforts to obtain a nice car, to finally receive it at the end of my life, and only then to discover that no fuel is available for me to use to operate it? That would be a terrible and tragic waste! And, indeed, that is how we are when we spend our lives chasing things that don't last, while neglecting the condition of our soul, the one thing that does last.

I really don't like snakes, and perhaps like most people, I have one or two snake stories that haunt me to this day. In one, it scared the willies out of me; in a second, it defeated me; and in the third, I was left the hero (and wishing the whole thing had been videoed for my great-grandchildren). As a teenager, in Korea, one summer we visited the touristy, volcanic, Jeju island, off the south coast of the country. One day, we decided to hike up to the top of the volcano, which involved a very gradual, grassy ascent of several hours, if I remember correctly. The path was covered in about a six inch blanket of lush grass, and, therein, slithered the danger. After walking a good way, our group was spread out, up and down the mountain, and I found myself alone, and wondering, frankly, where everyone else was. Were they ahead of me, or behind me...I wasn't sure. I decided to just stop and wait; someone was bound to catch up with me, sooner or later... So, I stopped in the middle of the trail, probably trying to think up some brave Scout song to hum, as the minutes ticked by. After a bit, I glanced down at my feet, and there, perfectly laid out between them, was a long serpent. Yiiikes! Reflexively, I glanced to my left, where a bunch of brambles were, right next to the path. And, there, just about at eye level, sitting right smack in the middle of the bushes, two glistening eyes sat, staring back at me, no doubt, belonging to the mate of the one that was about to bite my leg off. I don't really remember anything else about that trip...but, that moment, I'm sure, I'll never forget. Some years later, in college, just below the campus, which was high atop a mountain, lay a wonderful trail, a favorite destination for guys interested in gals. So it was, that one day, a certain young lady and I were walking together along this trail. We suddenly came upon a coiled and rattling snake, very clearly, not pleased with our presence there. I tried to shoo it away with sticks and stones, but they didn't faze the snake, much less break any of its bones. We were defeated, and had to turn back. Some further years later, with the same gal as before, now my wife, we were walking along a trail in Los Angeles, above the Pacific Ocean, which lapped at the rocks, far below us. As we walked along, you guessed it...another snake. This time, the snake was not going to defeat me. I looked about, and found a small stone. Who needed five smooth stones, when one jagged, sharp one would do? I scaled the slope above us, leaned way over a giant rock that I had climbed onto, stretched out my arm, and held it above where the snake was coiled. I let go of the stone...and this is where Indiana Jones could not have done it any better than I did. The stone connected with the snake exactly behind its head...and the head shot off in one direction, while the rest of the reptile went in the other. That moment was as satisfying as any tennis match I ever won, even if it lasted only about three seconds. A direct hit, and the danger exploded away from us.

In Zechariah 11, there is a most curious verse that reminds me of all these snake stories. Zechariah is listening to a message from the Lord, and, in the middle of it, he tells us that he picks up his staff, "Favor". Now, I just love that as a name for a walking stick. I still like to walk the mountain trails, and I never leave without taking one of my walking sticks with me, a legacy of all those snakes that entered my life, uninvited. I just don't want to countenance a rattler on the trail, unarmed, ever again, if possible. Next time I go, I'll have to invite "Favor" along with me. Walking sticks, or shepherd staffs, in the Bible, often refer to a tool or implement that gives guidance, direction, or protection to us (or rather, to the defenseless sheep they are protecting). God has given us his Word for exactly the same purpose. His Message is our "Favor", that guides and protects us along the paths of life. Let's be sure we never neglect to carry "Favor" with us, as we head out, into the big wide world, today.

SEPTEMBER 10

Day/Date   Be sure to remember five things to be grateful for every day.   September 10

John 14:6 NCV   Jesus answered, "I am the way, and the truth, and the life."

History and the Bible contain many evidences that Jesus is who he claimed to be. But it is our decision whether we choose to believe him and to accept the renewed relationship with God and the peace that he offers.

I guess, like members of any profession, whether pastors, policemen, politicians, or pole vaulters, when missionaries gather, they sometimes put their heads together and share funny, sad, agonizing, or triumphant war stories with one another. I remember one elderly saint sharing with us that one of her supporting churches used to send them used tea bags as gifts. We all got a good laugh out of that. Perhaps, everyone feels under appreciated at times, and we were no different. How come missionaries always seem to get the leftovers, what no one else wants, the bits people can afford to live without, their used tea bags... Honestly, though, if I am truthful with myself, I must confess that we have been dealt with rather lavishly over the years. In fact, occasionally, just on occasion, I'll whisper to my wife, "Better not tell our supporters where we are right now. Don't want them to think we are living too high off the hog!" (Actually, when we were in quarantine, in Korea, I was feeling a little like that, as the government facilities were really comfortable, much better than we would have expected.)

But, as I reflect on all these things, I am stopped dead in my tracks by Matthew 3:4. It's a verse we just pass right over, without a second thought, but this verse refers to the man Jesus talks about, as being the one closest to God, John the Baptist. John wore camel's hair and ate locusts. And it wasn't a big deal. He never complained about it. He didn't have a deserving, entitled mind-set. Neither did Paul. Both men laid down their lives for their Savior, for God. Never mind, what they did or didn't have, how badly they suffered or were mistreated. It was their privilege to serve the Almighty God of the universe. Is that my attitude? Sometimes, but, probably, not nearly enough. The Good News is certainly about God's unsurpassing love for us. But, it's also about God's sovereignty and rule over all things. It's about eternity, not my comfort today, including whether I get new tea bags or not. It's our infinite privilege to know and serve God. I hope we will always remember that. And, I hope we, missionaries, will realize how blessed and well cared for, we have been.

SEPTEMBER 11

> **Day/Date** *Be sure to remember five things to be grateful for every day.* September 11
>
> **Romans 12:1 NCV** Since God has shown us great mercy, offer your lives as a living sacrifice to him. Your offering must be pleasing to him, which is the spiritual way for you to worship.
> God has given us a great and unattainable gift — forgiveness and a restored relationship. Not only for this life, the gift will go on forever. Our only response to his generosity should be to offer and live our lives each day for him.

During several days of an international conference in Mexico City, we took a needed break from the meetings, to get out into the city a bit. I love history, and so, I was happy that the group was taken on an excursion to some of the ancient architectural ruins of part of the city. As we walked along, there were sellers of all kinds of souvenirs, eager to connect with any tourist, who happened by. One lady was there, selling hats, with a huge leaning tower of them on top of her head. Perhaps I glanced at her for a second too long, but apparently, she thought she had my wallet hooked, so we got to chatting for a moment. I don't know if I gave her a Gospel, or exactly how the subject came around, but, at one point, she reached for her necklace, with a cross attached to it, and beaming, exclaimed, "I'm a Christian, too!" It was only a passing moment, but precious, nonetheless, as we realized that, though we shared virtually nothing else in common, we had what mattered most in life, and that is what bonded us together. It spoke to me that, here was this lady, on the streets of Mexico City, laboring to support her family, and also, walking with God through her life, right where she found herself.

Psalm 128 says something about that, as well. We are told that, we will be blessed, as we walk with God, trusting him, following him. Perhaps that's a good reminder to us, every now and then. God looks down on us, and blesses us, as we serve him, and walk with him, right where we are.

SEPTEMBER 12

Day/Date   Be sure to remember free things to be grateful for every day.   September 12

Romans 3:23 NLT   For everyone has sinned; we all fall short of God's glorious standard.

God's standard is perfection because he is perfect and is the opposite of evil. So when we become contaminated with the smallest amount of evil (due to a lie, anger, greed, selfishness, or unkindness), we — along with everyone else — fall short of God's standard. But thanks to God himself, he has covered our sin and contamination so that we still are able to have a relationship with him.

My siblings all knew that I had it easy, going off to boarding school. When my older brother first left home, he was in a whole new world that, in many ways, he just wasn't ready for, and that gave him a lot of tearful nights. By the time I came along, all my older siblings had been there, or were still there, so it was more of an exciting adventure, when I climbed aboard the train, to head off for school. My older siblings had prepared me well. They told me how to navigate the system, who to watch out for, what to do to stay out of trouble. But, mostly, it was an exciting new world, and I felt secure, not being alone there. I also sighed in relief that one particular, scary, drill sergeant teacher was no longer there, had moved on, so I felt like I had dodged a potential cannonball. Many years later, long after I had completed all my schooling, I met this drill sergeant my siblings had warned me about, all those years before. It was the first time I recalled ever actually meeting her...and, I was surprised to discover that she just seemed like a very sweet lady, who cared about us and wanted the best for us. (Granted, now that she held no power over us, my perspective might have changed, but still...)

Many times, when I've read the book of Malachi, I've come away, thinking, "Man, God kind of sounds like a stern drill sergeant!" Don't forget to tithe! Don't divorce! Don't be so careless! Follow my laws! It's easy for us to miss God's opening words: "I have loved you." All the seeming sternness has to be viewed in light of his overarching love for us. A lot like that high school teacher many years ago, who, no doubt, was there, serving, only because she cared about all the students. That's how God is with us. He warns and chastens us when he sees us wandering off toward danger, heading into trouble, without realizing it. When seen from that perspective, we realize that God ever, only, wants what's best for us, even if it occasionally squeezes us. Sometimes we had been so focused on the squeeze, that we forget why God is allowing it to happen in our lives. It's for our good. It's because he loves us. It's to get our attention when we're heading toward danger. Let's thank him for being the caring, loving God that he is.

SEPTEMBER 13

Day/Date Be sure to remember five things to be grateful for every day. September 13

Psalm 139:17-18 NCV God, your thoughts are precious to me. They are so many! If I could count them, they would be more than all the grains of sand. When I wake up, I am still with you.

Our children are always in our thoughts, and even when they are grown, hardly a day goes by when we are not thinking about them and sharing their experiences in our thoughts. God loves us so much more than we can imagine, and day or night, we are always in his thoughts. What a wonderful comfort!

The Chinese language has to be one of the most fascinating and interesting in the world (as long as I don't have to speak it!). I (what I thought was diligently) studied it for two years, after we first arrived on China's shores back in 2010. Then, I hit a brick wall, and just couldn't absorb anymore. (If you want to learn a language, take my advice...don't wait till your 50s.) I was left, hardly being able to say much of anything. And, it didn't help that we lived in a remote spot in China, where most of the minority tribes had also decided to live. Nearly every time we went outside, we likely would encounter one minority or another, none who were speaking Chinese. Plus, all the college students wanted to learn English. How in the world could anyone expect me to learn the language in that environment? Still, it was and is an interesting language. In addition to being made out of oodles of characters, some of which, kind of look like the word they represent, there also are a good number that, with a little imagination, you could guess, came from the Bible. So, it leaves you scratching your head, and wondering, when the Tower of Babel came tumbling down, and the folks on the scene were scattered far and wide across the globe...could some of them have found their way to China, where they decided to incorporate some of the stories about God that they would have known, into their new (Chinese) language? You do wonder. Take the word for boat, for example. It is composed of three smaller characters: eight + person + vessel. Why? Well, you do remember how many people were on Noah's big boat, right?? Or, how about the word for covet: two trees + a woman. What was it that got Eve into trouble in the Garden of Eden? Then, there's the word for blessing, or good luck…probably the most popular word you see posted in China, especially during the New Year, when they all wish each other good luck, or blessing. This character for blessing seems to be made up of: one + person + field + God. Could that be telling us that, when we are working the land, and have the Lord as our God, that we are blessed? I do wonder…

As I read down chapter 5 of Matthew, I think of that Chinese character for blessing. It talks about a lot of folks, conditions, circumstances, when we are blessed. But, it's interesting, because it doesn't talk about being blessed when we have money in the bank, when we are healthy, when we have secured a great job… Odd as it may sound to us, it seems to suggest that, whatever our situation, when God is in the picture, when we are walking through life with him, then, we are blessed. Sort of reminds me of the Chinese character. Nothing fancy or exotic. Just you, the soil, and God. That's all we really need to be happy, to be blessed. A good reminder not to be distracted by all that the world throws at you. Just you, your situation, and God…that's really all you need. Lord, wherever we are, whatever situation we find ourselves in, help us to remember that with you, only with you, we're blessed. We have enough. Amen.

SEPTEMBER 14

Day/Date Be sure to remember five things to be grateful for every day. September 14

2 Corinthians 5:15 NCV Christ died for all so that those who live would not continue to live for themselves, and was raised from the dead so they would live for him. A slave is someone who lives utterly and completely for his master. His entire existence is taken up by serving and pleasing his owner. Paul describes himself as a slave to God. But interestingly and ironically, when we give our lives to God, it is only then that we are truly free and experience the freedom from sin that God intended for us from the beginning.

Early in our marriage, my wife and I lived in Delaware, which was like a foreign country to this Korean and Southern boy. But, it wasn't all bad. One thing I liked about it was that, up there in the North and East, a lot of things are fairly close together. Just like when we lived in France, without too much fuss, when we could hop over to this country or that, while we were in Delaware, we could journey to New England, Washington DC, New York City, and other places, all without a lot of effort. In fact, we got to where we would take weekendly excursions to any place we wanted, and we would call them our second, third, or fourth honeymoons. It might have been about on our seventh honeymoon, that we decided to take off on an Easter weekend visit to the nation's capital. Coming from Korea, seeing all these impressive and amazing monuments and sacred places was pretty awe inspiring. To see the Apollo space capsules, the Wright Brothers' airplane, the Lincoln Memorial...wow, wow, and wow! We even, one day, got to venture into the holy of holies...the White House. I don't know if you still are allowed in, but we got to enter this sacred place. Mind you, it was only one or two of the outer rooms, and they had carefully rolled back the red carpet so that we wouldn't contaminate it, in any way, but still, we were in...right there, where Lincoln had been, Jefferson, FDR, Kennedy, even Jimmy Carter. This is where they had walked and lived, and, in Teddy R.'s case, let their kids ride their ponies. Obviously, there was a whole lot we weren't allowed to see (nearly all of it, actually), but, to get even a glimpse into this place was amazing.

Reading Genesis 1 & 2, I get the sense that God is allowing us to get a glimpse into his "White House", as it were. It's only a little peek, but, still, it's truly awesome. What does God show us? He reveals to us that he's always been around, even before the show we're a part of began. He shows us his stunning power...greater than Superman, when God speaks, things are created, set in motion. His creativity and scientific genius are also displayed, showing a dazzling array of plants, animals, nature, astronomy, and much more, all perfectly in tune, all working together as perfectly as the most perfect Swiss time piece. This passage shows us that God is good, that everything he does is good...and that the most precious thing he made, was us! We are the high point of what God created, he made us good, to live full lives, in harmony with him, to work and enjoy the universe he created. We have managed to mess things us pretty bad along the way, but, still, God is good, he loves us, and wants us to live full lives with him. Thank you, Lord. May we do just that, in our poor, weak way, with your help and guidance.

SEPTEMBER 15

Day/Date Be sure to remember five things to be grateful for every day. **September 15**

Ephesians 5:8 NCV In the past you were full of darkness, but now you are full of light in the Lord. So live like children who belong to the light.

When people do not know God, their lives are marked by, and often driven by, guilt, fear, and shame. Many people live as captives to these consequences of sin. When we accept God's salvation, he breaks the control that these things have over our lives. We will always have some evil in us while we live on earth, but we don't have to be dominated by it as we live for God.

Maybe every generation has a day or a year that will "live in infamy". Ours, no doubt, will be the year 2020. (I mean, let's hope it doesn't get any worse than this!) Actually, though, if we step out of our own skins for a minute, out of our own little corner of history and geography, there really have been some pretty awful other moments in history. We only have to look for a moment at God's chosen people, the Jews, to put our own day into sharper, more balanced, perspective. A Jewish slave, Joseph, once upon a time, saved Egypt from famine, and had all the surrounding nations eating (literally) out of Egypt's hand. How were the Jews rewarded for that dramatic rescue? By 400 years of slavery. Finally, finally, God brought them to their special land that he had long before promised to them. But, then, they kept being pestered by surrounding empires, and finally, they were carted off as exiles, while God's holy city and sacred place of worship were ransacked and desecrated. Much closer to our day, the Jews have continued to be chased and hunted down, as if they were the lowest of animals…and suffering the greatest butchery during the years of the Holocaust.

It almost sounds as if Psalm 129 is referring to some of these atrocities. "They plowed my back," it says, "making long furrows." I'm not sure exactly what that's talking about, but it certainly sounds unpleasant. Yet, even in our worst trials and afflictions, the psalm is telling us that we're not forgotten. "The Lord is righteous. The blessing of the Lord is upon us." If the Jews, God's select people, could believe that, then, all the more, so can we. God's precious and perfect Son paid for our ransom from slavery. He continues to pour blessings on us, perhaps, most notably, with his Spirit to guide us, and with his Holy Word to direct us and change us. Down through much of history, people didn't have the whole Bible, and perhaps only had a priest reading bits of it to them, once a week, maybe not even in a language they could understand. We have been truly blessed. Maybe we should pause today, count our blessings, name them one by one, and offer up sacrifices of thanksgiving to our righteousness and loving God.

SEPTEMBER 16

Day/Date — Be sure to remember five things to be grateful for every day. September 16

Psalm 73:25 NCV — I have no one in heaven but you; I want nothing on earth besides you.

This psalm writer was tempted to look at the lives of those who don't believe in God and imagine that their lives were easy, wealthy, and blessed. But looking more closely, he realized that their security and prosperity didn't really last, and that their lives were not as stable as they first appeared. He was reminded again that true worth and security are found in God.

Life really seems to be stacked against kids sometimes. I mean, why don't they ever let a kid run the government? Think what a nice world it would be everywhere, if a kid was calling the shots... When I was young, I wondered whether the grown ups had it in for us. We always had to do what they wanted, what they thought was best, what was most convenient for them. Then, to top it off, after a grueling school year, they would make us put on these silly skits and plays and performances. How come they could never bend to us for a change? Most of elementary school, I had only one classmate, in our quasi homeschool, in the missionary community. This gal, LBL, was taller than me, and seemed to be ahead of me in just about every way. Especially when it came to memorization. Then it really wasn't fair. We would have to memorize a psalm or some verses from Matthew, and they would just effortlessly roll off LBL's tongue. Did the teacher deliberately pick verses that she already knew? I wondered. For me, every word was painful, every word learned was like pulling one more tooth out, nothing was easy about it. Even after we'd been given plenty of days to learn them, I would stumble and bumble my way through, while the words just slid out of LBL's mouth.

There is something that is curious about this whole thing, though. Those passages I labored through, in Psalm 8, and parts of Matthew 6, I've never forgotten. Decades later, they have hung around, stuck with me, given me endless comfort. "O Lord, our Lord, how majestic is your name in all the earth." "Do not lay up for yourselves treasures on earth. Do not be anxious about your life. Seek first the kingdom of God." How thankful I am today that Aunt Sally and the other teachers didn't give up on us, didn't quit when we sure gave them every reason to, knew the treasure of God's Word, and that it was more valuable than the struggle to learn it. I hope we parents are continuing that discipline of teaching God's Word to our children, even when they're not interested in learning, knowing that to hide God's Word in their hearts is of such great value. Let's keep persisting, just like my dedicated teachers did, many years ago.

SEPTEMBER 17

> **Day/Date** Be sure to remember five things to be grateful for every day. September 17
>
> Isaiah 57:18 NCV I have seen what they have done, but I will heal them. I will guide them and comfort them and those who felt sad for them.
>
> God sees what we think and do, and he knows that many of us choose to turn away and disobey him. Yet, because of his great love for us, he desires to comfort, forgive, and heal us. And he promises to do so when we turn back to him.

Sometimes we long for the easier, less frantic, simpler days of past generations. Days when there were less cars on the road. When a gallon of milk was just that, not one of 37 options that you have to sift through, just to take some milk home. When a burger was simply a burger, not a minefield of decisions before you can sink your teeth into one. In truth, though, there are a lot of good things about this complex, modern world we live in. As a boy, I would lie, sweltering in my bed, unable to fall asleep in the heat. Dad would come into the room and fan me with a little paper contraption, and eventually, I would doze off to sleep. Now, at the touch of a thermostat, I can decide whether I'll sleep in coolness or not, thank you. Today, I'm not dependent on the few thousand titles that the neighborhood bookseller chooses for me. I can look at and choose from zillions of books, finding precisely what I want, at a better price than I had to pay ten years ago, and have it delivered into my hands within days, or even hours, without hardly having to get up out of my chair. And then, there are laminating machines. Laminating what?? Lest anyone is perplexed by this cool gadget, I just had to obtain one some years ago, and I love printing out permanently protected Bible verses, Bible reading plans, family photos to keep tucked into my Bible...I love my little machine. If there is a need for a chief laminating machine operator in heaven, I'll definitely stand first in line for the position. Mostly, I just love my stiffly covered cards because, through their verses, they remind me of what's important in life. Through their photos, parked around me, here and there, they remind me of those I love, those who are dear to me.

God, also, sends us reminders of what is important. Probably not in the form of a plastic covered verse, but reminders, nonetheless. When Adam and Eve got sidetracked, and were in danger of becoming derailed altogether, in Genesis 3, God sent them a reorienting compass...himself, as he walked in the garden where they lived. His presence definitely redirected their focus, right when they needed it. Those laminated verses get my attention, too, sometimes right when I need them. The sunrise, sunset, mountains, and birds also remind me daily of the one who is watching over us, the one who is directing the flow of history. The most important reminder he has given us, of course, is his Word, the Bible. I guess I have been reading it for the better part of 60 years, and strangely, it speaks to me more now than it ever has before. It's not the same old, same old...it really is new every morning. What is it about this old piece of literature? It's God's Word, God's breath, his heart speaking to us. Alive, active, life changing, it waits silently for us to turn to it for guidance, just as God waited quietly in the garden for Adam and Eve to stop and listen to his wisdom and love to enter their lives. Our Bibles sit quietly, waiting patiently for us to hear their truth. Will we? Will we keep them waiting? It will be our loss, and the loss of our family and friends, if we do.

SEPTEMBER 18

Day/Date — Be sure to remember five things to be grateful for every day. September 18

Psalm 51:12 NCV — Give me back! the joy of your salvation: Keep me strong by giving me a willing spirit.

This is both a tragic statement and a wonderful statement. It is very sad to realize that we can stray so far from God that we lose the awareness of being God's children. But the way back from this bad place begins by understanding and acknowledging before God that we have turned away and that we need his help to turn back, and even to want to turn back. God hears and answers us when we approach him with this attitude.

We can learn a lot from animals...their persistence, their quiet patience and contentment, the beauty displayed in them through their Creator, their intense loyalty to their offspring. And then there are pet dogs. I feel a tinge of guilt at times, when the pet dog of some family member or friend looks up at me, eagerly, expectantly, longingly...willing me to play with them, to share a crumb of my attention with them, to just give a nod or a wave or a whistle...and I brush on by, without so much as a smile. If there's one thing an old pet dog is, it's loyal. They are as loyal and devoted as Monday is long, and that's what makes them so precious to us. Sometimes I wish I had some of that same eager anticipation and attentiveness in my life.

Psalm 130 just breathes that longing expectation that we should have toward God. Listen to what it says to us: "Out of the depths I cry to you, O Lord. Let your ears be attentive to the voice of my pleas! I wait for the Lord, my soul waits, and in his Word I hope. Hope in the Lord! For with the Lord there is steadfast love!" Do you hear it? Do you hear that same longing expectation of your pet dog, coming out of those verses? These words tell us to look and listen eagerly to God's Message to us. Here is where we find peace, joy, God's enduring love. Let's turn our attention to him with anticipation. The psalmist, and all through the Bible, other people as well, found God to hear, to understand, to weep with them, to answer them, to be with them. Lord, help me to look to you, to wait eagerly for you, as patiently and attentively as a pet dog waits for his owner's response.

SEPTEMBER 19

> Hebrews 7:25 NCV — He is able always to save those who come to God through him because he always lives, asking God to help them.
>
> Sometimes we may think we are too far gone, our lives are too much of a mess, we are beyond saving. But this way of thinking makes two mistakes. It supposes that normally we are good enough to be saved—but no one is. And it also greatly underestimates God's power and love to be able to save the lost who come to him.

My Grandpa taught me that there was an easy way to remember Matthew 7:7:

"Ask, and it will be given to you;

seek, and you will find;

knock, and it will be opened to you."

The key was in the three main letters of the verse: A-S-K. Pretty easy, eh! That's where the easy ends, though. The harder part is understanding what it really means, figuring out how it fits into our lives, making it work the way it's intended to. In another place, Jesus says, "Ask for whatever you wish, and you'll get it. (Assuming my Word remains in you, that is...)" That sure sounds like an awfully colossal, wide open, promise, doesn't it. So, what does God really mean, when he tells us this? It probably helps to think of my own children asking me something. "Dad, can I have a car? Dad, can I date that guy I saw on the street? Dad, can you move my little brother out of the room, so I can have it for myself?" No, no, and no. And on it goes. Or...what if my kids ask me this: "Dad, should I go to this Bible study? Dad, can you explain this passage to me? Dad, can you help me figure out which college to go to?" Yes, yes, and yes! In the first series of questions, the child really is not on my wavelength, not thinking the way I think, does not have my same goals, or values, or commitments in mind...or, we might say, they don't have my words in them. The second series of questions are in line with what is important to me, reflect the same things I value, dovetail with what I know is good for them.

What is it, then, that is in God's heart? What is it that he wants? What should I be asking for, that lines up with his heart's desire, with the truth within him? He does tell us, over and over again. Am I listening? Or am I so focused on what I want, what is my priority, that I mistake mine for his priority, that I imagine that it is what he wants for me, for his world? What does God want? He wants me to love others as much as, and in the same way that, Jesus did. How did Jesus do it? Well, to begin with, he gave himself, his future, his comfort, his personal pleasure, up for others. Am I doing that? Am I asking God to make that happen in my life? Additionally, God wants to save everyone, not wanting anyone to perish in hell. So, am I praying for everyone who is lost? Am I praying for the many folks in China, in Russia, in North Korea, in Saudi Arabia, who still need to hear that God loves them? I'm pretty sure that's in line with God's heart. I wonder how he will answer those prayers of ours, if we A-S-K him on behalf of these people? Shall we commit to that? Shall we ask and ask and ask...and wait to see what he does? I expect that's really more what Jesus is meaning, when he tells us to ask, rather than for me to get the snazziest car that I could possibly imagine owning.

SEPTEMBER 20

Day/Date *Be sure to remember five things to be grateful for every day.* September 20

Isaiah 1:18 NCV Come let us talk about these things. Though your sins are like scarlet, they can be as white as snow, white like wool.

Red can remind us of blood and pain and suffering. When we turn away from and disobey God, our lives are colored by evil, and the pure, clean hearts God desires for us are tainted by sin, stained with blood. But all through the Bible, and through our lives, God invites us into his presence so that he can show us how to be clean again.

We MKs (missionary kids) were a strange lot. Clearly not nationals, like the local folks where we lived, we also were not quite the same as the citizens of our home countries. In a very real sense, we didn't fit in anywhere, maybe something like those folks we read about in Hebrews 11, who didn't quite fit in with the people around them. Our oddity drew us together, and frequently, those of us who were in the US might come together just to hang out, during holidays or periods of vacation. I remember one such gathering in Nashville. Earlier, during that Christmas holiday, I had been at my brother's rural home in South Carolina, and attempting to give him a bit of a hand, I thought I would cut some firewood for him. Only, I gave my hand to the saw instead, and it bit into my thumb. A few days later, when we were gathered in Nashville, my thumb was angry and infected. Fortunately, we were congregated at the home of a gentleman who had started a Christian hospital in Korea, so I carried my thumb directly to him. As he gently tended to it, I asked him a question. "What was it like, being among those men?" "Oh, they put each leg in their pants, just like we do," he responded, in a matter of fact way that caught me by surprise. You see, this gentleman, who had also himself grown up in Korea, and was a wizard with the language, had interpreted for President Lyndon Johnson, when he received the Korean president at the time, on an official state visit. Rather lofty company to be among, I could only imagine. But, the way he sounded, it was just an ordinary day for him. He certainly didn't seemed to have been overawed by their presence, the way I most certainly would have been, if I had been there that day. The challenging thing about being in the presence of prominent folks, is that it can all easily go to our heads. Maybe that's what happened to Peter, when, full of bluster, he shared the grand idea of erecting monuments to Moses and Elijah, when they appeared on the mount with Jesus, who had brought Peter along with him. But the doctor in Nashville didn't seem overly impressed by the inspiring company he found himself in, that day with the two presidents.

In a similar sort of way, King David might have been forgiven for getting a little heady being in company with himself...when he went down the list of all the great exploits and accomplishments that God had used him to carry out and produce, after his humble beginnings as a squirt in a family of older brothers. But, what is truly astounding, is the tone we hear from David in Psalm 131. Any one of us would excuse David for being just a mite proud of who he was, of the way God had raised him to the pinnacle of God's own people. But, listen to his words in verse 1: "O Lord, I do not occupy myself with things too great and too marvelous." How could he have said that, given all the great and marvelous things he had actually done, things that are recorded for all of history to read, no less, as they are included in God's inspired Word? I think the only way he could have uttered those thoughts was to realize who he was talking to...the great God of all eternity...and he knew that he was nothing, next to God. I seem to forget every minute whose presence I am in. Anytime I do the tiniest little inconsequential goodness, my head and chest swell up, and I instantly forget who is enthroned above me, how small I really am, next to him. David did not forget that. After all his grandest accomplishments, he knew he was actually nothing, next to God. Lord, how quickly we forget that we are dealing with, in the presence of, you, the Almighty God, who is over all things. Help us to remember who we are...and who you are. Amen.

SEPTEMBER 21

> **Day/Date** Be sure to remember five things to be grateful for every day. September 21
>
> Isaiah 12:1 NCV   At that time you will say: "I praise you, Lord! You were angry with me, but you are not angry with me now! You have comforted me."
>
> After we turn from our sins and receive God's forgiveness because of what Christ did for us, God wipes our dirty record completely clean. Nothing is left of our sinful life in God's eyes, and his anger against our sin exists no more. When God looks at us, he sees Christ's righteousness in place of our sin.

Do you get discouraged, like I do, when you scan the news headlines? Corruption. Tragedy. Horrific, senseless accidents. Massacres. Cruelty. Unspeakable abuse. Really, at my age, I just about feel ready to graduate from this tired old world, and to move on to the next stage. When I feel that way, several times a day, I'm forgetting one big thing. Who's in charge. I am giving into the temptation to imagine that fate and randomness are in the driver's seat. How badly I'm mistaken. How quickly I forget. God is not asleep at the wheel, as I might imagine. He hasn't walked away and turned his back on us, as I sometimes think.

We're reminded emphatically of who is in charge, in Genesis 5&6. At the beginning of chapter 6, it sounds like God has about given up on people, that he's ready to throw up his hands and write off this bad experiment as a lost cause. But two passing comments tell us something different, open our eyes to what is really going on, just like when Elisha asked God to open his frightened servant's eyes to the true picture of things, and suddenly the servant saw God's fiery chariots surrounding them on all the hills encircling their position. Way before chapter 6, when Noah was 500 years old, in chapter 5, we read that, when he was born, his father proclaimed, "This one shall bring us relief." Talk about the understatement of that millennium...Noah was certainly going to play the key role in bringing relief from the sin that was strangling the world at the time. What's remarkable to me, though, is that God already, in chapter 5, knew about the mess that humanity was set to create in chapter 6...and he was already preparing and sending his instrument of deliverance...hundreds of years before it was even apparent that Noah was going to be needed. Is God unaware of the evil around us today? No. Has it caught him off guard? Not likely. Is God scrambling to put out all the fires here and there, around the globe? No, he already knew about them, and planned to deal with them, long, long ago. And one day, it will become clear to us, evident to us, when he opens our eyes, as he opened Elisha's servant's eyes, to what he is doing in the world. The other passing thing we see in chapter 6 is that God says that his Spirit will not contend or strive or wrestle with men forever (due to their sinfulness). But, what that tells us, is that, even though we often, perhaps even usually, aren't aware of it, God's Spirit is at work in the world. He is active, carrying out his plans, making things happen, drawing people to himself...again, even though we very often are not aware of it. The fact that God says that his Spirit will not keep working forever...tells us that, in fact, he is now working. So, when we get to feeling down about the world we live in, let's remember...God was working out his plans long before we, and the messes we see around us, ever arrived on the scene. And, also, God's Spirit is working right now, today, everywhere. That's something we can bank on, have confidence in, draw strength and encouragement from. Hallelujah! Come, Lord Jesus!

SEPTEMBER 22

Day/Date Be sure to remember five things to be grateful for every day   September 22

2 Peter 2:9 NCV   The Lord knows how to save those who serve him when troubles come.

If God set the uncountable stars in place, if he fit everything on earth to work together in harmony, do we doubt that anything is too hard for him to deal with? Are any of our little difficulties too great for him? No, of course not.

I had an amazing epiphany one day in Dhaka, in Bangladesh, when I was there on a work and ministry trip. That moment will always stay with me, and it opened my eyes to something about Jesus that I just hadn't appreciated before in such living color, in such a vivid experience. Toward the end of my days there, my host took me to a well known souvenir market, where tourists like me enjoy spending our last few takas on something we don't need, but that will help us to remember the journey, once it's all over. Of course, the locals know this place quite well, also, and, in any of these places, there are a handful of beggars congregating, seeking the attention of a generous foreigner. (Apparently, some of these folks mistook me for being generous.) On that particular day, I saw one old lady, terribly crippled, lying on her back on the ground, with her legs, tangled and twisted above her. So sad to see. Some of these folks, I'm fairly sure, have been maimed intentionally by criminals, a horrible method of trafficking to fleece unsuspecting tourists out of a few dollars. (At least, that's what some of the news articles tell us.) As I was poking around the shops, a little boy, about as tall as my waist, perhaps 7 or 8 years old, approached me and looked up into my face. He had the saddest expression on his sweet little face. But, what was much more sad than his expression, was his arms. Missing. Cut off, it looked like, neatly in the same place, on both sides. I had to wonder if they had been sliced off intentionally. Without even thinking about it, I reached down and frumpled his thick black hair. And something happened that I guess I just never expected. The sad little boy broke into the biggest, sweetest, happiest grin that covered his whole face, that you could imagine. And suddenly I got it, why Jesus always reached out and touched people, like we see him doing in Matthew 8. He could have kept at a distance, and proclaimed healing, from a safe few paces, on these terribly diseased lepers. But, no way Jesus was going to do that. A big, big part of their healing was to be recognized as being members of the human race, to be seen as persons of value. That was colossal. Jesus knew it, even if no one else did. So, invariably, he reached out and touched these lowest of the low. It was the lesson I was given that day, by that little boy, though I hadn't expected it or looked for it. Although, no doubt, there were plenty of scary diseases floating around them in those days, Jesus always looked right past the illnesses, to the person, who was not only physically ill, but, just as important, needing the healing of acceptance from another human being. Obviously, that's not the same as someone receiving healing for their sins, but, still, receiving compassion in God's name is an important step in the right direction. It's what we also need to do, as we go through life, in this diseased and uncomfortable world. Reach out to people with compassion. Touch them. (With our masks on, of course...) Lord, help us to take on your eyes, to view others as the ones you love and gave yourself for, to treat them as Jesus showed us how to do.

SEPTEMBER 23

Day/Date · Be sure to remember five things to be grateful for every day. · September 23

Romans 5:20 NIV · Where sin increased, grace increased all the more.

Some people are bad, others are really, really bad. And some people appear to us to be good. But God knows our hearts, and he can see that we are all, however good or bad, affected by sin. No matter how messed up by sin we may be, God's grace is adequate to meet our need.

There were certain rites of passage when we were young, that could not be avoided. They came around with clock like regularity, some were good, some were downright scary. One of the most exciting days of the year was when a cardboard box would arrive from Calvert School, in Baltimore, Maryland. I remember excitedly carrying our box home, hardly being able to wait to open it. It contained our new supplies for the soon to begin school year...new textbooks, new pencils, pads of writing paper, colored construction paper, rulers...everything we would need for our next level of school, all brand new, all for us personally. Next to Christmas, and my birthday, it was the best day of the year. But there were other days that also came around with regularity, scary days, days that you hoped Mom and Dad might forget this year...(They never did.) Chief among those days were the shot or vaccination days...and the dental appointment day. Haircuts with hand clippers weren't much fun either...those things seemed to delight in shortening our hair by the roots. But the dentist was hands down the worst. Now, our dentist back then was nothing like it is today. Today, you nestle into a cozy padded chair, you get to choose your favorite music to listen to, the assistant chats with you about whatever you like, and you never really feel a thing, while the dentist apologizes the whole way through that they might just possibly be causing you even a hint of discomfort.

Then, when you're all done, they send you on your way with a goody bag, and with a wave of the hand, you're on your way home. I guess somebody pays the bill, but it doesn't seem like I do. As I was beginning to say, that's not what the dentist was like when I was a kid. First of all, it was too close to home...I could walk over to the clinic from our house, which made it just a little too uncomfortable. You entered a waiting room, with a game or two laid out on a coffee table, and some stiff, uncomfortable chairs against the walls. They thought they could distract or charm you with the games, but, of course, we all knew better. All the waiting patients sat grimly, fidgeting uncomfortably until their names were called. Finally, when the call was announced, I got up and headed into the appropriate room. Various smells and occasional screams or groans reached out to my senses. The dentist we had, Uncle Dick, was the kindest, most professional, most expert dentist anyone could ask for. The problem, though, was that he was also a wizard at languages, and he just couldn't help himself. He would chatter and ask questions the whole time I was sitting there, staring up into his nostrils. But how did he expect me to respond, when he kept my mouth pried open to the near breaking point? Several numbing (hopefully) shots later, the high pitched drilling began. It seemed like hours later, that I would spit out blood, and then stagger home, like a boxer who had just been pummeled for 15 rounds. Why did we have to go through all this? It was good for us, the powers over me seemed to believe. I had to take that on faith. But, remarkably, decades later, many of those fillings are still with me. It did turn out, after all, that the entire torturous procedure was, indeed, good for me. I finally get it now...many, many years later. Though it had been a fearsome experience, I knew I could trust Uncle Dick, and I didn't have to be afraid.

When we read through Genesis 7 & 8, the hair raising trauma that Noah endured reminds me of my dental visits back in those days in my youth. God called him to an urgent task, and he obeyed willingly. He knew he could trust God. He spent 100 years (!) building a boat, with no apparent place where it was going to be launched. When the day came, as the heavens let loose their torrents of rain, it would have been terrifying to watch the water rise, and rise, and rise...until nothing was left...not a single other living person or animal or plant. How scary would that have been? Definitely, a fearsome experience. Noah must have wondered what was going on. But he trusted God, and was able to see God's good plans unfold slowly, over time. In the middle of what was happening, it was terrifying, and God even allowed Noah's family to, no doubt, experience fear and anxiety...knowing that he was working out something better to come. And just like my scary dental experiences as a boy, that my parents allowed me to endure, with a good long term purpose in mind, God may, and does, at times, allow us to go through hard times, as part of his long term good plans. But, like Noah, who trusted, and obeyed, God, we, too, can trust him for what we can't see or understand. We are in his good and safe hands. We don't need to fear.

SEPTEMBER 24

> **Day/Date** Be sure to remember five things to be grateful for every day. September 24
>
> 2 Peter 3:18 NCV Grow in the grace and knowledge of our Lord and Savior Jesus Christ.
>
> No doubt there are some professions or disciplines that, given enough time, we can learn most all there is to know about them. But to really know Christ and the changes he can make in our lives is a full time, life long occupation, and even then we will only be starting to understand him. We will not fully know him until we pass from this sinful world into his perfect presence in heaven.

As we watched "The Crown", about the young, newly enthroned, Queen Elizabeth 2, it was entertaining to observe the sparring, dancing, and intrigue that went on between the ancient, vastly experienced, Prime Minister Winston Churchill, and the young, completely inexperienced, yet, very determined and independent minded, Queen Elizabeth. The PM wanted to ensure that she made no missteps, that she didn't tarnish the throne, that she would not be the cause of some international scandal, embarrassment, or disaster. QE2 would listen to his sermonizing and lectures, then promptly make up her own mind (mercifully, usually in accord with the PM's wisdom). What was mildly amusing to watch, for this rebel from the former colonies, was how Mr. Churchill, in his declining 70s, would shuffle into the Queen's chamber, and teeter there, bent over his wobbly cane, in her august presence, waiting for QE2 to be seated…so that he could then collapse into a nearby chair. As she stood chatting and rambling with her pleasantries, the poor old man had to stand there, swaying like a leaf, waiting for her to take pity on him. But, however weak and wobbly the ancient PM was, it would have been unthinkable for him to seat himself before she sat. That was entirely out of the realm of proper, acceptable, correct royal protocol. And he certainly lived for the monarchy. It was not in his DNA to cross its institution, in any way.

In a somewhat different manner, but also very similar, we observe King David behaving the same way in God's presence, in Psalm 132. David had suffered much, battled much, conquered much. The kingdom had been consolidated. He was well due a much earned rest and pampering. But, he wouldn't think of it. He would not allow himself to rest, if God's house of worship had not been prepared and made ready. David understood, perhaps similarly to how Churchill recognized whose royal presence he was in, that his sovereign Lord came first...that whatever he as king had accomplished, was actually nothing, when compared to who was really over all, all important, all powerful. Lord, as I begin each new day, help me remember whose presence I'm in. Help me keep my priorities focused on you, as David also did, as the PM did before QE2. Whatever I may think of myself, remind me who I'm living for, in whose presence my life is lived.

SEPTEMBER 25

> **Day/Date** Be sure to remember five things to be grateful for every day. **September 25**
>
> **2 Peter 3:9 NCV** The Lord is not slow in doing what he promised. God is being patient with you. He does not want anyone to be lost, but he wants all people to change their hearts and lives.
>
> Sometimes God seems so long in answering prayer or in accomplishing what we think he should be doing. But we can be sure that he is still working out his good plans. This may mean that he is delaying or being more patient than we would be in giving some people more time or additional opportunities to turn to him.

I heard my name being called, and I turned to see who it was. The instant I saw him, I am ashamed to admit, I spun around and got out of there as fast as my feet would carry me. I felt bad, but also terrified, and had to get away as quick as I could. Many years ago, when we resided in Korea, the living conditions were not quite what they are today, in the 21st century. Families cooked over open fires, right on the dirt floors of their homes. As the mothers busied themselves preparing their rice and kimchi for the family, they would bundle up their little babies and lay them close to the fire, where they could stay warm. Tragically, on occasion, these babies would roll too close to the fire, and disaster would meet them. My two teenage sisters began visiting the patients who had survived such fiery accidents, in the children's ward of the hospital where our father worked. I remember seeing some of these little kids, who loved my sisters, as they waved out the windows of the room where they were recovering, at a distance, as we walked by. On that day, when my name was called, it was one of these little boys. He was excited to see one of the friendly foreigners coming by, and ran straight out to meet me. But as soon as I saw, right up close, his horribly disfigured, ruined face, I couldn't handle it, and I ran.

Jesus also encountered someone horrific in Matthew 9. But, in contrast to me, Jesus looked past the exterior, and saw the individual person who was precious in his sight. Who did Jesus see? He saw a traitor, a sleazy robber of God's people, a man who everyone avoided like the Corona virus. He saw a disgusting tax collector. This man's name was Matthew (the writer of this very Gospel), and Jesus saw in him, not the blooding sucking scoundrel that everyone else saw, but a sinner in need of a Savior. And Jesus invited this apparent scum to be his friend, to come join him, to spend life together with him. I wish I could go back and rewind that day in the hospital, when I was a boy. I wish I could go back, sweep that little burned boy off his feet, and let him know how precious he was. Lord, help us to see others as you do. Not as a person who is unattractive or unpleasant, someone who is in my way or messing up my life. Help me to see that they are individuals that you love, died for, and want a relationship with. Help me to convey that to them, with all that I am. Amen.

SEPTEMBER 26

The idea that God gives "talents" or gifts or strengths to people in different amounts, in different kinds, is all a bit of a mystery to me. Wouldn't it make sense that he would start all of us humans on the same level playing field? Why would he give some people unfair advantages over other folks? Why would God give some people (folks who may be severely disabled, people born in terribly disadvantaged situations, people who are left-handed) seemingly so little to work with in life? I expect that part of it, at least, is that God delights in variety and creativity. After all, the world would be a pretty boring place if all the plants everywhere...were banana trees. And if the whole world was full on nothing but the lowly slug, in terms of animals. How much better and wonderful that the universe if full of a magnificent variety of colors, designs, abilities, and so on...what a fascinating and potentially God-honoring landscape he has made.

In Genesis 9, after God has created everything, he says, "All right, now be fruitful and multiply! Explode with the potential I have given you!" I can just imagine God's excitement, creating all the massive variety of things in the universe, all with abilities, purposes, and possibilities...and then, God stepping back and declaring, "OK, now go for it! Be all that you can be. Be all that I've created you to be. Explode with all the possibilities I've placed in your hands!" I think God made all of us created things for the purpose of blessing and honoring him, of bringing him glory by performing as he made us to do, and also of blessing one another as we are fruitful and multiply. I can't imagine that God made us with the ability to produce...so that we would just sit on it or even produce so that we could store it all up for ourselves. I'm sure that a big part of the talents God has placed in our hands is for the purpose of sharing, scattering, spreading. I love the story I read about the other day of a pig farmer in Britain... who saw it as part of his purpose to give away a portion of what he produced each year to support God's ministry. We might wonder what raising pigs has to do with using our talents for God, or whether it even is a talent worth mentioning. But this farmer was deliberate and determined in doing so, and found a way to do it. We can also do the same. How much better it would be if all of us multiplied the talents God has given us by sharing and spreading them...rather than by simply using them to build up a big empire for ourselves. Lord, help us to do that, with whatever big or little you've chosen to put in our hands, so that, in whatever way we come to, we might bring glory to you by putting to work what you've given us.

SEPTEMBER 27

Day/Date Be sure to remember five things to be grateful for every day. September 27

Psalm 91:15 NLT   When they call on me, I will answer; I will be with them in trouble. I will rescue and honor them.

These are perhaps the most comforting words a child can hear from his parents and feel security from, in knowing. They are also comforting to hear from God, and much more profound and meaningful when spoken by him. For he means he will always be with us, from now through eternity. He answers us according to our real needs, not according to what we desire at the moment. And he rescues us from the death of sin forever.

In 1995, we landed on the shores of England, to a future we were excited about, but that was also highly uncertain. How would it be, after living in a community in France, to transition back to living fully in the general secular society? How would the dynamics be different for our children, without the protective and nurturing environment they had been blessed with in France? Would my wife find a group of kindred spirits to surround herself and share life with? And what would a job be like for me, going from working within a team, to working all day, every day, with only one person, my boss? Although my boss and I both shared a connection to Asia, I having grown up in Korea, he having worked in Japan, which was certainly helpful, we also came packing our differences…different personalities, temperaments, energy levels, priorities…a number of factors, really, that could have easily derailed our working relationship anywhere along the track. I don't know how much it helped, but fairly early on, I decided that I would try to serve my boss by lightening his load, attempting to make his job easier by serving him. I like to think that, thanks to my gracious, servant attitude, we got along splendidly. But, truthfully, I know that he also toiled tenaciously to work as a team with this moody, uncommunicative, contrary, self-centered guy with an Asian chip on his shoulder toward Europeans.

Perhaps, it was remarkable that we were able to survive and carry on at all together, for so long as we did.

Psalm 133 is a beautiful picture of what can happen...except that it rarely does! Brothers dwelling in unity?? Precious like fresh dew in a parched land? Hardly! It's beautiful...if it were only true. But I think back to my working relationship with my boss in England...and it reminds me of these verses. Thrown together unexpectedly, unlikely office mates, we nevertheless shared the same goals, the same commitments, and we both managed, by God's grace, at least on occasion, to get along, to work together, to serve each other...so that we could honor God and better serve the larger ministry and team we were a part of. It does tell me that, as beautiful as the verses in this brief psalm are, they don't occur by accident, by chance, or on a whim. It more likely happens as a result of hard work and laying down our lives...and that is when God gives his blessing, when he lavishes his good graces on our lives.

SEPTEMBER 28

> **Day/Date** Be sure to remember five things to be grateful for every day. September 28
>
> Philippians 2:5, 7-8 NCV Think and act like Christ Jesus. He gave up his place with God and made himself nothing. He humbled himself and was fully obedient to God, even when that caused his death on a cross. We are given new life and many precious promises from God when we turn our lives over to him — including his promise to always be with us. But at the same time as we turn from being slaves of sin, we become slaves of God, to serve and live for him, not as we please to serve ourselves.

Something strange happened to me once, and I still, all these years later, don't quite know what to make of it. While we were living in England, I was down in London for something or other, with the usual passel of kids in tow, and I hit upon the grand idea of showing them Big Ben and the Houses of Parliament, the pinnacle of British power, knowing, of course, that we wouldn't really be able to see much, other than the exterior of the buildings, but that would, at the very least, permit us to tell posterity that we had "been there"... But a funny thing happened, as they say, on the way. We arrived there, and a friendly employee happened to have some leftover or unclaimed tickets to a private "reading" within the chambers of Parliament. I had no idea what that meant, but being the foolish American that I am, I jumped at the opportunity to get our ten or twelve feet in the door. We were ushered in, up some stairs, and into a private room. Shown to some seats, we settled down, and I glanced around, wondering what I was doing and where I was. A few of the more genteel, shall we say, Britishers, gathered in the room, looked our way, and nodded politely (or was it annoyingly, I wasn't sure??), as if to say, "What in the world are you doing here? And who are you, anyway?" Moments later, a well known British celebrity entered our presence and graced us with his audience and with a highfalutin reading. I squirmed uncomfortably, knowing I was way out of my element, clearly in the wrong place on the wrong day, while our kids wondered even more where their Dad had brought them. Mercifully, there was a brief pause in the proceedings not too long later, and as quietly and unpretentiously as a rambunctious, noisy American family can do, I pushed our kids as quickly as possible out of the room. Whew...still don't really know what happened that day!

Matthew 10 must have been a very similar day for the twelve disciples. Jesus called his ragtag followers together and picked out an unlikely group of them to stick with him as his close confidants. Then he gave them a precise, highly specialized job that I imagine they felt unprepared for. But, Jesus knew them, knew the task, and he had confidence in them. Amazingly, we are in the same boat as those twelve guys were in, back then. We are out of our element, in strange company, a little disoriented. But God knows what he's doing. He's working out his plans, and we are part of those plans! And he believes in us and will give us what we need to do the job. Are we ready? Shall we dive in, as his disciples did? He tells us in this chapter in Matthew what he wants us to do.

SEPTEMBER 29

Day/Date   Be sure to remember five things to be grateful for every day: September 29

1 Timothy 6:7-8 NCV We brought nothing into the world, so we can take nothing out. But, if we have food and clothes, we will be satisfied with that.

There are many things that are pleasant and enjoyable in life—friends, books, travel, to name just a few. But none of these things are lasting or are capable of fully satisfying us. When we have the basics that we need—food and clothing—what really satisfies is a life of serving and knowing God.

Do you ever wonder how the world's languages could have all become so different? I've never enjoyed languages, and they were always among my least favorite classes in school. I just couldn't get the French accent when we lived there. Thankfully, enough of the words were similar to English that you could kind of fumble your way along. I tried to study some Russian when we were, at one time, considering moving to Central Asia. The alphabet, I more or less got. But I was totally confused by how the spellings of words changed, for example, the many different ways to spell "Moscow", depending on how it's used in a sentence. Then, there's Chinese. A fascinating language to dig into if you're a linguist, it seems like a lost cause before you even begin to study it, for someone like me, with less than great hearing and no ear for music. With something like 50,000 characters, but only 400 sounds, it means that a single character can have about 100 different meanings. So, you can have, for example, the story about the poet and the lion...and the whole tale is all made up of the one sound, "shi". Of course, they have tones, which help a little, if you can hear them. I couldn't, and when the Chinese speak at conversation speed, the tones all blur together to my ears. When we first arrived in China, my wife boldly would tell people she encountered, "My name Els." She would invariably be met with the strangest puzzled reactions. What she didn't realize is, because she didn't have the tone quite right, it sounded to the Chinese like she was saying. "My foot Els." Whew...so confusing! The one sentence I sort of mastered was: "My Chinese is not good." Of course, if you can say that, they know that you really can speak good Chinese, and they immediately rattle on to you in their language, and you're hopelessly lost. But, it wasn't a total lost cause. I did come away, after seven years, with one or two choice words that I still enjoy tossing out, every now and then. All this language craziness certainly makes one wonder how it all came about. How in the world did people come up with so many convoluted ways of communicating? Did the early speakers deliberately try to make things difficult for everyone else?? Some languages seem so counterintuitive (like English, for example), that you almost wonder if it's all due to some secret plot.

Then, you stumble on the outlandish story in Genesis 11, about the Tower of Babel and the languages getting all mixed up...and you come to the conclusion that this crazy story must actually be what happened. How else can we explain all the confusion in the languages...unless God intentionally did it? When God created people, earlier in Genesis, he directed them to be fruitful and to spread throughout the earth. But, they didn't. Instead, they all hung around in one place, and started to think too highly of themselves. So, to stop them in their tracks and to stymie their pride...God confused and scattered them. And therein is the explanation for all the crazy languages. One thing that the confusion caused, in addition to smashing the rising pride of people, is that the scattering of people resulted in the knowledge of God also being spread across the globe. We certainly see hints of that in what appear to be biblical references in the Chinese language, possible suggestions of God that may be traced all the way back to Babel. Perhaps, one lesson we can learn from all this messy mixup is that God is working out things for good, even when it all appears to be only chaos and destruction. Most likely, the Babelites were befuddled and dismayed by what was suddenly happening to them, when, one day, they couldn't understand each other. But God was working out his good plans behind the scenes. Just as he still does today. As they say, looks can be deceiving. And, God is, no doubt, the Master of accomplishing things that are way beyond any appearances. So, let's trust him, in spite of the confusion we may, from time to time, see around us.

SEPTEMBER 30

> **Day/Date** Be sure to remember five things to be grateful for every day. September 30
>
> **Psalm 50:23 NLT** Giving thanks is a sacrifice that truly honors me.
>
> Sometimes life throws things at us which are excruciating to endure. When my wife had life-threatening cancer, I wondered how I would care for our nine children on my own. It is a real effort and sacrifice to give thanks in such circumstances. But when we are thankful, God receives our thanks as a pleasing offering to him. It shows him that we trust him even in the hardest situations and that we know he is working out his good plans even in the midst of difficulty.

He motioned me over, pointed to his iPhone, and showed me videos of himself boxing. Next, he showed me photos of a recent "Miss Cambodia", and told me that she was now his wife. Who was this famous boxer I was talking to? Well, my wife and I were walking the beautiful road, next to a tree filled park in Seoul, on our one hour jaunt to teach at one of the schools for North Koreans where we are volunteers. It was the autumn, and all the golden ginkgo leaves were falling and filling the streets. So, the street sweepers were out in full force. A little girl was next to one sweeper, appearing to be helping out her Dad, so I paused to say hello and tell her she was doing a great job. That's when her sweeper father motioned me over to show me who he really was. What an interesting and unexpected surprise! That was a fun few moments for the both of us. Whenever I see cleaners and sweepers on the streets, in the restrooms, in the subways, I make a point to pause and thank them for their service to us. I figure most people walk right past them, in a hurry, without ever noticing them. I remember one lady I thanked, in an airport, and she smiled a bit shyly in response. Then, several more times she passed by, and kept smiling at me. I almost felt like I had made a new friend. And then there was the boxer I met.

Some of these instances come to mind when I read Psalm 134. This brief psalm refers to people who served God in the Temple at night. Would most people walk right past them, as they kept watch during the long, lonely hours passing slowly in the dark? Were they people who others may have looked down on and thought little of? It's interesting that they are mentioned here in the Bible. Clearly, God doesn't think they are insignificant. And, more remarkably, the psalm tells us that these servants, when they lift their hands to God, they bless him. He is blessed by them. They sure aren't unimportant to God! As much as I sometimes try to be aware, I still walk past most people, overlook folks, don't notice them... Lord, help us to see people as you do, to value them as you do, to honor and love them as your Son did and showed us how to do.

MONTH 10

Quarantine day 10...

Thoughts from Mark, Luke, and John:

*Everywhere he went, Jesus made people happy, uncomfortable, angry, and terrified.

*Jesus was constantly followed by crowds who wanted food, stories, healing, and miracles.

*Whenever he encountered them, Jesus reached out and touched the sick, which was culturally improper to do. He touched the most vile, diseased, and unclean. He was always patient and compassionate with them.

*Whenever God or a heavenly being appeared, people were terrified. But he always told them not to be afraid.

*God uses each of us to share his Good News.

*The Gospel is overwhelming and all encompassing…and is difficult for us to grasp fully.

*God could have supernaturally told everyone on earth individually the Good News. Instead, Jesus trudged along one dusty road after another, talking sometimes to crowds, but also to many people one by one. Now he has given us the very same task and privilege.

*Jesus couldn't help being compassionate and involved in people's lives.

*People found it very hard to believe in Jesus as the Messiah.

*Matthew was passionate about sharing with the Jews that Jesus was indeed the Messiah that the Old Testament had foretold.

*Mark told his Gospel story of Jesus who was actively and energetically the Son of God.

*Luke showed how Jesus brought salvation to all people.

*John emphasized that Jesus was indeed God.

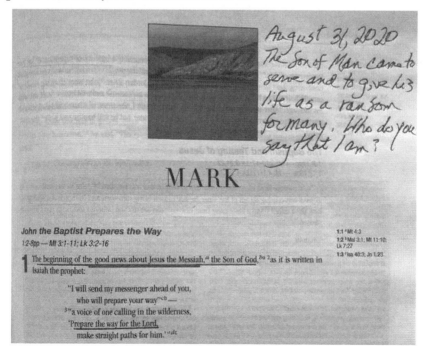

OCTOBER 1

Hebrews 13:14-15 NLT This world is not our permanent home; we are looking forward to a home yet to come. Therefore, let us offer through Jesus a continual sacrifice of praise to God, proclaiming our allegiance to his name. Heaven will make this earth pale and fade away in comparison. We will have no sorrows, no pain, no loneliness, and no unmet needs there. What a wonderful place it will be! So we can already begin now thanking God for what he has promised to us in the future.

Charles Spurgeon churned out an unbelievable amount of writings, sermons, and other activities in service to God, during his lifetime, including opening a Christian college and an orphanage. His influence still strongly lives on, and he probably preached to more people than anyone else had, up to his day. But, perhaps surprisingly, Spurgeon also struggled with deep depression at times, so severe that it drove him to feel like hanging it all up. He was also harshly attacked by the media, and even by other believers. Did he wonder why God permitted him to suffer so much? Undoubtedly, he did. But, as he wrestled, he began to realize that God allows us to struggle in order to strengthen and mature us, and for us to experience suffering in some of the same ways that Jesus did, and to better understand what Jesus endured for us. He discovered that suffering helps us to turn our attention back to God, and helps us to place our hope and trust in him alone. As challenging as it was, Spurgeon was able to see God's good hand in it.

I have sometimes puzzled at the story of John the Baptist, in Matthew 11. After his dramatic baptism and worship of Jesus earlier in the book, John now had been thrown in prison. He was probably perplexed, wondering why God had abandoned him, wondering if he had been all wrong about who Jesus actually was. He must have been depressed, tossed into a dark jail cell and deserted. So, from prison, John sent a message to Jesus, asking if he really was, after all, the promised Messiah. Jesus responded by describing John as being the greatest in God's kingdom; yet, here he was, questioning who Jesus was. If nothing else, this should show us that it's probably pretty normal for us to struggle. If Spurgeon and John the Baptist struggled and doubted (and never mind, so many of the Old Testament prophets, who also wrestled tremendously), why should it surprise us that we sometimes struggle with who God is, or why he allows hard things into our lives? The question is, will we trust him, even as Job did, even as Spurgeon did, when trials and struggles are great in our lives? Lord, give us strength to be able to trust you.

OCTOBER 2

Day/Date   Be sure to remember five things to be grateful for every day.   October 2

Mark 5:19 NCV   Go home to your family and tell them how much the Lord has done for you and how he has had mercy on you.

When we receive good news, we want to share it with those we know. When we receive great news, no one has to tell us to share it — we will do so with great enthusiasm. In this story, Jesus instructed the person to go and tell his family about his healing and forgiveness. This news was too good not to share, and what the man received could also be given to his family members.

In the early 1990s, when our kids were all sprouting and little, we lived out in the beautiful foothills of the Alps in France. It was the perfect place to raise a small and growing brood, even if Yanks were a bit out of their element in a French environment. All around us, in every direction, fields were overflowing with gorgeous lavender, sunflowers, poppys, rapeseed, and whatever else they were growing out there. A couple of miles away from our small community was a quaint little French village that had a local primary school which our kids could attend, to make a few friends and pick up some French. We parents would take turns driving the kids to school, packing the kids into a tiny Renault jeep, and winding our way through the fields on the tiny roads that snaked through the landscape. One such day, as I was navigating my way through the maze of country roads, and two particular twin boys were blasting out their favorite YWAM chorus at the top of their lungs, I turned a sharp corner where two little lanes intersected, the rear right tire caught the jagged concrete curb, and it quickly went flat. (Why does this kind of thing have to happen to good folks toiling out in the harvest fields, I wondered??) I don't really remember what happened next. Did I change the tire? Did someone come rescue us? (We didn't have cell phones back then, so I couldn't exactly call for help.) Anyway, somehow the kids got to school, and I limped back home, feeling chagrined about the tire. Worse was to come, however. I thought I could just turn the jeep over to one of the helpful French associates to let them handle it, but, no, no, that's not how they did things in France. They followed the biblical example...he who sins will be punished...not some associate. So, I had to do the deed. Now, under any other circumstance, this would have been simple. But in this case, it meant that I had to drive the car to the bigger town, find the tire dealer, and...in French, mind you...ask for a new tire for the vehicle. That sounds easy, but when you're already stressed to death about uttering more than a "salut" in the language, it becomes tantamount to scaling the nearby Mount Blanc in the Alps. This would require all my nonexistent language skills. So, I studied and toiled and practiced for several days how to say, "I would like to buy a tire", but in French. Finally, the dreaded day arrived, I climbed shakily into the car, and rattled off down the road to Montelimar. With my navigational skills at high alert, I located the tire dealer, and confidently walked in. Up to the counter, I marched and blurted out in my carefully choreographed French: "I'd like to sell a tire!" Those guys had the most puzzled look on their faces. Somehow, I secured the needed tire, and hightailed it back home, carefully avoiding any nearby curbs.

A similar thing happened to Abraham one day, in Genesis 12. OK, so he probably wasn't driving a Renault, but something occurred that left him wondering, why do things like this have to happen to good people. God appeared to the patriarch and told him to pick up and move far, far away. Back in those days, that was a monumental, life changing decision to make. Few roads, fewer rest stops, hostile clans...what awaited him was mildly more challenging than having to blurt out a few words in French. So why would God require him to do this? God had a greater good plan in mind than the temporary uncomfortable inconvenience suggested. When God gives us something hard to do...even if it's something as mundane as a flat tire, we can be safely certain that he has good plans in mind. So what were they, for Abraham? God was working out his special plans for his chosen people, and more precisely, to save the world from their sins, from eternal destruction. That's a slightly bigger plan than Abraham's mild inconvenience entailed. And, why, then, did God send a flat tire my way? Well...I'm still trying to figure that out... To trust him more? To realize I needed to buckle down on my French studies? To give me a needed break in town, away from all our kids? (Probably that was it.) Anyway, for whatever reason (and there may have even been several), God, no doubt, have some good plans in mind. Can we trust God, for now, when we don't quite understand why something may be happening to us? He can be trusted. Lord, help us, when we're fearful and uncertain about what is going on around us.

OCTOBER 3

John 4:34 NCV — Jesus said, "My food is to do what the One who sent me wants me to do and to finish his work."

Jesus was so focused on fulfilling the task his Father had given him, that he was not distracted by other things. Amazingly, Paul, also, though he was beaten, imprisoned, and suffered greatly in many ways, was not distracted from serving God by these things that happened to him. It was as if serving God was what gave Jesus and Paul their reason for living. And so it should be with us.

Is God good? Perhaps that's THE big issue we all think about, wrestle with, get derailed by, flip flop over, walk away from God over, wonder about from time to time...several times a day. I don't know about you, but I am terribly forgetful, my eyes tend to focus on things I don't like or that frighten or worry me...and I begin to wonder whether God is really good. But if I really reflect on it, I am reminded at every turn how good God is. Two small moments in the last 24 hours come to mind. We arrived yesterday at the home of one of our daughters. She lives in Idaho, about a million miles from the rolling Tennessee hills we call home in America. As we pulled up, I looked out the car window and saw her two little twin girls, romping and rolling in the snow. I had to go join them. This scene brought back immediately my childhood in Korea, rolling around in, sledding over, digging through, the snow. As I squeezed between two fence posts, to the slope where they were playing, one of them hopped on a sled and sailed down the slope, standing erect like a Roman soldier in a chariot, all the way down. "I gotta have some of this, I thought!" I jumped in with them, taking countless rides down the hill with them, sitting, lying, standing, reclining, together, separately...doing as many crazy things as I could think of. They were having a ball. I was having a ball...and getting myself soaked and winded, pulling the sled back up the slope numerous times. Who could have asked for a better time? Was this snow, the slope, the cold, the laughter, the connection with the girls...was this all a gift from a good God, or what? I certainly thought it was. Then, early this morning, as I was sitting on my bed, reflecting on several Bible passages, I looked up and saw the most exquisite, beautiful flower I could imagine, in a jar just to my left. Of course, it had been sitting there all along, but its stunning elegance grabbed a hold of me at that moment and wouldn't let go. Its unbelievable delicateness, beauty, intricateness, was just amazing. Again, at that moment, it reminded me of the good God we have...who loves beauty and creativity...and who desires to share it with us.

That's what we are told in Psalm 135, too. "God is good. God is great. God does whatever he likes to do." Thankfully, for all of us, but especially for those who know and follow him, he is good all the time, as they say. And when we look around us, even in this sad and broken world, we see his goodness everywhere.

OCTOBER 4

Probably two of the more tricky and contentious topics among Christians are baptism, and how we handle the Sabbath. Is the Sabbath on Saturday, or Sunday, or does it matter? And what do we do on the Sabbath? When I was a boy, playing cards and dancing were pretty big no-no's. I think I remember the older generation telling us that on Sundays, they had to sit quietly, knitting or reading...and not much else. Playing rowdy games was clearly off limits. And of course we had to always dress seriously up when we headed off to church. The first time or two I saw people sipping Starbucks coffee in church, I was scandalized. Now, it's just pretty ordinary, even served by some churches out in the lobby. If my grandparents walked into one of these services, they would surely wonder what was going on. It certainly wasn't a church service...but what was it?? So often, at least in the old days, keeping the Sabbath was about doing, or not doing, this thing or that.

In Matthew 12, Jesus talks about the Sabbath. And about all he says is that he is Lord of the Sabbath...and that it is for the purpose of doing good. That's an awfully wide open playing field, it seems to me. Most of the things back then that people were upset at Jesus for doing, were because he was not doing this or that thing, which seemed very important to them. Not so much about doing good, which, of course, was what Jesus was all about. Apparently, our biggest problem, down through the centuries, has been that we try to turn the Sabbath into an external list of does and don'ts. But, in reality, Jesus said it was about the heart...doing what is good, out of a heart committed to God, doing the good things that honor him, and the things that bless other people. Something I do know is that when I am obedient to God, it honors him. And that makes it a good thing. One of the things that's very clear, all the way through the Bible, is that following God is not a solo event. He made us for each other, for relationship, for gathering together to worship him as a group. So, I think a pretty good place to start with the Sabbath is to visit, and become committed to, to fellowship of believers...a church. Are we doing that...(aside from any COVID restrictions)?

OCTOBER 5

Day/Date   Be sure to remember five things to be grateful for every day.   October 5

Psalm 27:14 NCV — Wait for the Lord's help. Be strong and brave, and wait for the Lord's help.

The accounts in the bible of believers' experiences are filled with action, suffering, trauma, and much uncertainty and suspense. Though God's followers knew they could trust him, their extreme circumstances at times caused them to forget God or to run from him to seek help elsewhere. Because God's plans and timing are different than ours, he repeatedly reminds us to trust and have confidence in him

When we started to have kids, it was a whole new world, and we wanted to do it right; and we also realized that we needed all the help we could get. Thankfully, there was oodles of help to be had. There were plenty of books on parenting, with a lot of helpful and useful tips on ways to raise a family successfully. When I check today at the resources available, I discover a whole new crop of books that are for sale now...I'm sure with a lot more additional useful information to help us along this tricky and treacherous path. I'm so grateful to the many authors...and parents...who have shared their wisdom, tips, and even their failures, with us. Something interesting, and quite surprising, really, at least for me, was what we encountered when our kids grew up and branched out on their own...as they would certainly be expected to do. What I hadn't anticipated, and which I haven't found many books addressing, is the changing relationship and dynamic that takes place, once the kids grow up and leave home. From the parent's perspective, somehow your kids are still your kids...and you perhaps assume that life, and the relationship, will carry on, business as usual. So, it can be a startling wake up call, and for me, anyway, slow learner that I am, a rather painful process of discovery, as well, to find out that it doesn't all stay the same. A lot of things change. What happens, when the kids grow into adulthood, is that they "come into their own", you might say, discover who they are, and also, especially when they get married, become different people, understandably, influenced by their spouses. I guess, when you step back and think about it, that certainly makes sense. I mean, my wife and I are both different people, for having married each other. She ended up living in China, which was undoubtedly a startling and unexpected turn of events for her parents, and that happened in large part because of who she married, a boy from Korea, who was probably more Asian than Western, under the skin. And the same kind of thing has happened with our kids, so I'm still trying to figure out exactly what that means and where that will take us and our relationship together.

I wonder if the same dynamic was happening in Genesis 17. God was speaking to Abraham, and he promised that Abraham would have a blessed family, starting soon, at least, that's what Abraham understood. As it turned out, the process took longer than Abraham had expected. But, what I find interesting, is how God goes to such great lengths to make sure that his relationship with Abraham stayed the same, even as Abraham was about to undergo some big changes in his life. No doubt, God knew that with the upcoming changes, new priorities, distractions, and focuses would grab Abraham's attention. And so, God wanted to be sure that their basic relationship stayed intact. A lot like how we feel as parents when we sense that our own kids are on the edge of jumping off into whole new aspects of life, and wondering how it will change our relationship. I am still not sure how to handle it all...even though we have experienced it nine times! But, clearly, God had the same worry, and his relationship with us was critically urgent to him. So paramount, in fact, that he wanted the relationship to be sealed in blood, literally! He absolutely didn't want to lose Abraham, and he doesn't want to lose us. He wants to be sure that he maintains a relationship with us, no matter whatever else happens in our lives. He wants to hold on to us. He makes that clear in his Word, by showing us how to do it. The question is, how will we respond? Will we respond to God by following through on a continued relationship...or will we allow the distractions and cares of life to derail our relationship with him? That is the big question that we all face in life...and which continues to stay with us, all through life.

OCTOBER 6

If there's one thing that parents try to drill into their kids, it's to say, "thank you", it seems like, every time they turn around. Didn't my grandparents know I was happy by my expression or response, when they bought me a watch or an ice cream? Why did I keep having to say "thank you" every time? Didn't they get it? And why did I have to thank my teachers, when about 97% of what they gave me, I didn't really want anyway? But, there it was...apparently, growing up to be a ten year old required saying "thank you", anytime we should, anytime we didn't know what else to say, anytime, anytime...just in case it was the right time!

Maybe that's what God is also trying to tell us in Psalm 136. It starts out immediately by telling us to say "thank you" to God. Then, now that the necessary duty is behind us, he explains why, in the next 26 verses, we need to do it. The writer does so, by telling us 26 times, just in case we might forget along the way, that we are to thank God...because his love for us in permanent. You would think once might be enough. But, apparently, we're hard of hearing. We're forgetful. Sometimes, we even wonder if God really does love us. Well, this psalm puts that question permanently to rest. In 26 verses in a row, God tells us the exact same thing...he loves us forever...that's what we should be thankful for.

That's just about as certain, sure, and emphatic as he can get. Shall we just accept it? And perhaps refer back to it, throughout the day, whenever we forget or wonder? Remember: Psalm 136.

OCTOBER 7

Day/Date   Be sure to remember five things to be grateful for every day.   *October 7*

John 8:11 NIV   Leave your life of sin.

Turning to God and following him is a simple choice and decision. However, it is not easy. Due to our selfishness and weakness, as well as the tempting things around us that distract us, turning to God can be difficult for us and is an ongoing, lifetime process and occupation. So the Bible reminds us frequently to turn away from sin.

My sister and brother and I were in the back of the minibus, bouncing along the dirt road, on the way back home from the beach, or somewhere. As I saw a Korean woman trudging along the edge of the road, I reached for a Gospel of John, and flung it through the open window. It sailed, pages fluttering, through the air, and landed a few feet in front of her. She immediately dashed forward to grab it up. We spent a good bit of the trip, rocketing out Gospels, trying to see how close we could land them to the people we were aiming at. I wonder, sometimes, what happened to all those booklets. Did the people read them? Did they make a difference to them? I suppose we'll never know. My Dad loved passing out John's Gospels everywhere he went, to whoever he encountered. Some people said that this method wasn't appropriate, wasn't effective, wasn't strategic, just wasn't fitting, as Mammy declared in "Gone With the Wind". But the real question, to me, is, what is it we're relying on? Is it God's Word, which is living, and sharper than a two edged sword, or is it the method or strategy or plan we are using?

Matthew 13 tells us what God thinks. He tells us to scatter his Word, far and wide, here and there, appropriately and inappropriately, in season and out. Yes, some will fall by the wayside, but some will bear extravagant fruit, not because of the method, but because of what it is...it's living and is God's Word. When we bend over backwards to get the strategy or method right, we are declaring that what is really important is the vehicle, not what the vehicle is carrying. The vehicle is just a vehicle. What it is carrying is life, life in God, new life that he offers to each one of us...and that he wants us to pass on to everyone else. So, let's pass it on. For in it, is Jesus, who is all the treasures of wisdom and knowledge.

OCTOBER 8

For about ten years, we lived in the Knoxville, Tennessee area. Actually, we lived south of the city, close to the airport. The airport was next to the main highway coming south of the metropolis. And then, right next to the airport was a military airbase, which was back and off to the side of the main airport. Our neighborhood was down a long road called Airbase Road, a small two lane road which went directly to the off limits airbase. As big cities go, Knoxville did not really apply. It was under 200,000 people, not far from the Smoky Mountains, but pretty far from anything else important that ever happened. Then, one day, we heard that something very big was going to take place in our city, and, in fact, it was going to originate right on Airbase Road, practically in our own back yard. President George H. W. Bush was coming to town. I don't remember what for, and he was in and out so quick that you dared not blink an eye during his visit. I just knew that he was coming...and Airforce One, with the President on board, was to be landing at the military base right at the end of our road, which, of course, meant that his presidential motorcade would pass directly in front of our neighborhood. This could be our great moment to grab a slice of history! As the appointed hour arrived, I took one or two of our kids and waited by our neighborhood entry. After some minutes, two black vehicles with dark windows went sailing by. Did he see us, as we stood there waving? Did we see him? I wasn't sure... And he never wrote me about the pivotal moment, so I still don't know. That briefest of moments barely registers in my catalog of memories; certainly, it was not the life defining moment it might have been. Oh well, maybe the President will pass by our neighborhood in Chattanooga one day, and we'll have another shot at it.

A similar event occurred in Genesis 18. OK, so it was slightly more dramatic, but still, it was a one time, passing moment. God showed up on Abraham's tent flap. God told him what he planned to do in nearby Sodom...and then he was gone. But, wow, what an amazing encounter. How could anyone top that? But Abraham's life did move on from there...children, relocations, conflicts, testings...did he regularly think back on that meeting with God? Did it help and encourage and support him through all the ups and downs that came at him in the days to come? Maybe...but I don't know. Yes, it was exciting to see the President's car go zipping by...but I can't exactly say that it was life changing. Probably that's why God chose to give us his Word. The Bible is the very words of God...what we need everyday. Not a one time, dramatic encounter, but daily guidance to show us the way to navigate through life. As exciting as it would be to have a meeting like Abraham did, most of the dramatic and pivotal moments I've ever had are passing and don't usually have a big affect on me from day to day. But the words God speaks to me everyday do make a big difference to me, do give me the direction and guidance that I need. Truly, they are life to me. They are what God has given us, knowing that we need daily nourishment, not a one time Mount Everest memory. God's given us food for each day...let's eat our fill of it!

OCTOBER 9

When I worked at CLC's international headquarters in England for ten years, the bulk of those years was with the International Director at the time. It was a little surprising to me that, coming in with as little experience as I had, he was as open and transparent about everything as he was. He wanted to be sure that we were both current and up to date with all things CLC, so that whatever came our way, we would both be as informed of the situation as possible. With that in mind, he wanted to have printed off every communication that passed through our four walls, so that neither of us missed anything. It sometimes seemed a bit more than was really necessary to me, but at least this way, we could both have access to everything CLC around the globe. We would both be able to walk the road together, both be able to support each other, discuss things, and deal with everything together. If nothing else, it certainly made me feel very much part of the inner workings of the organization.

I wonder if maybe that is part of the reason why we have been given Psalm 137. Some of its words can make us wince uncomfortably...smashing babies against the wall?? Good grief! Seeking disaster for their enemies? How about turning the other cheek? Shouldn't that fit into the picture somewhere? Israel had certainly been devastated. God's holy city, his sacred place of worship, his people, wives and children...all plundered, desecrated, abused, ravaged... Perhaps it's not a surprise that God's people, now enslaved, wanted some justice, wanted their older brothers, so to speak, the Edomites, to be punished for not coming to Israel's aid, in their hour of need, and jeering at them instead. Certainly, they deserved to be punished. But one thing I do find significant about this psalm: the writer is very open and transparent about unloading all his lamentable thoughts, feelings, and sorrows before his holy God. Perhaps like my former boss, God wants us to bring everything to him. He wants us to share all our hurts and pains and sorrows with him...because he loves and wants to experience our lives with us. Some of the psalms, and this one as much as any, share our deepest pain and sadness...which are examples to us of how far we can go in unloading our hearts to God. He welcomes all that we are, into his presence. He receives us with open arms when we come to him.

OCTOBER 10

As my wife and I are out for our daily walks, I always enjoy observing the creativity and imagination that people put into restoring their homes, landscaping their property, and making something beautiful out of what, not long before, appeared to be run down and nearly beyond salvaging. The beautifully manicured lawns, bordered by colorful flowers, bushes, and gardens, are also a banquet for our eyes. When I look at those lawns, I recall the first big lawn I had to keep up with, at the house we moved to as we were starting a family. It was a pretty good sized yard, I guess, and at the height of the warm spring grass growing season, it seemed even more enormous...given that I had to cut it weekly with our cheap Sears muscle powered lawn mower. I remember many a sweltering afternoon, pushing and puffing, sweat pouring off me, dust and grass blades flying up all around me. Thankfully, though, our energetic and enthusiastic young son would not allow his struggling father to go it alone. He would run out of the house, grab hold of the handle I was pushing with both his little hands, which he could just reach from below, and help me complete the task stretching out before me, by practically hanging on and enjoying the ride. It seemed that my load and sweat both increased greatly when he showed up to offer his help.

I have to smile when I read Matthew 14. The accounts of Jesus' activities are dazzling, breathtaking...feeding a stadium full of hungry people with a couple of loaves from Panera Bread, wandering across the waves of a storm tossed lake in the middle of the night, healing people here and there. It's incredible...but, interestingly, it doesn't seem to be quite enough. Jesus didn't break a sweat even once, doing all these stunning feats...but he seemed to want something else. Maybe, like when I saw my son come running out, it lifted my heart and my spirits, even if it also increased my load...Jesus just wanted his friends to come along with him and share his life and adventures. Feeding 5,000? No problem. But, he didn't quite do that, did he? He told his friends, "Here, you give it a try!" Did he really imagine they could do what he was able to do? Hardly. "Come on, Peter! Come join me out here on top of the hurricane!" Was he perhaps hoping the pesky Peter would drown? Most likely not. I think Jesus just wanted to share his daily walk with his closest friends. Same as he wants to do with us today. Does he really need my help reaching the whole world? Of course not. But does he want my flimsy, pathetic, fumbling support in his big game plan? Oh, yes, he does! He really does...just because he loves us and wants to share the ride with us, wants us to be in on his exciting plans for a big world out there. So, pack your Panera sack lunch, and come join the adventure! Jesus is waiting for you.

OCTOBER 11

Day/Date Be sure to remember five things to be grateful for every day. October 11

John 7:38 NCV If anyone believes in me, rivers of living water will flow out from that person's heart.

When we believe in Jesus and turn our lives over to him, he sends us the Spirit to live in us and to change us. When the Holy Spirit is controling and guiding our lives, spiritual life-giving water will come out of the lives that we live.

The start of the Korean War caught all the missionaries serving in South Korea by surprise. Many were in meetings, away from home, and they had to immediately leave, pack one suitcase only, and be ready to evacuate, to flee, the next day, to head to the port city of Pusan and a rapid exit from the city. My parents were separated; Mom took my infant brother and left for Japan, while my father stayed back to (initially, anyway) look after the mission compound. One car of evacuees bounced along a southern road toward Pusan, when they came to a split. The road went in two directions, there were no signs to tell them which way they should go, and so they didn't know what to do. They paused to pray, asking God for wisdom, and then headed down one way. Eventually, they arrived at the port, and to safety, and it was there they learned that, in hiding to ambush them as they passed, a band of enemy forces was waiting for them on the other road. God had directed them to take the way that was clear and safe. I don't know how often God directs our steps in this way, unknowingly to us, but, I expect that it may be more often than we realize. One day in heaven, we'll probably be surprised and awed when we hear the accounts of the number of times God directed us away from disaster, or directed catastrophe away from us.

That's exactly what we see happening in Genesis 20. Abraham was journeying with his clan through unknown and potentially hostile territory, in obedience to God's command to him. Abraham's wife, Sarah, was apparently a beautiful lady, and Abraham knew well the customs of the day, one of which was that, if you were the king or the leader of a nation, you could choose whichever (i.e. more than one) pretty lady you liked, to be your wife. Now, I have no idea what I would have done in Abraham's sandals, but he hatched out a clever plan (rather shocking to Western ears) that would hopefully maintain his clan's integrity and continuity, which, as the patriarch, was his overarching responsibility and duty. Everyone in a clan sought the family's longevity and future, and that even meant, at times, that one individual's life might be sacrificed for the greater good of the whole group. That seems shocking to Western ears, where each individual is valued equally, and, if anything, the leader would lay down his life for everyone else. But in Eastern, Asian culture, it's just the opposite. The leader's life is protected at all costs, so that the integrity of the clan is safeguarded. Abraham, of course, understood that well; it was part of his DNA. Even though he loved his wife, Sarah, he understood that his duty meant that she might have to offer up the ultimate sacrifice of herself. So, the plan Abraham hit on was to tell any king that came along, and who set his eyes on Sarah, that she was Abraham's sister (which, technically, she was, because they had the same father...which is also pretty strange to Western ears!). And, not entirely surprisingly, that is exactly what happened. King Abimelech saw Sarah and decided that she would be a nice addition to his growing lineup of royal spouses. He took her into his palace...and then, just in the nick of time, God intervened. Now, I doubt if King Abi prayed about his decision, as the missionaries did that day at the fork in the dirt road, but, clearly, God decided that this unfolding of events was too important to allow the King to pursue his desires with Sarah. So God met the King in a dream, telling him, this would only happen over God's dead body. Even unbelieving Abimelech understood what that meant. God's don't generally just keel over dead, and the God of all the universe was definitely not about to. So, the King did his sensible duty, returned his latest wife, and Abraham's family was saved. Like I said, we really don't know how often God intervenes in our lives, from day to day. But given his unmeasurable love for you and me, given the fact that he knows everything, even what's going on in the minds of evil people...and, given the fact that he's all powerful...well, it's just terribly, terribly unlikely that he's going to fall asleep on his watch over you. No way that's going to happen. It's just not. God does allow us to bounce along some pretty bumpy and rocky roads at times, that's for sure, but he won't take his eyes off you, that's something you can bet your sandals on, whether you're Eastern or Western.

OCTOBER 12

October 12

2 Corinthians 6:2 NLT At just the right time, I heard you. On the day of salvation, I helped you. Indeed, the right time is now. Today is the day of salvation.

How does God know when we need him? How can we be sure that he will be listening when we call to him? Because God knows everything about us — our thoughts, desires, needs, and prayers. He says that when we come to him with sincerity, he will hear and answer us. The best time to call to God is now — so that we don't waste another minute of our lives.

A knock rapped at the door, and I turned around and looked out our picture window. There, crowded around our front entrance, stood four or five uniformed policemen. I had about half a second to sift through my options, but, in that short time, I really didn't see any, so I moved toward the door to invite them in. My wife was seated at our dining room table, along with 8-10 university students, all with Bibles opened to the story they were digging into at that moment. As I opened the front door, and the officers filed in, my heart stopped beating, time stood still, and I stood watching to observe what they would do. From time to time, unannounced, mind you, the police would pay foreigners a visit in China, just a friendly little visit to ensure that the foreigners were obeying their end of their visa deal. Ours stated that we were English teachers. The officials looked around the room, saw the students, saw the open Bibles, and also our floor to ceiling bookshelves, packed out with English books that we loaned out to the students. "I see, yes, you are teaching English," one of the officers stated. They all turned, and filed right back out of the room. My heart restarted itself back up again. I don't know if I let out a "whew" audibly or under my breath, but, I'm sure one came out of me. Maybe even the angels in heaven were holding their breath, I don't know.

In Psalm 138, David makes some curious statements. He says: "Before the gods I sing your praise. All the kings of the earth shall give you thanks." These were not empty, trifling, words for David. Frequently, the kings of the earth were after his hide. The gods of the earth, in the form of their thuggish followers, were against him, too. Yet, remarkably, David knew that God was interested in these people, too, and that one day they also would bow before their sovereign God. So, though it certainly gave us a few unnerving moments, I was happy, nonetheless, when the powers of the day heard about what we were doing, and perhaps heard the Good News in the process. Some of the university students who gathered with us, studying just across the road from our "gated neighborhood", would declare to the guards at our gates that they were entering our neighborhood to come study the Bible with the foreigners. I was definitely torn in two directions by such events. On the one hand, they were mildly unnerving. On the other hand, though, I think of these words of David, and am keenly aware that the kings and rulers of the world also very much, maybe even more than most, need the Gospel. Perhaps, as a start, at least, we can pray earnestly for our rulers, that one day, they will sing God's praises, just as David hoped they would do.

OCTOBER 13

If there's one thing my father was (among probably a few other things), it was that he was unconventional. It's not so much that he was a rebel, determined to upset finely crafted traditions and formalities. It was more that, he just seemed oblivious, clueless, about them. He didn't seem to realize what the conventions were. He must have missed that course in college. I was once making a presentation and was talking about the unconventional, and used by Dad as exhibit A. At the end of the presentation, the leader of the group stated, "Well, that was unconventional!" My Dad had a way of ruffling feathers everywhere he went, but, in doing so, he had the air of a two year old: "What? Oh, really? Did I do that? Jumping Jehoshaphat, I had no idea!"

What is interesting, as we are shown in Matthew 15, is that it was the trampling on the conventions of the day by Jesus, that so infuriated the religious leaders, the Pharisees, of that day. Does it seem mildly odd that they didn't seem to pick up on the fact that he was restoring people's vision, healing lepers, giving people back their ability to walk, feeding crowds with crumbs, sending storms fleeing?? Astonishingly, the conventions of the day were so, so, so utterly sacred...that even God himself wasn't allowed to bend or breathe on them. No, oh, no. That all sounds pretty ludicrous. But, that gives us a rather eye opening glimpse into the priorities of those religious leaders. The uncomfortable question is: are we much different in our day? My father (a little like Jesus) would drop everything when he spotted someone with any kind of need. I tend to size a person up. More carefully. More deliberately. More prudently. Will he cramp my day? Will he dent my wallet? Will he dirty my foyer? Perhaps, just maybe, after he has surmounted all the initial screening, then I will check my calendar to see if I can squeeze him in. That's probably how the Pharisees would have done it as well. And if the sandal didn't fit, well, then, forget that needy dude. But, Jesus just couldn't do that. Scattering all conventions to the wind, he saw a soul in need of a Savior, and that's what trumped all else. That is what drove him to people...and what infuriated the Pharisees. Lord, my heart so frequently looks just like the Pharisees, wanting to have all my choice ducks neatly and tidily lined up together. Please, change my heart. Give me a heart like Jesus, even a little more like Dad's, one that would see the world, would see the people you love and that your Son died for, and to reach out to them with your love, with your Great News. Amen.

OCTOBER 14

The 1920's and 1930's must have been wild, crazy, exhilarating, and hopeless years, all mixed up together. Maybe something like when Nero fiddled, as Rome burned, there were spectacular highs and terribly deep lows during those years, before World War 2 came crashing in on us and drew everyone's attention away from all the craziness. One reality, back then, was the power of organized crime, especially in Chicago. It is truly frightening when forces grow beyond the reach of legitimate and expected norms and structures. I remember once being in Central Asia. I was driving along with someone, and a policeman, standing on the side of the road, waved us down. But the driver of our car kept right on driving. "He's just going to take money off of us," my friend commented, as we carried on down the street. I thought to myself, "Wow, life gets scary when you lose confidence in the forces who are supposed to be protecting us, when crime pushes aside the law." Perhaps one of the stories that epitomizes best the crazy 20's and 30's is the movie, "The Untouchables", about the seemingly invincible Mob in Chicago. They built up an empire of crime, but, like everything else human, looks can be deceiving, and even the impenetrable crime bosses could not last forever.

But, do you know what is truly untouchable? You are. Just read Psalm 139. The Almighty God of eternity tells us that he hems us in, never takes his eyes of us, no matter how dark things may seem, that he goes before us, and watches our back. In other words...we are untouchable. Anything that does happen to us, that does touch us, passes through his hands first. He is holding us, guiding us, covering us...that's really all we need. Thank you, Lord!

OCTOBER 15

Day/Date Be sure to remember five things to be grateful for every day October 15

1 Corinthians 6:19-20 NCV Your body is a temple for the Holy Spirit who is in you, from God. You do not belong to yourselves, because you were bought by God for a price. So honor God with your bodies.

When we surrender our lives to God, all parts of us belong to him — our minds, our hearts, our emotions, the direction of our lives, our bodies. His Spirit is living in us to conform our lives to God. But if we are living as we choose, rather than to honor God, we squeeze the Spirit out of our lives and out of influencing us.

At sporting events, I will watch little children walking into the stadiums and onto the courts or playing fields, holding the hands of the most powerful and talented of athletes, and I think, "Goodness, how did they manage to get in that position? How did they get noticed, get picked, to participate in that ceremony?" Maybe it's luck, coincidence, a connection to the athlete, or to someone else...who knows...

Sometimes I wonder how the disciples got chosen to their positions by Jesus. Here they were, selected to be God's closest confidantes...and who were they? Lowly fishermen, tax collectors, fanatics..not exactly Harvard or Oxford material, not exactly household names. Did they ever wonder what they were doing there, in the presence of Jesus, whom God had foretold thousands of years before? I don't know, but they probably should have wondered what they were doing in that astounding company. In Matthew 16, we read about when Peter dramatically proclaims who Jesus was, the promised Messiah for the whole world. His words still ring in our ears today, thousands of years later. A remarkable statement of Jesus' true identity. Still, after that, though, Peter demonstrated his identifying colors, fumbling, bumbling, and betraying his way through the rest of the story. But, if nothing else, Peter's declaration in this chapter shows us who God counts on in his game plan: the misfits and losers of society. (That's us!) Thank God that he doesn't only include the perfect. I don't know about you, but that certainly wouldn't include me. Thank God that his grace covers, includes, and involves any of us who fall into his arms in trust. Thank you, Lord, for your mercy and grace, your love, for us all.

OCTOBER 16

Day/Date   Be sure to remember five things to be grateful for every day.   October 16

1 John 5:14-15 NCV   This is the boldness we have in God's presence, that if we ask God for anything that agrees with what he wants, he hears us. If we know he hears us every time we ask him, we know we have what we ask from him.

This is an amazing promise, but one that is easily misunderstood. It is not saying that God will give us whatever we ask for. Though we don't know everything about God, there is much we do know. So we are invited to ask him for things in line with his goodness, righteousness, and holiness. There is much we can ask God for ... and he tells us to ask!

When we lived in China, we met and got to know many university students. As with university students everywhere, I suppose, many of them fell in love with classmates. So we got to know some of them as couples and always wished them well in their futures together. Almost always, however, these relationships didn't last. It wasn't because the couples weren't suited for each other. It wasn't because they didn't love each other or share common values, commitments, or goals. They very often did share these things together. But, in contrast to the West, where we would have considered these couples well matched for each other, they lacked one critical and essential element. They were not from the same hometown, the same province. And for the parents, who had the final veto power regarding a marriage partner, this was what clinched it. No way they were letting their child marry someone from a far off location, an outsider. They had to come from the same place. It crushed us, on occasion, to see couples so well suited for each other, not permitted to stay together, and then to be pushed into a relationship and marriage with someone they didn't really love, someone from their own town. It was essential that the children married a local spouse so that, as the parents aged, the young couple would be close by to take care of them in their old age. If their son or daughter married someone from another place, then they would likely move away, and the parents would be left alone and uncared for in their declining years. That was the critical issue.

The story that unfolds in Genesis 24 is a beautiful story of marriage...and the Chinese would understand it perfectly. Of course it would happen this way. How else could it? Abraham, as his son Isaac approached the age of needing a wife, sent his trusted servant on a long, arduous journey, back to his home, to find a hometown girl for his son. He wanted a wife from the people and place that he knew, never mind, specifically, which girl that the servant found. Just one from back home. And, in this dramatic story, the servant did indeed, with God's help, find the right, satisfactory wife for Isaac that Abraham would be perfectly pleased with. It's very debatable whether Isaac's wife, Rebekah, was in fact, the best choice for him. Later, she would seriously deceive and trick her own husband...but that's a tale for another day. So, never mind...the point was, she was a hometown girl. I suppose in most relationships, there are one or two key factors that determine whether the partners (and their parents!) are happy with the choice. God, also, chooses us for a relationship as well. But, he doesn't do it the way we do. He isn't looking for brains, potential, beauty, background, or anything else we may have to credit us in his sight. He simply decides to love us...permanently. He loves us, stays with us, regardless of who or how or what we are, and he places his love on us, come what may. Now, isn't that a wonderful love story?? East or West, it doesn't get better than that.

OCTOBER 17

Day/Date Be sure to remember five things to be grateful for every day. October 17

Philippians 3:13-14 NCV   There is one thing I always do. Forgetting the past and straining toward what is ahead, I keep trying to reach the goal and get the prize for which God called me.

Paul's attitude is a good example for us. He was so focused on living for God, both because he wanted to honor God and because he knew that sharing the Message was so urgent, that he would not allow himself to be deterred or distracted from his goal. In that sense, he maintained the same intensity that an athlete has when he is striving to win a prize.

Cultures and customs are critical to any society, and it is imperative to learn and understand them when we are visiting or living in another country. Sometimes, what is fine in one country is deadly in another, or vice versa. Having grown up in Korea, I learned many of their customs intuitively...they just became part of who I am. On occasion, that backfired when I returned to the US for college. For example, it's important in Korea not to appear to be too greedy. So, if someone offers you something, you politely decline (Never mind that you want it desperately!), waiting for their second and third offer before you finally agree to receive it. Growing up in that environment, to me it just seemed normal...and downright impolite to do it any other way. Where it got me into painful trouble, though, was when I landed in America, and someone offered me ice cream. Are you kidding, of course I want some! But, no, even though that was exactly how I felt, I had to politely refuse the first offer. Then, the American would turn and move on to something else, while I impatiently waited for their second offer...which never came. (Stupid Americans! Didn't they understand etiquette??) That was one cultural norm that I learned quickly not to stick to...the cost was just too great. A different, and colossal, faux pas in Asia is to touch an elder on the head. That is just way too close and familiar. You would never do that. Maybe on the arm, that might be OK...but never on the head.

It's interesting and enlightening, in Psalm 140, how King David says to God, "You covered my head." He would never have told one of his soldiers or guardians, "Cover my head." The King's head was always open to all, so it was clear who was supreme, that there was no one else above or over him. But, David knew where his real protection lay...under God's protective hand. He knew that all his soldiers were not what was critical to his safety and well-being. No, it was God's protective hand covering over him. That is what he counted on. And, I expect that David shared that point with us so that we would understand the same thing. God offers to cover us, to protect us, as well. Will we choose to live under his covering? It's the best place to be!

OCTOBER 18

A number of years ago, we were sharing about our overseas work in a prayer meeting at an acquaintance's home in Nashville. While there, the telephone rang, and surprisingly, it was for me. How did someone know I was here, I wondered? I got on the phone, and a voice told me, "This is 'John Smith'." I knew the name immediately. He was a well known personage in Christian book and publishing circles. Everyone in my organization knew the name. He wanted to see me. Me?!? "Of course, yes, sir, I'm free!" So, I drove to his company, was ushered into his grand office and into his presence, and thought, "What in the world am I doing here??" I tried my best to act savvy and knowledgeable. We had a pleasant visit, I was ushered back out...and I never heard from him again. Apparently, I blew my one chance to get my toe inside a significant door.

Peter had better luck than I did, in Matthew 17. At least Jesus was already on his side in this story, not like the one who invited me in my encounter. Peter was at his bumbling best when Jesus brought him and his buddies to the top of a hill to meet up with Moses and Elijah. Peter recognized them somehow, but he also knew that they were long dead, as in, over 1,000 years dead. But, he tried to keep his calm, so suggested, "Hey, how about if I just throw together a nice shady shelter for each of you?? Wouldn't that be grand?!" Jesus, of course, was on the most critical, pivotal mission in history...the rescue of all humanity, no less. And it would cost him dearly, it would come right out of his hide. No doubt, understanding the gravity and weight of his task, Jesus needed encouragement from others from time to time. So, on this day, he called on Moses and Elijah to join him from heaven. And Peter was right there, up to the challenge, ready for the moment. But, aside from Peter's usual antics, the remarkable thing about that day was that Peter was there at all. Jesus probably knew already that Peter would make a nut of himself...but he wanted Peter along anyway. And that's an important reminder to us. Jesus wants us along with him. Never mind if we're not savvy or altogether with it. He just wants us there with him. He wants you. He wants me. I mean, really, I doubt if either of us could do worse than Peter. And he loved having Peter around. He invites us, too, to hang around in his presence, to go through life with him, to learn about him, to learn from him, to learn to love him. If Peter was invited, well, then, I know we are, too.

OCTOBER 19

> Day/Date Be sure to remember five things to be grateful for every day. October 19
>
> Psalm 48:14 NCV This God is our God forever and ever. He will guide us from now on.
>
> What a wonderful comfort and truth. Friends, loved ones, or other supports in our lives can fail us or not be there when we need them. But God promises, when we trust in him, to stay with us and guide us through our lives and into and through eternity.

During the last few years, when I've returned to Korea, I've discovered a place and a country that is unrecognizable with where I lived and grew up 50 years ago. From being one of the poorest countries in the world, it has clawed its way to becoming one of the richest. The transformation has been from stone age to space age. What I hadn't realized, but also started to notice, on recent visits, was the change in the perception of my father as well. As we were growing up in my hometown, I remember my father as a busy, caring, engaged, and probably disorganized, father, physician, and missionary. When I run into people today, I'm surprised at how many randomly encountered Korean people know about my father, and how many even view him as a saint. What happened? Why the seeming change? It's what we call "legacy", and it can be a sobering, even frightening, reality that happens to us unawares. It creeps up on us without our notice, and once it appears, it can be awfully hard to change or tidy up. There are some sad stories in the Bible of people with talents and God's blessing on them, but, who, with a few careless decisions along the way, very much altered the course of their life...and their legacy. Samson and King David are two people who come to mind. How they must have wished, as they looked back near the end of their lives, that they would have been a little more careful, a little more attentive, a little more willing to listen, and just a little less reckless, when seemingly innocent moments came along and grabbed ahold of their attention.

Two insignificant, or so it appeared, bits of information in Genesis 25 came back to haunt Abraham and his descendants...even for thousands of years, right up to the present day...in tragic and painful ways. "Abraham married another wife. Abraham gave everything he owned to his son Isaac." Well, he had become prosperous and recognized, and in that culture it was his due to pick up another wife. What was the big deal? And, in that Eastern culture, the oldest son had the responsibility to carry on and head up the clan, so, of course, he would get everything. What else could Abraham have done?? No doubt, those were the thoughts that filtered through Abraham's mind during those days. But, how costly was the fallout, the left behind legacy of his life. Abraham introduced discord and dissection, malice and deceit, into his family, and that was the legacy he left behind. It leaves me thinking...what will be my legacy? Will I pass on selfishness, rudeness, focus on temporal things, judgmental ways of behaving, missed opportunities? Life can certainly seem like a mind field at times. And what makes it doubly scary is that, like a cancer, we may not realize what a mess we've made until we are too far down the track to do much of anything about it. It does warn us that we need to be careful, deliberate, intentional, wise... What will I leave behind at the end of my life? It's a question that perhaps we all need to ponder and reflect on, more often than we do.

OCTOBER 20

I came up the driveway in a puff and a panic, looking for Mom urgently. Our 5th or 6th grade teacher had given us an assignment to present an oral speech before the class (which was composed of just one other student), that afternoon, and I only had our lunch break to prepare for a task that scared me to death. Mom calmly sat me down and went through a demonstration of how I should do it, even down to showing me how to wring my hands, I seem to remember. Almost instantly, the tension and stress drained out of me, and I realized I would live to see another day. Maybe Mom had been through this with a few of my older siblings before, I don't know. She certainly seemed to take it all in easy stride and was not unhinged by it. However, I also can't imagine that she would have received my anxious plea with anything like a sense that it was a pleasing offering to her.

Yet, crazily, that is the scene that unfolds before us in Psalm 141. King David comes into God's presence in a panic, demanding that God listen, hear him out, and fix his problem pronto. Before he can even catch another breath, David further tells God to receive his urgent demand as a holy offering and sacrifice to God. I don't think David was joking with God, but it does seem just a little audacious for him to approach God in a panic, demanding that God deal with his problems, and then to immediately add, that God should receive this plea as a holy offering. What is going on here is that David knew, from oodles of experiences before, that God wants to hear from us, he delights in it, that no problem is too much trouble for God, and that, on the contrary, God loved to hear from him, and loves to hear from us. What a crazy, loving God we have, who holds our rantings and ravings as something special! Shall we test time out today?

OCTOBER 21

> Day/Date Be sure to remember five things to be grateful for every day. October 21
>
> John 15:31 NIV "My son, you are always with me, and everything I have is yours."
>
> When God saves us, it is purely and entirely based on his grace, and not on something we've done. But the older son in this story Jesus told was upset that his younger, less deserving brother, was given a lavish party. The older one believed that since he had lived a better life, he was more deserving. But if we really understand our own sin and God's grace, we will know that everything good we do is not really righteous enough in the presence of a holy God. We all are dependent on his grace.

Sports was a big thing in high school, at least the one I went to. Never mind that it was an intentionally and outspokenly Christian school. If you didn't make it big, or at least pretty big, on one of the sports teams, then you could just forget about it...(and forget about attracting the interest of one of the fairer females at the school). Now, I was smart. I knew I would be crushed and tossed out and trampled on, in football, baseball, basketball, or soccer. But there was still tennis. And in tennis you have a big net separating you and the other guy...and there's only just one other guy against you...so I figured I at least had a fair chance to make something of myself. It really helped when my older brother went off to King College...and then sent me back a brilliant red windbreaker, perfect to wear out onto the court at the start of a match, with "King" stenciled right on the back. My Mom happened to be up for one of our games once, and she told me afterwards that she overheard two of the elementary kids as they watched me play. "Why is that 'King' on the back of his jacket, anyway??" "Because he's the king, man, don't you know that?!?" Now, that was just the kind of publicity I could do with. I'm sure that jacket helped me win lots of matches, and maybe even the heart of one or two girls... Looking back on all those years, I do wonder what the administration and teachers must have thought of us guys, as we swaggered and strutted our way through that Christian school. I hope we didn't embarrass or shame them too severely. But as silly and self absorbed as we were, I can't believe what the disciples did, those guys who were Jesus' really close buddies.

In Matthew 18, we get at least part of the story. Here Jesus was, about to embark on the greatest rescue mission ever, an excruciating task for him, and which he had told them about, and one warm Galilean day, they came sauntering up to him, in the most casual, disinterested sort of way, and asked Jesus: "By the way, who do you think is the greatest in God's kingdom?" Now, we know, and they knew, and Jesus even knew, that they were really only referring to themselves. "Who of us, Jesus, is going to edge out the rest? Who gets to wear the 'King' jacket? How are you going to reward us, huh? Have you thought about that yet??" You would think that Jesus would have sacked them all, then and there, and brought in the second string, hopefully some guys who were more serious and less clueless. But he didn't. He stuck with the losers that he began with. He kept them close, shared his deepest thoughts and hurts with them, and treated them as if...well, kind of like they thought of themselves, like they were really, really special. I don't know if Jesus intentionally chose these losers especially to send us a message, or what. But it certainly does send us a message. The message is that God is a God of grace...of undeserved mercy and love...and he just can't help himself, because that's who he is. God is love...and so that's what he shows to us today, what he showed us yesterday, and what he will keep right on showing us forever. I don't know about you, but this is one God we can worship and fall on our faces before. He is an awesome God.

OCTOBER 22

We lived in a very different world when I was a boy; and I never could have imagined how much it might change in a few decades. Everything was very labor intensive, took a lot of sweat, and was also quite time consuming. For example, if we wanted to have chicken for dinner...which is not so unreasonable, right?...it meant that our gardener would have to pedal his bicycle into town, head for the big market, and bargain for the right chicken to buy. He would then lash it to the back of his bike (It would still be alive, at least for now.), and pedal his way back up the hill to our house. Once he returned, he would grab the chicken, take it around to the back of the house, pick up the axe, and pin down the chicken's neck on a stump of a tree. Chop! The head would fling off onto the ground. I think I remember (unless my memory is getting the best of me, which could also be possible) on one or two occasions, the chicken jumping up, headless, and taking off around the yard for a few meters, before it finally collapsed, really dead, at last. Then the body would have to be plucked, gutted, the feet chopped off, and finally, it was ready to be cooked. It was a pretty big job, from start to finish. The one entertaining part was when it ran around with its head cut off, thanks to its final spastic muscular reflexes. If you didn't know better, you might think it was still alive at that moment.

Genesis 27 reminds me of chickens with no heads. If they are running around, you really can believe that they're still alive, even if your brain tells you they shouldn't be. In this chapter, the patriarch Isaac recognizes that he is approaching the end of his life, and so he wants to carry out his responsibility of passing the family baton on to his eldest son, who will then become the next head of the family. But this is where deceit enters the picture, and Isaac gets confused. He's pretty sure he's not seeing his oldest son, Esau, but his vision is dim at this point, and his younger son, Jacob, is trying to steal the blessing from his brother by confusing his father. Jacob was confident that could fool his brother and get away with it...but just like the chicken with no head, sooner or later, reality was going to catch up to Jacob, and his life of deceit was going to stop running and collapse, forcing him to pay the penalty for his deception. Do we sometimes imagine that we can fool or deceive God, I wonder? We may kid ourselves into thinking we can pull the wool over God's eyes on occasion. But actions have consequences that return on us eventually. Jacob's deceit had painful consequences, both in his relationship with his brother, and in the way his own children treated each other in the years to come. We would be wise to remember that our actions and choices do cause consequences, and these consequences will come calling, sooner or later.

OCTOBER 23

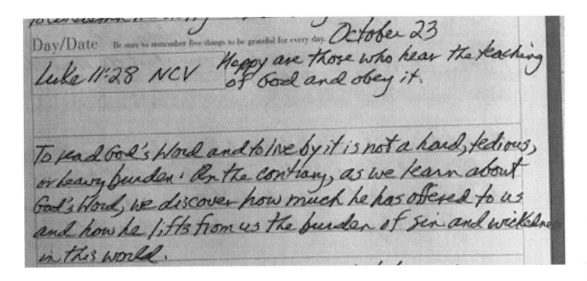

Day/Date   Be sure to remember five things to be grateful for every day.   October 23

Luke 11:28 NCV   Happy are those who hear the teaching of God and obey it.

To read God's Word and to live by it is not a hard, tedious, or heavy burden. On the contrary, as we learn about God's Word, we discover how much he has offered to us and how he lifts from us the burden of sin and wickedness in this world.

Some people are good at keeping up appearances. Others just can't seem to do so. Maybe one of the best examples of not being able to keep up appearances was Abraham Lincoln. Year by year, as he pushed and pulled the country through war that was destroying the nation, Lincoln aged visibly, looking more wrinkled and worn with each passing month. Even in the best of times, I don't know how leaders manage to juggle and deal with all the issues, problems, and crises that face them daily. President Lincoln had to have faced the most trying period in American history. I'm sure there were times when he was at the end of his strength, the end of his reserves, the end of his human abilities. He was remarkably transparent, though, when he acknowledged that he had no place he could turn to except to God. He found that no other solutions helped him in the same way.

King David, in Psalm 142, found himself at the same place that Abraham Lincoln did...at the end of his reserves, with nowhere else to turn...except to God. So, he poured his heart out to his Almighty God. Although God generally doesn't magically make all our problems go away, he does know what's best for us, and he has our best interests in mind. Wouldn't it make sense for us to go to him as well...perhaps even before we come to the end of our rope? If it worked for Lincoln, if it was good enough for King David, then I'm sure it will be right for us as well!

OCTOBER 24

Day/Date Be sure to remember five things to be grateful for every day October 24

Exodus 15:11,13 NCV There are no gods like you. You are wonderfully holy, amazingly powerful, a worker of miracles. You keep your loving promise and lead the people you have saved.

When we read through the Bible, and when we look around us and see all that he has created, God is revealed as a holy, righteous, all powerful being who we are not able to fully comprehend. But he promises to love us and care for us when we turn to him for salvation.

I was so sure of everything in life in my 20's and 30's, but it seems that with each passing year, things just aren't so certain anymore. We are saddened each time we hear of a marriage or a family which has collapsed under the pressures of life, the years, the things that come against us. When I was young, I thought that marriage was a sure thing. I mean, what could go wrong to derail it? It's a good thing I didn't know all the things that can show up to attack a marriage...otherwise I may never have jumped into the game. Even in the old, old days, like back in Bible times, marriage was a challenge. Some of the religious leaders of the day quizzed Jesus about it, trying to figure out what was required...or what they could get away with. The Old Testament is full of examples, as you read between the lines of the stories, of strains in marriages, of marriages gone wrong. Our human tendencies just seem to be always moving in the opposite direction of what is needed for a strong and healthy marriage.

When people came to Jesus with their questions in Matthew 19, he responded firmly and unequivocally. Even though he was never married, I'm sure he understood the challenges inherent in making a success of two selfish and broken people coming together to build a life. I doubt if Jesus was being hard on them just for the sake of being ornery. But he was well acquainted with our weaknesses and failings, our tendencies toward self-centeredness, so he didn't gloss over what was involved. He emphasized that marriage was made by God, for our good, but also with established boundaries. And, when we cross those boundaries, or shrug our shoulders in reaction to what God has put in place, we are setting ourselves up for trouble. And, with marriage, in particular, we set ourselves, and those around us, up for big trauma when we imagine that we know better than God, or that we can get away with being careless about what he's put in place for our own good. Marriage is hard in the best of times. Let's commit ourselves to making it work, shall we?

OCTOBER 25

Day/Date — Be sure to remember five things to be grateful for every day — October 25

1 Thessalonians 5:16-18 NCV — Always be joyful. Pray continually, and give thanks whatever happens. This is what God wants for you in Christ Jesus.

These can seem like hard things to do all the time! But if we are trusting God, if our hope is in him, and if we are living for him, then these activities should be an outflow from a heart greatly blessed by God, and not a heavy activity to perform.

I really didn't realize the significance of sharing the name of the man I called, "Dad". We were in the same house, the same family, ate the same food...but, I'm not sure I understood what a deep, profound, and enduring connection it would be. Even after he is long gone, and now I am an old man, I am still attached to him and who he was. Some bonds are enduring and not easily broken.

When God appeared to Jacob in Genesis 28, I don't know if Jacob understood fully his own connection to Abraham, his grandfather. Probably he didn't. God was about to enlighten him. Can you imagine belonging to a family that would be a blessing to everyone in the whole world? What would it be like to be a person who, just because of your grandfather, received a message from God Almighty saying that God would be with you permanently, that he would always watch over you? That is even greater care and protection than being the grandson of the Queen would give you. It must have been mind blowing enough to Jacob to hear these words about the family he belonged to. But, these words are still true for us today. These words apply to us. When we belong to God's family, he promises to always be with us, to always watch over us, to always protect us. We don't have to worry; we don't have to be afraid. Lord, help us to understand what it really means to be in your family, for you to be our Heavenly Father. Open our eyes to the reality of who you are, and the reality of who we are, because of that relationship.

OCTOBER 26

1 John 1:1 NCV   We write to you about the Word that gives life.

The Bible is a book, but it is different from any other book in the world. It is a book written by God, that tells us about him, about us, and about Jesus, who can restore our relationship with God and give us real life.

When I think back over my life and try to remember the worst situations I've been in...in the company of snakes, feeling over my head in an exam classroom, in a car accident, experiencing severe airplane turbulence, going through cancer with my wife, being lost in a strange land...and so on...as bad and as uncomfortable as some of those conditions were, I don't think I've ever come close, or ever will, to what some of the folks in the Bible endured. I wonder if God purposely came up with some of the craziest, most bizarre, ruthless, horrendous situations he could think of, to include in the Bible...so that none of us could say, "Well, God just doesn't understand my circumstances. He's never encountered what I'm going through. He just doesn't get it. His strength and ability to rescue or intervene can't touch a case like mine." Think about what some of those chosen characters had to live through: a global flood that killed everything around you, being sold as a slave by your own brothers, heaved into a band of snarling and starving lions, tossed into a flaming furnace, told to marry and love a prostitute, flung overboard by your shipmates, and on it goes! These are so outlandish that it would be hard to even dream up these types of situations.

Imagine the worst possible scenario you could be in...and then multiply it by about 300 times. That's where King David found himself in Psalm 143. Running for his life. Hiding in a dark, dank, dirt cave. Armies coming against him. His own son gunning for him. Even though he knew God, and was talking to him in these verses, David had arrived at the point where he said: "I'm out of hope. I've come to the end of the line. I don't even think God can help me." But, then, in mid-prayer, he catches himself, is able to regain his balance, and remembers who he is talking to, who is, as a matter of fact, the only one who can help him. So this is what he says: "Actually, God, I'm thinking about what you have done over the years. I do remember who you are. You are great. I need you and I'm desperate for you. I will be lost without your help. Remind me that you love me. Show me where I need to go. Teach me, lead me, guide me!" I really can't imagine going to any human with these requests, with this kind of desperation, in this degree of hopelessness. There's only one place to go, and David knew it, when he regained his equilibrium. Only God loved him, understood his dire circumstances, and had the ability to deal with them. It's the same with us today. We have the same loving and powerful God. He knows us and wants to help us. All we have to do is follow David's example. That's why he's in God's book. Not so we'll see all his blunders. Not even so we'll see what a great fighter he could be. No, God kept him in his holy book as an example to us when we have reached the end of the line (and hopefully long before) and have nowhere else to turn. When we are beyond ourselves, when the forces or the cards are stacked against us, let's follow David's example. He's there, not at all because he was smart or perfect, but because, when he was desperate enough, he did finally turn to the right place. The same place we can turn to today.

OCTOBER 27

1 John 2:3,6 NCV We can be sure that we know God if we obey his commands. Whoever says that he lives in God must live as Jesus lived.

Many people live honorably and in ways that appear to be good. But they may not be followers of God. However, if we truly are followers of God, there will be evidence of it in the way we live. Our lives should be guided by the Bible in ways that can be seen.

When we've had meetings in recent months, I like to tell my coworkers that they're better than the 12 disciples. They keep answering the bell and showing up, even when times have been severely trying and testing, and when the future looks bleak. The disciples all scattered and fled when they felt the heat. They were even worse than that. Not only did they skedaddle, they came to Jesus with a request. "Can we be numero uno in your kingdom?" Jesus might have thought they were joking...a lame attempt at humor like I am prone to do...except that, in Matthew 20, James and John, two of the key inner circle members, enlisted their Mom to carry out the task. They must have been certain that Jesus would comply; it's not likely that they would place their Mom in the awkward position of making this request, and then potentially being rejected, unless they were pretty sure it was a done deal. Not only were they thinking of and wanting to elevate themselves in front of everyone else, they also had the audacity of thinking only of themselves right at the moment that Jesus was heavy burdened with the ordeal that was hanging over his head, that of laying down his life as a ransom for many. They really were rascals. But their embarrassing and outrageous behavior actually gives us great hope and assurance. If Jesus was so patient and loving with those guys, even at his heaviest moment, think how he must be toward us now, seated in heaven, and interceding on our behalf. What an amazing God we have. What an amazing Savior. What an eternally loving God is looking down on you and me today!

OCTOBER 28

Day/Date Be sure to remember five things to be grateful for every day. October 28

1 John 1:6-7 NCV If we say we have fellowship with God, but we continue living in darkness, we are liars and do not follow the truth. But if we live in the light, then the blood of Jesus cleanses us from every sin. If we are living with God and are truly following him, this fact will make us different people in the way we live. We will not continue to live selfishly for ourselves and it should be evident in our lives that we are following God.

During the terms in high school, we had one break, in the fall and in the spring, when we could return home for a long weekend, and get cashed up again for the next couple of months. This entailed a long, slow train ride, back and forth to home. On one such trip, several of us foreign teenagers were traveling together. I don't remember with who or what the connection was, but there was also a young Korean guy who was with us. At one point, he came over and sat next to me to chat for a moment. He told me that his father was a pastor, and that probably he would follow in his Dad's footsteps...eventually. For the moment, he wanted to have some fun and enjoy himself and sow a few wild oats. There would be ample time to get serious and spiritual later on in life. The next time I saw that Korean boy was in the hospital. I went with a friend to visit him. We couldn't see his face - it was completely swathed in wide, blood-stained bandages. I heard the story of what took place. He and a buddy were drinking and having a good time. At one point, something must have happened between them that tipped the friend over the edge. He took an empty beer bottle, smashed it to jagged smithereens, and then came at our Korean acquaintance with the top end, slashing his face into shredded ribbons. He was now laying in a hospital bed, immobile and unable to see or speak. I wondered what it would be like for him now, to go through life with grooves of scars all across his face. What had he done to his father's heart by his behavior? What would his future look like now? It was a terribly sobering and silent, yet loud, parable to me about life, about choices, about the friends we gather around us, about the things we desire in life.

There is one little bitty phrase in Genesis 30 that is also sobering and tragic: "She became jealous." Those small words set in motion devastating actions and consequences. Division, distrust, hostility...so many nasty and ugly fallouts from that one simple sentence, culminating in some of the offspring of these women selling the son of the other woman (her own sister) as a slave. And my thoughts go back to this Korean friend. He observed the apparent good times of his friends and wanted some of it for himself. He was jealous of what they had, and he wanted it as well. And it destroyed his life. Probably without exception, when we become jealous of what others have, we are setting ourselves up for serious trouble. Why can't we just be content and happy with what we have...with what God has given us? Life would be so much simpler...we would be so much happier! Isn't it ironic and odd that we so often choose the more damaging and costly path? This kind of behavior, so common to us all, is a big part of what confirms to me what the Bible also tells us...that we're all broken by sin, that, without God's grace and intervention in our lives, we are all pretty likely to make a mess of things. Lord, help us to see the folly and foolishness of following our own selfish tendencies. Keep us from our own destructive jealousies and desires. Help us to choose your path for us in life. Amen!

OCTOBER 29

Day/Date Be sure to remember five things to be grateful for every day. October 29

1 Chronicles 16:10-11 NCV — Be glad that you are his; let those who seek the Lord be happy. Depend on the Lord and his strength; always go to him for help.

When we belong to and follow God, we can be very thankful that he is always with us and available for us to go to when we are in need. God invites us to come to him in our time of need and desires to help us.

When we are back home from some time overseas, I love taking old photo albums off the shelf and flipping through the chapters of our former lives. These random images bring right back to my mind those moments of years gone by, when our kids were little bitty toddlers, scampering around the house. I remember the days...but wonder where all the years went to. Such quickly passing glimpses into our existence. Where did they all disappear to? When we were going through our lives then, it felt like they would last forever, that they would always be with us. But as I look back over those old pictures, I discover that they've all vanished, seemingly in a moment, never to be recovered. We don't believe it at the time, but it's true what the Bible says: life really is fleeting and a vapor.

David was pondering these same thoughts in Psalm 144. Life was so brief. It left him wondering why God would even bother with us. If we vanish so quickly, why does God even care about us? But, he does. And, he cares about us deeply. Like my old photos of times long past, to me they are reminders of what is precious. Though they quickly went by and are now long gone, these images of my children are still what is important and precious to me. So, in that sense, I can understand God's perspective. Though our lives are quickly passing, it does not mean we are without value to God. As rapidly as we move off the scene, still God treasures us. That is something that doesn't change with God. He has always loved us...he always will love us. Thankfully, God doesn't change! He has always treasured us...and we will always be precious to him. That is great news, a great reality.

OCTOBER 30

Do you want to imagine something ridiculous?? What if we walked out onto the street...and we saw a king or queen or prime minister or president, passing by on a donkey. Wouldn't that be astonishing? We sometimes see impressive, regal, over the top processions passing, and perhaps wonder what great personage it is that is passing by. Is it the President, the Queen, or someone else?? We tend to make a pretty big fuss over celebrities, politicians, royalty, or other famous people. Now, what if it would ever happen that there was some leader who was over the entire world? In addition to being kind of scary, it would be rather mind blowing and would justify some very serious fuss over the individual.

Actually, Matthew 21 tells us that this is exactly was Jesus, God in human form, chose to do. As the head over the whole earth, he, nevertheless, came into the royal city, Jerusalem, riding on a lowly, borrowed donkey...not even one raised especially for this grand entrance...just one picked up, literally, off the street. What does that tell us? Why did he do it? I don't really know. But, at least, it's worth some serious reflection on our part. The disciples wanted places of honor in heaven. No wonder Jesus told them that they didn't understand what they were asking, didn't know what they were talking about. God's way is the low way, the humble way, the sacrificial way. Could you ever imagine the

Queen or President giving up their life for you? (No offense, but, I can't either.) But that's what the Almighty God did for us. That should give us long pause...to reflect on his love for us...as well as his servant, slave really, posture toward us. And we are supposed to follow his example. I do not see that in myself, nor in leaders, Christian included, for that matter. Lord, help us to meditate on this, on who you are, what you did for us, and what you have told us to do for you...and for others. How greatly we fall and fail every day. Help us, we ask. In your Son's holy, and lowly, name. Amen.

OCTOBER 31

Along the Kentucky-West Virginia border, in an area that saw many split loyalties during the Civil War, a rivalry developed at that time between two family clans. This Hatfield-McCoy feud has become legendary in American folk tradition, to the extent that it is now the subject of tourist sites and attractions. I think it has finally been laid to rest, more than 100 years after it originally flared up, but it is still referred to as an example of a irreparable rift between two parties. Actually, though, there is a much bigger division between two families, that has rumbled on for thousands of years, and is still alive and well in the world today. It involves the hostility between Jews and Muslims, whose footprints can be tracked all the way back to the split between Isaac's sons, Jacob and Easu. It would seem that things could be patched up without major difficulty, if the sides wanted to. But, without some pretty serious concessions and humility, these kinds of divisions are hard to mend.

Not only did Jacob butt heads with his brother, he also had difficulty with his in-laws. We read about the sad tale in Genesis 31. It got so heated and dangerous that even God had to get involved. As I read through this account, one reality jumps out at me: there was an absence of grace. I suppose we could debate about who, in the story, exhibited more or less grace, who was the primary party at fault, but clearly grace was lacking...and without it, they just couldn't move forward together. The result was an uneasy, suspicious truce between the two groups. At any rate, it's a very tragic story that is worth us thinking about still today. Most divisions we observe or experience, most family separations we hear of or live through, come down to this: no grace, or at least, an unwillingness to demonstrate it recklessly and with foolish abandon. And that's really what it takes. I see this lack in myself every day. I wish God could just fix it easily. Unfortunately, that's not possible. It's such a deep rooted disease, that healing it requires radical, invasive surgery. It scares me to think about it. But, it's what we need. Lord, help us. We need your grace. Inject it into us, whatever it takes. We don't want to be like Jacob and his father in law, Laban, nor like the Hatfields and McCoys. Heal our disease...and hold on to us as we undergo your treatment!

MONTH 11

Quarantine Day 11:

Thoughts from Acts, Romans, 1&2 Corinthians, Galatians, Ephesians, and Philippians:

*As Jesus warned, his followers will be persecuted.

*Prayer...soliciting God's help as they reached out with the Good News...was essential to the early church.

*Knowing they would suffer and be persecuted, the apostles shared the Good News anyway.

*They considered it a privilege to suffer for the Gospel.

*The early Christians looked for every opportunity...regardless of the danger-...to share the Message.

*God provided through Christ what we could not do for ourselves.

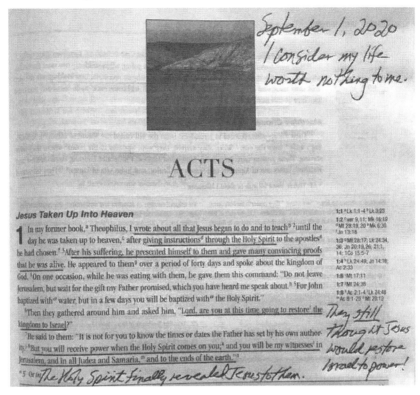

NOVEMBER 1

Day/Date   Be sure to remember five things to be grateful for every day.   November 1

Psalm 62:1 NCV   I find rest in God; only he can save me.

Experiences in life use up and sap our energy to different degrees. We can be left feeling very depleted or very stressed, depending on the circumstances and our ability to cope with various dynamics. Yet even in the midst of difficult, trying experiences, God can give us quiet rest and peace in our hearts without necessarily removing all the difficulties.

Sometimes I wonder if God doesn't look down from heaven and shake his head as he looks at us and our behavior. We must look like little three year olds who know better than anyone else. One time I watched, rather amused, as one of our grandchildren lectured her daddy and told him how he was all wrong about something and that she clearly knew better. It was rather comical to observe, considering how small her world, her experience, and her knowledge really was. Surely, we are exactly the same with God. We are so certain that we know what is best, and yet we stubbornly refuse to do the one thing that is needful, the one thing that will bring our world back into harmony.

The words of Jeremiah 4-5 remind me of this same thing. God is saying to the people, "You created the mess you're in. All you gotta do, is turn back to me, and I will set things straight." And it's not like God is a severe taskmaster (as we tend to think he is, and as I well remember thinking my parents also were at times)... In fact, he says to the people, "Just find me one decent person in Jerusalem...only one!...and I'll forgive the whole city!" Now that is pretty amazing compassion if I've ever heard of it. It's like a judge telling a murderer, "OK, just tell me about one thing you did good in your whole life...and I'll forget this whole case. I'll sweep it all away and declare you innocent." God's love and compassion for us, his patience with us, is really way overboard. It's way too much. We would never treat each other this generously, this lavishly. It just wouldn't be correct, it wouldn't be proper, we would be out of line. But really, that's how God treats us. His mercy and grace is out of line. It's inconceivable. It's beyond understanding and comprehension.

So, what about it? Wouldn't it be something if we all decided to turn back to God, to recognize our disobedience and selfishness, and repent, and return to God, like the Ninevites did unexpectedly in Jonah's day?

We seem to all be fervently praying these days that God will clear away and remove our troubles and inconveniences...but maybe we need instead to take a closer look at our failings, our self centeredness, and turn back to God so that he will heal our world... Is that what he is waiting for us to do?

NOVEMBER 2

> **Day/Date** Be sure to remember five things to be grateful for every day. *November 2*
>
> **1 John 3:3 NCV** *Christ is pure, and all who have this hope in Christ keep themselves pure like Christ.*
>
> *Christ is holy, without sin and evil. When we give ourselves to him, God attributes his righteousness and holiness to us. But while we are still living in our bodies, we live with our sinful nature, thus we must daily turn our lives over to Christ so that the Spirit can work in us to make us pure.*

Sometimes we are like little kids with their parents in terms of how we relate to God and view him. As kids, we seemed to spend much of our time trying not to get into trouble with our parents...as if they were our main obstacle, hurdle, or opposition in life. How much could we get away with, how much of life could we enjoy...without getting caught by Mom and Dad?!? It's as if we view them as the bad guys. Many, many years later, hopefully, we will see and realize that, in fact, they were just trying to care for us, to guard us against all the pitfalls and sinkholes that life throws in our way... They were barring and blocking us...from getting own ourselves into a lot of trouble. But as they did that, we at times saw them as being the troublemakers to our happy lives.

Acts 24 uses that same word: troublemaker. Paul is going about his usual business...doing all he possibly could to speak truth into people's lives, to share God's love, to warn of God's judgment against disobedience. But in doing so, he was upsetting many people's comfortable apple carts. They had nice, tidy, fun lives, and Paul came along, trying to throw them into disarray. Plain and simple, Paul was a troublemaker.

And Jesus tells us as well: If we choose to follow him, if we choose to shine the truth into people's lives, they will see us as troublemakers. They won't like us. They will come against us. That's one of the hard realities of following God.

People won't necessarily cheer us on. If fact, they will very likely oppose us. I don't know about you, but I sure don't like it when people are against me. But am I willing to stand for truth, even if it brings people against me? I certainly hope so. I would hope that I would not compromise truth and what is right...so that people will like me. God, help us to stand for the truth! Help us in our weakness and self centeredness!

NOVEMBER 3

> **Day/Date** Be sure to remember five things to be grateful for every day. November 3
>
> Malachi 3:1-3 NCV "I will send my messenger. He will be like a purifying fire and like laundry soap. Like one who heats and purifies silver, he will make them pure like gold."
>
> Our human nature tells us that we can be good, improve ourselves, and make ourselves acceptable to God. But when Christ came, he showed us that all our own righteousness was really only dross that needed to be purified away. It is only by accepting his righteousness that we are considered to be pure by God.

No doubt from his reading of the Old Testament, the apostle Paul knew how seriously important it is for us to pass on what we have learned, as he admonished his listeners to do, in 1 Corinthians 15. We forget so quickly, we turn so far from our moorings, when we aren't regularly reminded of what is important in life, what we need to know and hold onto, about God. And it reminds me, too, of all those who have gone before us, who have reminded us of what is of utmost importance...many times at heavy cost to themselves...

Ancestors who have:

·left their home country

·fled their homes

·risked their lives

·lost family members

·given up promising careers

·suffered hardship

·lived in poverty

This, and even more, so that you and I could hear the Great News. Are we continuing what they did for us, and what Paul tells us to do? Are we passing on, to those who are coming after us, the News that is uppermost in importance in the world? It is terribly sobering in the Bible to read that "a new generation rose up who didn't know God", because the older generation neglected to do what they should have done. Let's not let that happen to us. Let's not shortchange those who follow after us...the stakes are too grave and too great.

NOVEMBER 4

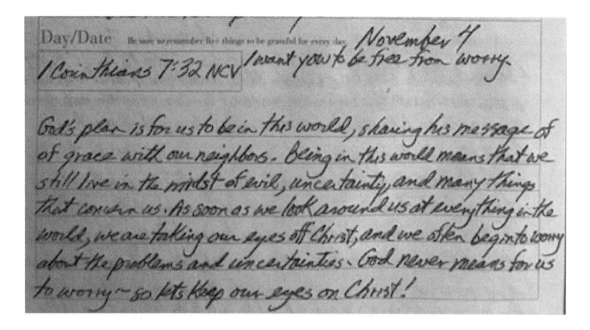

Day/Date — Be sure to remember five things to be grateful for every day. November 4

I Corinthians 7:32 NCV — *I want you to be free from worry.*

God's plan is for us to be in this world, sharing his message of of grace with our neighbors. Being in this world means that we still live in the midst of evil, uncertainty, and many things that concern us. As soon as we look around us at everything in the world, we are taking our eyes off Christ, and we often begin to worry about the problems and uncertainties. God never means for us to worry — so let's keep our eyes on Christ!

"The eyes of all look to thee,

and thou givest them their food in due season.

Thou openest thy hand,

and satisfieth the desire of every living thing.

Every day will we bless thee,

and we will praise thy name forever and ever."

I can still hear my grandparents reciting this prayer from the King James Version at mealtimes, when we were visiting them. They were missionaries in China for many years and had suffered a lot from bandits, loss, separation, illness, and evacuation. I only knew them in their retirement, but they still clung tightly to God's Word, and his promises sprinkled all through the Bible. These assurances from God were very real to them, were priceless, even, and my grandparents could not be separated from them. The verses above are from Psalm 145, which has become one of my favorite psalms, and my Grandpa's voice still sounds in my ears when I again read those words. The verses contained in David's words are filled with the abundant goodness, generosity, and compassion of God. Listen to these descriptions, taken from several different versions: "The Lord is very patient, full of love, good to everyone." "You lavish your favor on all creatures." "He showers compassion on all his creation." What a great God we have. He expresses his love to us by pouring out his goodness and compassion on us everyday. Let's give him our thanks.

NOVEMBER 5

> Day/Date Be sure to remember five things to be grateful for every day. November 5
>
> Ecclesiastes 2:11 NCV Then I looked at what I had done, and I thought about all the hard work. Suddenly I realized it was useless, like chasing the wind. There is nothing to gain from anything we do here on earth.
>
> Solomon was a very wise man who undertook a careful study of life to discover its real meaning. After accomplishing many things, he decided that they really had little significance. His final conclusion was that the most important activity we can do is to believe in and obey God. Everything else passes quickly away.

I'm sure my wife will tell you, with a roll of her eyes, that I count richness by the number of Study Bibles that a person owns. And I have several. (OK, a lot.) I love accumulating them, and love giving them away just as much, or even more. I especially like the ones that are well over 2,000 pages in length. We are so blessed, in our day, to have the benefit of the decades of study invested in God's Word by many teachers and theologians, all nicely laid out with their study notes. But, the Bible is a big book, and one wonders at times, whether God couldn't have just told us all that we needed to know in 2-3 pages. Why is it necessary to load us down with 2,000-3,000 pages? Especially when we are looking at the Bible with Chinese or North Korean friends, who have very little background or knowledge of it, it can be daunting and overwhelming.

Actually, Jesus did narrow the whole message down to just a few words, which he tells us in Matthew 22: "Love the Lord your God with all your heart. Love your neighbor as yourself." There it is…the whole thing in just 14 words. Of course there's a whole lot more in the Bible: where we came from, how God works in people's lives, how we should spend our lives, how to work out our marriages and families…and a good bit more. But, if we could just get those 14 words down, I'm sure everything else would fall neatly into place. A whole lot of the other minute details and stories wouldn't matter so, so much. So, what do we say? Shall we arm wrestle with this little verse? It's pretty lean and simple. But, I bet, actually, that we would meet our match right here. We can ask God to make these words real in our lives...we should, in fact. But, I expect that they will be a lifelong wrestling contest that we will never quite overcome. These words are just too counter to our natural tendencies. But we can certainly try...and ask for God's help in doing so.

NOVEMBER 6

Day/Date   Be sure to remember five things to be grateful for every day.   November 6

1 John 3:11, 16 NCV   Love each other. We know what real love is: Jesus gave his life for us. So we should give our lives for our brothers and sisters.

Our natural inclination is to care for ourselves before we think of others. In addition to saving us, Jesus was an example to us in how we should live. He gave up his life for others, not only when he died, but daily in the way he lived. We also ought to live this way to show others what God's love looks like.

At least in our Western society, we frequently go to great lengths to hush up any hint of scandal in an individual's life, for the sake and protection of their reputation. Although it can be uncomfortably embarrassing and awkward, I am thankful that God did not gloss over such things in the Bible. Can you imagine the potential humiliation or discomfort, if you were the most celebrated king of a nation, when God included your greatest misjudgment and failure for all the world and all of history to see and read about? (David and his shenanigans with Bathsheba.) Or for your colossal failures, as a leader in the church, to be splashed across the pages of Holy Scripture? (Paul's ruthless persecution of Christians; Peter's unthinkable, cursing denial of his own sacrificial Savior.) Surely, God could have used a trifle more decorum in sharing these stories with us! But, he didn't. And why didn't he? As it tells us in Romans 15:4, these things were written down for our instruction. God doesn't waste things - even our failures. As my wife and I were out walking once, we came across an elderly man, and we introduced ourselves to each other. He said, "I am Joe Blow, and I am an alcoholic. I haven't had a drink in 27 years." I don't actually remember his name, or the number of years he mentioned. But, I really admired the way that, with humility, and without shame, he acknowledged his failures, and realized that they could be a blessing and an example to others. There was no cover up there.

At the beginning of Genesis 32, we read that an angel came to visit Jacob, with a message from God. And who was this Jacob, whose name is so well known to us? He was known as "the deceiver". He lied to and tricked his father, in order to steal the inheritance and position of honor in the family from his older brother. God told Jacob that he would give Jacob a great family of descendants. Jacob got tired of waiting around, so, instead, impregnated two of his slave girls, to help God along with his promise of offspring. In this chapter 32, we read of Jacob's meeting with his older brother again, who, understandably and justifiably, after his brother's theft of the honor and position due to Esau, Jacob was scared to death of. Again, not long after the angelic visit from God, Jacob misled his brother, making excuses and half truths about why they should not travel together, and then skedaddling away from where he told Esau he would meet him. With Jacob, it seemed to be one deception after another, even while God was reaching out to and blessing him. At least two thoughts come to mind from this passage. God's love for us is deep and wide, as his Word tells us. Even as we all mess up big time, God still loves us and doesn't write us off. And the other, more sobering lesson, is that our sins follow us. Jacob found deception to be a useful tool from time to time. But that pattern and its fallout followed his family and descendants in heartbreaking ways for years and generations to come. What I may choose to do today is bad enough on its own...but it is even tragically worse in the example and legacy it leaves my children and descendants. Lord, stop us in our tracks, whenever we foolishly imagine that selfish disobedience to you will somehow work for our and everyone else's good. Have mercy on us!

NOVEMBER 7

Day/Date *be sure to remember five things to be grateful for every day* November 7

1 John 3:4-7 NCV Sin is living against God's law. Christ came to take away sins, and there is no sin in Christ. So anyone who lives in Christ does not go on sinning. To be like Christ a person must do what is right. We all know that, however good we are, we are not perfect. This means that we all fail to obey God's law completely, and we are not acceptable to him. This is exactly why we need to accept Christ's perfect sacrifice on our behalf in order to avoid God's punishment. Although God then accepts and forgives us, we still have sin in us. But we must not give ourselves over to living a completely sinful life — in which case we would not be able to live for Christ.

"I want to stay faithful and finish well." It was not long after the COVID virus started to get out of hand and rampage across the globe. We were marooned in our little apartment in Tennessee, instead of being in Korea, where we had planned to be. Not knowing yet what this pandemic would entail, I became worried about the other residents in our neighborhood, most of who were retired folks who fell into the high risk category for the virus. (Here's a tip for when you are approaching retirement age: if you are worried about your advancing age and your future, just move into an elderly community…you will feel a whole lot younger!) I didn't know if they would feel isolated or abandoned or unable to shop for food. So I carefully made up a list of all the residents in our community and decided I would go around to each one, to check up on them. (I was less meticulous about actually carrying out my good intentions!) One of the first residents I visited was a widower in his 90s. I was especially concerned for someone in his advanced age, all on his own. I needn't have been. Bounding down his staircase in shorts, when I asked him if I could do anything for him, he responded: "No. Can I do anything for you??" He also said that he wanted to finish his race, the life God had given him, well, and strongly.

I don't know if the writer of Psalm 146 was elderly or not, but he does make an interesting comment in passing. He says, "I will praise the Lord as long as I live." Then, he lists a few things he is grateful for: God being his helper, giving us justice, freeing us, healing us, giving us a helping hard, and protecting us. So, he planned to stay close to God, and to have a thankful attitude, for as long as he lived. What a great way to live your life. Even as life may get harder, and more challenges may come across your path, it's a wise goal to hold onto, to keep a thankful attitude and to carry on faithfully to the end.

NOVEMBER 8

Day/Date Be sure to remember five things to be grateful for every day   November 8

Psalm 24:9-10 NCV   Gates, open all the way. Open wide, aged doors, so the glorious King will come in. Who is this glorious King? The Lord All Powerful — he is the glorious King.

Here we are given a picture of a city welcoming a king by opening its gates for him to enter. But it also shows us what we should do in our own lives in response to Christ's offering of new life to us. We should open our lives wide to him so that he can come in and live with us!

I wonder if Paul at times may have enjoyed being in prison... "What?? Are you crazy?" Perhaps that's a normal response to a dumb question like that. But, think about it. When he was in prison, Paul didn't have to sew any tents, didn't have to travel or get shipwrecked, didn't have to worry about his next meal, and could read and write uninterrupted, all day long, if he wanted to. Sounds like a pretty good deal to me! When we landed in Seoul last August, we knew we would likely be in for a two week quarantine in a government facility. We were hoping the Immigration folks might have mercy on us and allow us to quarantine in our own apartment, but, though they were all smiles and politeness, they were also firm. "No dice. Nada. Ain't gonna happen on our watch, amigos." But, what we began, with a good measure of fear and trepidation, turned out to be a spiritual highlight that we will never forget...being able to read the whole Bible through in two weeks. It's a little embarrassing to admit that God had to jail me in order to get me to do this...but, still, it was a wonderful experience, and it makes me wonder about Paul's sojourns in prison. (Granted, he probably didn't have clean sheets, AC, delicious Korean food, or a beautiful bay view like we did...) We are about to head back to Korea again, and once more we're hoping to quarantine at home. But, we're preparing for the alternative jail sentence, as well, which means not seeing anyone, and not being able to leave our room the whole time. Actually, this time around, I'm excited about the prospect. I want to do something different from reading all the way through the Bible. I love the Psalms, which teach us so much about God and our relationship with him, and so, I'm planning to read all the way through them, every day, for ten days. I'm preparing myself already. I've picked out ten different versions of the Psalms to take with me...mostly pocket sized, so they won't be too much of a burden to carry. The ones I've selected are:

Christian Standard Bible,

Contemporary English Version,

English Standard Version,

Good News Bible,

King James Version,

Message Bible,

New International Version,

New Living Translation,

New Revised Standard Version, and

Schottenstein Tehillim Interlinear Translation.

I'm excited to see what God may have in store for me as I delve deeply into his Word once again. Digging through all my Bibles makes me realize how terribly rich we are in the current generation to have so many good choices of God's Word. From the list above, only one or two were even available when I was a boy. So, what will we do with all this richness we have in our hands? God wants us to use it for good, for worshipping and honoring him, for reaching out to others.

Jesus, in Matthew 23, was talking to a group of folks just like us...folks who, in their day, had been entrusted with much in the way of spiritual things. And he wasn't happy with what he saw. They had used their privilege and blessing to look down on others, to load people up with burdens, to set themselves in high places for their own benefit. Jesus was angry at them for not using well the blessings God had given them to pass on to others. It's a serious reminder to us: God hasn't blessed us for our own fatness or pleasure...but so that we will use all in our hands to bless others and honor God. That is what he desires, that is what he will check for, one of these days, when we encounter him face to face.

NOVEMBER 9

Day/Date Be sure to remember five things to be grateful for every day. November 9

1 John 3:22 NCV God gives us what we ask for because we obey God's commands and do what pleases him.

When we belong to God, we obey and live for him with the help of the Spirit in us. As our lives are increasingly in line with God's priorities, so will our prayers be. As we desire to please God, our prayers will also be for the things that concern him, and he promises to answer us.

On hindsight it was a pretty foolish thing to do, but I just had to... I was in North Korea with a small group of visitors from a humanitarian aid group. Each moment of everyday was carefully choreographed and monitored by a group of government hosts who looked after us 24/7. But one night, we were staying at a traditional inn that was in the form of an old Korean home, where we slept on the floor. After our minders turned in for the evening, I had a few moments to myself. I couldn't let the opportunity slip away. I snuck outside, just to take a short walk down the country lane, to see what was there. As I walked along the path, high walls rise up on both sides of me, surrounding private homes and courtyards. As I approached one house on my left, I could hear a woman inside the house. Perhaps her window was open, I don't know, because the wall was too high to look over. But she was speaking out loud with tremendous passion and fervor. I stopped to listen to her. Her voice sounded exactly like the impassioned prayers I remembered as a boy, when we attended Korean churches. "Goodness," I thought, "Does she realize that people passing by out here can hear her praying...and that she could get into a bunch of trouble if anyone reported on her??" I listened some more...and, with shock and sadness, realized that, though it sounded like the prayers of old, she was actually praying her heart out to the North Korean leader, Kim Il Sung. My, oh my, how terribly tragic, I thought. And no wonder she was praying aloud with her window most likely open. She was wanting people to hear her, and to note her loyalty and dedication to the god-like leader. That was a shocking and sobering encounter-...and, wisely, I quickly scurried back to my room, after offering up a prayer for that lady.

As I read the very sad and tragic accounts of Jacob's family in Genesis 34-35, I'm reminded of how badly things can go wrong when we wander away from God's ways. Jacob's relatives fell into dismal behavior, largely because they had turned away from the ways of God. And when I look at North Korea today, I see the same thing. A people who have turned away from God, abusing their own people, and suffering miserably. Will you pray with me, that God would open their eyes, that his light would shine into that deathly dark land, and that God's freedom will be poured out there? They need their Heavenly Father desperately, though they don't even realize it.

NOVEMBER 10

Day/Date Be sure to remember five things to be grateful for every day. November 10

Job 19:25,27 NCV I know that my Defender lives, and in the end he will stand upon the earth. I will see him myself; I will see him with my very own eyes. How my heart wants that to happen!

In the midst of horrific and seemingly unending suffering, Job clung to his hope in God and in the promise that one day he would live with God in heaven. As we also experience difficulties, it is a great encouragement to know that this life is passing, and that one day we will live pain free with God.

We were thankful for the church fellowships we were able to plug into during the years we lived overseas. In so many ways, they supported, blessed, and encouraged us. While they've been wonderful experiences for us, as the years pass, we do miss the fellowships that we enjoyed and were used to back in the US, as well as the worship services we had been used to during much of our previous lives. I remember on one or two occasions, when we were back in the US, feeling tears rise in my eyes as I became so moved as we again heard and sung the familiar old hymns. They were so precious to us. They recalled to us special times of worship and fellowship during many years in the past.

As precious as these songs of praise are to us, it's astonishing to realize that our songs of worship also bless God. It's hard to imagine that our wobbly music would be able to compete with the heavenly, angelic choirs. But God says, in Psalm 147, that our praises to him and good and delightful to him! We are told some of the amazing things that God does for us: he heals us, sustains us, provides for our physical needs, blesses us, gives us his Word…and, to seal the deal…he delights in us! And, too, he delights in our praises. Shall we please him today with them?

NOVEMBER 11

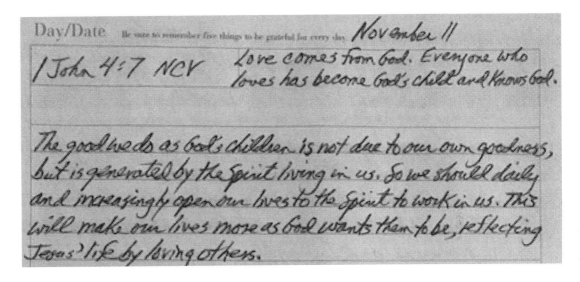

Day/Date *Be sure to remember five things to be grateful for every day.* November 11

1 John 4:7 NCV — Love comes from God. Everyone who loves has become God's child and knows God.

The good we do as God's children is not due to our own goodness, but is generated by the Spirit living in us. So we should daily and increasingly open our lives to the Spirit to work in us. This will make our lives more as God wants them to be, reflecting Jesus' life by loving others.

Corrie ten Boom used to tell the story about asking her father for details of what would happen in the future. He gave this wise and beautiful illustration as an explanation, as told by her:

Father sat down on the edge of the narrow bed. "Corrie," he began gently, "when you and I go to Amsterdam, when do I give you your ticket?"

I sniffed a few times, considering this.

"Why, just before we get on the train."

"Exactly. And our wise Father in heaven knows when we're going to need things, too. Don't run out ahead of Him, Corrie. When the time comes that some of us will have to die, you will look into your heart and find the strength you need, just in time."

Often in life, we wonder about things as Corrie did. "I wish I knew what I will be doing next year. It sure would be handy if I knew where we will be living in a couple of years from now." And so on. But, I expect that God gives and reveals to us just what we need to know...and no more. In Matthew 24, Jesus explained to his disciples about a number of events that would take place in the future... some of them, pretty scary. But, there were also many details he didn't reveal to them. They didn't need to know about it all yet. When I look back over my life,

I am thankful now that I didn't know much of the future before it happened. It probably would have been too much for me to handle or bear all at once. So, in his gracious providence to us, to Corrie, to the disciples, and to me and you... God tells us enough to live on for today. It's the best for us that way. It also gives us plenty of (not always comfortable) opportunities to trust him for whatever will happen to us in the future.

NOVEMBER 12

Day/Date   Be sure to remember five things to be grateful for every day.   November 12

Jude 1:3 NCV   I want to encourage you to fight hard for the faith that was given the holy people of God once and for all time.

God entrusted us with the Good News of his love for the world. At the same time, the devil and many things in the world distract people from hearing and believing God's message. So we need to keep working hard to share with people the Good News; it can't be done half-heartedly.

"The same way you do!", he laughed, with a great grin on his face. When I was a boy in Korea, I had an Uncle Lewis, whose family was missionaries in Japan. So, when we traveled back and forth between the US and Korea on furloughs, we would at times stop by for a visit with my Mom's younger brother. He was named after his father, Lewis Lancaster, and I was also named after his father, my Grandpa. I knew precious few people named "Lewis" when I was young, so when I met my Uncle Lewis, I got pretty excited. I knew there were two ways to spell the name: Lewis and Louis. I just had to find out how he spelled his name, and so I asked him that question. Somehow I neglected to put one and one together and deduce that, since we came from the same source, it was fairly certain that we spelled our names the same way. Apparently, he already knew more about me than I realized! He knew where I came from, and that, obviously, our names were the same.

Speaking of names, we are given a huge dose of names in Genesis 36. Oodles and oodles of names that we know little, if anything, about. But God recorded them there because he knows each one, and they are important to him. He also knows about each one of us, even more than we realize, just like my Uncle knew more about me than I realized. It's a great comfort to understand that our Heavenly Father knows all about us. He knows our needs, our desires, our shortcomings, our future, where we are at now...and, most of all, he cares deeply for us. That's a wonderful place to be...and I'm reminded of that every time my tongue gets tied up in knots, trying to wade through these lists of names that mean so much to God.

NOVEMBER 13

Day/Date Be sure to remember five things to be grateful for every day. November 13

1 John 4:10 NCV This is what real love is: It is not our love for God; it is God's love for us in sending his Son to be the way to take away our sins.

We love God because he has changed us and placed his love in us. But God loved us long before this, not because of anything good in us, but just because he chose to love us. He loved us though we were unlovely and filled with sin.

Mothers-in-law are given a pretty bad rap, aren't they. I won't go into too much detail about mine (After all, I still have to live with her daughter!), but I will say that I always enjoyed visiting my mother-in-law, as well as my wife's mother-in-law. I'm treading on dangerous ice here, because it may suggest something that's not true, but it was always a delicious experience to feast at their homes for dinner. My, I do have good memories of those times. Those two ladies just didn't seem to know how to cook up anything bad...always a delight to the taste buds. It was never difficult to praise their meals.

Psalm 148 is very interesting, as it also talks about praising. In this case, it says that everything, even many things we wouldn't normally imagine, offer up their praises to God. Fire praises him, hail does, snow, wind, wild animals, clouds... It seems to be telling us that everything God created has the task, in the way that they operate and behave, of praising him. Now, I don't know about you, but I could probably, if forced at gunpoint, come up with one or two things not to praise my mother-in-law about. But, apparently, there is no thing, and no occasion, when we shouldn't be able to praise God. Am I doing that? Every day? All the time? Sometimes, I have to confess, I find it easier or more convenient just to complain about my mother-in-law (at least in former days), instead of counting my blessings and all the ways I should be praising God. But, if the hail and wild animals can do it, surely I can as well.

NOVEMBER 14

> Day/Date — Be sure to remember five things to be grateful for every day — November 14
>
> Isaiah 13:11 NCV — The Lord says, "I will punish the world for its evil and wicked people for their sins."
>
> God is a just and righteous judge who punishes evil. It is a frightening thing to be punished by him. But, thankfully, even though we are all sinners, through Christ he has provided the way for us not to receive the punishment that we deserve.

When our kids were little, it was a mammoth job getting all the duffel bags prepared for our journeys back overseas, to wherever we happened to be living at the time. My wife would set out plastic bags for each child, marking them, "So and so's shirts", "so and so's sister's dresses", "so and so's big brother's school books", and on and on it went, for each so and so we had at the time. It must have been something akin to Christopher Columbus preparing for his crossing of the ocean...trying to anticipate every eventuality, carefully planning for each conceivable need that might arise.

Jesus had a long conversation with his disciples in Matthew 25, instructing them carefully, as well, regarding an upcoming voyage. This is a voyage that we, also, will one day journey on...the trip to eternity. Jesus' words emphasized the seriousness of packing our bags well, so to speak, of making certain we were ready for this all important journey. We were so thorough and meticulous and careful about preparing for our travels in past years. How about the biggest trip of all, coming up soon? Are we ready? Are we preparing? Jesus' words definitely had a sense of urgency and importance about them. We would do well to listen to them and prepare for this specific, greatest of all, voyages that we will one day embark on.

NOVEMBER 15

Day/Date Be sure to remember five things to be grateful for every day. *November 15*

Jude 1:21 NCV *Keep yourselves in God's love as you wait for the Lord Jesus Christ with his mercy to give you life forever.*

One day, perhaps even during our lifetime, Jesus will return to carry those believers who are still living on earth back to heaven with him. It is a wonderful day that we are waiting for. Until then, we should be faithfully living for God by sharing his love with others.

I didn't really enjoy it, and I never could get the pronunciation down, but, nevertheless, I took five years of French in high school and college. It didn't bother me for the teachers to call on me in most classes, but I dreaded being asked a question in French. I knew that I would get the words and pronunciation all tangled up, and feel very humiliated and embarrassed. The one perk, however, is that the tests seemed easy to me, I did well in the classes, and so they boosted my GPA. But, secretly, I really did not enjoy the classes and figured they were a big waste of time. The day I finally walked out of my very last French class and, with a big sigh of relief, kissed the language goodbye, I never in my wildest dreams would have imagined that 16 years later...I would be living in France, thankful, finally, that I had studied French once upon a time. I supposed that God had a funny sense of humor, to throw me into the lion's den of language anguish, following after five years of tortuous study, and figuring I would never have to see French again. It did occur to me, though, that perhaps God had led me to get some French under my belt, knowing long before I did, that some day I would be needing it.

I don't know if the same thoughts went though Joseph's mind in Genesis 39, or sometime later. But, he certainly went through the wringer...sold by his brothers, falsely accused, and finally, tossed into prison. It's one thing to have to take a less than riveting class in school and then to discover that God can use it in your life after all. It's a completely different level of anguish to suffer, and, at the same time, to trust that God knows what he's doing, and will use it all for his good purposes. Did Joseph understand that? I don't know. But, he certainly held on to God, even during his darkest days. Can we do that? Much of life includes things we don't enjoy. Can we trust in God's goodness in these uncertain moments?

I believe we can. Lord, help us to trust you.

NOVEMBER 16

> **Day/Date** Be sure to remember five things to be grateful for every day. **November 16**
>
> **2 Corinthians 5:7 NCV** We live by what we believe, not by what we can see.
>
> There is a dramatic account in 2 Kings 6 of Elisha and his servant surrounded by an enemy army. The servant was filled with fear. But Elisha told him not to be afraid, that their power was greater than the army opposing them. Then God opened the servant's eyes and he saw that the hills around them were filled with chariots of fire from heaven. Elisha knew that God was with him, even though nothing was visible. He also can live without fear, knowing that God is with us.

Our kids seemed so innocent and sweet when they were little. For the most part, we really enjoyed them, even delighted in them. Now that they are all grown up, when they visit us, they recount to us some pretty startling and distressing stories about their childhoods that we never would have believed or imagined when they were little. How they avoided certain foods, snuck in the pantry to pinch their favorite snacks, were unkind to their younger siblings... I am scared to think about what other stories may still come out in the open in the future. But, we still delight in our kids (most of the time!)...

What is really astounding to me is a little phrase we read in Psalm 149: "The Lord delights in his people." It's one thing if we were cute, like our kids were, once upon a time. But, we're not. We're, in a very real way, little devils. We're selfish, judgmental, impatient, angry... And the remarkable thing is that God knows us totally, exactly as we are. He knows all our thoughts, all our attitudes, all our actions...and he delights in us! It's incredible. What a wonderfully safe place to be. God knows us completely...and loves and delights in us, nonetheless.

NOVEMBER 17

The day our doctor in England told us that my wife had cancer was a day we will never forget, a day that changed and defined our life from then on. We were in for a steep learning curve, a lot of bridges to cross, a long and grueling journey to travel. One of the things that our doctor told us was rather shocking, and revealed the true colors of men, anyway. He said that in Britain, when men get cancer, their wives stay with them. When women get cancer, 80% of their husbands bail on them. What a shocking statistic, and how shameful toward men. Sometimes, I suppose, it takes times of crisis or testing to bring out people's true loyalties and commitments.

That was certainly the case in Matthew 26. It was getting very close to the end of Jesus' life. He wanted to spend a good part of these last days on earth with those he was closest to. His words were intimate, painful, from his heart, and shared with great love and feeling with his dearest friends. As he explains to them the upcoming, unfolding events, how he would suffer and die for the world, he interjected a couple of startling points. He said that one of his closest friends, right there among them, was about to turn traitor, betray him to his enemies for cash, so that Jesus would be put to death. Then, a little later, Jesus added, "Oh, and by the way, my dear friend Peter, you are going to deny you even know me, not once, but three times, to save your own hide." They were shocked to hear this about themselves, and had a hard time believing him. They couldn't seem to imagine that they themselves could stoop to such low levels. Apparently, they didn't even know their own hearts as well as they thought they did, as well as Jesus knew them. And, that, really, is what is so startling about this account. The disciples were repulsed to hear of their own behavior. But Jesus wasn't. Though he knew them inside and out, he knew all their thoughts, and knew what they would do tomorrow, still, he loved them dearly, wanted to spend his last moments with them, and wanted to share his heart with them. He was going through unimaginable trauma and agony, something they couldn't begin to wrap their heads around, and in spite of knowing their treachery and disloyalty, he wanted to be with them, he still loved them. I can't begin to fathom that. Could I love and share my heart with someone I knew was, in short order, going to betray me? I can't imagine it. All I can do is fall down in awe and worship of him.

NOVEMBER 18

> Day/Date Be sure to remember five things to be grateful for every day. November 18
>
> Revelation 1:17 NCV When I saw him, I fell down at his feet like a dead man. He put his right hand on me and said, "Do not be afraid. I am the First and the Last."
>
> If we were to see God today, his greatness and brightness would strike us blind and put us in a coma. What an amazing thought that this same God loves us, promises to be with us, and is the ruler over all things.

I don't remember the exact occasion, 40 some years ago, but I can still hear the words as if they were spoken this morning. RFS was being honored for his years of service to the college. Being a man of precious few words, he rose to his feet and said only this: "The lines are fallen unto me in pleasant places; yea, I have a goodly heritage." The words he quoted were from Psalm 16:6. In addition to that image still being set in my mind, what most impressed me by what he said was that he did not acknowledge or receive or comment on the fact that he was one of the most stalwart, faithful, longest serving members of the staff, for which he was clearly being recognized. It was simply that he stated and believed that it was all due to God's grace and provision on his life. Anything he may have done or accomplished or could boast about...was really due to God, and thus, that was where honor should be placed.

I love the story of Joseph, recounted for us in the waning chapters of Genesis, with so much drama, so many unexpected highs and lows. Plenty of peaks and valleys in chapters 40&41 as well. Joseph is given wonderful and supernatural opportunities by God, then he is cruelly forgotten, instead of honored or rewarded. Much later, he is finally remembered...and, sensationally, recognized. But, instead of, quite understandably, fluffing up his own proud feathers, he calmly and matter of factly pointed out that everything that happened was due to God's greatness and provision, not at all because of any cleverness or wisdom on Joseph's part. My goodness, it must have been tempting to at least give himself a small pat on the back, especially after all the injustice he had cruelly suffered from his own brothers and from his employer...but he didn't. He only acknowledged God. He only gave God the credit and recognition for any honor that came his way. Would I have done that, in his place? I don't know...I hope so. But, thank God for Joseph, for RFS, and for others like them who God sends our way, to remind us that it is really him who is behind the events of our lives, who is controlling and steering all that happens to us, sometimes seemingly randomly, at other times, very uncomfortably. Let's keep our eyes on him.

NOVEMBER 19

> **Day/Date** Be sure to remember five things to be grateful for every day.
>
> November 19
>
> Isaiah 57:15 NCV — God lives forever and is holy. He is high and lifted up. He says, "I give new life to those who are humble and to those whose hearts are broken."
>
> When our pride is broken by the knowledge of our sinfulness and bankruptcy before God, he then gives us forgiveness and a new life. This is most amazing when we realize how far above us God is in his being, power, and holiness. That he would want to stoop down so low to have a relationship with us is beyond our understanding.

Our grandkids are all different. Some are quiet as field mice. They sneak into the room, I look up from my reading, and there they are, just quietly standing there, staring at me, as silently as a mouse. Then there are others. Boy, there are others... They come crashing into the room (figuratively, you understand...they're not really destroying anything...) and seize your total attention with a trumpet blast, or like a charging rhino. They grab your attention whether you give it to them or not. God seems to enjoy making them all different and unique.

We would think, especially the way many elegant churches hold their somber and serious services, that God would prefer the field mouse approach as we enter into his presence. But, we would be mistaken. No, Psalm 150 tells us how God really likes us to approach him. Never mind that he's handling and directing world affairs, global leaders, universal events and crises. He tells us that he wants us to come crashing into his presence, interrupt all his urgent and important meetings and summits, with all the noise and gusto that we can muster, clanging cymbals, blaring our trumpets, banging on our drums! Shall we go grab God's attention today?? He's waiting for us.

NOVEMBER 20

During and after high school, for many years, I was a diehard Atlanta Braves baseball fan. You had to be pretty committed to stay with them for so long. Those were mostly lean years, save for one World Series championship in 1995. Long after that championship year, they were once again in the doldrums, facing an impossible mountain as they entered the final, ninth inning of a game against the Cincinnati Reds. Down 9-3, it was just a matter of committing three more rapid outs, and then walking out of there as quick as possible, with their heads hanging down. Improbably, I mean, really improbably, the first guy to bat that final inning got a hit. So did the next, and the next. Soon the bases were full of runners, and the poor pitcher just couldn't locate the "out" button. A couple of runs scored, and eventually, the Braves were behind only (only!) 9-6 in their final inning. A second string infielder, one of those guys who are good with their hands and notorious for being poor hitters, came up to bat...and hit a long, towering drive to left field. The outfielder was perfectly positioned to snag it right at the playing field wall. He lept up, the ball hit his glove...and then bounced out and over the fence...a four run, grand slam, final at bat, game winning hit. The Reds were in shock. Minutes earlier, they were up 9-3 and were planning their game ending, told you so, celebrations. Moments later, they stood stunned, watching in unbelief as the Braves wildly celebrated their, snatched from defeat, victory. What a crazy game.

When we read Matthew 27, we can taste the depressing aroma of defeat and death hanging in the air. Jesus was being abused and mistreated by those whose job was to uphold justice and the law. They knew he was not guilty. But their job would be easier, and they would be cheered, if they skewered him and hung him out to die, never mind his innocence. The events roll, one on top of another, heading toward a train wreck, infinitely worse than a 9-3 baseball defeat. Though Jesus knew the script beforehand, being fully human, as well as divine, he tasted in full agony and brutality, what felt like the abandonment of his Heavenly Father, the one who ultimately held Jesus' life in his hands. His own Father had turned and walked away, abandoning him in his exact moment of need. Why in the world would God do that to his only Son, whom he dearly loved? For you. Totally for you. All this pile of agony, brutal torture, betrayal, pain, and death...because he loved and still loves you. As the events winded down on a dismal day, the impossible happened. Jesus was brought back to life. He beat back death and secured our salvation. An improbable, no one could have expected, victory snatched out of the deepest defeat. Far better that a passing baseball game, his pain and unlikely triumph secured the greatest victory ever in history. All that...done for you. What an amazing story. Amazing truth. Amazing history, reality, love, and utter game changer. Let's get out there and cheer with all the angels! He gave us our lives back.

NOVEMBER 21

Our dentist in Korea was a remarkable man. To me, he was just one more father among the handful who lived clustered together in our missionary community. But, aside from being a most competent dentist, he was a scholar and inventor, teaching dentistry and patenting new dental advances, taking dental teams out to the rural countryside, and training dental assistants. But, that was not all. He was a wonderful, creative Bible teacher...I still remember his Sunday school lessons, nearly 60 years later. He would create board games to illustrate Paul's missionary journeys, and to keep us squirmy kids entertained and mesmerized. On top of all that, in his spare time, he was a wizard at languages, and he developed study techniques to aid the other foreigners who wrestled with the puzzling Korean language. He was also a great athlete. We used to play softball games down on a sprawling field below where most of us lived. During one such game, while he was pitching, I still remember him snagging two balls belted above his head, and at his belly...with his bare hands. They are the only two plays I remember from all those games. (I remember feeling relieved that he was pitching. I had wanted to pitch, but when I saw him grab these two hit balls, I knew instantly that I would never have been able to do the same.) But perhaps his greatest talent was entertaining the other missionaries. On special occasions, we would meet up at a local Chinese restaurant in town, and the show would commence. The good dentist would, with a big smile on his face, start to tell us one joke after another. Those, I also remember, after all these years. He specialty was ones with a twist at the end. Such as this one:

"A famous German pianist arrived in the U.S. several days before his concert. Upon sitting at the concert grand in the music hall, he played several notes. He walked away and refused to touch the piano again until his beloved tuner and technician from Germany, Opporknockity, was summoned to make the piano right. Opporknockity was flown to the States and set to work on the piano. At last, the finishing touches were in place. The pianist played the piano and found it perfect.

Early on the morning of the day on which the concert was to take place, the pianist came to rehearse. When he began to practice, something was wrong. Something had happened to the piano! He found out that the stage hands had moved the piano in order to replace some floodlights above. The pianist was outraged and insisted that the beloved Opporknockity be flown back to the States to set all right with the piano before the evening concert. The in-house tuner simply would not do! All involved with the concert knew that there was no way around it. They contacted Opporknockity at his home in Germany, explaining the circumstances. Opporknockity responded by saying, 'The Maestro should know better than anyone... Opporknockity tunes but once!'"

I love the story of Joseph, near the end of Genesis. The drama, intrigue, twists and turns...it all reminds me of one of Uncle Dick Nieusma's tales with a final, unexpected jolt. Things go badly for Joseph, a glimmer of hope appears, then things get worse, and, at some points, we wonder how in the world it will all be resolved. But, through it all, God is working, guiding the events improbably, until, right at the end, the details come together, fall into place, and we can finally see God's plans all working together for good. The one ingredient we need, as we walk through our own life story, is to trust God when we don't yet see or understand how the pieces are going to all fit together. They will, in God's time, but for today, we have to hold onto him, and leave the details in his hands.

NOVEMBER 22

November 22

Revelation 2:2, 4-5 NCV

I know how you work hard and never give up. But I have this against you: You have left the love you had in the beginning. Change your hearts and do what you did at first. God knows all about us. He knows the good things we do, as well as the not so good. But because he loves us, he shines the light of his Word on our lives to show us where we need to change. Do we desire to honor God enough to acknowledge our faults and ask for his help in changing?

After being in a small Christian boarding school in Korea, with the same 8-10 students in all my classes, it was an utterly contrasting and bewildering world to land in a massive public high school in ninth grade in Atlanta, during a furlough. Diverse teachers in each class; 20-30 different students in every one; confusing halls to navigate between each class, jammed with students; rest rooms smoking like a freight train from all the pupils sucking on cigarettes (against the rules) between classes. Thankfully, at least the classes were in English (except for French), so I could mostly understand what was going on...although I found plenty of my fellow students bewildering also. One day, our geography teacher took us outside on a mini field trip. I don't remember what we did out in the woods, but it was nice to get out of the cramped classroom for a bit anyway. What I do remember about that day, though, is coming around a bend, and seeing a couple of grinning students, hanging out together on the grass. One of them was in our class, so he was playing hooky...AWOL from class. Our teacher wasn't too pleased or amused by his behavior, but didn't say much. He grinned rather sheepishly, but also didn't say anything. As we moved on, I felt a bit like a straight laced nerd, obediently attending class with our middle aged matron of a teacher, and missing out on a cool, fun afternoon with some buddies. I don't know what happened to that guy...he seemed to skip school frequently. In the meantime, my boring plodding graduated me from high school, took me through college, on into graduate school, and into some decent jobs. Fine, they haven't been the most boasting about positions on earth, but, still, as I glance down at our belly, I am reminded that I haven't been hungry either. And I wonder about that other student. Did his fun in the sun get him through university, help him snag a good job? I have to wonder.

Psalm 1 kind of talks to us about the same thing. It talks about walking along God's path, meditating on his law, growing and bearing fruit like a tree... These are all activities that take persistence, diligence, faithfulness...not exactly adjectives that we associate with having a good time. In the short run, they may appear tedious and dreary, but the psalm tells us clearly that this kind of long obedience, as Eugene Peterson says, does bring prosperity, well being, security, joy, and pleasure to God. This is very much a picture of life. Most things of value require a healthy dose of hard work and discipline, and none more so than our spiritual lives. Lord, help us to focus on you and your Word, keep us from being distracted or derailed by all the pleasures that come our way, keep us walking straight along your pathway. Amen.

NOVEMBER 23

Day/Date: Be sure to remember five things to be grateful for every day.

Exodus 19: 4-5 NCV I carried you out of Egypt as if on eagle's wings and brought you here. So now if you obey me and keep my agreement, you will be my own possession, chosen from all nations.

God cares for us and carries us many times more than we are aware of. He wants to adopt us as his children, and as his children, we need to live according to his Word. When he frees us from sin, we cannot continue to live in sin and be under its control.

We've traveled, it seems like, in every way possible, to every place possible. Not entirely true, but it can seem like it at times. Especially when the kids were little and all needing attention (I really don't know how my wife did it!), it sometimes felt like we had been wrung out so far that we couldn't take anymore. On one trip back to England, the airline had overbooked and didn't let us board our flight. So, with all the little bitty kids, we had to pass most of the day sprawled out in the airport, already exhausted from the transatlantic flight, and with our youngest still under a year old. Somehow, the hours crept by, my wife and I tag teamed napping, so at least one of us could always keep an eye on our eight kids and innumerable bags. After trips like that, finally staggering home was akin to reaching the finish line of a double marathon. Finnnnally, we could collapse, relax, let the kids roam through the house...all was right with the world again.

After all the shock and trauma of the preceding few days leading up to Jesus' crucifixion, you would think that the soldiers who had marched with him through all the floggings and other events would be numb to anything else. What else could possibly shock or startle them? Yet, in Matthew 28, we are told that an angel showed up before them from heaven. I mean, how scary could a couple of angelic beings appear to these battle and brutality hardened military guys? Inconceivably, when they saw the angels, they were so utterly beyond themselves that they passed out and fell over. It occurred to me as I was reading these verses that, just as a messenger from this heavenly paradise was vastly different from anything the guards had experienced before, it will be the same for us when we arrive in heaven. After our lengthy journeys with our children, just walking through our front door at home was a complete game changer for us. Suddenly we were relaxed, we could let our intense focus down, we could breathe easily again. When we show up in heaven, one day, it will be as shocking to us (in every good way imaginable) as it was for those Roman soldiers. Instantly, all traces of our sins will evaporate, all our worries will fall away, my arthritic hands will be whole again, stress will be gone, loneliness, anger, bitterness, sadness...all done away with. It will be as much of a game changer, in positive ways that we can't even begin to conceive of now, as anything ever could be. It will be a great day, and we will be stunned beyond all imagining, by all the dazzling goodness and love all around us.

NOVEMBER 24

November 24

Luke 2:29-31 NCV   Now, Lord, you can let me, your servant, die in peace as you said. With my own eyes I have seen your Salvation, which you prepared before all people.

What a clear testimony to who Jesus is and what he would bring for the world. He may not have known entirely what he was proclaiming, but surely God placed into Simeon's mouth these words that express so well Jesus' mission on earth.

The old hymns I grew up on are beautiful to listen to, and they are all the more rich and wonderful when we read about the stories that precipitated them. One of the hymn writers whom we have received the most blessings from is Fanny Crosby. By an unfortunate remedy given for an eye infection she had as an infant, she was left blind for the rest of her life. She married a blind man, they had a less than ideal marriage, her only child died in infancy, and Fanny lived in poverty during her declining years. Yet, remarkably, she also was able to say about her blindness: "It was the best thing that could have happened to me. How in the world could I have lived such a helpful life had I not been blind?" One of my favorites, of Crosby's 8,000 some hymns, is, "All the Way my Savior Leads me", written after she prayed for her needed rent money. Shortly afterwards, an unexpected knock at her door brought a stranger, who handed her the exact amount she was lacking to pay her rent. If we are willing to, we can see God's hand in even our seeming pain and misfortune.

We notice exactly the same pattern in the story of Joseph, recounted for us in Genesis 44&45. After all the misfortune and mistreatment that he had experienced and lived through, he was able to say to his brothers, who had started his tragedies rolling by selling him into slavery, "It was God who sent me here ahead of you to preserve your lives." Even after enduring excruciating hardships and misfortunes, Joseph was able to see God's directing hard in it, to see how it had been for a good purpose. When bad things happen to us, do we pray for God to get rid of them...or can we , like Joseph, like Fanny Crosby, look to God for how he will use, even our suffering, for his good plans in the lives of others? That takes courage, faith, a dying to myself. Lord, may it be so in my life.

NOVEMBER 25

Day/Date   Be sure to remember five things to be grateful for every day.   November 25

Revelation 2:9/10 NCV   I know your troubles and that you are poor, but really you are rich! Be faithful, even if you have to die, and I will give you the crown of life.

A life of following God may not be rich by the world's measure, nor trouble free. But a relationship with God makes us rich in ways far beyond and more lasting than anything the world can offer us. Let us keep being faithful in following him!

During the period when we were in China, I seemed, one year, to get a burst of writing energy that then fell off again after those months. One of the writing projects I worked on was to interview a variety of people...co-teachers, students, elderly folks on the streets, laborers...to learn their stories. I wanted to share with our American friends what the ordinary Chinese were like...really, folks just like us, wanting jobs, families, peace...individuals needing the Gospel just as we do. The stories that willingly unfolded for me were fascinating...and amazing. Stories of suffering under the Japanese, the turmoil of the Communist takeover years, starvation during the Great Leap Forward...amazing stories, really, that nearly all of them shared openly and freely with me. Just one example was a young university student who studied English and the Bible with us. Her family was from a minority group, though you couldn't tell it by looking at her. Her family had been farmers; they were always hungry, there was never enough to eat, they would wear their one set of clothing until they were too tatty and needed replacing, and their housing was poor. Her grandfather lost both his parents at a young age, and so he had to farm, being unable ever to attend school. Our friend's mother remembers always being hungry, and they lived mostly on corn stalks and husks. But she was lucky. She was one of only three girls from her village who was privileged to attend middle school.

Mostly, the girls stayed home until a marriage could be arranged for them. Today, our friend's grandparents are happy because they can eat rice and meat every day. It's the best time of their lives. Our friend wanted to get her university degree so that she could help her parents have a better life. I must admit, after hearing the stories in China that I did, it's hard for me to appreciate some of the things that today we complain loudly about. Someone took my favorite parking spot! I had to wait eight minutes in line at Walmart! That child sure was noisy in church!

Maybe God feels the same way about us. In Psalm 2, he says, "What is everyone so bent out of shape about? Why is everyone so up in arms? Have they already forgotten how much I've done for them? Have they forgotten the peace and protection I give to them?" This is a good reminder to us to pause and count our blessings. There are things we can be thankful about. When my wife had cancer, it helped her to stop and make a list of what she could be thankful for...instead of being consumed by the one thing that was weighing on her mind. I expect we all have more to be thankful for than we realize, and certainly more than many people have been blessed with.

NOVEMBER 26

Day/Date · Be sure to remember five things to be grateful for every day. · November 26

Jeremiah 3:12 NCV "I will stop being angry at you, because I am full of mercy," says the Lord. "I will not be angry with you forever."

God cannot tolerate sin, evil, and disobedience because of his righteousness. But though he knows all our faults, it does not mean he won't forgive them. He has mercy enough, and more, to forgive us of all our disobedience against him.

It seems that every culture and place in the world is different and has its unique set of dynamics, power, complexities, and prejudices. I may visit one locale and be invisible, another place and be honored, still another area and be discriminated against. In some places I am fearful, in others I feel right at home (in Asia, of course). Even in the crowded and small old city of Jerusalem, you can sense a different dynamic and atmosphere, as you cross the invisible boundary between one sector and another, within the Old Town.

It must have been the same in Jesus' day, and he certainly stumbled into trouble numerous times as the flaunted the existing and accepted protocols and culture of the day. We see it again in Mark 2. We find him hanging out with the uncool dregs of society, and the high level religious leaders said, "What in the world are you doing, hanging out with that scum?" Even as religious leaders, God's people, they knew that there were certain boundaries that respectable people wouldn't dare cross. How did Jesus respond? Well, clearly he was people blind. Prostitutes, money hungry tax predators, lepers, outcasts...they were all just people to Jesus. And not "just" people. They were the folks he loved, came to die for and rescue, the folks he loved best to hang out with. So, on this day, Jesus responded, "Sure, you religious folks have your friends, and that's fine. But I came to spend time with the ones who need a hand, those who need saving. I didn't show up just to have a good time. It's the sick of society who need help, not those who already have it all together." What about us? Are we like the guys who only enjoyed hanging around with their buddies? Or are we living for something more than that? Does our schedule include some of the misfits of society, some of those on the margins, some of those headed down the broad road, as Jesus called it? I hope so... I hope it's the case with each one of us.

NOVEMBER 27

It wasn't quite the same as Jacob's clan, including all the women, children, sheep, and cattle, crossing the precarious and desolate land from Canaan to Egypt, related to us in Genesis, but in December 1993, our family loaded up our six little kids, including our youngest three month old, into our rattily red Ford Transit van, and headed north for Holland. Our small CLC community in the south of France became a deserted ghost town at Christmas, as all the French workers returned to their homes for the holidays, and we didn't want to sit the days out alone. So my wife hatched the plan to drive across Europe to visit her relatives and cousins in the Netherlands during those days. I had my own secret agenda. I wanted to visit my former beloved Bible teacher who I remembered from my school days in Korea. Kees Glas grew up as a boyhood friend of Brother Andrew (God's Smuggler), lived through the German occupation of his country during the Second World War, and later moved his family to Korea as a missionary with WEC, following the Korean War. And, now, he was retired, back home in his beloved Holland. Mr. Glas was a most passionate teacher of the Bible, preaching to the handful of us disinterested students as if his life (ours, really) depended on it. I can still see his focused face, his impassioned words, his wavy Dutch head of hair, and I remember today the cherished verses he had us memorize (2 Chronicles 16:9; Luke 24:32; 2 Corinthians 4:17-18), all, as if it were yesterday. His stories of the seething slave boy, Ben Jacob, in Egypt, stay with me still. As students, we snickered at his stories...but they went down deep into my heart, and I wanted to thank this man of God for his dedication and service to us. I wanted him to know, in his latter years, that his diligent teaching to this seemingly uninterested group of teenagers hadn't been for naught. We had a wonderful visit together on that last day of 1993, and I can still picture his grinning face, as we sat in his Dutch home and remembered together those long ago days in the classroom in Korea. Thank God for dedicated servants like Kees Glas!

In Genesis 46-67, we read the story of Jacob and his family traveling to Egypt to join his son, Joseph, now the leader of the whole land, second only to Pharaoh. It's a dramatic accounting of how God is steadily working behind the scenes, not only in the lives of his own people, but in the lives of pagans as well, to bring to fruition his divine, good plans. That is worth us remembering and holding onto as well. We can be tempted to place our trust and hope only in what we see around us. But let's not forget God. He's directing the drama, not anyone else, and we can trust in his goodness and justice, even on days when we can't see it.

My beloved teacher, Kees Glas, was welcomed into his Heavenly Father's presence with the greatest of "hartelijk" (heartily!) on January 20, 2021.

NOVEMBER 28

Day/Date Be sure to remember five things to be grateful for every day. *November 28*

Revelation 3:11 NCV Continue strong in your faith.

In Ephesians 6, Paul shares with us some tools that God provides for us to keep us walking closely with him. These include reading and obeying his Word, prayer, trusting in God, and living righteously. It is up to us, with his help, to use those tools in our daily life.

I seem to remember my son telling me a funny joke that goes something like this: "Don't feel so bad...the whole world is really not against you. A couple of the smaller nations are neutral!" It is helpful to have a laugh every now and then, to help loosen up the stress and anxiety we may be facing on a given day. The apostle Paul certainly, at times, felt like everyone had turned against him. And King David was the same way. From being the great, powerful, beloved king of a united Israel, a few short decades later, he was running for his life, fleeing from his own son, no less.

He says, in Psalm 3, as he calls out to God, "O Lord, I have so many enemies; so many are against me." Apparently, David felt like even the small neutral kingdoms had abandoned him. Thankfully, though, David didn't stay struck in his quagmire. He quickly jolted himself out of his lethargy by recalling who and what God is. Here's what he shares with us: "You, O Lord, are a shield around me. You are my glory, the one who holds my head high. I cried out to the Lord, and he answered me from his holy mountain. I woke up in safety, for the Lord was watching over me. I am not afraid of ten thousand enemies who surround me on every side. Victory comes from you, O Lord." We are so blessed that David preserved and shared his experiences, his ups and downs, with us. Because we, also, as we journey through life, travel through frightening highs and lows. But we have the same God that David had. He hasn't changed. When David spoke to him by addressing him, "O Lord", he was speaking to God, not as some far off deity. He was affirming that God was his God, close at hand, with him, listening to David, taking care of him. Ten thousand armed and dangerous enemy soldiers? No big sweat...the Almighty God of all the universe was with him, caring for him, watching over him. He's the same God we have with us, on our side, today. Amen, David, amen!

NOVEMBER 29

John 14:21 NCV   Those who know my commands and obey them are the ones who love me, and my Father will love those who love me. I will love them and will show myself to them.

Many people down through the ages have claimed to know and follow God. John explains to us that the real test of whether we belong to God is whether we are obeying and following his Word — not simply saying that we know him. As we obey God, he will reveal to us more and more of who he is!

During one of the court cases I participated in, when I was called up for jury duty, many years ago, I was surprised at the two sides drawn up against each other. On the surface, it looked like the case was stacked very much in favor of the one side. They had a set of polished, trimly suited, slick looking attorneys who put fear into you just glimpsing them. The other side came bumbling in, a lone lawyer with a rumpled suit, frumpled hair that needed clipping, an over-weight and overaged gent who looked to my untrained eyes that he was in for a legal lashing. I felt a bit sorry for the guy he was defending. Well, surprise, surprise, to me anyway, the over the hill Lone Ranger took it to the other side and tore them to ribbons. They filed out, at the end of the case, with their ties tucked between their legs. Lesson one: Looks will be deceiving. Lesson two: Fire power is not always all it's cranked up to be.

I was just reading in Mark 3 about how Jesus went off to a quiet place to choose his Cabinet, those closest confidantes and experts who would be key to him successfully carrying out his mission, his term on earth. And, so, who did Jesus select, out of the thousands who followed in his train? Twelve bumbling idiots, if you really want to know. Unskilled (no offense to fishermen), untrustworthy (tax collectors), impulsive and unreliable (Peter, the future head of the church), treacherous (Judas I.), and prone to anger and conceit, it certainly looked like

Jesus carefully thought through his Cabinet options...and chose the most idiotic candidates. Now, why in the world would he have done that? Don't forget...looks can be deceiving!...something Jesus apparently learned before I did. Earlier, this morning, I read in Psalm 3 about how David, alone, on the run, with only his God at his side, felt perfectly safe in the middle of 10,000 armed enemy soldiers. It occurred to me that Jesus could have wisely chosen 10,000 of heaven's top angels as his partners. Instead, he picked twelve idiots. He also knew lesson two: firepower is not everything. Jesus, seemingly, went way out of his way to make it emphatically clear to all of us, that God's plans, his ways, his work...is not dependent on the fast, the first, the clever, the smart, the strategic, the most educated. Jesus knew (I wonder why we still haven't figured it out...) that God's plans for the world, for you, for me, do not hinge on the greatest and the best of what we have. He already has it in the bag. It's already accomplished. And, to our eyes, at least, God is taking his time, to give as many of us as want to join him, time enough to do so. But the time won't last forever. Let's get on board, if we haven't already.

NOVEMBER 30

Day/Date _Be sure to remember five things to be grateful for every day_ November 30
Revelation 3:19-20 NCV I correct and punish those whom I love. So be eager to do right, and change your hearts and lives. Here I am! I stand at the door and knock. If you hear my voice and open the door, I will come in.

God's teaching, training, and punishment, done because he loves us, can be quite trying and painful at times. How much better it is to honor God with our lives and to show him our gratitude and love by how we live. God wants to fellowship with us, but he does not fellowship with evil.

In 2003, we were on furlough from England, visiting supporting churches and friends, and spending time with our family. My father's health was declining, and he was becoming increasingly frail. As the day approached for our return to Sheffield, it occurred to me that I would likely not see my father again on this earth. Mom had already just passed on to heaven only a few months before. Knowing we were about to leave, I wanted to tell my father goodbye, to pray with him one last time, and to thank him and tell him how much he and his life well lived had meant to us all. It was a very sweet moment that I was grateful to spend with him on that June day, only one month before he did indeed leave this earth. It doesn't always happen that we realize in advance that we are with a person for one final time, so I was very thankful for this unique opportunity.

We see the same thing happening at the end of Genesis. Jacob comes to the end of his life in Egypt, and he is able to spend time with all twelve of his sons and to give them his blessing. The blessings he gives are interesting, informative, and, I can't help feeling, must have been uncomfortable for some or all of the sons. Jacob was glowing in his assessment, particularly of Judah (Jesus' forefather) and Joseph (the one who had been horribly mistreated by his older brothers, but had been used by God to rescue them all). But his final "blessing" to some of the others must have left them feeling pretty sobered and shortchanged. It's a reminder to me that God uses weak human beings to carry out his plans, that he does things very differently than we would likely do them, and that his good and amazing ways will prevail, in spite of any human plans that can appear disastrous to God in themselves. It is a most dramatic picture we are given in this story of Joseph in Egypt of what a great God we have.

MONTH 12

Quarantine Day 12:

Thoughts from Colossians, 1&2 Thessalonians, 1&2 Timothy, Titus, Philemon, Hebrews, James, 1&2 Peter, 1&2&3 John, Jude, and Revelation:

*Christ makes us alive and gives us hope.

*We will suffer and be persecuted.

*Even in trials, there are opportunities.

*Faith, Hope, and Love are the three tenets of the Christian life.

*God saves us because he loves us. He entrusts us with the Gospel, not only to save us, but so that we will pass it on to those who have not yet heard.

*Paul didn't view trials as something to be avoided, but as a natural part of our following Christ.

*Live like Christ did.

*Live faithfully while we wait for Christ's return.

*God will make all things right one day.

What a wonderful privilege and experience to read through God's Word in 12 days! I would recommend it to everyone!

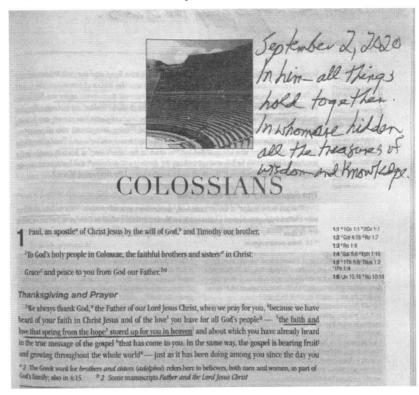

DECEMBER 1

Day/Date Be sure to remember five things to be grateful for every day. December 1

Proverbs 11:30 NCV A good person gives life to others;
the wise person teaches others how
to live.

Although this verse is challenging us to live well and right,
it is also a perfect description of the life Christ lives.
He came expressly to lay down his life for us; and by
his example, he showed us exactly how to live. Let
us follow his example!

What a rich blessing we possess from those who have gone before us. I am so thankful for Warren Wiersbe's Transformation Study Bible, which I am reading through at present. He shares with us some wonderful thoughts from the eight verses of Psalm 4. David, in one of his frequent desperate conditions, urgently calls to God for help. He knows that he can come to Almighty God at any time. He understands that, though he is a big sinner, God has accepted him and declared him "not guilty" because of David's trust in God's grace. Because of that, and knowing as well that God is with him...and in spite of his present circumstances...David is joyful and able to sleep peacefully.

Here are Wiersbe's thought from the psalm:

1) Fear the Lord. We don't need to be afraid of anything else.

2) Don't sin. Don't let it get the best of us.

3) Think about it overnight. Good, practical advice.

4) Remain silent. Reflect and meditate before God.

5) Offer sacrifices. Give thanks to God.

6) Trust in God...instead of in anything else.

Wise words, all!

DECEMBER 2

Day/Date Be sure to remember five things to be grateful for every day. December 2

Revelation 4:8, 11 NCV Holy, holy, holy is the Lord God Almighty. You are worthy, our Lord and God, to receive glory and honor and power, because you made all things. Everything existed and was made because you wanted it. God is perfect and pure, and he made everything that exists. As people he created and who are dependent on him for our every breath, we should be spending our lives honoring him and living for him.

The stories of suffering and hardship I heard from the Chinese I talked with during our time there were hard to imagine. There were periods in their recent past when food was so scarce that the people had to scrounge in the hills for bark, weeds...anything they could possibly try to boil or make into something that they could swallow. Those were tragic years.

In Mark 4, Jesus shares several parables about farming and about seeds. What strikes me about these stories is how extravagantly God sows his seed...his Word, his Gospel, his love, to those he created. Jesus tells the story of farmers, seemingly recklessly, scattering seeds all over the place, so that many of the seeds didn't even land on the plowed field. They just threw it out excessively, as if they had way too much to plant, so they flung bunches of it into the wind. It's a beautiful picture of God's overflowing love for us, and for those still waiting to hear about his love. He wants so much to share it with us, with the world, those he scatters it everywhere, to any possible place where someone might just happen along to pick it up. How ecstatic those hungry Chinese would have been back in those hungry days, to stumble on piles of seeds like this. And how happy still, when people hear today of God's love, and comprehend what that means to their lives and their existence.

DECEMBER 3

Day/Date — Be sure to remember five things to be grateful for every day. — December 3

Isaiah 61:10 NCV

The Lord makes me very happy; all that I am rejoices in my God. He has covered me with clothes of salvation and wrapped me with a coat of goodness, like a bride dressed in jewels. Surely one of the happiest moments in life is when a bride is dressed in her wedding clothes. When we come into God's family, He wraps us in love, forgiveness, and salvation as if we were in wedding garments. We are clean because of what Christ has done for us, and our life is beginning anew.

Hiroo Onoda was a 22 year old intelligence officer when he arrived in the Philippines near the end of World War 2, having been given the assignment to hamper the Allied forces from landing on the islands. Onoda was also commanded never to surrender, never to take his own life. After the US forces landed, Onoda headed for the hills to hide out. He was not about to surrender. He had total confidence in and loyalty to the empire of Japan, and even when leaflets were dropped, urging him to come out of hiding, he refused, believing that it was only a ploy to induce him to surrender. Finally, in 1974, near 30 years after the war ended, Onoda's old commanding officer had to be dispatched from Japan specifically to convince him that the war had indeed ended, and to order him to surrender his sword, and to give himself up. What an amazing loyalty and dedication to the cause, even if it turned out to be misplaced.

As we look at David's life in the Old Testament, we encounter someone perhaps as tenacious as Mr. Onoda. David had plenty of instances when he could have been expected to surrender, when all visible hope was expended. Still he persisted. In Psalm 13, David does sound weary. "How long do I have to hang on and keep going, Lord?" There was no apparent reason to expect deliverance...still he hung on, as he declared: "But I trust in your unfailing love. I will rejoice because you have rescued me." Even without visible relief on the horizon, David was so confident of God's rescue, that he stated that God had rescued him, as if he knew it had already happened. In his mind, it had already happened, because he knew that God keeps his promises. May we also, when the going gets tough, when the way is unclear, hold on to God, and trust in his deliverance. He can be trusted!

DECEMBER 4

Day/Date _Be sure to remember five things to be grateful for every day._ December 4

Joel 2:1, 11-12 NCV Let all people shake with fear, because the Lord's day of judging is coming; it is near and is an overwhelming and terrible day. The Lord says, "Even now, come back to me with all your heart."

God's justice must punish sin. His love for us provides us with an escape from that punishment. But what a tragic day it will be when God comes in judgment on those who have not accepted his salvation. We must tell as many as we can!

Charlie showed up quietly to our men's Bible study, invited along by one of the other participants. He had an easy grasp of languages, and he loved books. Charlie's grandparents were elementary school teachers who suffered and faced many hardships. His grandfather was from a cultured and educated, land-owning family, but those advantages invited trouble and hostility, at that time in China's history. Regularly, their home and property were pillaged, and eventually, they lost everything and were reduced to poverty. Why all this suffering and hardship? It's very perplexing and difficult to make sense of. But, one day, Charlie met his Savior. His story did not end with the legacy of suffering.

God does permit us to suffer. In Exodus 17, the Israelites were trudging through an unforgiving desert area, where no water was to be found for themselves and all their animals, which were their livelihood. It's not easy to understand all they experienced. But all the events did give them opportunities to see God and to trust in him. Perhaps the same can be said for Charlie and his family in China. And how do we respond to hardship and trials? We can turn to God, or away from him... As hard as trials may be, the story is tragic for those who choose to turn away from God and to go their own way. We get a picture of some of those folks who the Israelites encountered on their journey to the land that God promised to them. Most all of them ended badly, for turning away from God. Lord, as we pass through this troubled world, and experience ups and downs, storms and moments of calm, help us to keep our eyes on you, to trust you, to wait on you, and to hope in your salvation.

DECEMBER 5

One of the hard things about being in missions full time is that, in spite of the best intentions, in spite of wanting to honor God in everything, in spite of wanting to advance the Good News…sometimes things don't go well or according to plan. I suppose we're in good company. I doubt Paul exactly expected everyone in Asia to desert him. And Jesus (of course, he knew ahead of time since he was divine) wouldn't have wanted or expected all his closest buddies to run when the going got tough…but, they did.

In Mark 12, Jesus told a story. He told about a farmer who planted a field. Later, the farmer sent someone to check up on things. But when he got to the field, the messenger was beaten up and sent on his way. The same thing happened several times. This reminds me of when our organization starts a project at times. Later, someone is sent to check up on it. Generally, things are doing OK. But, just occasionally, it seems like the local guys will beat up on the visitor and send him packing. Maybe it's due to some misunderstanding, maybe the goals were misunderstood…or, just maybe, the locals decided that they wanted to keep for themselves what was intended for others or for the greater ministry. At any rate, it doesn't seem to end well. That's about what it looks like in Jesus' parable. The tale turns into a disaster. But, then, Jesus tells us the "end of the story", so to speak. And this is what he tells us…the end result is wonderful to God. And

God gets what belongs to him. In other words, the unhappy occurrences are used, transformed, and turned around for good. Obviously, the prime example of this is Jesus' own death in the worst possible manner. God supernaturally turned it all around for good. Or, you could say, God got what belonged to him all along. Now, think about it, if God could do that with the worst calamity in history, with all the forces of the devil arrayed against him...do I really imagine that he can't turn around a hiccup or two in my life for his spectacular good? It all belongs to him anyway, right? Yes, absolutely! When we offer our work, our efforts, our lives, to God...he will get what belongs to him. We don't need to worry. The glory belongs to him...and will come to him.

DECEMBER 6

Day/Date Be sure to remember five things to be grateful for every day. December 6

Hebrews 2:14-15, 17-18 NCV Jesus became like them so that, by dying, he could destroy the power of death and free those who were like slaves. Jesus had to be made like his brothers so he could be their merciful and faithful high priest. Then Jesus could bring forgiveness for their sins, and he can help those who are tempted, because he himself suffered and was tempted. Perhaps we will never fully comprehend what Jesus did for us until we get to heaven. He was perfect, holy, and all powerful, yet he laid that all aside and came to earth as a simple man so that he could suffer excruciatingly on our behalf. And even after saving us, he continues to help us in daily following him.

I discovered I needed glasses at an evening service at our church. I don't really know why...maybe our song leader was an optometrist on the side and was looking for more business, who knows...but, for some reason that I don't remember, he told everyone to cover one eye, as we looked up at the screen which displayed our song. Then, a few moments later, he told us to cover the other eye...and, right then, the whole screen went blurry for me. And, that's when I discovered I had a vision problem, in one eye, at least. (Now, doesn't that sound like a clever ploy by an undercover eye doctor?? I bet he had appointments lines up for months after that!) At any rate, I dutifully made an appointment, and my vision has never been the same since. (Well, actually, it keeps getting worse, but at least, I can keep going back to my eye doctor...not the same fellow as the song leader, mind you...paying my dues, and getting my sight corrected again.)

All of this sight saga reminds me of the tale we read about in David's words in Psalm 12. David's all in his usual panic. "Help, God! Help! All the good guys are disappearing!" God calmly replies: "I can see. I can hear. Don't worry, I'll deal with it." When God speaks, it's like when we get our vision corrected. Suddenly, everything becomes clear...we can see things sharply in focus again. And what do we see? We discover that...believe it or not...God really is controlling things. He really does know what is going on. And, that looks can be very deceiving, downright misleading, even. What looks like all a blur, what looks like everything is utterly out of whack, is really just due to our bad vision, the incomplete picture that we have, without God's 20/20 clarity. So, whenever I'm feeling panicky about what I see around me...I probably need to remind myself of what David needed reminding of. Things really aren't careening out of control. It's just my vision that's out of whack. God knows what he's doing...everything is actually in his good and perfect and capable hands. No worries!

DECEMBER 7

Day/Date — Be sure to remember five things to be grateful for every day — December 7

1 John 4:11 NCV — Dear friends, if God loved us that much, we also should love each other.

When we are slow or reluctant to love others, we forget how deeply God loved us and what he suffered for us even when we were unlovely and sinful. A real test of how much we understand God's love for us is how much we love others who he also loves.

She was a quiet girl, when she started attending a Bible study in our home, with some of the other university students. Slowly, we came to know her, and gradually her story came out. In those villages where her family lived, and where she was raised, boys were prized, because it was assumed that they would stay in the area and take care of their elderly parents some day. Lily was one of three daughters, not so well appreciated, as well as a prized single son. When Lily was ten, her parents moved to the big city to look for work. From that time on, she saw her parents only sporadically, mostly living on her own, cooking and fending for herself. Each Monday morning, she would walk the three hours to school, carrying the rice on her back that she would need to cook by herself, as she spent the week days and nights at the school. It was a hard, tough, lonely childhood.

I think about our sweet friend, Lily, as I read about the arduous journey of the finally free Israelites, trudging their way through the hostile desert wilderness, as recounted for us in Exodus 15&16. They knew God was with them...something Lily was unaware of as she grew up in China. Still, it was laborious for them, and the hardships caused them to quickly forget God and to become impatient with and complaining toward Moses. But, God regularly sent reminders to the people that he was still with them, guiding them, aware of their needs, and that he would continue to provide for them. God provided for Lily, too, though it was not without suffering. And, if we will observe and acknowledge it, we will see how God provides for us as well. Sometimes unexpected, sometimes even comical, but God cares and is looking after us. He came to the aid of the Israelites, using a stick, dew, and quail, lots and lots of quail, in these two chapters. How has he been providing for us in these days? Will we notice? Will we remember? Will we thank him? Lord, open our eyes to your care and provision. May we not forget you, as the children of Israel were sometimes quick to do. Help us to always be mindful of your presence and your care. Amen.

DECEMBER 8

Day/Date Be sure to remember five things to be grateful for every day December 8

Isaiah 55:9 NCV Just as the heavens are higher than the earth, so are my ways higher than your ways and my thoughts than your thoughts. The heavens extend as far as we can see — and then keep going. No one fully understands God; he is so much above and beyond us. The few people who were allowed to encounter him closely while on earth were nearly overwhelmed and killed by the experience. It is a good reminder for us to trust God and to not be too quick to question his ways.

After studying Chinese for two years (and struggling to get to first base with it), I needed a different visa, rather than a student one, so that we could continue to stay in the country. Through a tip from a student we knew, I was introduced to the headmaster of an English school in our city. I had never thought about teaching before, but it seemed like one of the best options at the time. The headmaster, Mr. Zhao, interviewed me and offered me a position at the school. Anywhere in Asia, respect for authority and position is important. General staff aren't on the same level as the boss. It's just understood and accepted by everyone. But, Mr. Zhao was unusual in this regard. He told me that, as a boy, when his family, along with many others, was struggling to survive, some of his neighbors would share their food with his family. Everyone was trying to make ends meet, so, clearly, this was a costly sacrifice for his neighbors. This generous sharing of what they had by his neighbors had a powerful impact on Mr. Zhao, and he never forgot it. Our headmaster didn't just say that he cared about people...he demonstrated it everyday, all day, year after year. Did I need a drink? No problem. Did I need money? No problem. I would walk down the hallway, after a class, ready to chill and grab an ice cream. And then I'd see Mr. Zhao. What was he doing? Emptying the trash. Sweeping the hallways. While some headmasters and officials "knew their place", and dressed and behaved accordingly, Mr. Zhao dressed simply and was always ready to stop and help anyone. He trained the other teachers, took them on outings during school breaks, advised them about life. Very simply, he laid down his life for everyone, it seemed.

In Mark 11, we read about Jesus' entry into Jerusalem, shortly before his death. In some ways, his entry into this great city reminds me of how Mr. Zhao would also have entered...quietly, forgetting who he was, focusing on others, not making a big fuss over who he was and the honor and ceremony that were rightly due him. Isn't it striking, in this account, that the Lord of the universe would come into the great city of God, where he was right to have expected a grand entrance, quietly, riding on a bleating donkey? At the very least, he could have chosen a black stallion, and with surely a couple of decked out guardians... It's remarkable that Jesus, Almighty God, made his grand entrance in such a simple and ordinary way. But, really, his whole life was like that. He came to serve, rather than to be served...a lot like how Mr. Zhao viewed and lived his own life. It's truly remarkable to see someone live their life that way...the way we are also supposed to live our lives.

DECEMBER 9

Day/Date Be sure to remember five things to be grateful for every day. December 9

1 Peter 4:7 NCV The time is near when all things will end. So think clearly and control yourselves so you will be able to pray.

We don't know when our lives will end, or when God will bring us to heaven. Because of this, we should always be ready for when it happens by living for God and by using our days in being faithful to serve him.

As 1999 wound down, the whole world seemed to hold its breath. What would happen when the world clock turned over to 2000, to Y2K, to a whole new millennium? Rumors, forecasts, predictions, and panics swept through the media, and there was palpable fear in the air. Would society collapse? Would the world as we knew it come to an end? In one sense, it seemed silly to listen to all these wild rumors? But...you just never knew... There was a lot of talk, a lot of unease, real fear, in fact, within the science and techy communities. What would happen to the computers, which were not calibrated with a 2000 year in mind? The thought was that, with computers unable to register "2000", everything would grind to a halt. Trucks would no longer transport our food, our Amazon orders, everything really, as they had always done before. Other things, also...banking, hospitals, schools...would grind to a halt. There would be anarchy...every man for himself. It could be a disaster. Some people were taking it seriously, planning ahead. We heard of some who sold everything, built bunkers underground, and stored up a year's supply of food for, come what may. Others, figuring that life as we knew it was going to end, decided that they would take advantage of it while they still had it, and went on spending binges, before they lost everything. Looking back now, over 20 years later, it all seems pretty silly. But, in the thick of it, it really was pretty scary. Well, especially with the responsibility of a large family of 11 lives under my roof, I certainly was not going to be caught off guard. I would be ready. I selected about three of our cleanest, most sturdy plastic milk jugs, and carefully filled them with sanitary drinking water. I stored them on the steps going down to our basement. I was ready. The extra water would surely carry us over for the few extra hours necessary, before everything settled back down to normal. And then, I waited. We invited a family over that evening, on December 31, 1999, for a time of prayer, as we saw the New Year of 2000 come upon us. And what happened? Nothing. Nothing happened. Trucks kept right on delivering. Computers kept right on humming. And I quickly got rid of my three extra water jugs so no one would think I had been duped like everyone else and gone to all the trouble of preparing for nothing. I remember earlier in the day, that a friend in Australia had written, and said, "It is now 2000 here, and I can assure you: there is nothing to worry about. There is life after 2000."

When I read Psalm 11, my mind goes back to those frightening, uncertain days. And I am reminded of where our true security is. It's not in extra water bottles, or hunkering down in a bunker. We are told: "The Lord is in his holy Temple; the Lord still rules from heaven." Really, that's all that matters. Life can be scary at times, certainly it can fill us with fear. But, our real hope is not in bunkers or bankers or bullets. Our hope is in the God who controls everything. So what do we have to worry about? Lord, help me to remember this, to remember you...everyday when, once again, I forget it.

DECEMBER 10

Day/Date Be sure to remember five things to be grateful for every day. December 10

Mark 9:24 NIV   I do believe; help me overcome my unbelief!

We are told numerous times in the Bible to trust God and to believe in him. But God knows that we are weak humans with weak faith. He invites us into his presence even as we are struggling to understand and believe in him. And he wants us to acknowledge our struggles to him.

My, oh my, the stories I heard from the older generation in China! Without exception, they agreed that the present was the best time of their lives...when they had enough food everyday, when they could eat meat if they wanted to. They had endured and survived through a time and age that is hard for us to conceive of today. One elderly man I talked to recalled, decades earlier, during the "hard times", having to get up before dawn, to hike way up the high mountain nearby, to scrounge sticks, which they could then bind together to construct brooms, and then could sell on the side, so that they would have enough food to eat. They had to climb very high, because all the vegetation and branches had already been stripped from the lower parts of the mountains. Life was so hard, so grueling...but, somehow they kept going.

The children of Israel suffered greatly as slaves in Egypt as well. Then, as we read in Exodus 13&14, right as God finally showed up to rescue them, their suffering was not yet over. As they were finally able to breathe a sigh of relief...the whole Egyptian army, all their soldiers and chariots, appeared out of the desert, trapping the Israelites against the sea that was facing them. At the moment all seemed lost, we read of the dramatic rescue of God, as he brought to bear his power and presence in a miraculous way. The Israelites surely had many moments, many years, even, when they wondered where God was, what the purpose was of all their suffering, whether it would ever end. The Chinese of a generation or two ago must have felt the same way. What was the purpose of all their suffering? Would they ever be rescued from it? God does, in his sovereignty, allow us to suffer. But, it's not without purpose. He wants to see if we will trust him. Will we, in our most difficult moments, turn to him for help? He also allows us to suffer so that we can experience his rescue, his greatness, his power. Many of the Chinese who survived their most severe years have now had opportunities to hear about and turn to God. Even the Egyptians, following all the calamities in Exodus, were given an opportunity to observe God's power and turn to him. And, of course, as they were suffering, the Israelites were never to forget God's powerful arm of deliverance on their behalf. Lord, help us, also, to see you, to trust you, to believe in you, during our hours and days of testing and struggle. Help us to trust you and to look to you for salvation, when times seem at their most severe.

DECEMBER 11

"Don't speak until spoken to. When you speak, say, 'Your Royal Highness.' After that, say, 'Ma'am.' Don't sit in her presence, unless she sits. Don't touch her, except to take her hand, if she extends it to you. Bow when you first come into her presence. Bow when you prepare to leave. She will ring a buzzer, then I will come back in and escort you out." As we've been watching, "The Crown", about the British monarchy, these were the instructions given, not to a janitor or driver, but to the Prime Minister of the whole country. It seems astounding that the highest official in the land would be required to bow and scrape in this way for another human being.

In Mark 10, we observe a different situation altogether. The contrast could not be more stark. First, Jesus invites people to bring their squirmy, noisy kids to him so that he can hold them and bless them. Later, a blind beggar calls out to Jesus, and he stops and heals this social outcast. No waiting in line, no bowing, no fancy titles... Almighty God came down to be with us, to live with us, to love us, and to treat us as equals. Remarkable. The contrast is stunning, as compared with the monarchy. This truly shows us how much God loves us, values us. He is the Almighty Sovereign of the universe, and yet, we are invited and welcomed to come into his presence anytime, just as we are. That's an offer well worth pursuing!

DECEMBER 12

Most of the time, I don't, but, just occasionally, I wish I could go back and convey to my parents that they really did know what they were doing, after all. They've been long gone, and now it's my turn to be an old, over the hill, geezer that doesn't know anything, just doesn't get it. That's pretty much how I viewed them once. Now that I've been around the block more than once, increasingly, I see the wisdom and good sense of their ways. The moments that I would puzzle over or question something, and Dad would kind of mumble something incoherent, I realize now that it wasn't because he was senile. It was because he was calmly saying, in his own way, "Just be patient. Hang in there. Don't worry, you'll understand it someday. You won't be entirely clueless forever." The frustrating aspect of this whole growing up process is that, by the time my kids grow up and get a life education, I will be gone...I won't have the great pleasure of being able to say, "Surprise, surprise! Now, you understand. See, I wasn't so dumb after all!" (But, then, of course, my parents are no longer around to finally be able to tell me that, either.)

I kind of suspect that in Psalm 10, David, or whoever wrote it, was processing the same thoughts. "Earth to heaven: wake up, please! As in right now! Don't you see what's going on down here? The bad guys are running roughshod over everything. They're having a field day, trampling over my turf. Hurry up! Show up! Set things in order! Yesterday, already, if possible!" To his credit, David (and the other writers) did still turn to God, did still look to him for help. So, they were not altogether on the wrong track. They just had the problem, in this psalm, anyway, that a lot of younger folks have (that I had!)...they think that enthusiasm and "new" ideas trump wisdom and experience. It might, just on occasion. But, for most of life's defining, lasting, and critical situations, I'll take the wisdom and experience. That's why Proverbs and other places in the Bible tell us to be patient, listen to counsel, seek out our parents' advice. It's hard for us to see it when we're young, but other people have actually gone before us, have dealt with the same issues and dynamics we are dealing with, and most likely, have already made the same mistakes we are about to make (but could avoid, if we were willing to listen). Who knows...maybe one day, much later, David looked back over his impatient rantings with a little more understanding, a little chagrin, even, at the impertinence of his younger days. God, help us to listen! To be patient. To be teachable. Most of all, to seek out your wisdom, your advice, and your help...rather than bulldozing ahead toward a train wreck. Amen!

DECEMBER 13

I've always enjoyed visiting a new place for the first time. Everything is there to be discovered, a feast for the eyes, nose, ears, taste...invariably, I click loads of photos on that first visit. If I come to a place for the second time, I take a whole lot fewer pictures because it's not all new anymore. By the third time, I hardly take any photos, at all. But, it is definitely fascinating to experience how cultures, peoples, and societies are all so varying, so diverse. And China must surely win first prize in that department. In the south corner where we lived, most of the minority tribes seemed to congregate, and there was an explosion of colors, clothing, traditions, and tastes, everywhere you looked. Perhaps one of the most striking and prevalent items that caught our attention was the doorways. Nearly every house had a protective wall surrounding it, with an impressive gate to close in and protect the family that resided there. These gates and walls spoke silently the message that this was a family's sacred, secure, private domain. And the gates and doorways were often elaborate beyond what would seem warranted...but they conveyed the important message of being someone's fortress. What was nearly universal, though, was the color around the door posts of the gate. Crimson banners were afixed, usually glued, around the door, providing a dramatic sign. These banners were so striking that every time I read about the Passover in Exodus, I am reminded of China. When I asked someone local why they posted these brilliant red banners around their doorways, guess what the explanation was? They are for the purpose of warding off evil spirits. Does that sound like the Passover to you??

Whenever we read through this portion of Exodus with our students, chapters 11&12, the story of smearing blood around the door posts, to guard against the angel of death, would jump out at them. We told them that their tradition of red banners may very well have originated right here. It certainly was a dramatic teaching moment. The blood around the doors provided a sign, indeed, for the "evil spirit", it also distinguished between those who chose to obey God and those who did not, and they provide a reminder, still in China today, of what God did in rescuing his people from slavery, and that we are to teach those who come after us about who God is. God emphasized to Moses: "Make sure the people remember and celebrate my rescue, my salvation, of them, forever." Thankfully, God gave us his Word to remind us and teach us. Today, as much as ever, we need to remember and to pass the knowledge of God on to those who come after us.

DECEMBER 14

"One day the government officials arrived and completely destroyed our home and took away our pig, which was our main item of value, in punishment for what we had done." I met Frank on my epic bike trip in Shangrila. He was one of the English students on the trip, so we got to know each other a bit. When his mother became pregnant with him, she had to flee to the forest and hide out until it was time for Frank to be born. That's because he already had an older brother, and his parents were permitted to have only one child. When word got out that his mother was again pregnant, after the birth of his brother, the police arrived and took his mother away by force, for the purpose of forcing her to have an abortion. Inconceivably, she was able to squeeze her body through the jail bars, jump to safety, and flee to the woods. But, ultimately, the family would pay a heavy price for attempting to flaunt the official policy. Given this family history, Frank felt burdened to complete university, secure a good job, and contribute significantly to the support of the family.

Jesus saw children differently. They were precious in his sight. Jesus was God, and demonstrated that fact, sometimes in very dramatic ways. In Mark 9, we are told that the disciples with him were terrified. Later, the crowds were overwhelmed with awe when they saw Jesus. Even his presence and appearance were staggering at times. But, at the same time, Jesus was not too lofty to care for what was important here on earth. He greatly valued little children, and made it quite clear that he expected us to do the same. Everyone was precious to him. Are we the same way? Do God's people, even those right around us who don't seem to have much going for them...do these people have value to us? They should. If they are precious to God, then they need to be precious to us as well. Are we demonstrating God's love to those around us, even the unimportant ones? Lord, please help us to do so!

DECEMBER 15

I was at my favorite used bookstore, McKay's, with three of my grandkids. See, grandparents can be more clever than they appear. They willingly take the grandkids out on an excursion...so they can really do what they want to do...but with the little ones in tow to make it look very serving and magnanimous. One of the best things about McKay's is their throwaway bin. It's as if Santa came along, saw me there, opened up his sack of goodies, and then dumped them into the bin just for me. Well, yesterday was a bonanza day. I really hit the jackpot, which will strain by bookshelves even more than they already were groaning. Some guy came up, huffing and puffing, hauling several hard plastic boxes full of books. He dumped them into the bin, telling me, "We just took over an older church building, and we need to get rid of their library books. Help yourself!" Like I said...Santa just showed up. As I was sifting through their commentaries, Bibles, and all manner of books about Christian living, I caught a glimpse of another book, buried beneath a pile of others. I saw just enough of it to recognize what looked like a Chinese drawing on the cover. Naturally, that grabbed my attention. I pulled it out: "Chinese Idioms and Their Stories". Now, the Chinese are every bit as good as Plato, Aesop, Jesus, or Confucius, when it comes to parables, proverbs, and idioms. And there's one mystery one that my Nai Nai used to recite to us, that I've been trying to track down for years. No Chinese person I've asked has ever recognized my mumbo jumbo when I've tried to repeat it to them. As I remember, and I can still hear my grandmother saying it, it sounded something like this: "Gerren you, gerren you, gway ju". Yeah, I didn't think you would recognize it. Anyway, she used to enjoy saying that with a twinkle, and then tell us, it means, "To each his own. Everyone does things in their own way." As I was flipping through the pages of the book, I stumbled on an idiom that certainly sounds like my Nai Nai's. The story the book includes with the idiom is about two generals who didn't coordinate their plans for battle...and thus were both wiped out, in the ensuing battle. Clearly, doing things your own way can be a very bad idea at times. Or, put another way, when we don't work together, we are asking for trouble.

When I look around the world today, it does seem like a lot of that way of operating is in evidence. Chaos here, disaster there, confusion everywhere. Perhaps the same thing was going on in Psalm 9. David observes the nations scrambling this way and that, but God's coordinated plans get the best of them. God's strategies are just too carefully planned and thought out for us to think we can get the best of him. It's far better, far wiser, as David learned early on, to stick with the winning side, to get on board God's train, and to follow his lead. May we all have the good sense to do just that!

DECEMBER 16

Psalm 62:8 NCV   People, trust God all the time. Tell him all your problems, because God is our protection.

This verse tells us that God protects us. But at the same time, it acknowledges that we have problems and difficulties. God does not keep all hardship from us, but he helps us in and through them, and when we come to him, it shows that our trust is in him.

"It will only happen over my dead body!", the female Communist bureaucrat snorted. We were working on a longtime dream of CLC...to open a Christian bookstore in Moscow, Russia, in the bastion of the Communist empire. What had once seemed like an unimaginable, ludicrous dream, began to feel like it just might be possible in the early 2000s. We had put together a strong team of committed folks to make it happen. Moscow, perhaps along with all the large cities in Russia, was segmented into specific administrative areas. The local official assigned to each one held complete sway over all that took place in their little dominion. Our team found a sturdy two story building that looked to be very suited to operating a bookstore. It was also located close to a key subway stop, near one of the city ring roads. It looked very promising to us, and we were very grateful to be able to purchase the building with gifts received specifically for this project. Now, we needed to obtain the necessary permission to operate a business in this part of the city. Our team leader entered the office of the appropriate official and explained to her our plans and desires to open a Christian bookstore in her jurisdiction. Her response was that there would be no way in the world, barring her own death, that this would ever happen. Our leader, a courageous, tough guy who was not easily deterred, had a sudden inspiration. "What if we opened a bakery on the ground floor...and had our bookshop upstairs??" The whole demeanor of the grim lady changed. "Well, that just might be possible," she responded. Remarkably, many months later, when we were finally able to have our grand opening ceremony for the bookstore, this same Communist lady showed up for the occasion. She approached our leader, and told him, "You know, it really is a miracle that this is happening today. Normally, there is no way I would ever allow a Christian bookstore to operate on my watch, within my turf!" As it has happened, the bakery idea turned out to work very well for us. It drew customers in, and the rent it provided for us, from those operating the bakery business, was a support to our book ministry.

I wonder if Moses, in Genesis 9 & 10, felt the same way our Moscow leader did. God sent him repeatedly to Pharaoh to ask for permission for the Israelites to leave Egypt. Even in the face of spectacular and devastating plagues and destruction, Pharaoh held his stubborn ground and basically responded, "You'll only leave here over my dead body!" What in the world do you do in a situation like that? Jonah ran...I probably would have joined him. But Moses didn't budge. In the presence of a completely defiant emperor with absolute authority and full of scorn, Moses held firm. So did our team leader in Moscow. A Marxist atheist with no desire for what we had to offer, and full of scorn for us, didn't deter our leader. He was convinced of the right of what we were doing, and he was going to see it through, even in that tough and great city. There must be a lesson in there for us somewhere! It certainly shows us the importance of standing for what is right. Of trusting and believing in God...even when the situation appears to be impossible. Ultimately, things are in God's hands...even the heart of the Pharaoh and the heart of any hard bitten Communist bureaucrat. God is the decision maker. We can trust him, even when he gives us terribly hard assignments that seem beyond our abilities at times.

DECEMBER 17

> **Day/Date** Be sure to remember five things to be grateful for every day. December 17
>
> Psalm 106:13 NCV But they quickly forget what he had done; they did not wait for his advice.
>
> It is very sad when people do not know God and have not heard of his love. It is even more sad when they know God and have experienced his love, yet still turn from him and choose to go their own way. How important it is for us to support and encourage each other so that this does not happen.

Aunt Sally was special. Rightfully so, during those grinding, post Korean War days of scarcity, hardship, and a nation struggling to rise and in need of the Gospel, most of the missionaries seemed a mite grim and sober to this little boy growing up during that period. But, not Aunt Sally. When she taught us, it seemed more like an adventure, not the glum lessons some of the other teachers drilled us in. She had a twinkle in her eyes, as if she knew about or was planning something fun, just around the corner. She coached us in how to pass the time more easily during lengthy church services. Told me about some clever components to her house, easily overlooked, but designed especially for her advantage. If there was some fun happening somewhere, more than likely, Aunt Sally was in the middle of it.

And then there is Psalm 8. Every time I come to it in my daily readings, Aunt Sally comes to mind. She gave my lone classmate and me the assignment to memorize it. She might have been asking me to scale Mount Everest. My female classmate absorbed and regurgitated it effortlessly. What was it about girls, that they had it so easy, anyway? I'm sure my marble playing, outdoors scampering around, and sorting my stamps endlessly had nothing to do with why I wasn't learning it. For me, it was a long, long battle, to get down one word at a time of that endless and arduous, nine verse passage. Somehow, with my Mom's continuous drilling, I did learn those verses, at least passably. Aunt Sally let me get by, and didn't even make me feel bad or frown at my imperfect recitation. Today, though, well over 50 years later, those words from Psalm 8 are still with me...and so are Aunt Sally's twinkling and affirming eyes. She gave us a gift...she was a gift. And it was a lesson to me of the importance of planting God's Word down deep in our hearts when we are young. For, then, it stays with us. And we continue to be blessed by it all through our lives. Are we doing that with our children, our grandchildren? Are we helping them hide God's Word in their hearts?

DECEMBER 18

I don't know if it's just me, but it seems like my whole world revolves only around...me. I guess I can understand that, in a sense, I see things from my own perspective, because, after all, I am only looking out at the world through my own set of two eyes. (I don't even have the advantage of four eyes, like some people seem to have...) But, why, I wonder, does my brain work the same way as my eyes do? Why do my thoughts not go further beyond myself than they do? Why am I so small minded? When I was a boy, my entire life was sifting through and soaking the paper off my stamps, counting and recounting my handful of Korean coins, or running through the neighborhood to find out what the rest of the gang was up to. That was about it, for my gigantic, little world. Meanwhile, my Dad was saving the planet, healing all manner of diseased individuals, raising folks miraculously out of poverty. But, the only thing I seemed to notice about him was that he got the two or three cubes of ice that our kerosene refrigerator produced, in his drink...and we didn't get any.

I wonder if Jesus sometimes felt the same about the folks who gravitated around him. We are given a glimpse into some of that dynamic in Mark 8. Here he was, healing people left and right, feeding the whole countryside...and his disciples were worrying about their next meal, wondering whether one of them was greater than the other, whether it really was the right thing to heal a person in this way or on that day. Jesus' eyesight was much bigger than that...he seemed to take in everything, seeing the big picture, even seeing other people's thoughts. He saw the needs, he saw the solution, and he toiled daily to serve and help people. Why can't I be like that? Why am I more concerned about the interest on my bank account...than whether someone knows the meaning of life? Lord, have mercy on us...and help us to see things and people as you do...and with your loving heart, as well!

DECEMBER 19

"Food was always scarce. The USA helped China with guns and money for fighting the Japanese. There were no happy times during that period; we were just trying to survive. I never went to school." These were some of the words I remember an elderly man (Well, he couldn't have been that old...I'm his age now!) speaking, as I was interviewing him several years back in China. Such hard memories...a while generation in China missed the opportunities and experiences we take for granted and assume are our natural right. So many sad stories like that among the older generation in China. At the same time, some of these older folks mention the presence of American soldiers and pilots passing through. Occasionally, I would meet an older person who spoke remarkably good English, very much surprising me. Invariably, they would have learned it from the few American soldiers who passed through during the war. Certainly, some of these soldiers may have been Christians. Did they take the opportunity to pass on their faith? And, if the Chinese observed it, did some of them remember, and take it on board? An intriguing question...

In Genesis 7&8, we read about the beginning of some of the plagues God sent against Egypt to get their attention, show them who the real God was (not one of the many deities they worshipped), and squeeze them to the point where they would free God's people. I have to wonder, as I read through the dazzling and pervasive plagues that God sent...how much of this did the Egyptians remember? Did they absorb and believe in the God of Israel, as they observed these plagues and as the Israelites lived among them? I wonder. And it also makes me consider...what do we leave behind when we pass through people's lives? Do we leave them with a picture of who God is...something of the Gospel? Jesus, for sure, arrested the crowds' focus as he passed through their lives. Are we doing the same?

DECEMBER 20

December 20

Ephesians 4:1-2 NCV I am in prison because I belong to the Lord. God chose you to be his people, so I urge you now to live the life to which God called you. Always be humble, gentle, and patient, accepting each other in love. Let us be as focused and driven as Paul was, who was so intent on sharing God's Good News that the threat and even the reality of prison did not deter him. With God's help, we can live for him and show people his love by how we live.

I leaned over and said "hello" to the little girl. And that passing encounter is what started one of the most interesting and fruitful friendships of my years in China. I had been walking down a sidewalk on what we called "Carpenter Street". Our town of Dali was known for three things: it's marble, it's tie dye creations, and its amazing carpentry. All the exquisitely carved wood we saw everywhere was made on this Carpenter Street, by hand, with all the same tools we would have imagined that Jesus used in his carpentry shop, many centuries ago. When I greeted the little girl, her father responded in excellent English. I invited him to my men's Bible study, and from then on, this devout Marxist was one of my most loyal attendees, inviting along many of his non believing friends to our lively studies and discussions. Roger believed that Marxism liberated him from the philosophies and constraints that bound so many others. People like me, and others in the West, were slaves to their money. Only Cuba and North Korea were truly free, he told me with confidence.

Jesus explained to us, in Mark 7, that the real problem was inside of us. Certainly, there are plenty of problems around us and outside of us...but, Jesus said, what we really need fixing, is our broken heart. I'm still hoping Roger will one day understand that.

DECEMBER 21

When we look at China today, it may seem that it has been strong and stable as a nation for a long time. But the people went through a lot of upheaval to arrive at where they are today. One shopkeeper I encountered while we lived there told me of losing his parents at a young age, of struggling through life on his own, attending school only till about age ten, of selling firewood from the mountainside to feed himself, and then learning road construction. Life seemed like a scramble, just trying to figure out a way to survive. He recalled hearing stories of American pilots, flying into his area during World War Two, to help against the Japanese. Some of the Americans built a "Good News Hospital". He said to me, at the end of our conversation, "Tell the Americans that they are welcome here!"

David, in Psalm 7, must have experienced some of the same sense of scrambling for security and survival that I heard from the older Chinese man. His words sound desperate: "I come to you for protection. Save me! Rescue me! Stand up! Wake up!" Even in his desperation, David did know where to turn. Time and time again, he received help from God, and, after his frantic pleas, he adds: "God is my shield. I will thank the Lord because he is just; I will sing praise to the name of the Lord Most High." Perhaps somewhat like the Chinese, David frequently experienced a mix of hope and desperation. He knew where to turn...but he still had plenty of desperate moments. Lord, help us as well, when we are feeling panicked and at the end of our tethers, to always be mindful of where our true help lies. Turn our hearts to you in our moments of greatest need. Amen.

DECEMBER 22

When British Prince Charles was thirteen, he was sent to Gordonstoun private boarding school in the bleak and remote wilderness of Scotland. It was known as a rough, no nonsense, institution that taught its boys toughness and independence. Perhaps, it did. Charles later described it as "Colditz in kilts" (referring to the German prisoner of war castle in World War Two). It makes one wonder why his parents would send Charles to a place that would be so difficult for him, especially as a member of the royal family. Well, his father, Prince Philip, had also attended there, had a tough time as well, but believed that it had shaped him into the person that he was to become. So, he wanted his son to have the same formative journey. It was indeed a challenging experience, and, no doubt, Charles must have felt very alone, deserted even, during his sentence there. But was he? Was he abandoned? His father knew exactly what he was enduring...the pain, ridicule, hardship, loneliness, spartan conditions. Certainly, he was daily, moment by moment, in his parents' thoughts. They cared for him dearly, knew what he was suffering and going through...and, yet, they sat back silently and allowed him to live it out.

We see the same thing happening, in a way, in Exodus 5&6. God directed his chosen and dear people, his children, in a very real sense, to relocate there, to that inhospitable, desert region, far away from home, roots, everything that was familiar. And God sat back and watched them suffer...living through 400 years of hell as the lowest of slaves. Eventually, he rescued them, but they sure went through the crucible before their term was over. Mostly, God was silent. When he finally sent a lowly shepherd to rescue them, the screws were clamped down by Pharaoh even harder, leaving them barely gasping for survival. So, why did God operate like this, allowing his precious people to suffer so painfully? I suppose we can learn a lot from Prince Charles' experience. It was not because God didn't love the people...he loved them dearly. It was not because he had forgotten them...they were in his moment by moment thoughts. It was not because God is not good or because he is unjust...there is nothing bad or unjust in him. The same could be said of Charles' parents. And, when we endure bewildering, excruciating circumstances, we, also, may not understand what is happening, and why a loving, all knowing God would allow these things in our lives. But, we do know this: God is good and loves us. He hasn't forgotten or given up on us. His good plans will be carried out...most likely with a measure of pain and discomfort thrown in. He has the final word. His good plans won't be derailed. (And, hopefully, it won't take us 400 years to discover what he's doing!)

DECEMBER 23

One of our dearest friends in China was a young college student who spoke very good English. He especially was close to my wife, and would enjoy hanging around with her for hours, talking about the Bible and all sorts of other things. He was not an English major, but his knowledge of the language was exceptionally good, to the point that he entered an English speech contest at his university, and won. We sure were proud of him. He continues today along his successful path as a lawyer in one of China's great cities. The story our friend, Pancho, told us about his family background was tragic. Being property owners at the wrong time meant that they suffered a lot, lost everything, and were fiercely discriminated against. But, for Pancho, it didn't stop there. In addition to outside scorn, he also suffered greatly from his own grandmother, who mistreated him, and eventually, kicked him out of the house when he was 14. It was a lot for a young boy to endure and suffer.

I thought about Pancho when I read the story of Jesus' rejection in Mark 6. He also was rejected and scorned wherever he went, and no place worse than in his own hometown, by his own people and family. They just couldn't live with his success, prominence, and attention. Pancho's rejection has not kept him from being the person he wants to be, securing a valuable education, and moving beyond his hard life story. He's done a great job. The suffering Jesus endured, for me, for you, and, yes, for Pancho, he walked into with his eyes fully open. He left the perfect dwelling he inhabited in heaven, came down to our dirty planet, and tasted and endured and was martyred in the worst way...for what? Only because he loves you and wanted to rescue you from sin and its consequences. That was all. That was enough. For you, me, and Pancho...that was enough for Jesus.

DECEMBER 24

Day/Date   Be sure to remember five things to be grateful for every day.   December 24

Proverbs 4:18 NCV   The way of the good person is like the light of dawn, growing brighter and brighter until full day light.

When we follow God and his Word throughout our lives, he works in us to make us more like him and reflecting his love and his character. When we live in our sinful and dark world, someone whose life has been changed by God stands out brightly next to the evil and darkness around us.

There is some uncertainty about the letter, as well as the family and circumstances it referred to, that was apparently written by Abraham Lincoln, and that was quoted in the movie, "Saving Private Ryan". It does sound like the eloquence we would expect from our 16th President, and other than Lincoln, King David comes to mind, in terms of matching Lincoln's mastery of words, but, of course, David was a few centuries before the Civil War, so, most likely, they did originate with Old Abe. My parents lost two children, and I can't begin to imagine how some of the parents in the Civil War, or any war, really, cope with those kinds of losses.

David, also, had his excruciating share of pain and sorrows. And, he expressed his suffering in Psalm 6, with words that one who is suffering deeply can relate to: "I am weak. My bones are in agony. I am sick at heart. I am worn out from sobbing." Crushed. Flattened. Devastated. Destroyed. That's what David sounds like. I don't have many words for someone who is journeying through an experience like that. All I can do, really, is refer you to how David dealt with his decimation. He came weeping to God. That is where he found consolation, comfort, rest, and a sympathetic ear. Jesus also was crushed and destroyed...even by some who should have stood with him. He understands us. He knows us. Let's go to him, in the same way David did, in his hour of greatest need.

DECEMBER 25

1 Corinthians 15:10 NCV God's grace has made me what I am, and his grace to me was not wasted. I worked harder than all the other apostles. But it was not I really; it was God's grace that was with me.

Paul was one of the greatest and most dynamic followers of God of all time. But he was always aware of who he had been — a persecutor of believers. He was keenly aware, as we should be, that any good that was in him was due to God's mercy and grace in his life.

Our first son showed up at the same time as we moved to a new city, took on our own Christian bookstore, and purchased a new home. Things were falling into place nicely. Clearly, I had life by the tail, and it was all going to unfold according to plan...my plan, that is... One day, decades later, we look back and smile at all our nicely laid out schemes for the rest of our life. If there's one thing you probably realize in your latter years, it is that things didn't, don't, and won't, go according to our carefully choreographed game plan. God just seems to enjoy upsetting our pristine apple carts a little too much.

I expect that's exactly what happened to Moses in the early chapters of Exodus. He realized that things were getting a little too heated for him in Egypt. So he skeedattled to the far off wilderness of Midian, where no one knew him, no one could find him, and where he could start all over with a completely new game plan. Things did tick along smoothly for a long time...for 40 years...until God showed up and stomped big on his sheep and apple cart. Moses' quiet life would never be the same. The balmy days of Midian would be forever gone...and Moses' life and legacy...as well as the entire history of Israel...would be totally shaken up. Now, probably Moses' life is a bit more dramatic than what the rest of us will experience in our lives. Chances are, you may not be changing the course of a nation's history, or freeing a couple million slaves, anytime real soon. But, still, that is how God tends to work, through every page of the Bible. We might all do well to be alert to his call on our lives. Hang on for the ride...but don't hold on too tightly to your apple cart...

DECEMBER 26

Day/Date Be sure to remember five things to be grateful for every day. December 26

Galatians 5:1 NCV We have freedom now, because Christ made us free. So stand strong. Do not change and go back into the slavery of the law.

Even when we know and follow God, our self-centeredness constantly wants us to believe that we are good on our own, that we can please God on our own, and that we can manage on our own without Christ's redemption.

As China's population exploded in the late 1970s, and crept toward one billion inhabitants, the government intervened and proclaimed that only one child would, from then on, be permitted per family. This created tremendous pressure and anxiety for a Confucian driven society, where it is expected (much as in the Bible) that the oldest son will care for aging parents in their declining years. What if a family had only one daughter? Then what? Who would one day care for the parents, as their sole daughter would by then be married and caring for her in-laws? This was a tragic reality that we saw lived out in the lives of some of our friends, that later caused an over abundance of men (due to many girls being aborted), and has continued, to this day, to have ramifications for surrounding countries, such as North Korea, whose women are lured to China as wives. We heard more than one young lady tell of her family, where she was the first (or surreptitiously, the second or third) daughter to be born, and felt clearly unwanted and unloved by her parents. Some girls behaved as the boys that they knew their parents desired, resulting in aberrant sexual behavior as they grew up. The unanticipated fallout of the one child policy was at times very tragic. It is a terrible shackle to grow up in a family, knowing you are unwanted.

In Mark 5, we also read about someone who was unwanted; in this case, a severely deranged, demon possessed man, who was feared by all and a clear danger to himself and to everybody else. Everyone steered far away from him, giving him wide berth, anytime his screams, yells, and moanings were heard in the distance. Everyone, that is, except Jesus. Seeing Jesus and his gang approaching, the deranged man exited his cave hideout and started to call out to Jesus. Instead of doing the expected, and clearing out of there fast, Jesus went straight toward him, talked to him, healed him, and gave him a mission to carry out. I think of those unwanted girls in China, and I know Jesus would have embraced them, welcomed them, treated them as friends and loved ones...because that is what Jesus does. That is who he is. For that demonic man long ago, for those one child girls, and for you and me today, Jesus embraces us, loves us, and accepts us.

DECEMBER 27

Day/Date · Be sure to remember five things to be grateful for every day. · December 27

Matthew 16:24-25 NCV · If people want to follow me, they must give up the things they want. They must be willing even to give up their lives. Those who want to save their lives will give up true life, and those who give up their lives for me will have true life.

These seem like hard words for us to hear. But in reality, the things we give up to follow God are not the most important and are not permanent. What we receive from God as part of our new life are the most important aspects of life — joy, love, peace, and a hope for the future.

We were privileged to become acquainted with many university students during the years we were in China. For a number of reasons, many of them did not feel close to their parents. Sometimes it was the Confucian culture that prevented warm relationships between parents and children. Others were raised by grandparents, while their parents were away at jobs in far off cities, so they didn't know their parents well. Some of these students would call us "Mom" and "Dad"...and perhaps we were the closest they had experienced to real parents. At any rate, we tried hard to reach out to them and treat them as our own children, and they responded in kind. When the chaos of the Corona virus began swirling across China, one of our former students, whom we had gotten to know well but who had persisted in refusing to give her life to Christ, wrote me and said, "I realize now, with all that is happening in the world, that some things are simply beyond, outside of, our ability to control. So, I realize now, that God really does, indeed, exist. There is no other explanation for what is happening in the world right now. There is nowhere else for me to turn." I was amazed to read her words. I had been praying that God would use the disruption and distress of the pandemic to open people's eyes to him...and here was someone, a close friend, that had experienced that exactly! It was so very exciting to see how God worked...in her...through distressing circumstances...to bring her, at last, to him.

I think of our sweet friend when I read David's words in Psalm 5. David was distressed (not much new there). He said that he had nowhere else to turn. There was no other solution to his situation that he could see...just like our Chinese friend...than to turn to God. And so he did the only thing he could see left for him to do. In the beautiful words of Eugene Peterson's Message Bible, verse 3 quotes David in this way: "Every morning I lay out the pieces of my life on your altar and watch for fire to descend." Isn't that simply beautiful! And that is exactly what God invites us to do each day...when we're at the end of our rope...and, of course, even before...to lay our whole selves, our whole situations, before him, and to wait on him for his response.

DECEMBER 28

One summer, shortly before my 60th birthday, I was invited on a bike trip. I don't know how many decades it had been since I had seriously ridden a bicycle, but it had definitely been a while. A friend of mine in China was invited to take an excursion with about a dozen university students who were studying English. Their tutor wanted them to have further language practice, and he thought up the creative idea of inviting along a native English speaker on a bike outing with the whole group. A great idea, really. Only, my friend wasn't free to go, so he called in the second (more like the fourth) string sub to take his place. That's how I ended out on a bus to Shangrila, in the far northwest corner of our province, very close to Tibet. In fact, most of the people living around Shangrila are Tibetan, recognized by their headdress, striking houses, and other customs and habits. So I tagged along on what was to be a one hour pedal around a lake in the area. I enjoyed getting to know the students as we traveled together on the bus, and, since they were a captive audience, managed to interview all of them about their lives, as well. Clearly, they were a new generation in China, privileged to attend university, choose their life careers and direction, things their parents and grandparents knew nothing about. One of the girls I talked to shared about her grandparents' experiences in the late 1950s. The country was suffering through one of its most challenging periods, when there just wasn't enough food to go around. This student told me that she had heard stories of people being reduced to eating each others' dead babies in order to survive. I can't even begin to imagine reaching that point of desperation, but we have heard similar stories like that from other sources as well, so I know that those kinds of things did happen.

Perhaps the closest we come to, for a similar situation in the Bible, is in Exodus 1&2. The Egyptians were feeling intimidated by the burgeoning Israelite population in their midst, so the Pharaoh decided to turn them into slaves, in order to subdue and control them. Still their numbers grew. Eventually, he decided to dump the Israelite newborn boys into the Nile River. They surely must have wondered where God was in all this. But even in these darkest, most grave days, God hadn't forgotten them, and he was putting a rescue plan into motion. It's hard to fathom the hardship that they...or the Chinese, years ago...endured. But, however bad or dire our situations may become today, let's remember that God hasn't forgotten us. He hadn't forgotten them...he hasn't forgotten us. His plans are underway. He is working his plans out, and he will reveal them to us at the right time.

(As it turned out, returning to my intrepid bike event, our over enthusiastic leader didn't quite know the way around the lake near Shangrila, we became hopelessly lost, and the one hour excursion became a ten hour epic marathon. I had no idea where I was, in the middle of all this Tibetan countryside, so I told myself that I had to put my head down and just keep pedaling. Remarkably, I think to everyone, including myself, I arrived first back at our hotel at the end of our staggering day.)

DECEMBER 29

> **Day/Date** Be sure to remember five things to be grateful for every day. December 29
>
> Psalm 39:7-8 NCV — Lord, what hope do I have? You are my hope. Save me from all my sins.
>
> This is a desperate plea from a man who seems to be drowning or losing hope in life. But actually, it is a good place to find ourselves. When we realize we are unable to save ourselves and to overcome our sins on our own, we are finally at a place where God can help us when we call out to him.

I was sorry that I never saw him again. After I had interviewed more than 100 people in China over the course of a year, I wrote out and compiled the interviews into two little books. Part of the ongoing task (and quite fun as well), was to return to the place where I had interviewed people, sometimes just out in the street, try to find them, and then give them a copy of the little book which featured their story in it. They were usually pretty excited to get them...especially if a few of their friends were around, so they could see that their friend had been featured in a book. But, this one man, a security guard, I never found again. When I returned to where he had worked, and the place where I had interviewed him, he was no longer there. I asked some folks nearby if they knew him, and they said he had retired and moved away to another town. His was a particularly sad story. He told me that whenever he thought of his parents, he would break down in tears. Basically, they were beggars. But, today, as a security guard, he felt very well off. Life was so difficult when he was young, and without enough food to be had, that his parents would rummage through garbage bins, in search of anything that might be edible. Or, they would look for weeds in the fields and forests to eat. His parents had suffered so much for him, that he couldn't help weeping as they came to mind.

Jesus tells us a similar sad story in Mark 14. The details he gives make it abundantly clear that he knew exactly what he was heading into. "Go into the village, and find a man carrying a pitcher," he told his disciples. He knew every step of the upcoming torturous journey. He would be mistreated, betrayed, abandoned, beat up, and finally executed. On top of that, this was not an ordinary execution. No, he would literally be carrying the entire weight of the world's sin and disobedience on his shoulders. And it terrified him, crushed him. Still, he did it, for you, for me. Like the security guard I interviewed, whose parents suffered humiliation and pain for him, Jesus was suffering for us. I don't very often, but, I should probably weep, as well, when I think of all that Jesus suffered and carried for me. Lord, give us a fresh understanding of your love and suffering for us. Help us to see it and to thank you with our daily lives, lived forever you.

DECEMBER 30

I looked across the counter at his chest, and my head tilted back as my eyes followed his body up, up, up, till they reached his eyes...and I thought, "Who in the world is this guy??" It was a typical, slow, quiet day in my little Christian bookstore in Alcoa, Tennessee. A couple walked in and started browsing through the books. I didn't especially notice them until they approached the check out to purchase a few items. It was then that I was overwhelmed at his size. Only after a check had been filled out and slid across the counter did it suddenly register with me. The check was in the name of "Reginald White". Goodness, so that's who it is! Reggie White was one of the most feared defensive players in the National Football League of all time, and he was at his peak during the 1990s, when he visited my humble store. He was perhaps the greatest defensive end to play the sport, and opposing quarterbacks were terrified of him, knowing they would be meeting this tower of a man on numerous occasions throughout the game. But there was another side to Reggie White. He was a Christian pastor, earning himself the nickname, "The Minister of Defense". At one time, an opposing lineman started cussing at him, perhaps as they did, when trying to rattle each other during games. Reggie looked the guy in the face and said, "Jesus is coming." Then, during the next play, Reggie totally flattened the guy in front of him. He then stepped over and reached down to help the guy up, greeting him with these words: "Jesus is here!" In addition to being an inner city pastor in Knoxville, near my bookstore, during the off-season, Reggie and his wife lived in a sprawling ranch house about a mile from where we lived. They took in unwed mothers, who lived under their roof, right along with their own family. Inside of this fearsome athlete lived a man who cared deeply for the marginalized and needy in society. (I only wish I had held onto his check as a souvenir...but being the penny pinching shop clerk that I was, I wasn't about to forego the $1\[?]-20 that he spent on his visit!)

As we wade through Exodus 21&22, we are met with a tedious listing of does and don'ts, details we need to be cautious about and aware of, as we interact with other folks. But, beyond all the meticulous fine points, what is communicated to us is that we are to love our neighbors as much as we love ourselves. And that is what Reggie White did so well. He cared about other people, even mean-hearted opponents on the football field. What does loving our neighbor look like in our own lives? As I look around the world, as well as within my own heart, it's very apparent that it could use a whole lot more of what Reggie demonstrated throughout his life. A care, a concern, a love, for others, in the same way that we care for ourselves.